1991

W9-ADI-250

Principles of risk management   v.2

3 0301 00070509 1

Principles
of
Risk Management
and
Insurance
Volume II

C. ARTHUR WILLIAMS, JR., Ph.D.
Minnesota Insurance Industry
Professor of Economics and Insurance
University of Minnesota

GEORGE L. HEAD, Ph.D., CPCU, CLU
Director—Risk Management/Loss Control Education
American Institute for Property and Liability Underwriters

RONALD C. HORN, Ph.D., CPCU, CLU
Professor of Insurance and Professional Studies
Baylor University

G. WILLIAM GLENDENNING, Ph.D., CPCU
Professor of Insurance and Risk
Temple University

LIBRARY
College of St. Francis
JOLIET, ILLINOIS

Second Edition • 1981

AMERICAN INSTITUTE FOR
PROPERTY AND LIABILITY UNDERWRITERS
Providence and Sugartown Roads, Malvern, Pennsylvania 19355

© 1981
AMERICAN INSTITUTE FOR
PROPERTY AND LIABILITY UNDERWRITERS, INC.
All rights reserved. This book or any part thereof
may not be reproduced without the written
permission of the publisher.

Second Printing • August 1982

Library of Congress Catalog Number 81-66112
International Standard Book Number 0-89463-023-7

Printed in the United States of America

368
W658p
V. 2
2ed

Table of Contents

v

Physical Aspects of Insurance Contracts ~ *The Self-Contained Policy; Common Provisions Approach; Manuscript Policies; Collateral Documents*

Procedures for Coverage Analysis

Insured Entities ~ *Entities Specifically Identified By Name; Entities Identified By Relationship to Another Insured; Summary of Insured Entities*

Introduction

Insured Events Under Property Insurance Policies ~ *Covered Properties; Covered Causes; Covered Consequences; Covered Locations; Covered Circumstances; Covered Time Periods*

Insured Events Under Liability Insurance Policies ~ *Covered Activities; Covered Causes; Covered Consequences; Covered Locations; Covered Circumstances; Covered Time Periods*

Introduction

Policy Limits ~ *The Rationale of Policy Limits; Types of Policy Limits in Property Insurance; Types of Policy Limits in Liability Insurance; Types of Policy Limits in Multiple-Line Insurance*

Loss Valuation Provisions and Limits ~ *Loss Valuation Methods in Property Insurance; Loss Valuation Methods in Liability Insurance*

Introduction

CHAPTER 8

Insurable Interests

INTRODUCTION

Volume I examined many basic principles of risk management. It also examined insurance as an important risk management technique, both from the viewpoint of the individual risk manager and from the perspective of society as a whole. Volume II will concentrate on the structural and legal aspects of property and liability insurance contracts. Chapters 9 through 14 will explore the following subjects:

- The general structure of property and liability insurance contracts;
- The entities and events insured under these contracts;
- The contract provisions and legal principles that govern the amounts of recovery; and,
- The contract conditions that may affect the intended coverages.

Chapter 15 will apply the material in the preceding chapters to analyze the standard fire policy.

The study of insurance contracts logically begins with an understanding of the particular interests that are legally insurable. This chapter:

- defines insurable interest;
- examines its purposes;
- catalogs the various types of insurable interest in property and liability insurance; and
- comments on some of the problems that may arise when the insurable interest requirement is not satisfied.

1

DEFINITION AND SCOPE
OF INSURABLE INTERESTS

In a broad legal sense, an *insurable interest* may be defined as "the kind of financial interest a person must possess in order to have *legally enforceable* insurance coverage." A person is said to have an insurable interest if the occurrence of an event to be insured would cause financial loss or injury to that person. Thus, whether a person has a legally insurable interest depends on the relationship between that person and the property, life, or event in question. If the relationship exposes the person to financial loss, it is sufficient to support an insurable interest. Such a relationship *creates* the insurable interest. The *interest* itself is the holder's legitimate interest in purchasing insurance to cover his or her exposure to loss. In short, the law defines an insurable interest in much the same way that a risk manager would define a loss exposure (a set of circumstances that presents a possibility of loss). The holder of the insurable interest is the person or entity exposed to loss.

The mere fact that a person has a *legally* insurable interest does not necessarily mean that his or her specific loss exposure will be considered insurable from the viewpoint of a particular private insurer or private insurers generally. It has already been demonstrated that a number of exposures of considerable financial importance to persons or firms are regarded as not commercially insurable.

Furthermore, even on an exposure of a type generally regarded as commercially insurable, each insurer has the right, in the absence of a contrary statute of regulation, to accept or reject applications for insurance based on its own underwriting standards. Thus, in the context of a discussion of insurable interest, the term "insurable" should be viewed in a legal sense, as opposed to an underwriting sense.

A legally insurable interest is required if the insurance contract is to be enforceable in the courts by the parties to the contract. In that sense, its existence is as desirable from the underwriter's point of view as it is from the insured's.

The full scope of the insurable interest doctrine is best appreciated by applying it separately to (1) life and health insurance and (2) property and liability insurance. This division will also facilitate some useful comparisons.

In Life Insurance

The previously introduced definition of insurable interest is applicable to life insurance, provided the following important refinements are taken into account:

(1) *A life insurance policy purchased by a person on his or her own life (at his or her own initiative) is valid and enforceable in favor of any beneficiary named by the insured-policy-owner, regardless of the amount of the policy or whether the beneficiary has an insurable interest in the life of the insured.* This general rule has led many writers to suggest that a person has an "unlimited" insurable interest in his or her own life. While it is true that the *law* imposes no upper dollar limit on the amount of life insurance a person may purchase on his or her own life, there are practical upper limits set by insurer underwriting practices and the ability and willingness of the insured to pay the requisite premiums. Moreover, it is probably stretching a point to view an insured as having an insurable interest in his or her own life. The insured does not really suffer a financial loss from his or her own death (or at least does not survive to claim any compensation for the loss). It thus seems more accurate to say that when a person applies, in good faith, for life insurance on his or her own life, the question of insurable interest is normally not involved because it is legally immaterial.[1]

(2) *When the applicant wishes to purchase life insurance on the life of another person, the general rule is that the applicant must have an insurable interest.* Since in most such cases the applicant is also the beneficiary, the courts want to be assured that the insurance is not likely to provide a motive for murdering the insured. However, if there is a close enough family relationship between the proposed insured and the applicant-beneficiary, the latter does not have the burden of proving exposure to financial loss in a narrow sense. Most courts *presume* that family members have insurable interests in the lives of others who are closely related to them by blood or marriage. While the range of relationships covered by this presumption varies somewhat among jurisdictions, in general:

   (a) each spouse has an insurable interest in the life of the other;
   (b) each spouse has an insurable interest in the life of a child and a child in the life of a parent;
   (c) brothers and sisters have insurable interests in each others' lives; and
   (d) grandparents have insurable interests in the lives of their grandchildren.

Even if not within the range of relationships presumed to give rise to an insurable interest, mutual insurable interests may also exist between any two family members, even if distantly related, or any two individuals if one of them is in fact financially dependent on the other. The economically dependent person has an insurable interest based on the financial support that presumably would have been received from the other person, had he or she lived. The person providing the support also has an insurable interest in the life of the dependent, as a means of recouping the costs of having provided that support.

In addition to individual and family relationships, there are many business relationships that give rise to insurable interests in life insurance. Among those insurable interests recognized and commonly used to support the purchase of life insurance are:

- the interest of an employer in the life of a key employee,
- the interest of a creditor in the life of a debtor, and
- the interests of both a partnership and the individual partners in the lives of each working partner.

In each of these situations, the business entity is both the applicant and the beneficiary but *not* the insured. Each situation clearly involves the possibility that the business entity will suffer substantial financial loss upon the death of the insured. Hence, each of the above exposures to financial loss clearly gives rise to insurable interest.

Statutes in some jurisdictions, as well as the underwriting practices of many insurers, require the written consent of the proposed insured before issuing an individual life insurance policy to an applicant-beneficiary who is not the insured. Consent of the insured normally is not required (1) in group life insurance, (2) when one spouse applies for individual insurance on the other's life, or (3) when a parent applies for individual insurance on the life of the parent's minor child. The reason for generally requiring the insured's consent should be rather obvious. It is an attempt to reduce the likelihood of murder, by allowing the insured to refuse his or her consent for the issuance of a policy to a person whom the insured has reason to mistrust.

(3) *In life insurance, the insurable interest is legally required to exist only at the inception of the policy.* This general rule normally has no practical effect on the applicant-beneficiary who is a close family member (since the insurable interest is presumed) or on the applicant who is also the insured (since the

insurable interest is presumed or is considered legally immaterial, depending on which legal rationale is accepted). But the rule
does mean that the applicant-beneficiary who is not a close
family member must have an insurable interest only at the
inception of the policy, not necessarily at the time the insured
dies. One result is that an employer may retain a life insurance
policy on the life of a key employee, even after the employee
resigns and goes to work for another employer. Similarly, life
insurance obtained on a spouse during marriage remains valid
and enforceable after a divorce.

To summarize, the broad definition of insurable interest is best
applied to life insurance by acknowledging several important
refinements. A person may have one or more legally enforceable
contracts providing an unlimited amount of life insurance on his or her
own life. Some authorities explain this general rule by saying that we
each have insurable interests in our own lives, while others insist that
the doctrine of insurable interest is legally immaterial when the
applicant is also the insured. When the applicant is not the person to be
insured, the law stipulates that the applicant-beneficiary must have an
insurable interest at the inception of the policy. Generally, a person has
an insurable interest in the life of another if (1) they are closely related
by blood or marriage, (2) one of them is financially dependent upon the
other, or (3) they have a business relationship of such a nature that
premature death of the insured would cause financial loss to the
business (beneficiary).

In Health Insurance

The broad legal definition of insurable interest, presented earlier, is
generally applicable to the field of health insurance. However, the
specifics of its application depend primarily on the type of health
insurance policy in question.

For health insurance policies written either (1) to pay stated sums,
regardless of the amount of loss, or (2) to provide specified medical
services upon the happening of the insured event, the insurable interest
requirements are basically the same as those applicable to life
insurance. That is, the insurable interest needs to exist only at the
inception of the policy, it is normally the applicant-beneficiary who must
have an insurable interest, and the persons who have insurable
interests in health insurance are essentially the same as those who
would have insurable interests for life insurance purposes.

For health insurance policies written to pay (up to the policy
maximum) no more than the insured's actual loss, on the other hand,

the insurable interest requirements follow the rules that are applicable to property and liability insurance and elaborated upon throughout the remainder of this chapter. Here, suffice it to say that with respect to health insurance policies for which payment is not allowed to exceed the amount of the loss, it is the *insured* who normally must have the insurable interest *at the time of loss*. The insured may satisfy the requirement by having, at the time of loss, a right to income (in the case of disability income insurance) or a liability for medical expenses (in the case of medical expense insurance).

In Property and Liability Insurance

In applying the broad legal definition of insurable interest to property and liability insurance, it is helpful to begin by stressing three important points:

(1) it is the *insured* who must have an insurable interest,
(2) the insurable interest must exist *at the time of loss*, and
(3) there are *many* relationships that give rise to insurable interests in property and liability insurance.

Each point will be considered in turn.

Insured Must Have Insurable Interest The insurer is one party to a property or liability insurance contract. The only other party to the contract in a specific situation is the insured claiming entitlement to benefits. Consequently, it is the insured who must have an insurable interest in order to have a contract that is legally enforceable against the insurer. In contrast, in some life insurance situations, the party claiming entitlement (the beneficiary) may not be the party on whom the insurable interest requirement is imposed.

Insurable Interest Must Exist at Time of Loss Except by statute in a few states, property-liability insureds are not legally required to satisfy an insurable interest requirement at the inception of the policy. While insurers routinely impose the requirement as a matter of underwriting practice, the *law* generally requires an insurable interest of the property-liability insured only at the time of loss. This is in keeping with the prevailing view that most property and liability contracts are legally *contracts of indemnity*. Such contracts are designed to make whole or indemnify the insured for *loss actually sustained*. The courts will not enforce an indemnity contract in favor of an insured who did not have an insurable interest at the time of loss. To do so would violate public policy by unjustly enriching a person who did not really suffer a loss.

This same reasoning is not applied to life insurance situations, largely because life insurance contracts are not considered contracts of indemnity. Instead, life insurance contracts (as well as some health and property insurance contracts) are referred to as *valued policies* or as "contracts to pay a stated sum." The life insurer pays a stipulated sum of money at the insured's death, regardless of the amount of the dollar loss, if any. Enforcing this agreement is not considered contrary to public policy, as long as the insurable interest requirement was validly presumed or otherwise satisfied at the inception of the contract. The courts seem to feel that the primary purposes of insurable interest in life insurance—to prevent wagering and murder—are served adequately by requiring it only at the inception of the policy.

Many Relationships Give Rise to Insurable Interests There are many relationships that create or give rise to insurable interests in both liability insurance and property insurance. Remember that our general definition of insurable interest referred to relationships between a person and the life, property, *or event* in question. A property owner has a rather obvious insurable interest in owned property. However, as will be shown, the notion of insurable interest is not restricted to property "owners." There are many rights and interests, beyond mere ownership, that also create valid insurable interests. The phrase, "or event," was included to make the insurable interest definition applicable to liability insurance, since it is well established that people are exposed to the possibility of financial losses from their potential liability to others.

Grouped together into logical categories, the various insurable interests in property and liability insurance may rest on any of the following foundations:

(1) property rights,
(2) contract rights,
(3) exposures to legal liability,
(4) factual expectations of loss, and
(5) "representative" status.

Each of these categories will be explored in detail later in the chapter. First, the basic purposes of the insurable interest requirement will be examined.

PURPOSES OF THE
INSURABLE INTEREST REQUIREMENT

It has been argued that the insurable interest requirement is a restriction on the freedom of buyers and insurers to enter into any contract of their own choosing.[2] The courts and the legislatures have imposed the requirement for many years, nonetheless, in the belief that the purposes it serves are ultimately in the *public* interest. The three main purposes of requiring insurable interests are to:

(1) prevent wagering through insurance,
(2) minimize intentional losses, and
(3) enforce the principle of indemnity.

As will become apparent, the third purpose is applicable only to contracts of indemnity.

Preventing Wagering Through Insurance

If an entity were permitted to insure a life, property, or event in which it had no insurable interest, insurance policies could be used to disguise gambling contracts. For example, anyone could gamble that a prominent person would die within one year by taking out a one-year life insurance policy on that person's life. If the insured lived, the insurance company would simply keep the premium paid for that policy. The applicant for the policy would have lost the bet. If the insured died, the applicant-beneficiary would have won the bet and would collect the face amount of the insurance policy. A similar gamble could be made on whether a particular building would be damaged by fire during the term of a fire policy. If fire insurance were written to pay the insured the amount of the damage to the building, even though the insured had suffered no loss from such damage, the insured would stand to gain from what is essentially a gambling transaction or agreement.

Early English law permitted insurance contracts on lives and property to be written and enforced without proof of an insurable interest,[3] or with a clause indicating that the insurance of the policy was itself conclusive proof of the insured's valid insurable interest.[4] Allowing anyone to insure against events in which they had no other interests apparently led to undesirable behavior. This can be inferred from a statute, enacted in 1746 by the English Parliament, requiring a valid insurable interest in all marine insurance contracts. After recognizing that policies not supported by a true insurable interest had "been productive of many pernicious practices, whereby great numbers of ships, with their cargoes, have either been fraudulently lost or destroyed, or taken by the enemy in time of war," and after noting "a mischievous type of gaming or wagering, upon the pretence of assuring the risk of shipping," the law declared that, for all types of marine insurance, "no assurance or assurances shall be made ... interest or no interest, or without further proof of interest than the policy, or by way of gaming or wagering, or without benefit of salvage to the assurer." It further stated that "... every such assurance shall be null and void to

all intents and purposes."[5] In 1774, Parliament extended the requirement of an insurable interest from marine coverages to all types of
insurance coverages, with a statute declaring that "no insurance shall
be made on the life or lives of any person or persons, or on any other
event or events whatsoever, wherein the person or persons for whose
use, benefit, or on whose account such policy or policies shall be made,
shall have no interest...."[6]

From the earliest decisions of American courts, an insurable
interest has been required in the United States under all types of
insurance policies. Without one, the policy is *unenforceable* by either
the insurer or the insured (or applicant, in the case of life insurance).
The refusal of courts to enforce insurance policies not supported by a
valid insurable interest is consistent with their general refusal to
enforce a wagering contract. In general, contracts that have been made
illegal by statute or that are considered by the courts to be harmful to
the public interest will not be enforced by a court. Rather than try to do
justice to the parties to any illegal contract, courts will do nothing to
help or hinder any of the parties. Private wagering contracts are illegal
in the United States, both because they are declared so by statute in
every state and because such contracts have generally been judged by
the courts to be contrary to the public interest. Any insurance contract
not supported by a valid insurable interest is a wagering contract and,
hence, is unenforceable.[7]

Although the insurable interest requirement does not eliminate
every kind of insurance profiteering, it does work rather effectively in
the narrower sense of preventing those who do not have legitimate
insurable interests from wagering through insurance. Few people even
attempt to purchase insurance covering lives, property, or events in
which they have no legally insurable interest. Some who might
otherwise be tempted are aware that the contract would be unenforceable. Furthermore, those who do attempt such purchases are likely to
be declined by alert underwriters, and those who slip through the
underwriting screen are likely to find that the insurer will use the lack
of an insurable interest as a defense in denying their claims.

Minimizing Intentional Losses

The second purpose of the insurable interest requirement is to
minimize the number of intentional losses that may be attributed to
moral hazards. As noted in Chapter 1, hazards are conditions that tend
to increase the frequency and/or severity of losses. Moral hazards
generally refer to the conditions that lead some people to exaggerate
losses or intentionally cause them to occur in order to collect insurance

proceeds. Intentional destruction of property and lives is quite obviously wasteful and otherwise contrary to the public interest.

Complete elimination of all intentionally caused and exaggerated losses would be far too much to expect from the imposition of an insurable interest requirement alone. Indeed, merely imposing the requirement on the *insured* should not have any appreciable effect on the volume of intentionally caused or exaggerated losses covered by liability insurance. Virtually everyone legally has an insurable interest in the events covered by liability insurance policies, which normally exclude intentional acts of the insured anyway, and a third-party claimant is not required to have an insurable interest. It is also unlikely that the insurable interest requirement itself has any effect on those persons who simultaneously have (1) valid insurable interest in property or lives *and* (2) criminal inclinations. This proposition is attested to each year by the number of persons who reportedly burn their own buildings or murder close relatives with the apparent motive of collecting insurance benefits.

In spite of the aforementioned limitations, it is believed that the insurable interest requirement does serve the important purpose of "minimizing" the intentional losses of property and life—at least in the somewhat loose sense of reducing them to a number below what they would have been in the absence of the insurable interest requirement. This result is achieved by attempting to prohibit the purchase of insurance by persons who would have everything to gain and nothing to lose by the occurrence of the event insured.

The insurable interest requirement restricts the purchase of *enforceable* insurance to people who stand only to lose if the insured event occurs. For example, the life of a person would probably be in great danger if any stranger could collect substantial life insurance proceeds on the death of that person. So also would the Empire State Building be quite vulnerable if any person could buy and collect on an insurance policy covering explosion damage to the building. A buyer with no insurable interest would surely not be willing to pay the premium unless he or she had every intention of either causing the explosion or wagering. Either would be deemed undesirable from both the public's and the building owner's points of view.

Preventing wagering and minimizing intentional losses are closely related and overlapping objectives. If the reader doubts whether the insurable interest requirement is very effective in reducing intentional losses, it should be remembered that the requirement does help prevent wagering and would probably be imposed by the courts for that reason alone. If it also does at least some good in preventing crimes like arson and murder, as it is believed to do, so much the better. Some contribution toward the control of intentional losses is at least a "function" served by the insurable interest requirement, if not a basic purpose.

Enforcing the Principle of Indemnity

The third purpose of the insurable interest requirement is to assist in enforcing the so-called "principle of indemnity." The *principle of indemnity* is the universally accepted presupposition or assumption that the proper function of insurance is to do no more than indemnify, make whole again financially, or put the insured back into the same financial position that he or she enjoyed before the occurrence of the insured event. Stated in the negative, the principle of indemnity means simply that a person should not profit from an insured loss. If insurance were to be written in ways that would assure easy profits for insureds, there would be strong incentives for them either to make certain the losses occurred or abandon their own loss prevention and reduction efforts. Society would suffer a resulting increase in arson and other forms of damage and destruction. Thus, the proper function of insurance is to indemnify, not to enrich insureds.

The insurable interest requirement assists in enforcing the indemnity principle only with respect to insurance policies that are legally classified as *contracts of indemnity.* In all such contracts, the extent of the insurable interest serves as an upper limit on the amount the insurer will pay to the insured for a covered loss. One cannot actually lose more than he or she stands to lose, and what one stands to lose can be measured by the dollar value of one's insurable interest. The insurer will pay at a maximum, subject to any other limits that may apply, no more than the amount of the insured entity's insurable interest. For example, under the insuring agreement of the standard fire policy the insurer agrees to pay "to the extent of actual cash value at the time of loss—but not exceeding the amount which it would cost to repair or replace—*nor in any event for more than the interest of the insured....*" Similar provisions in other contracts of indemnity likewise specify that the extent or amount of the insurable interest of each insured is a maximum amount payable to that insured. (Additional contract provisions and legal principles that also help preserve the principle of indemnity will be discussed later in this text.)

The insurable interest requirement does not serve to enforce the principle of indemnity in life insurance, since life insurance policies pay a stated sum of money regardless of the actual dollar loss to the beneficiary. In a *legal* sense, life insurance contracts are not in most cases regarded as *contracts of indemnity.* Nor does the insurable interest requirement enforce the indemnity principle in those health or property insurance policies that are also written on a valued or stated-sum basis, where the amount payable upon the occurrence of the insured event is agreed to in advance. Consequently, valued policies may result in violations of the indemnity principle, unless underwriting safeguards and other techniques are used by insurers to prevent "overinsurance." Overinsurance has not been a serious problem in life or property insurance, but it is not uncommon in health insurance.

TYPES OF INSURABLE INTERESTS IN PROPERTY AND LIABILITY INSURANCE

As noted earlier, in the field of property-liability insurance an insurable interest may be based upon (1) a property right, (2) a contract right, (3) a potential legal liability, (4) a factual expectation, or (5) a representative status. While these five categories overlap in some respects, they serve as logical and systematic headings for presenting explanations and specific examples of some of the more common insurable interests. The specific examples will make frequent use of the generic term "entity," which is broad enough to include a natural person, a corporation (an artificial entity legally recognized as a "person"), a partnership, a charitable organization, a governmental body, or any other entity that may have an insurable interest by virtue of its exposure to financial loss.

Insurable Interests Based on Property Rights

The concept of "property" has a variety of meanings. In ordinary conversation, the term is most commonly applied to buildings, autos, and other tangible objects having a physical existence. Although this usage may also be found in the law, the legal concept of property is more accurately defined as an aggregate or "bundle" of *rights* that have an economic value because they are guaranteed and protected by law. Some of these rights pertain to physical objects of a tangible nature; others do not. Copyrights, patents, trademarks, and corporate stock certificates are properly called intangible "property," for example, because they *represent* valuable economic rights, but do not have intrinsic value themselves. Indeed, there is an important sense in which the concept of "property" includes every valuable right that is capable of being owned, whether or not such a right pertains to intangible objects or to real or personal property.

Real property refers to rights in land, including rights to water, minerals, things permanently attached to land (e.g., buildings), and things growing on the land (e.g., trees). It also includes rights that are closely related to land, such as the right to cross the land of another, called an "easement." *Personal property* refers to all other rights or, in other words, to all property that is not real property. Rights in personal property are also referred to as "chattels."

An entity may possess the *entire* bundle of rights in relation to an object of real or personal property, in which case the entity is the sole owner. Or, the bundle of rights may be divided among several entities, each with one or more rights, in which case there is incomplete ownership by any one entity. The right or sum total of several rights a particular entity possesses is often referred to in legal circles as that entity's "interest" in the property. This usage is merely a short-cut way of referring to an entity's *property* interest, its *legal* interest in property, or the particular right or combination of rights the entity possesses.

The term *estate* also has a variety of meanings. In the field of estate planning, for instance, "estate" ordinarily means the whole of all property owned by a person, including both real and personal property. However, "estate" is also used as a synonym for a particular legal interest in property, and it is frequently combined with another word or phrase to describe a classification of property and convey the nature and/or extent of the interest. For example, a *simple estate* is an estate owned by one entity, whereas a *concurrent estate* is co-owned by two or more entities. At common law, an estate in land is called a "freehold" estate if it has an indefinite termination date or duration. An "estate less than freehold" has a definite termination date or duration. There are numerous additional classifications and subclassifications of estates in the highly complex field of property law.

For the purposes of identifying and analyzing some of the more common insurable interests that are based on property rights, it is not necessary to catalog all of the systems of classifying estates. But it is important to acknowledge that full "ownership," in its ordinary conversational sense, is by no means the only bundle of rights that gives rise to an insurable interest.

With respect to a specific item of property, the most comprehensive estate normally consists of two elements: (1) complete, outright, and full ownership (the *extent* of the rights), and (2) an unlimited time (the *duration* of the rights). This total estate can be carved up to create lesser interests, either as to the extent of the interest or its duration. While these lesser interests are not always called estates, they are all property interests or bundles of rights, just as the colloquial notion of ownership is really a bundle of legal rights. Furthermore, just as the so-called "owner" has an insurable interest in a building because of the owner's exposure to the possibility of financial loss from fire or some other peril so also is it generally true that any entity has an insurable interest in property whenever:

(1) the entity possesses a property right and
(2) the value of the right would be diminished by the damage, destruction, abstraction, or loss of use of the item of property in question.

Specific examples of such rights are provided in the following pages. Under each heading, the description of the estate or bundle of rights will be no longer than necessary to convey the nature and extent of the corresponding insurable interest.

Fee Simple Estate The legal phrase "fee simple estate" refers to the estate commonly called full ownership of property. Though applied more frequently to estates in land, the phrase is broadly applicable to virtually any kind of property. A fee simple estate is the largest estate (i.e., it contains the most rights) of any estate in our legal system. The term *simple* indicates that one entity owns the estate; the term *fee* indicates that the estate is of an "eternal" nature, thereby permitting it to be passed along to heirs or persons named in a last will and testament. The holder of a fee simple estate also has the right to sell, give away, lease, or use in any lawful way all or a portion of the estate. The holder of a fee simple is, of course, subject to zoning, pollution, and other laws governing the use of the property. He or she is likewise subject to the ultimate power of the state to exercise its right of "eminent domain" and take over the property for public use. Additionally, if the holder of a fee simple estate dies without a will and without any heirs, the property ownership "escheats" (reverts) to the state. Such limitations and restrictions mean that the holder of a fee simple estate is not truly an absolute and uncontrolled owner in a literal sense. Nontheless, the holder of a fee simple estate will hereafter be referred to as the "owner" of property. This yielding to common usage is merely for the sake of expositional convenience. It does not alter the fact that the fee simple estate holder is an owner only in the somewhat loose sense of having the largest number of property rights available.

Full Value. It is well established that the owner of property in fee simple has an insurable interest equal to the full value of the property. The property has an economic value to the owner only because he or she has the power to exercise all the rights of ownership. Total destruction of the property would result in a corresponding dollar loss to the owner, then, because the value of the rights would likewise be destroyed.

While it is generally agreed that the extent of the owner's insurable interest is the full value of the property, the courts do not always define "full value" in an explicit and precise way. What does seem clear is the intention of the courts to reinforce the principle of indemnity by limiting the amount of an entity's insurable interest in property to the maximum dollar loss the entity could sustain from the property's total destruction. It can thus be inferred that, *for insurable interest purposes*, the "full value" of property (the maximum dollar amount the owner could lose from its destruction) is generally equal to the sum of

(1) the loss of the property's *intrinsic value* plus
(2) the loss of the property's *value in use.*

For example, consider a building that has been totally destroyed by fire. What total dollar amount would truly indemnify, make whole again, or fully reimburse the owner for the destruction of the building? This total amount would be the owner's maximum potential financial loss, which would also be the amount of the owner's insurable interest. One element of the total would consist of the labor and materials cost of a building of identical size, kind, and quality. This replacement cost amount would be sufficient to restore the building's intrinsic value. But it might take up to, say, six months to build a new structure. In the meantime, the owner will be deprived of the building's economic value in use. Suppose, for instance, the owner has been conducting a business in part of the building, renting another part of it to a tenant, and residing in the remaining part. During the period of time it will take to restore the building and get it ready for occupancy, the owner may lose money he or she would have otherwise enjoyed in the form of business profits and rental income, and he or she probably will incur additional expenses to secure alternative living quarters. The building owner's total potential loss, the full value which the courts say is the insurable interest, would be the sum of (1) the replacement cost of the building (the direct loss of intrinsic value) plus (2) the lost profits, lost rents, and extra living expenses for the period of restoration (the indirect loss resulting from the loss of the building's economic value in use). Knowledgeable insurance people may note that insurance *practice* typically segregates these two elements, but that fact is not germane here. As a legal matter, the fee simple owner's interest encompasses both.

Effect of Mortgage. The fee simple owner has an insurable interest equal to the full value of the property even when the property has been mortgaged or otherwise pledged as security for the payment of a debt. Since total destruction of the property would not relieve the owner of the obligation to repay the entire debt, the extent of the owner's insurable interest is not reduced by the amount of the debt. The owner may therefore insure the property for its full insurable value. In addition, the lender also has an insurable interest in the property that has been pledged as collateral security for the debt, and the lender's interest is normally based on the amount of the debt (as will be discussed later under the heading of contract rights). The result is that the sum of the two insurable interests actually exceeds the full value of the property. To illustrate, suppose a building with a replacement cost of $100,000 has been mortgaged for $60,000. The owner's insurable interest of $100,000 (in the building itself, ignoring its value in use) plus the lender's insurable interest of $60,000 equals $160,000, considerably more than the building's intrinsic value. Such situations are common when more than one entity has an insurable interest in the same item of property. Underwriting safeguards, contract provisions, and other techniques must be used by insurers to combat the obvious potential for overinsurance and abuse.

Property Owned by a Corporation. With respect to property owned by a corporation, there is no question that the corporation, as a legal entity distinct from its stockholders, has an insurable interest in such property to the extent of its full insurable value. American courts, with few exceptions, hold that a stockholder also has an insurable interest in the property of the corporation, even though the stockholder has no enforceable title to the corporation's property. The stockholders have the right (1) to receive dividends (once declared by the corporation), and (2) to take a proportionate share of the corporation's net assets, after discharge of corporate debts, should the corporation ever be dissolved. The courts reason that, because substantial damage to the corporation's assets could significantly lower the value of the rights of a stockholder, a stockholder's potential loss is sufficient to prevent insurance on corporate property from becoming a mere wager. American courts will therefore enforce an insurance contract secured by a stockholder on corporate assets, but only to the extent of the actual loss the stockholder might sustain if the insured item(s) of corporate property were totally destroyed.

Life Estate A life estate is an estate that lasts for the lifetime of a specific person. The holder of a life estate is known as a *life tenant.* The life tenant may possess, use, and enjoy the property during his or her lifetime. However, the life estate terminates at the death of its holder (the life tenant) or, less frequently, at the death of someone other than the holder. In either case, at the termination of the life estate, the property passes to another entity known as the *remainderman* (or it reverts to the grantor of the interest, if no remainderman has been named or the specified remainderman is not legally qualified to take the property).

To illustrate, suppose a husband who owns a house in fee simple stipulates in his will that his wife is to have a life estate in the house for as long as she lives; thereafter, his daughter is to have a fee simple estate in the house. The husband then dies. In this situation, the daughter is the "remainderman" (sic), and she becomes the holder of a future interest known as a "remainder" at the time her father dies. The wife is the life tenant or the holder of the life estate. The life tenant (the wife, in this case) is entitled to possess and use the property during her lifetime, but she cannot pass it along to others in her will, since her interest terminates at her death. Similarly, though the wife theoretically could sell her life estate while she is still alive, it might be very difficult to find a buyer, because the buyer's interest would likewise terminate at the instant of the wife's death. This is consistent with the general rule that the holder of a particular type of estate cannot transfer any greater estate to another person.

A life estate can be created in ways other than through a will. For example, a son may make a gift to his mother of a life estate in property that the son holds in fee simple. If the son does not name a remainderman, the property reverts back to the son at the mother's death. During the mother's life tenancy, the son's interest in the property is a future interest, known as a *reversion* or *reversionary interest*, and he is referred to as the *reversioner* or holder of such an interest. If, as is likely, the mother dies before the son, the son would take back a fee simple estate in the property—the same interest he had held before he created the life estate for his mother. If the son dies before the mother, the value of the reversionary interest becomes a part of the son's estate at his death.

Insurable Interests in Life Estates. To understand the insurable interests that may exist in relation to a life estate, it is necessary to remember the various parties who may hold the property rights.

- The *life tenant* is the holder of the life estate.
- The *remainderman* is the holder of a remainder interest.
- The *reversioner* is the holder of a reversion or reversionary interest.

The life tenant is said to have a *present interest* which gives the tenant the right to possess and use the property currently. The remainderman and the reversioner in the earlier examples were said to have *future interests*, because their rights to possess or use the property did not become operative until some future point in time. Each of these three parties has valuable property rights, which may provide the basis of an insurable interest.

The *remainderman*, though holding only a future interest, could easily take over the rights of possession and use tomorrow, if the life tenant dies tomorrow. Likewise, the life tenant could die (1) in a common accident with the remainderman, (2) in a situation where no remainderman had been named, or (3) in a situation where the specified remainderman had died before the life tenant. In all three cases, the *reversioner* would immediately take over the rights to possess and use the property. In recognition of such realistic possibilities, the remainderman who holds a future interest generally has an insurable interest equal to the full value of the property. The same is true of the reversioner. Each of these two parties stands to lose the entire value of his or her rights, it is reasoned, if the property were to be destroyed by fire or some other peril. Accordingly, both the remainderman and the reversioner may each enforce a contract that insures the property for its full insurable value.

The *life tenant* also has an insurable interest in the property in which he or she holds a life estate. The amount of the life tenant's insurable interest is usually determined in one of two ways, depending on the legal jurisdiction. In some jurisdictions the life tenant's insurable interest is equal to the full value of the item of property in question. In others the life tenant's insurable interest is limited to the "present value" of the life estate, given the age of the life tenant (or other person whose life governs the duration of the estate). The latter approach requires a brief explanation. It is essentially a process of computing the lump-sum equivalent of the annual income that could be earned by investing, for a period equal to the life tenant's estimated life expectancy in years, a sum equal to the intrinsic value of the property. For example, assume that a property has an intrinsic value of $60,000 and that a reasonable rate of return would be 6 percent per year. Investing an amount equal to the property's value would generate an income of $3,600 per year. Assume further that the life tenant has an estimated life expectancy of forty years. The probable value of the tenant's life estate would be about $54,000. The mechanics of present value calculations are discussed elsewhere in the CPCU curriculum. The point for now is that the $54,000 amount is the present value or lump-sum equivalent of an annual income of $3,600 per year for forty years, discounted at 6 percent, the assumed reasonable rate of return. This present value of the tenant's life estate would serve as an upper limit on the amount of the life tenant's insurable interest, in jurisdictions that have adopted the present value approach. It is felt that, if the property were to be destroyed tomorrow, an immediate cash payment of $54,000 would fully indemnify the life tenant. The cash in hand is considered the financial equivalent of the right to use the property for forty years.

Some courts have rejected the notion of limiting the life tenant's insurable interest to the "present value" of the life estate. Such courts have insisted that the life tenant has an insurable interest equal to the full value of the property, on the theory that the life tenant is indemnified only by an insurance payment large enough to restore the property to its pre-loss condition and permit it to be used as it was being used before the loss.

Regardless of how the amount of the life tenant's insurable interest is determined, the life tenant is generally under no legal obligation to repair or rebuild the property after it has been damaged or destroyed, unless (1) the damage or destruction was caused by a negligent or intentional act of the life tenant, or (2) the documents creating the life estate specifically obligate the life tenant to effect repairs or replace the property. Nor is the life tenant legally obligated to insure the property for the benefit of the remainderman or reversioner, in the absence of an enforceable agreement to the contrary.

These general rules may appear to be unfair to the remainderman and the reversioner, since the value of their rights effectively is diminished to the extent that the property is both damaged and uninsured (or underinsured). Remember, however, that the remainderman and the reversioner may each purchase separate insurance for the full value of the property, if separate insurance is desired. Again, as in the owner-mortgagee case, the parties have insurable interests that collectively exceed the full value of the property.

When each party does purchase separate insurance—especially when it is purchased from three different insurers—the insurers are faced with the dangers of overinsurance and moral hazard, as well as the formidable problem of determining how much each insurer is legally obligated to pay to each insured. The latter problem is further compounded because the separate policies may provide different amounts and/or types of coverage. Moreover, the purchase of separate insurance policies may not adequately protect the respective interests of the parties, and duplicate coverage is unnecessarily expensive in any case. A more rational approach is to retain a competent attorney, preferably at the time the life estate is created, to prepare a legally enforceable agreement that requires the purchase of an appropriate amount of insurance to cover all the parties, as their interests may appear, in a single policy. Such an agreement will often specify, in addition, who is to purchase and pay for the insurance, who is obligated to repair or replace the property when it is damaged, that the insurance payments are to be used for this purpose, and the perils to be insured against. The details of such an agreement may vary according to the legal jurisdiction or the preferences of the parties, but the mere fact that the holders of the various interests are often close relatives does not eliminate the need for a formal understanding before a loss occurs. To the contrary, the grantor of a life estate who is made to understand its implications will normally want to exercise special care to protect the interests of loved ones and avoid any unpleasant disputes between them.

Estate or Tenancy for Years   An "estate for years," also called a "tenancy for years," is an estate that lasts for a definite period of time—such as three months, ten years or even ninety-nine years. The holder of this type of estate, the *tenant*, has temporary possession and use of property that is owned by another entity. A tenancy for years is most often created and governed by the specific terms of a lease agreement, which is usually in writing. The property involved may be an item of personal property—such as an auto, or an item of real property—such as a parcel of land, a building, or a portion of a building. In either case, the tenant is normally renting the property from the owner (landlord) for an agreed price. At the end of the specified period, the tenancy for years will terminate (unless it is renewed).

Insurable Interests in Tenancy for Years.   The insurable interests of the owner (landlord) were discussed earlier under the heading of the fee simple estate. They include the insurable interests of the fee simple owner in the full intrinsic value of the property owned, as well as the owner's valid interests in insuring against a loss of rental income, a loss of earnings associated with a business interruption, and the extra expenses which may be required to secure alternative facilities during the period it takes to restore the property's economic value in use. To these should be added the reminder that the tenant for years often makes so-called "improvements and betterments" which become a permanent part of the real property being rented from the owner. If so, the owner has an insurable interest in the improvements, though actual responsibility for insuring them may be stipulated in the lease.

The holder of a tenancy for years also may have several kinds of insurable interest in the property subject to tenancy. Since the existence and/or amounts of the tenant's insurable interests often are determined by the specific terms of a lease, there is a sense in which such interests could be discussed under the heading of contract rights, rather than under property rights. However, the two categories overlap in some respects (e.g., a right to possess or use property is very often granted by contract), and some of the tenant's insurable interests would exist, even in the absence of a corresponding lease provision. The argument over classifications will be left to others. The goal here is merely to identify some of the more common insurable interests that may be held by the tenant for years.

Some courts have said that the tenant for years has an insurable interest in the full value of the item of property the tenant is renting from its owner. As a practical matter, many owners prefer to insure the property themselves and pass the cost of the insurance along to the tenant(s) as a part of the rent. The typical tenant has no particular desire to insure the landlord's property, given the choice. However, the tenant would have good reason to consider purchasing additional insurance in the tenant's own name, if (1) the tenant has an option to buy the property, (2) the owner is known to carry inadequate coverage, or (3) the tenant is legally obligated by the lease to insure the property and/or return it in good condition at the end of the lease, especially if the lease stipulates that the tenant is not released from the latter obligation by damage to the property from certain specified perils.

Unless an explicit agreement imposes additional duties on the tenant, the tenant is generally not responsible for damage to the property, unless the damage was caused by a negligent or intentional act of the tenant or of someone for whom the tenant was responsible. Furthermore, in shorter-term leases the tenant is usually not responsible for the payment of rents, if the property is severely damaged, during the time it takes to restore the property to its pre-loss condition. In ninety-nine year leases the tenant is often required to continue rent payments throughout the entire duration of the lease, including the period during which damaged property is being repaired or replaced. In either long- or short-term leases, there may be specific provisions dealing with such matters as:

- who bears the consequences of loss to improvements and betterments made by the tenant;
- who is responsible for paying the costs of utilities, cleaning, and maintenance services;
- whether rent paid in advance is refundable if the property is severely damaged;
- whether and under what circumstances the tenant must pay a penalty for breaking the lease;
- and whether (as is often the case) the rental amount is subject to renegotiation after the property has been severely damaged or destroyed.

All this suggests that when the relevant property is damaged or destroyed, the tenant for years may suffer the kinds of indirect losses associated with the temporary inability of the tenant to *use* the property.

It is extremely difficult to formulate accurate generalizations about the indirect loss exposures and related insurable interests of tenants for years. They vary from tenant to tenant, and they are governed by a number of factors, especially the specific terms of the applicable lease agreement. For example, suppose a business tenant leases an entire building for ten years and the building is destroyed by fire at the end of the fifth year. The loss of the building's intrinsic value is borne directly by its fee simple owner, assuming no lease provision to the contrary. But what kinds of insurable interests does this tenant have? That would depend upon the loss exposures actually faced by this particular tenant. A business tenant undoubtedly would own furniture, inventory, machinery, or other items of personal property which could be insured for their full insurable value as *contents* of the building. The tenant clearly has a use interest in *improvements and betterments* made by the tenant. In addition, the tenant may have valid interests arising out of the substantial indirect losses that may result from the inability to use damaged or destroyed property for the period it takes to repair or replace the property and otherwise return to a normal level of business activity. Such indirect losses could be caused by direct damage to the building, direct damage to the contents, or both, and the losses could include those associated with leasehold interests, business interruptions and/or extra expenses.

A *leasehold interest* exists whenever the rent a tenant pays under its present lease is less than the rent the tenant would have to pay for the same or comparable property at today's prices. Suppose a business tenant had five years remaining in the lease at the time the building was destroyed. Suppose the tenant was paying a rental of $1,000 per month, though comparable facilities would cost $1,500 per month at the time the building was destroyed. The lease stipulates that the $1,000 monthly rent is subject to renegotiation whenever the building is damaged seriously enough to render it untenantable. The tenant will now have to pay $500 more per month for the five years remaining in the lease, whether the tenant stays in the same location or moves to another location. This excess amount is effectively a potential "loss" which can be insured by the purchase of leasehold interest insurance.

A *business interruption* loss exposure may be faced by the tenant, as well as the landlord. It exists whenever a business would be forced to cease or reduce operations as a result of damage to the building and/or contents, thus giving rise to loss which is in general measured by the decline in earnings during both the period of shutdown and the additional period of time it takes to reach a normal level of revenue after the business reopens. If the business is of the type that would want to continue to operate even at higher-than-normal expense levels, in spite of serious damage to the property, it would experience a loss equivalent to the *extra expenses* of operating the business while the property is being repaired or replaced.

Each of the aforementioned loss exposures is analyzed in greater detail in other CPCU texts. The purpose of mentioning them in this discussion is to stress that the tenant for years may have a variety of insurable interests arising out of the relationship to leased premises.

Some of the tenant's insurable interests are equal in amount to the direct loss of ownership rights, as measured by the intrinsic value of property owned by the tenant. Other interests of the tenant are equal in amount to the indirect losses of rights to use property which is owned or leased by the tenant. These indirect losses may far exceed the intrinsic value of destroyed property, and they are often based largely on the provisions of a lease agreement.

Joint Ownership and Insurable Interests Buildings, land, autos, and bank accounts are among the items of property frequently owned by two or more entities, in which event the property is said to be "jointly owned." A particular property interest or bundle of rights, if jointly owned, is called a *joint tenancy concurrent estate*. Though a joint tenancy does not have to be a fee estate or an estate in real property, the following discussion will assume that each estate referred to is owned in fee, and it will use the family residence as a familiar example.

Estates involving joint ownership include the common-law estates of joint tenancy, tenancy by the entirety, and tenancy in common, as well as a tenancy in partnership.

Joint Tenancy. A *joint tenancy* is an estate owned by two or more joint tenants and characterized by the fact that each tenant has an equal share and each has the right of survivorship. Thus, if J, T, and Y are joint tenants and Y dies, Y's share goes equally to J and T (the survivors). If T then dies, J ends up owning the entire estate. A living joint tenant could sever the estate by selling his or her interest. But a joint tenant's share cannot be willed to another, by definition, because at the instant of death the share of the deceased passes automatically to the surviving tenant(s). Generally, each joint tenant has an insurable interest to the extent of the full value of the property. Since any one of the joint tenants, as the only survivor, could quickly become the sole owner of the property, each tenant effectively stands to lose the full value of the property if it is destroyed. Note that we are concerned here with the extent of the legally recognized interest and not with the actual securing of insurance to cover any interest. We are saying that, in the *eyes of the law*, each joint tenant is deemed to have an insurable interest in the full value of the property. We are *not* saying that each should secure insurance equal to full value or that each could collect from insurance the full value of the property.

Tenancy by Entirety. A *tenancy by the entirety* is a special kind of joint tenancy which is applicable only to a husband and wife, and it cannot be terminated during their lifetimes unless both agree to do so. Like joint tenants, tenants by the entirety have survivorship rights. If the husband dies, his share of the property passes to the wife (or vice

between the unit owners and the association that serves as the operating organization on behalf of the unit owners.

Despite legal variations, each unit owner normally has an insurable interest equal to the total value of the condominium estate, including the unit owner's specified percentage interest in the building(s) and any alterations of (and additions to) a building which are effected by the unit owner.

Future Interests A future interest in property is a *present right* to take possession of the property at some specified future time. That time may be linked to a specified number of years—such as at the end of an estate for years, or to the occurrence of a specified event—such as the death of a life tenant. Examples of future interests include the previously discussed remainder interest held by a remainderman and the reversionary interest held by a reversioner. The precise nature of a particular future interest depends largely on the exact wording of the will or deed which creates the interest. In every case, however, the holder of the interest has a *present* right—not a contingent or possible right—to future possession of the property. Upon the occurrence of the specified event, or at the otherwise specified future point in time, what was once a future interest instantly "matures" and becomes a present interest in property. The holder takes possession of whatever kind of estate has been granted to him or her, whether a simple estate, a tenancy in common, or some other kind of estate.

The holder of a future interest has an insurable interest in the property the instant the future interest is *created.* The extent of the holder's insurable interest is the same as it would be if the future interest matured into a present interest immediately. For example, suppose father stipulates in his will that upon his death his wife is to receive a life estate in the family mansion in which father has fee simple ownership. When mother dies, daughter is to have a fee simple estate in the mansion. Father dies a few years after signing the will. At the instant of father's death, daughter acquires a future interest in the mansion. If mother dies immediately thereafter, daughter will take possession of a fee simple estate, and the holder of such an estate has an insurable interest in the full value of the property. Accordingly, daughter may insure the mansion for its full insurable value any time after her father's death, even if mother is still alive and healthy. It does not matter whether mother is thirty or ninety years old at the time. Daughter acquires her insurable interest at the instant the future interest is created for her—at the time of her father's death, in this case. The *amount* of daughter's insurable interest is not affected by the life expectancy of her mother.

It should be emphasized that in the above example the daughter would not have had any insurable interest in the mansion before her father died, even though the possibility of her eventual inheritance was clearly spelled out in her father's will. Since the person making the will (the *testator*) can always change the will as long as he or she is alive, any one named in the will is merely an *heir expectant* as long as the testator is still alive. An heir expectant generally does not have an insurable interest in the property covered by the will, because a mere expectancy does not in itself create a future interest. As soon as the testator dies, an heir does acquire a legally insurable interest in the property to be inherited, even before the estate is settled and the property distributed to the heir(s).

Equitable Title Generally speaking, there are two broad types of "title" in property law. The *legal title* to property is basically the enforceable right of its ownership and possession. The phrase is also commonly used to describe a deed, bill of sale, certificate of ownership, or other documents which may serve as evidence of title. An *equitable title* in property is the enforceable right of a person who is the real owner, as a matter of equity, to obtain the legal title from another party who is the owner of record without right of ownership. Through errors, misdeeds, or routine delays in consummating property transactions, the rightful owners of property often are at least temporarily deprived of legal title and/or custody and possession of the property. For example, the purchaser of an auto normally encounters some delay between the time of the purchase and the time the title document is received from the state. If an error occurs in processing, the owner may fail even to receive the title document. The holder of an equitable title may establish the facts in a court, if necessary, and obtain the legal title and the property.

In the meantime, it is well established that the holder of an equitable title to property has an insurable interest in the property, regardless of whether the holder has the legal title or has the property in his or her custody or possession. This rule has numerous applications in practice, especially in real estate sales transactions. In all situations involving holders of equitable title, the extent of the holder's insurable interest is the same as if the holder also had legal title. The amount of the insurable interest, then, depends on the particular kind of estate that is held.

Insurable Interests Based on Contract Rights

The material under this heading deals with insurable interests based on the rights an entity has as a party to a contract. An entity also is likely to have duties because it is a party to a contract. Some of these duties, which can be the origin of insurable interests based on potential legal liability, will be explained later in this chapter.

A contract may be defined as an agreement between two or more entities creating one or more obligations between them that the law will enforce. When one entity has a contractual obligation to a second entity, the second entity has a contractual right based on the first entity's obligation. Contract rights may be broadly classified as:

- Rights *in personam,* or rights with respect to persons. If one party to a contract has rights *in personam* against the other party to the contract, the first party does not have a claim against any *specific* property of the second party. However, the first party can require the second to use any or all of its property to satisfy its obligation to the first party.
- Rights *in rem,* or rights with respect to things or property. If one party has *in rem* contractual rights against a second party, the first party has a specific claim against *some particular item(s)* of property held by the second party. The first party can enforce its claim (if necessary) to satisfy any contractual obligation that the second party fails to perform.

Two examples, each involving a loan contract, will illustrate the differences between *in personam* and *in rem* contract rights:

- *In personam* rights are involved when a creditor makes an *unsecured loan.* (With an unsecured loan, the debtor does not pledge any property as security for repayment of the loan.) If the debtor fails to repay an unsecured loan, the creditor is only a *general creditor* of the debtor and has no more direct claim on any of the debtor's property than does any other general creditor.
- *In rem* rights are involved when a creditor makes a *secured loan.* (With a secured loan, the debtor pledges specific property as collateral to guarantee repayment of the loan.) The creditor is a *secured creditor* and has the right to take the property and sell it to satisfy the debt. This claim takes precedence over the claims of general creditors.

In short, an *in personam* right gives its holder a general claim against a person, but no claim against particular property. An *in rem* right gives its holder a specific claim against particular property.

Insurable Interests Based on Contract Rights In Personam Usually, contract rights *in personam* do not create insurable interests with respect to property-liability insurance. Because this type of contract right does not create any claims to specific property, it provides no basis for an insurable interest in such property. Thus, an unsecured creditor does not have an insurable interest in any property of a debtor as long as the debtor is alive. However, if an unsecured creditor obtains a court judgment against a debtor and is entitled, by the court's order, to proceed against specified property to satisfy the debt, the creditor now has an *in rem* right in the specified property and an insurable interest in it to the extent of the unpaid debt. Similarly, once a debtor has died, the rights of an unsecured creditor against the decedent become *in rem* rights against the property in the decedent's estate. The *in rem* rights give the unsecured creditor an insurable interest in at least some of the property (real property only in some jurisdictions) in the estate, to the extent of the debt outstanding when the debtor died.

There is one significant class of exceptions to the general rule that an *in personam* contract right cannot be the basis for an insurable interest in property. The exceptions involve situations in which the continued existence of a particular item of property is deemed by a court to be essential to that right. In these cases, the holder of the *in personam* right is ruled to have an insurable interest in the essential property. This was the basis for the rulings in the following cases, all of which resulted in a decision that an insurable interest existed:

- A person who was hired under a long-term contract as superintendent in a factory was held to have a valid insurable interest in fire damage to that factory. Without that factory, the value of the insured's *in personam* right to be paid for serving as superintendent would have been substantially lessened.
- A house mover was held to have an insurable interest in damage to a house the mover had contracted to move, but which burned before the move was complete. The amount of the insurable interest was based on the compensation the mover would have received.
- An insured had invented and patented a process used in drilling for oil, and had contracted with a drilling firm to allow it to use the patented process in return for paying the inventor a portion of the profits from particular oil wells. The inventor was held to have an insurable interest in damage to the machinery used to pump oil from the particular wells.

In each of these cases, the holder of the *in personam* contract right was said to have had an enforceable insurable interest equal to the profit the insured would have received had the insured event not occurred.

In contrast to the general rule in property-liability insurance, *in personam* contract rights do create insurable interests with respect to life insurance. For example, an employer, entitled by contract to the skills of a key employee (an *in personam* right), has an insurable interest in the life of that employee.

***Insurable Interests Based on Contract Rights* In Rem**   An *in rem* contract right generally is the basis for an insurable interest in the property subject to that right. The holder of the right is likely to suffer a financial loss from damage to the property. Two types of contracts are particularly significant sources of the *in rem* rights that are the foundation of corresponding insurable interests: (1) contracts in which the right secures payment of a debt, and (2) contracts for the sale of property.

In Rem *Rights to Secure Payment of a Debt.*   *In rem* rights may secure payment of two types of debt—those involving a secured creditor, and those involving a lienholder.

SECURED CREDITOR.   A secured creditor has an insurable interest in the property that secured payment of the debt. The creditor's insurable interest is the amount of the remaining balance of the debt. This general rule is the source of the insurable interest every mortgagee and pledgee has in property that secures the repayment of debts owed them.

The economic basis for this insurable interest is that damage to the mortgaged or pledged property can reduce the likelihood that the mortgagee or pledgee will be paid. While it is true that the debtor is still obligated to pay the debt even if the property is damaged or destroyed, the motivation to do so may be lessened significantly. If the borrower defaults, the creditor will not be able to sell the property in damaged condition for as much as the undamaged property could have been sold to satisfy the debt. This threat to the status of the creditor, though short of constituting a *certain* financial loss, is sufficient to support an insurable interest on the part of the creditor. The creditor's potential loss from the destruction of the property—the outstanding balance owed at the time of the damage to the property—is also the extent of the creditor's insurable interest.

LIENHOLDER.   A *lien* is a claim on property growing out of any contract on which money is owed; the *lienholder* is a creditor who has an insurable interest in the property involved to the extent of the debt. An entity may become a creditor because it is owed money for services performed for another entity. When those services involve work on the debtor's property, the entity performing the services may acquire a lien on that property. The lien may be based on a specific contract provision, or on the equitable principle that a party that performs services under contract ought to be justly compensated for those services.

The insurable interests of a lienholder are illustrated by a few examples:

- A hotelkeeper has a lien on a guest's luggage for payment of unpaid room charges; the insurable interest is limited to the extent of the unpaid charges.
- A landlord has a lien against a boarder's personal property for nonpayment of rent; the insurable interest is limited to the extent of overdue rent.
- A supplier of building materials to a construction site has a lien against the structure being built until the supplier is paid for the material; the insurable interest is limited to the extent of the unpaid bill for those materials.
- A moving and storage company has a lien against the objects being moved or stored; the insurable interest is limited to the extent of the customer's bill.

An exception to the general rule that a lien creates an insurable interest is the case of an employee to whom an employer owes back wages. Such an employee has a lien against the assets used in the employer's business, but the employee does not have an insurable interest in those assets. The reason for denying an employee an insurable interest in an employer's assets appears to be the judicial concern that an employee, disgruntled at not being paid promptly, might intentionally damage the employer's property in order to collect insurance on it. However, if the employee obtains a judgment against the employer, the employee takes on the status of a secured creditor. As such, he or she has an insurable interest, to the extent of unpaid wages, in the specific property authorized by the judgment to serve as collateral security for the payment of the debt.

In Rem *Rights Arising Out of Contracts for the Sale of Property.* The process of selling property involves transferring from the seller to the buyer the title, exposure to loss, and insurable interest in the property being sold. Before the selling process begins (as between the two parties) only the seller has any title or insurable interest in the property. The seller's insurable interest is then based on the seller's property rights. When the selling process is completed, the buyer has legal title to the property. The buyer's insurable interest is then based on the buyer's property rights. *During* the selling process, the seller, the buyer, and possibly both may have insurable interests in the property. These interests are based on legal title, on equitable title, or on a security interest in the property, but the principles governing ownership transfer and related insurable interests differ significantly between sales of real property and of personal property. Therefore, sales of these two types of property need to be discussed separately.

SALES OF REAL PROPERTY.　Sales of real property are governed in most jurisdictions by the common-law principle that loss exposure follows title. Since the holder of title of the property is exposed to loss, the titleholder has an insurable interest in that property. However, the title that brings with it the exposure to loss can be either legal or equitable in nature.

The buyer of real property has an insurable interest in it at several possible points in the selling process, before obtaining legal title to the property. For example, the *holder of an option to buy real property* has been held to have equitable title to that property and an insurable interest in it. By paying the option price and complying with the other terms of the option, the option holder may compel the owner to surrender legal title to the property. Under common law, a buyer of real property does not take legal title to it until the seller actually or constructively delivers the deed to the buyer. But the buyer has an equitable title to the property once the buyer and seller have agreed on the price and other terms of sale of the property. The buyer's equitable title supports an insurable interest equal to the full value of the property, which is the measure of the potential loss to the holder of the equitable title as a result of damage to the property.

During the time the buyer holds an equitable title to the property, the seller retains legal title until the deed is delivered to the buyer. This legal title is the basis of an insurable interest for the seller equal to the full value of the property. After delivering the deed to the buyer, the seller retains an insurable interest in the property if the seller has a security interest in the property as a mortgagee. (The same rule applies if payments are still due the seller under a conditional sales contract.) The insurable interest based on such a security interest is the unpaid balance of the mortgage (or purchase price in the case of a conditional sales contract).

SALES OF PERSONAL PROPERTY.　Sales of personal property are governed largely by the Uniform Commercial Code, rather than by common law. The *Uniform Commercial Code* was written by a large number of experts on American law under the auspices of the National Commission on Uniform State Laws. It organizes, clarifies, and in some ways changes the law regarding commercial transactions. The Uniform Commercial Code is only one of several codes on various phases of American law which, at the urging of the National Commission, have been adopted by many states. Adoption of the Uniform Commercial Code- with few, if any, variations in all states except Louisiana, the District of Columbia, and the Virgin Islands, has substantially reduced former variations among state laws pertaining to commercial transactions.

Article Two of the Code deals with sales of goods, including within the concept of goods all things that are movable except money. The Code applies to all sales, regardless of whether one or both parties to the sale is a business firm, a consumer, or some other entity. Thus, the only sales of personal property to which the Code does not apply are sales of intangible property. However, items of intangible property are not subject to damage by perils typically covered by property insurance. Only the documentary evidence of ownership of intangible property is vulnerable to physical damage. These documents frequently can be replaced at little cost. Or, if the cost is substantial, insurance against the cost of replacing them can be purchased.

The Code explicitly dissolves the common-law unity among title, loss exposures, and insurable interest, with respect to the kinds of personal property to which the Code applies. The Code permits the buyer and seller of such property to stipulate by agreement when title will pass between them. If they make no stipulation, the Code provides that title passes to the buyer at the time and place at which the seller completes physical delivery of the goods as required by the terms of the contract, even though the seller may retain a security interest in the goods. Precisely where and when the physical delivery required by the contract becomes complete depends on the wording of the contract.

Based on the rules regarding title, the Code sets forth three basic rules on insurable interests:

(1) The *seller* has an insurable interest in damage to the goods as long as the seller has title to the goods in accordance with either an agreement between the buyer and the seller or the Code provisions dealing with title.

(2) The *seller* retains an insurable interest in the goods while the seller has a security interest in them, even after title to the goods has been transferred to the buyer.

(3) The *buyer* has an insurable interest in the goods as soon as the goods have been "identified," that is, as soon as the specific goods the buyer is to take have been somehow distinguished from any other similar goods the seller may have. Identification may occur when the buyer and seller reach the mutual agreement which is the basis for their contract, when the goods are segregated in a package, or when they are delivered to the buyer. Identification can create an insurable interest for the buyer long before the transfer of title to the buyer or the satisfaction of the seller's security interest extinguishes the seller's insurable interest. Therefore, it is quite common for

both the buyer and the seller to have simultaneous insurable interests in the property.

The foregoing rules regarding the times at which a buyer and a seller have an insurable interest in goods also affect the extent of each entity's insurable interest in those goods:

- A *buyer* has no insurable interest in goods until they have been identified; thereafter, the buyer's insurable interest is equal to the full value of the goods, regardless of whether the buyer actually holds legal or equitable title to them.
- The extent of the *seller's* insurable interest in the goods depends on the point in the transaction at which the goods are damaged.

If the goods are damaged at a time when title remains with the seller and the buyer need not pay for the property, the seller's potential loss and insurable interest both equal the full value of the property. If the property is destroyed after title has passed to the buyer and the buyer has paid for them, the seller faces no potential loss from damage to the goods and has no insurable interest in them. If the goods are destroyed at any time when the seller has a valid security interest, the seller's potential loss (and insurable interest) is limited to the unpaid balance of the debt.

Because a buyer and a seller may both have simultaneous insurable interests in the same goods, and because the buyer's insurable interest is never less than their full value, the sum of a buyer's and a seller's insurable interests in the same goods may exceed their full value.

Insurable Interests Based on Potential Legal Liability

In general, an entity has an insurable interest in any event that may cause financial harm to that entity. Damage to the property of others or bodily injury to others is such an event whenever the damage or injury creates potential legal liability for the entity. An insurable interest that rests on potential legal liability does not depend on whether the entity has any legal or equitable title, but on whether the entity *may be* charged in court with liability for damage or injury stemming from the event in question.

Since *any entity has an insurable interest in any event that may result in liability for that entity,* the very fact that an entity has incurred a claim that comes within the scope of a particular liability policy is persuasive proof that the insured has an insurable interest in the event(s) that led to that claim. Even if the claim is groundless, the entity may still suffer a loss in the form of costs to provide a legal defense against the claim.

Auto ownership and operation provide several illustrations of insurable interests based on potential legal liability. The owner and the operator of an auto unquestionably have insurable interests in liability claims growing out of the use of that auto. In addition, a parent has an insurable interest in claims arising from a minor child's use of an auto owned by and licensed to the minor child in a jurisdiction with a law that makes a parent legally responsible for such use. Similarly, an employer has an insurable interest in claims arising out of an employee's use of the employee's own auto on business, since it is a well established principle of American civil law that an employer may be held liable for injuries and damages that result from the negligence of its employee while acting within the scope of employment.

Insurable interest arising out of potential legal liability does not require an insurable interest in the property (such as an auto or building) involved in the situation giving rise to liability. For example, a tenant has a valid insurable interest in claims arising out of injuries to visitors while in the public areas of an apartment house, even though the tenant has no insurable interest in physical damage to those areas. However, an entity must face a realistic possibility of legal liability due to the occurrence of the event in question in order to have an insurable interest in that event. An entity that faces no such possibility has no insurable interest. For example, a creditor that has merely loaned money for the purchase of an auto but has no other connection with the vehicle has no insurable interest in claims arising from the use of that auto. The creditor could not reasonably be subject to such claims.

Bodily Injury and Property Damage in General The typical liability insurance policy applies to claims for bodily injury and property damage under a broad range of circumstances. Before the fact, there is no precise basis for determining how large these claims might be. In recognition of this fact, the courts do not in general impose any dollar limit on the amount of an entity's insurable interest in the events covered by liability insurance. Either a natural person or a corporation theoretically could purchase an unlimited amount of enforceable liability insurance, if the buyer could find a willing insurer and the buyer was willing and able to pay the premium.

Damage to Specific Property An entity's insurable interest based solely on potential legal liability does have an upper limit when legal liability may arise out of damage to *specific* items of property. An example is when one entity is responsible for the safety of particular property that belongs to another. In such a case, the top limit of the responsible entity's liability, and of its insurable interest based on that liability, is the full value of the property, including the use value to the owner. Except that it may be held liable for its destruction, the insuring entity typically has no other insurable interest in damage to the property for which it is responsible. (An exception is an insurable interest based on a lien. For example, a warehouse may have a lien against stored property based on unpaid storage charges.)

There are many instances of liability insurance being issued to an entity that has an insurable interest based only on potential legal liability for damage to specific property of others.

- A bailee—one who takes temporary custody of property of others for a specific purpose, such as storage or repair—may insure its liability for damage to the property of others left in its custody. If the property is damaged under conditons which make the bailee liable, the bailee may collect the proceeds of insurance up to the full value of the property. However, after deducting any charges due the bailee for storing, repairing, or performing other services, the bailee must pay the remainder of the insurance money to the customer.

- A common carrier has an insurable interest in its liability for damage to goods of others which the carrier has agreed to transport.

- The executor of an estate has an insurable interest in liability for damage to property included within the estate.

- A hotelkeeper has an insurable interest in liability for damage to guests' property.

- A tenant has an insurable interest in liability for damage to premises the tenant has agreed to return to the landlord in the same condition as when the tenant's occupancy began.

- A warehouseman has an insurable interest in liability for damage to property being stored.

- A contractor has an insurable interest in legal liability for damages to a building under construction. Most construction contracts stipulate that the contractor bears the exposure to loss during construction even though the partially completed building is the property of the entity for which it is being built. Even after a building has been completed, the contractor may have an insurable interest in damage to the building. This would occur if the contractor is liable under the construction contract to repair or replace the building should it be damaged or destroyed within a specified period after completion.

- A person who has custody of property whose true ownership is unknown may insure against potential liability to the true owner if the property is damaged before the true owner becomes known.

Insurable Interests Based on Factual Expectation

Factual expectation is the most inclusive of all bases for insurable interests. It is the *expectation* of economic advantage to the insured, if the insured event does not occur, or, conversely, the expectation of economic harm to the insured, if the event does occur. The notion of factual expectation theoretically could serve as the basis for all insurable interests. Each type of recognized insurable interest involves the expectation of financial harm from the occurrence of the insured event or of financial benefit from its nonoccurrence.

Despite its logical appeal, factual expectation is not a valid basis for an insurable interest in property in the majority of United States jurisdictions. In the few situations where the courts have accepted factual expectation as a valid basis for an insurable interest, the insured does not need to have any property right, contract right, or potential legal liability in order to establish an insurable interest. The insured person only has to show potential financial harm from the event to be insured. For example:

- Wisconsin courts have held that a husband living on real estate owned solely by his wife has an insurable interest in that property. This insurable interest was based on the factual expectation that the wife will continue to let him live on the land and farm it.
- In Wisconsin a landlord has an insurable interest in damage to a tenant's crop when both the landlord and the tenant know that the proceeds from the tenant's sale of the crop are the only funds with which the tenant will be able to pay the rent to the landlord.
- An Illinois court ruled that a son has an insurable interest in buildings owned by his father when the father has orally expressed the intention to will the building to his son. This ruling is a rare exception to the general rule that an heir expectant has no insurable interest in his or her legacy until the testator has died.
- A commission merchant, it was ruled, may insure against loss of expected profits on the sale of goods being shipped to the merchant. Because the merchant made a contract prior to shipment with the owner of the goods to sell them on the owner's behalf, the court held that the merchant had an insurable interest in damage to the goods while at sea because

"nothing stood between the merchant and the sales commission except the perils of the sea." The merchant had satisfied the court that the goods would have been sold, had they arrived safely, because of the merchant's past success in selling goods of the same type.

The reasoning underlying the recognition of factual expectation as a basis for an insurable interest is summarized in the Insurance Law of New York State, which defines an insurable interest as including "any lawful and substantial economic interest in the safety or preservation of property from loss, destruction, or pecuniary damage."[8] The focus on the insured's *economic position*, rather than legal interest, is the distinguishing mark of factual expectation as a basis for an insurable interest.

In most American jurisdictions, some legal interest is deemed essential to a valid insurable interest. Factual expectation alone will not suffice. Although this legal interest may be based on any of several foundations—such as a property right, contract right, or potential tort liability—some legal interest is vital. For example, the California Insurance Code, in contrast to New York's, specifies that "a mere contingent or expectant interest in anything, not founded on an actual right to the thing, nor upon any valid contract for it, is not insurable."[9] However, in those jurisdictions that do require some legal interest, any legal interest is sufficient to support an insurable interest, even though it may be very unlikely that the legal interest will materialize into actual ownership or possession of the property involved. For example, in these states an eighty-five-year-old mother with a remainder interest in a home would have an insurable interest in that home even though it was currently occupied by a robust and healthy thirty-year-old life tenant. Though it is very unlikely that her future interest will ever materialize into actual possession and use, the mother would be held to have an insurable interest.

To justify denying an insurable interest based solely on factual expectation, some courts have simply held fast to the doctrine that a legal interest is essential to an insurable interest in all situations. Giving some logical basis for this conclusion is the assertion that recognizing insurable interests based solely on factual expectation would permit the purchase of insurance by strangers who would suffer no real loss from the property's destruction. Some of them might possibly wish to damage the property or to use their insurable interest to mask a wager.

In jurisdictions that deny insurable interests based solely on factual expectations, an entity with only a factual expectation but wishing to insure the particular property often can contractually arrange to have a legal interest in the property as well. For example, an heir expectant could enter into a contract with the present occupant to maintain, or help maintain, the property covered by a will under which the heir expectant stands to receive property. Such a liability for maintenance could create a clear legal interest for the heir expectant in the preservation of the property covered by the will. This legal interest would support an insurable interest recognized in any American jurisdiction. Thus, it can be argued that relying on factual expectation as the basis for an insurable interest when legally based insurable interests can be readily created by contract is dangerous to the insured.

Insurable Interests Based on Representative Status

As has been shown earlier, agents, trustees, and bailees often have independent insurable interests in property on the basis of contract rights or potential legal liability. Beyond these interests, the legal representative of a second entity may obtain insurance in its own name for the benefit of the second. For example:

- An agent may insure property in his or her name for the benefit of the principal.
- A trustee may insure property in his or her name for the benefit of the trust.
- A bailee may insure property in his or her name for the benefit of a bailor.

In these situations, the entity obtaining the insurance need not itself have an independent insurable interest in damage to the property. The entity derives its representative insurable interest from its relationship with the person(s) it represents. Although the insurance is issued in the name of the entity that obtains it, the "representative status" of the insured is customarily shown by inserting, after the name of the insured, phrases such as:

- "for the benefit of _____" (if the interest of a specific known entity is being protected), or
- "for whom it may concern" (if the interests of a class of entities are being protected).

Such phrases are not essential. If it can be shown by other evidence that the insurance was obtained for the protection of others, the validity of the policy is not jeopardized by the fact that the entity obtaining it does not have an insurable interest in the covered property. Further, there need be no specific grant of authority to insure from the interest being represented.

When legal capacity to insure the property is derived from status as the legal agent of another entity having an insurable interest, the entity obtaining the insurance must fulfill the duties of a legal agent. This means that the person obtaining the insurance must act in the best interests of the entity having the insurable interest and must pay over to that entity all insurance proceeds. When the person obtaining the insurance (such as a warehouseman) represents a group of entities (such as the warehouse customers), it is not necessary that each of these entities be identified or even specifically known to the person obtaining the insurance. To be covered by insurance obtained in this way, the protected entity must meet two criteria:

(1) it must be within the group the purchaser intended to benefit by insurance, and
(2) it must not have rejected the coverage.

PROBLEMS ASSOCIATED WITH
THE LACK OF INSURABLE INTEREST

An insurance policy that is not supported by a valid insurable interest is not legally enforceable. When an insurable interest is lacking, an insurer may raise this fact as a defense to any claim, thereby extinguishing both its duties under the policy and the rights which the insured (or other party, such as a mortgagee or beneficiary) had under the policy.

The possibility of an insurer's relying on the lack of an insurable interest as a basis for denying a claim raises at least three questions of public policy:

(1) Under what conditions may an insurer raise lack of insurable interest as a defense to a claim under a policy?
(2) Can an entity other than the insurer raise the insurable interest question?
(3) When a policy is declared void for lack of a valid insurable interest, what, if anything, is done to prevent the unjust enrichment of the insurer?

Use of the Insurable Interest Defense By the Insurer

Subject to very few restrictions, an insurer may, at any time, raise lack of an insurable interest to have a policy declared void. Successfully raising this defense has the effect of denying coverage for any loss the insurer has not yet paid. Because of the importance courts attach to removing any temptations for wagering, intentional destruction of property, or murder, the great majority of American courts even permit an insurer to avoid paying for losses which otherwise would have been covered under the policy. Yet, the courts do not always agree as to whether the lack of an insurable interest by the insured establishes sufficient grounds to justify denying a claim.

An example of the last point is the incontestable clause, found in virtually every life insurance policy. The usual incontestable clause bars the insurer from contesting the validity of a policy, for any reason except nonpayment of premiums, after the policy has been in force for two years. The purpose of the clause is to safeguard the insured and the beneficiary against stale challenges the insurer might raise to the policy many years after the issue date, perhaps when those who could successfully disprove an insurer's challenge would be unable to give good evidence to support the validity of a policy. The courts have interpreted incontestable clauses to be subject to only a very few implied exceptions, one of which is the lack of an insurable interest. The clause does not block an insurer from denying coverage under a life insurance policy because the applicant lacked an insurable interest in the life of the insured when the policy was issued.

That the majority of American courts allow an insurer to raise the issue of insurable interest despite the incontestable clause is strong evidence of the emphasis most courts place on preventing life insurance from becoming a temptation for wagering or homicide. Most courts are so concerned with preventing these crimes that they will allow the question of insurable interest to be raised after many years, even though this may deprive deserving beneficiaries of needed insurance proceeds after an insured has died. In a few jurisdictions, however, courts have ruled that a life insurer's right to raise the question of the applicant's insurable interest is limited by the incontestable clause.

In most jurisdictions, an insurer may deny coverage for lack of an insurable interest even though the insurer has been aware for some time of the lack of insurable interest and has accepted premiums for coverage the insurer has or should have known it could successfully deny. For example:

- When a life insurer's agent knew that the policy it had issued was truly a wager on the life of the insured, the insurer successfully defended against a claim by the beneficiary of the policy on the ground that, as a gambling contract, the policy could not be enforced by either party.
- In a case where an insurer's agent knew that a client had already sold, and had no legal or other interest in, a house the client asked the agent to insure, the fact that the agent (and, therefore, under the law of agency, the insurer) knew the client had no insurable interest in the house did not bar the insurer

from successfully denying a claim for damage to the house on this basis.

In situations involving policy conditions other than insurable interest requirements, courts often rule that the insurer's own conduct—letting the insured continue to breach a condition or especially leading the insured into a breach—bars the insurer from raising that breach as a defense against an insured's claim. For example, if an agent for a fire insurer knows that an insured has begun to store large quantities of fireworks in the basement of the building insured and yet the agent says nothing (or even tells the insured not to be concerned about the fireworks), most courts hold that the insurer may not deny the claim, even though the fire policy contains a provision that suspends coverage in the event of an increase in hazard. In contrast, when faced with evidence that an insurer or its agent knew of the lack of an insurable interest under a policy, most courts would allow the insurer to deny payment for an otherwise covered loss. Some courts have even stated that an insurer *cannot* waive an insurable interest requirement. Other courts have insisted that an insurer may waive, or be estopped (prevented) from asserting as a defense, a lack of an insurable interest. For example:

- It has been held that a life insurer is estopped from asserting the lack of an insurable interest in a cousin of an insured when an agent of the insurer persuaded the cousin to take over premium payments on a life insurance policy which was about to lapse, on the condition that the cousin be named beneficiary of the policy.
- Another court ruled that a fire insurer waived the insurable interest requirement by issuing a policy covering several buildings when the insurer's agent knew that the insured had no ownership or other legal interest in some of the buildings covered by the policy.

On the basis of the foregoing sampling of court rulings, it should be obvious that the courts do not always agree on the question of whether an insurer should be permitted to deny a claim on the grounds that an insured did not have an insurable interest. While conflicting rulings can sometimes be justified by differing sets of facts, the conflicts regarding insurable interest decisions also clearly reflect the differing judicial attitudes toward the relative importance of preventing gambling, intentional property destruction, and homicide (on the one hand), and fostering equity between insurers and insureds (on the other hand). In most jurisdictions the prevention of losses is seen as a more important objective than achieving precise equity between insurers and insureds. Accordingly, an insurer may use the lack of an insurable interest as an effective defense. Most courts will allow the defense, declare the policy unenforceable and void, and uphold the right of the insurer to deny the payment of the loss. In fact, insurers may prefer to use the insurable interest defense, even when they have other valid grounds for denying a claim, because it is often more difficult to prove fraud or breach of a policy condition than it is to establish the lack of an insurable interest.

Raising the Question of Insurable Interest By an Entity Other Than the Insurer

The question considered under this heading is whether an entity who is not a legal party to the insurance contract has a right to raise insurable interest questions for its own benefit. An event in which a particular insured has no insurable interest may still cause a loss to some other person or entity. Suppose, for example, that the former owner of a dwelling has forgotten to cancel fire insurance on that house. If it burns, the insurer may raise the insured's lack of legal or equitable title (or lack of any other basis for an insurable interest in the house) as a defense against paying the claim. The insured/former owner has suffered no loss. A significant loss has, however, fallen on the present owner of the house. If the present owner is not adequately insured against this fire loss, the present owner may try to collect some compensation through the former owner's insurance, either directly from the insurer or, if the insurer has already paid its insured despite the insured's lack of insurable interest, from the insured, on the grounds that the present owner of the dwelling is more clearly entitled to the insurance proceeds than is the former owner.

A similar question may arise in a life insurance setting. As pointed out earlier in this chapter, a parent has an insurable interest in the death of a child, but an uncle typically does not. Suppose that an uncle insures the life of a child, but the parents do not. If the child should die, may the parents raise the question of the uncle's lack of an insurable interest in the death of the child in order to collect the life policy proceeds themselves?

In either case, if the entity seeking compensation attempts to collect it from the *insurer*, the attempt will fail in all but (apparently) one jurisdiction. Because an insurance policy is a personal contract between an insurer and a particular insured, a general rule of insurance law is that no other party—no stranger to the insurance contract—has any rights against the insurer under that contract. For example:

- An employer applied for and was named beneficiary of a policy on the life of an employee and the employment relationship ended before the employee's death. The employee's widow was denied any legal standing to claim that the employer had no insurable interest in the employee's life, and that the policy proceeds should be held in trust by the insurer for her benefit.
- The heirs of a decedent's estate had no basis on which to sue a life insurer for paying the policy proceeds to the beneficiary named in the policy even though, the heirs claimed, the insurer could have refused to pay that beneficiary because of lack of an insurable interest. The right to question insurable interest was held to be the insurer's alone. If the insurer decides not to raise the insurable interest question, a person who is not a legal party to the insurance contract will not be permitted to do so.

One jurisdiction departs from this general rule by permitting any entity that has a financial interest in a loss to raise the issue of lack of insurable interest. The courts in this jurisdiction seem to feel that it would better serve the purposes of the insurable interest requirement if persons who suffer loss could use the doctrine to obtain compensation, even if such persons are not specified insureds or beneficiaries under the policies issued to those who do not have valid insurable interests. Moreover, these courts seem especially reluctant to permit a claim denial by an insurer that has received a premium for the protection.

While the vast majority of courts will not permit a person who is not a legal party to the contract to recover from the *insurer*, the majority of courts will permit such a person to recover from *insureds* who have *already been paid* for losses in which they allegedly have no insurable interest. That is, an entity seeking compensation usually may bring suit against an insured who has received insurance compensation for that loss without having had a valid insurable interest. An insured to which loss payments under an insurance policy have been made, despite lack of an insurable interest, has been ruled to be a trustee who must hold the funds for the benefit of the entity who is equitably entitled to the proceeds. The entity bringing such a suit may use the insured's lack of an insurable interest as evidence that the plaintiff is more entitled to the loss payments than is the insured. If a contest between rival claimants to insurance proceeds arises before the insurer has fully paid the loss to its insured, the insurer may, if it wishes not to become involved in such a contest, simply pay the amount of the loss to the court and let it resolve the conflicting claims.

Steps to Achieve Equity When a Policy Has Been Voided

When not supported by a valid insurable interest, an insurance policy is voidable and unenforceable. *Unenforceable* means that the contract will not be enforced by the courts. *Voidable* means that the contract may be declared by the courts to be void and of no legal effect. Where a court has declared that a particular policy is void, the general rule is that the insured loses all rights under the policy and is not entitled to any return of premium or any other benefit under the terminated policy. The reasoning underlying this general rule is that the insured's breach of the requirement of an insurable interest makes the insured responsible for terminating both the policy and any right to a premium refund or other equitable relief. Actually, this purported general rule is subject to two major exceptions which destroy much of the substance of the rule in many situations:

(1) In both property-liability and life and health insurance, the entity that paid premiums on the voided coverage is entitled to a full premium refund (although without interest) if the insurer, directly or through an agent, actively misled the insured or the applicant into believing that the insured or the applicant had a valid insurable interest.

(2) For life insurance, an exception originated before life insurance policies had cash values that might be returned to the applicant or the beneficiary if a life insurance policy was voided for lack of a valid insurable interest. Without the availability of cash values, courts confronted with a voided life insurance contract had the option (in the absence of any overtly misleading act by the insurer which would bring the case within the first exception given in the preceding paragraph) of either:

- declaring all premiums forfeited to the insurer and relieving it of all further obligations under the policy, or
- making the life insurance proceeds payable to the insured's estate.

American courts have adopted the second option, thus allowing the life insurance policy proceeds to be distributed according to the insured's will or the applicable law of intestacy. This rule prevents a potentially large forfeiture to the insurer of premiums paid over an extended period, and it also affords some indirect insurance protection to the insured's heirs. However, had cash value life insurance been common when this question first came before the courts, it has been suggested that the judges could have reached a more equitable solution by ordering the cash value of the policy, rather than its face value, to be paid to the beneficiary (or applicant, if the applicant is not the insured).

To repeat the general rules concerning property-liability insurance, *when a property-liability policy is declared void on the grounds of the lack of an insurable interest by the insured, the insurer is not obligated to pay the claim and the insured is usually not entitled to a refund of premiums previously paid.* The insurer could voluntarily pay the claim, if it wanted to do so, in which case a third entity who had a valid insurable interest, at the time of loss, might be able to recover from the insured who did not. Instead of paying the claim, the insurer could voluntarily refund the premiums paid by the insured. The voluntary refund of premiums would appear to be the most ethical approach, in the sense that it appears to avoid a windfall gain by the insurer, or the insured, but the insurer is not necessarily enjoying a windfall gain by keeping the premiums. In many cases the cost of the litigation would be much larger than the amount of the premiums involved.

Chapter Notes

1. For examples of writers who support this conclusion, see Robert E. Keeton, *Basic Text on Insurance Law* (St. Paul: West Publishing Co., 1971), p. 120; or Janice E. Greider and William T. Beadles, *Law and the Life Insurance Contract*, 4th ed. (Homewood, IL: Richard D. Irwin, 1979), pp. 135-136.
2. Keeton, pp. 101-102.
3. George J. Couch, *Cyclopedia of Insurance Law*, 2d ed. (Rochester: Lawyers Co-Operative Publishing Co., 1960), section 24:1.
4. Keeton, pp. 96-97. These clauses were variously known as "policy proof of interest," "interest or no interest," or "all interest admitted" clauses. Such clauses are no longer used except in a few specialized types of ocean marine insurance. See William D. Winter, *Marine Insurance*, 3rd ed. (New York: McGraw Hill, 1952), pp. 279 and 285-286.
5. Keeton, p. 95.
6. Keeton, p. 95.
7. Laurence P. Simpson, *Handbook on the Law of Contracts*, 2nd ed. (St. Paul: West Publishing Co., 1965), p. 454. A wagering contract is one in which at least one party is to receive something upon the happening of an uncertain event without giving an agreed equivalent or suffering an equivalent loss. Other major classes of illegal contracts include contracts in restraint of trade, contracts to defraud or injure third parties, contracts intended to harm the administration of justice, contracts harmful to the marriage relationship, and contracts charging usurious (illegally high) rates of interest on loans. Notice, however, that state-sponsored wagering (e.g., state-run lotteries and off-track betting) and wagering under special state license (gambling casinos) are practiced in some states. Contracts made in connection with such wagering are not made unenforceable by this connection.
8. New York Insurance Law, section 148, cited in Keeton, p. 113 (emphasis supplied).
9. California Insurance Code, section 283, cited in Keeton, pp. 113-114. For a discussion of factual expectations and other plausible bases for insurable interests in property, see Edwin W. Patterson, *Essentials of Insurance Law*, 2nd ed. (New York: McGraw-Hill, 1957), Chapter 3.

CHAPTER 9

Structure of Property and Liability Insurance Contracts; Insured Entities

INTRODUCTION

This chapter summarizes the general content and physical makeup of most property and liability insurance contracts. In addition, the last portion of the chapter describes the various methods which are used to identify and define the "insured entities," i.e., the person(s) or other entity(ies) for whom the insurer intends to provide the coverage under a particular policy.

GENERAL CONTENT OF PROPERTY-LIABILITY INSURANCE CONTRACTS

An insurance policy is structurally a written contract comprising numerous provisions. These contractual provisions, called *policy provisions*, express distinctive thoughts or stipulations in the form of clauses, sentences, or paragraphs in the policy. Some types of policy provisions are common to virtually all insurance policies, while others are found only in policies that are designed to meet a particular set of consumer needs. In either case, closely related provisions of a policy are normally grouped together in sections identified by headings.

In spite of the sometimes sharp differences among insurance policies, the contents of all property-liability insurance policies[1] can be broken down into the following component parts or categories:

(1) declarations,
(2) insuring agreements,

(3) exclusions,
(4) conditions, and
(5) miscellaneous provisions.

Every policy provision can logically be placed into one of these five categories. (A policy provision that does not seem to fit elsewhere could always logically be classified as a "miscellaneous" provision.) However, these five categories may not have precise counterparts in the language or structure of a given policy. Many policies do not group their provisions into sections with headings corresponding to these five categories. Other policies use some or all of these categories as section headings, but this does not mean that a provision that effectively serves the function of an exclusion will always be found in an "exclusions" section. A single provision might simultaneously function as a condition or an exclusion, as well as an insuring agreement, and the provision itself might be found almost anywhere in the several documents which together constitute the entire contract, especially when the basic policy has several forms and endorsements attached.

The five customary categories are preserved here because they provide convenient textbook headings for summarizing the general kinds of provisions contained in most property-liability policies. More specific and systematic frameworks for coverage analysis will be presented later in this text.

Declarations

The *declarations* of an insurance policy are the typewritten statements that are entered into what are otherwise blank spaces in the printed policy form. Declarations serve to personalize the policy by identifying the named insured(s) and describing each property or activity to be insured. In addition, the declarations typically specify:

- the policy number,
- the numbers of all forms that are attached,
- applicable policy limit(s),
- deductible(s),
- inception and termination dates of the policy,
- premium and the basis for its determination,
- additional interests covered (such as the interests of a mortgagee or loss payee), and
- (sometimes) the perils covered.

The declarations page may also contain information used by the insurer to rate the policy, issue it, and set up the necessary internal records.

Insuring Agreements

The *insuring agreements* are printed statements that summarize the insurer's obligation(s) by setting forth in broad terms what the insurer agrees to do under the contract.[2] For example, one insuring agreement obligates the insurer to "pay for damage during the policy period to the glass described in the declarations...." Another agreement obligates the insurer to "pay on behalf of the insured all sums which the insured shall become legally obligated to pay as damages because of A. bodily injury or B. property damage...arising out of the ownership, maintenance or use of the insured premises and all operations necessary or incidental thereto...." These two excerpts happen to be fairly concise; however, some insuring agreements are long and contain numerous clarifications and definitions.

Whether lengthy or concise, insuring agreements merely state the basic thrust or general nature of the insurer's obligations(s). The full scope of the coverage cannot be determined without examining the rest of the policy, since the insuring agreements are invariably explained or modified by exclusions, conditions, and other policy provisions—including those contained in forms and endorsements attached to the basic policy.

Exclusions

In the jargon of property-liability insurance, the term *exclusion* usually refers to a policy provision, clearly identified as an exclusion, that eliminates coverage the insurer does not intend to provide. However, the term is broad enough to embrace *any* policy provision that serves the function of eliminating unintended coverages, whether or not the provision is labeled as an exclusion. Both definitions imply that the primary function of exclusions is to clarify the coverages granted by the insurer, not to take away coverage from the insured. This point may seem academic and insincere to any person who does not become aware of an exclusion until after a loss. It is natural for such a person to feel that coverage has been "taken away," in effect, especially when the applicable exclusion is difficult to find in the policy. Even so, the drafters of insurance contracts are painfully aware how difficult it is to express an insurer's underwriting intentions in language that will not be misinterpreted by the courts. Specifying what an insurer does *not* intend to cover has proven to be one of several effective ways of clarifying what the insurer *does* intend to cover under an insurance policy.

A court may effectively eliminate *all* coverage whenever it declares a policy to be void and unenforceable, perhaps due to the lack of a valid insurable interest or for some other legal reason, but to call this a "coverage exclusion" would be stretching the concept to the point where it would lose its meaning. The term *exclusion* is more appropriately applied when an enforceable policy has been or will be interpreted to exclude a particular loss, although the policy continues to be enforceable.

What are the underlying purposes of policy exclusions? Why does the insurer want to clarify the coverages it does not intend to provide? Why does the insurer want to eliminate some coverages? Collectively, exclusions are said to serve at least six legitimate purposes. They may:

(1) eliminate coverage for uninsurable loss exposures,
(2) assist in the management of moral and morale hazards,
(3) reduce the likelihood of coverage duplications,
(4) eliminate coverages that are not needed by the typical purchaser,
(5) eliminate coverages requiring special treatment, and
(6) assist in keeping premiums at a reasonable level.

It should be stressed that a particular exclusion very often serves more than one purpose. Hence, in the explanations that follow, some of the examples used to illustrate one purpose could also have been used to illustrate other purposes.

Uninsurable Losses   One purpose of exclusions is to eliminate coverage for exposures that are considered uninsurable by private insurers. All exclusions of this type serve the basic purpose of eliminating coverage for loss exposures that do not adequately meet one or more of the various insurability conditions which were explained in Chapter 6. For example, virtually all property and liability insurance contracts exclude as uninsurable any losses arising out of war. While the exclusions in any particular contract depend on the nature and purpose of that contract, other common exclusions in this category involve losses due to intentional acts of the insured, nuclear radiation, earthquake, flood damage to fixed-location property, marring or scratching of furniture, normal wear and tear, mechanical breakdown, and *inherent vice*. (Inherent vice is a quality within an object that tends to destroy it, as when iron rusts, wood rots, or rubber deteriorates.) These exposures all fail to meet adequately at least one of the tests or characteristics of an insurable loss exposure. War and nuclear losses involve an incalculable catastrophe potential. Mechanical breakdown, intentional acts of the insured, inherent vice, and similar losses are not accidental or fortuitous in nature, but are controllable by the insured or highly predictable. Although some of these losses theoretically may be insured, the required premium is often so large that they remain uninsurable, as a practical matter, and are therefore excluded from the coverages offered by most private insurers.

Moral and Morale Hazards A second purpose of exclusions is to assist in the management of moral and morale hazards. Moral hazards refer to defects or weaknesses in human character that lead some people to exaggerate losses or intentionally cause them to occur as a means of collecting insurance proceeds. Exclusions can help manage moral hazards to the extent that they eliminate coverage for intentional acts of the insured. One example can be found in crime insurance policies that exclude coverage for any fraudulent, dishonest, or criminal act by any insured. Similarly, nearly all health insurance policies exclude coverage for losses arising out of self-inflicted injuries.

Morale hazards refer generally to the tendency of people to be less careful about preventing losses when they are insured. Exclusions can assist in managing morale hazards by eliminating coverages and making insureds themselves bear a financial penalty for their own carelessness. For example, many liability policies exclude coverage for liability arising out of damage to the property of others when such property is in the care, custody, or control of the insured. Under some contracts providing broad coverage on personal property, breakage of fragile articles is excluded unless caused by some specified peril such as fire, wind, explosion, and the like. The intent is to eliminate coverage for breakage caused by careless handling or misuse. Some policies exclude coverage for theft from unattended and unlocked vehicles.

Exclusions like these mentioned here do not entirely eliminate moral and morale hazards. However, they can assist in their management.

Coverage Duplications A third purpose of exclusions is to reduce the likelihood of unnecessary and wasteful coverage duplications. That is to say, coverage is eliminated from one kind of policy because it is likely to be provided by another kind of policy that is better suited to the task. For example:

- personal liability policies usually exclude losses arising from professional activities and business pursuits.
- glass insurance policies routinely exclude losses due to fire, because such losses typically are covered under the fire insurance policy on the building.
- fire insurance policies eliminate autos from the description of covered property, because auto physical damage insurance is readily available and widely purchased.

These are just a few of the many exclusions designed to avoid coverage overlaps among several different policies. Though exclusions alone do not entirely prevent coverage duplications, they do help reduce them, as do various other policy provisions.

Coverages Not Needed By the Typical Purchaser A fourth purpose of exclusions is to eliminate coverages that are not needed by the typical purchaser of that type of contract, thus enabling insurers to charge more equitable premiums to all their insureds. For example, the typical insured does not own or operate private aircraft, use his or her personal auto as a taxicab for hire, or use his or her home as a storage warehouse for business property. In recognition thereof, homeowners policies do not provide property insurance coverage for aircraft or business property in storage. Personal auto policies do not cover losses that occur while an otherwise insured vehicle is being used to carry people or property for a fee. People who need these coverages may obtain them separately, in most cases, by paying additional premiums. It would be unfair to reflect in the premiums paid by all insureds the cost of losses for these exposures not at all common to the usual insurance buyer. A significant degree of inequity is also likely to violate state rating laws and regulations, according to which insurance rates cannot be unfairly discriminatory. Exclusions are sometimes necessary, therefore, to achieve a reasonable degree of rating and premium equity.

Coverages Requiring Special Treatment A fifth purpose of exclusions is to eliminate coverages requiring special treatment. As used here, the term "special" means rating, underwriting, or reinsurance treatment that is substantially different from what normally is applied to the contract containing the exclusion. For example:

- Policies covering valuable personal property frequently exclude coverage for losses that occur while the property is on exhibition at a convention or trade fair. Paintings, stamps, coins, and other collectors' items are often on display for members of the public or other collectors to enjoy, during which time they are considered highly vulnerable to theft and other perils.
- The typical policy covering products liability excludes coverage of the insured's liability for the expense of recalling products that are or may be defective.
- General liability policies usually exclude the so-called professional liability exposure.

These exclusions pertain to coverages that require special rating, underwriting, and/or reinsurance arrangements. These same exclusions might also serve the purposes of eliminating coverages not needed by the typical purchaser and reducing coverage duplications.

Yet, excluding coverages requiring special treatment can be thought of as a somewhat different purpose of exclusions. It may be the primary or only reason a given insurer uses a particular exclusion. An insurer may exclude products recall coverage, for example, though it is needed by many insurance buyers and is not likely to result in duplicate coverage, simply because it is a highly specialized line the insurer does not wish to write. In fact, there are comparatively few insurers willing to write most specialty coverages. Further, some insurers would not be able to write highly specialized coverages, even if they wanted to, due to their inability to secure appropriate reinsurance protection.

Keeping Premiums Reasonable A sixth purpose of exclusions is to assist in keeping premiums at a level which a sufficiently large number of insureds (and prospective insureds) will consider reasonable. Keeping the premiums reasonable is an objective shared by insurers, rate regulators, and consumers alike. All exclusions serve this purpose to some extent. However, it is the only or primary reason for using some exclusions. For example, there is really no other compelling reason, under property insurance contracts, for eliminating the coverage of marring and scratching, wear and tear, mechanical breakdown, or other highly predictable losses. Such losses are not literally uninsurable. It is just that to cover them would require a higher premium than most people are willing to pay. They are uninsurable as a practical matter, therefore, because an insurer who automatically covered them under standard property insurance policies would undoubtedly "price itself out of the market." The premiums for routine dental expense coverage are also more than most individuals are willing to pay out of their own pockets; yet it has been marketed very successfully in recent years. The primary difference between the two examples is that the vast bulk of routine dental expense coverage is written on a group basis and is paid for by employers (as a tax-deductible expense). Since most property owners pay for their own property insurance, the aforementioned kinds of exclusions are retained in property insurance policies to keep the premium at a reasonable level.

Once it is acknowledged that the broader concept of an exclusion refers to any policy provision that functions as an exclusion, it becomes apparent that keeping the premiums reasonable in the minds of consumers is a primary purpose of many exclusionary features of policy design. In both property and liability insurance (including multiple-line policies), the consumer is given a fairly wide range of choice in terms of the breadth of coverage available from the same or different insurers. Generally, the fewer the exclusionary policy provisions, the higher the premium will be. That the reverse is also true reaffirms the point; namely, that one key purpose of exclusions is to keep the premium reasonable in the minds of a large number of buyers. Only when a sufficiently large number of people buy a given policy will the law of large numbers operate to make its sale a successful venture for the insurer. Exclusions may help achieve this goal, while simultaneously giving the consumer a choice of coverages and premium levels.

Conditions

Depending on the type of contract, the insurer agrees to pay the insured, to pay on behalf of the insured, to defend the insured, and/or to provide various additional services. The insurer's promises are invariably subject to a number of conditions. These conditions are so important to coverage analysis that all of chapter 14 is devoted to this subject. For now, conditions may be thought of as the various qualifications an insurer attaches to the promises it makes. They create duties on the part of the insured which must be met if the insured wants to hold the insurer to the insurer's part of the bargain. The insurer's promises are contingent upon both the happening of an insured event *and* the performance of various acts by the insured person(s). Examples of common policy conditions include the insured's obligation to pay premiums, report losses promptly, provide appropriate documentation for losses, cooperate with the insurer in any legal proceedings, and refrain from jeopardizing an insurer's rights to recover from responsible third parties (under "subrogation" actions) amounts equal to the payments it has made to its insured. If the insured does not do these things, the insurer may be released from its obligation to perform some or all of the otherwise enforceable promises it has made in the contract.

Miscellaneous Provisions

In addition to declarations, insuring agreements, exclusions, and conditions, insurance policies contain various "miscellaneous provisions" that generally deal with the relationship between the insured and the insurer. While these provisions help to establish working procedures for carrying out the terms of an insurance contract, they seldom have the force of conditions. Thus, actions that depart from the procedures specified in the miscellaneous provisions normally do not affect the insurer's basic duty to perform.

A sampling of "miscellaneous" provisions might include:

- a cancellation provision spelling out the rights and obligations of each party in canceling the policy and notifying the other party(ies);
- options giving the insured or insurer specified alternatives in receiving loss payments or discharging an obligation under the contract;
- valuation provisions setting forth standards for how losses under the policy will be measured (this is part of the insuring agreement in some policies);
- "other insurance" provisions spelling out the extent of the insurer's liability if other insurance covers the same loss; and
- a mortgage or loss payable clause specifying the rights and duties of the insurer and a mortgagee or other creditor of the insured.

Some miscellaneous provisions are unique to particular types of insurers. For example:

- A policy issued by a mutual insurance company is very likely to describe the right of each insured to participate in the divisible surplus, if any, and to vote in the election of the board of directors.
- A policy issued by an assessment mutual typically describes the nature and limits of an insured's potential liability for assessments. (As mentioned in Chapter 6, insureds may be required to make extra payments to the assessment mutual based on its loss experience.)
- A policy issued by a reciprocal insurer is likely to specify in each of its policies the authority of the attorney-in-fact to carry out its powers on behalf of the insured.

PHYSICAL ASPECTS OF INSURANCE CONTRACTS

An insurance policy may be assembled in a variety of ways. This section deals with an insurance policy as a physical document, explaining the function of each of the written instruments that is likely to be found in, attached to, or incorporated by reference into, any insurance policy.[3]

For the most part, insurance policies are

(1) *self-contained preprinted policies,*
(2) assembled through adding a "form" or "coverage part" to a preprinted document containing *common provisions,* or
(3) specially composed in a so-called *manuscript* (typewritten) policy.

This three-fold classification captures the major alternatives in insurance policy physical structure. Gradations within and among these alternatives are discussed in other CPCU courses.

The Self-Contained Policy

Some insurance policies are made up of a single document that contains all the agreements between the applicant and the insurer. A single, relatively standardized document identifies the insurer and insured, the property or other subject matter of insurance, and the amounts, terms, and conditions of the coverage provided by the policy. Tailoring coverage to the needs of individual insureds is achieved through the declarations and the use of endorsements.

A self-contained policy is appropriate when a large number of insureds face a loss exposure, or a set of related exposures that are essentially similar from insured to insured. Insurance written to cover losses arising out of the ownership or use of private passenger autos typically is written in a self-contained policy that can be used nationwide. In those states where no-fault auto insurance laws require the use of provisions suited especially to insureds located therein, the tailoring is achieved through the use of endorsements. Most life insurance and health insurance policies also are self-contained.

Common Provisions Approach

Many property and liability insurance policies are assembled by combining some document containing provisions applicable to a variety of coverages with one or more other documents providing a specific type of coverage and designated as *forms* or *coverage parts.* Historically, the best-known common provisions document has been the standard fire policy. Though referred to as a "policy," this document is not really a complete contract until one or more forms have been attached. Of later vintage is the use of the term *jacket* to represent a document containing common provisions and often serving as a wrapper or cover page. This nomenclature can be used to refer to documents in a number of types of insurance, including special multi-peril and general liability. In each case, one or more of a variety of forms (called "coverage parts" in general liability insurance) is combined with the jacket to assemble a complete contract.

Many inland marine and crime insurance contracts use the common provisions approach. While actual labels vary among insurers, many use a document called the "inland marine policy" in writing a wide variety of inland marine coverages, with the form(s) attached containing those provisions geared to meet a particular type of coverage need.

The special coverage crime policy and various forms serve the same roles in crime insurance.

Common provisions vary in length and complexity. In general, they contain provisions intended to be applicable to all or most insuring situations in which they are used, regardless of differences among insureds that may be recognized by the variety of forms used to complete the policy. With some, such as the standard fire policy, space for the declarations is an integral part of the document. In other cases, such as the general liability jacket, a separate declarations page is used.

Manuscript Policies

The two approaches described above both involve the use of preprinted material. In contrast, a manuscript policy, usually typewritten, is the product of negotiation between an insurer and an applicant (or the applicant's representative, such as a broker). Each provision in a manuscript policy is specifically drafted or selected for that one contract. While some provisions may be taken verbatim from printed or standardized policies, each manuscript policy as a whole is a "one-of-a-kind" document. The use of manuscript policies is largely restricted to entities of substantial size whose uniqueness of exposures and substantial bargaining power put them in a position of both needing and being able to demand individual treatment.

Because the wording of manuscript policies is developed through the joint effort of insurer and applicant, the two parties are more likely to be on equal footing in the event of a court's need to interpret ambiguities in the contract. In contrast, policies that the insurer framed with terms of its own choosing are likely to be interpreted against the insurer in the event of ambiguities. Provisions that may be interpreted in more than one way will be construed in favor of the insured, in other words, when the insured had no role in drafting the contract.

Collateral Documents

The immediately preceding paragraphs described the basic formats of insurance policies. However, several other documents—such as a written application, the insurer's bylaws, the terms of relevant statutes, or various miscellaneous documents—may be incorporated into a policy either by physical attachment or by appropriate reference. Any of these documents may become part of any particular insurance policy, regardless of its physical format.

Written Application   Although insurer practices vary widely, for some types of insurance a written application is rarely or never required. For these coverages, an applicant may request coverage orally, in person or over a telephone, and a representative of the insurer may create an oral insurance contract by immediately "binding" the requested coverage. However, for those lines of insurance that are relatively complex or involve particularly complex underwriting or rating, the insurer typically requires a written application. Jewelers' block coverage invariably requires a written application, as do all types of life insurance coverage. Even in some lines for which the insurer's representative has authority to bind coverage, a written application is required, and the submission is underwritten and rated by insurer personnel *after* coverage has been put into force by the representative.

Beyond its underwriting importance, a written application is legally significant because it contains the statements or representations the applicant makes to secure coverage. The truth of these statements may be critical to the validity of any insurance contract. Information on the written application often is the insurer's only basis for demonstrating a lack of good faith in securing the policy. However, to be able to rely on the application as a basis for having the policy declared void, the application often must be part of the policy. This requirement stems from statutes and court decisions which stipulate that a written insurance policy must incorporate all the agreements between an insurer and an insured. In some jurisdictions, statutes explicitly require that any written application be made part of specified types of insurance (especially life insurance policies). If a written application is not attached to the insurance policy, the policy remains valid. However, in such jurisdictions, failure to attach the application denies the insurer the right to have the policy declared void because of false statements in the application.

Endorsements or Riders   An endorsement, known as a "rider" in life and health insurance, is a provision that adds to, deletes, or modifies another document that is part of an insurance policy. Sometimes endorsements are labeled as a "policy change" or an "amendment." Many endorsements have only a descriptive title, like "loss payable clause." An endorsement may be a printed paragraph or series of paragraphs on a separate sheet of paper attached to the other document(s) making up the policy, or it may be typewritten or handwritten on a paper attached to those documents. An endorsement may even take the form of a handwritten note inserted into the margin of a basic policy, form, or coverage part, with the insurer's and insured's acceptance of this handwritten note being indicated by initialing and dating it.

There are thousands of standard endorsements available to meet the needs of particular insureds plus "all-purpose" endorsements, which are little more than blanks on which special agreements between the insurer and the insured are recorded in typewritten or handwritten form. Depending on the provision that an endorsement extends, deletes, or modifies, any particular endorsement may serve as (1) a declaration (such as by identifying an additional named insured), (2) an insuring agreement (such as by identifying additional properties or perils for which the insurer is willing to provide coverage), (3) an exclusion or deletion of an existing exclusion (such as an endorsement modifying the liability coverage of a homeowners policy by removing the exclusion of liability arising out of business pursuits of the insured), (4) a condition (such as an endorsement liberalizing the notice of loss requirement under certain circumstances), or (5) a miscellaneous provision.

In general, an endorsement takes precedence over any conflicting terms in the policy to which the endorsement is attached. Furthermore, a handwritten endorsement supersedes a preprinted or typewritten one. Both of these rules are based on the reasoning that alterations of the agreements between an insured and an insurer—especially alterations that they have indicated in handwriting—more accurately reflect their true intent than do the other terms of the policy.

An exception to this general rule arises in situations in which a statute or ruling requires that a particular policy be fully standardized, that it contain particular provisions whose wording or substance is specified, or that the policy not contain certain provisions whose wording or substance has been prohibited. In these situations, an endorsement cannot be used to subvert the purpose of law or regulation by modifying the terms of an entirely standardized policy, changing the wording or substance of a required provision, or inserting a provision whose wording or substance had been prohibited. Any portion of an endorsement that attempts to override decisions of a duly constituted public authority regarding the proper content of an insurance policy is void. The policy is read and applied as if those portions of the endorsement did not exist.

The Insurer's Bylaws and Relevant Statutes In certain circumstances, it is important that the bylaws of the insurer or the provisions of pertinent statutes be incorporated into a particular insurance policy. For example, when an insurer's organizational structure gives insureds some rights or duties associated with the management of the insurer's operations—as is the case with mutual insurers and reciprocal insurers—it is important that these rights and duties be made part of each insurance contract. Similarly, where an insurance policy provides protection against potential liability growing out of a specific state—such as a workers' compensation law or an auto insurance "no-fault" law—the provisions and amendments of these statutes actually define the insurer's obligation and must, therefore, be made part of each insurance policy. Furthermore, statutes in some states require that a particular type of policy contain provisions that differ slightly from the policies used in the majority of jurisdictions. These slight variations often are incorporated into the body of the policy through special provisions under the heading of "State Exceptions" to the standard policy. These state exceptions are effective only with respect to insureds whose losses come under the jurisdiction of a particular state in which the laws require such an exception.

The incorporation of relevant statutes normally is achieved by a general reference to them. For example, the usual workers' compensation policy defines the insurer's primary obligation to be: "To pay promptly when due all compensation and other benefits required of the insured by the workers' compensation law." Where pertinent, an insurer's bylaws may be incorporated by reference, although a copy of the bylaws may be physically attached to the policy. Most state exceptions are stated explicitly in the policy, and many policies contain provisions stating that any of their clauses which violate any applicable statute are hereby deemed to be amended to conform to that statute. Such a provision, along with the statement of state exceptions, recognizes explicitly the interpretation a court probably will give to the policy to make it conform to the legal requirements of any particular jurisdiction. When a policy incorporates a particular set of bylaws or applicable statutes, the policy is interpreted to change automatically with changes in these bylaws or statutes, rather than being frozen by the bylaws or statutes that pertained when the policy first became effective.

Miscellaneous Documents Subject to statutory and regulatory restrictions intended to standardize policies or otherwise govern policy content, an insurer and an insured may incorporate into an insurance policy virtually any documents they wish. Although these miscellaneous documents may be quite diverse, some of the more frequently incorporated miscellaneous documents include premium notes, inspection reports, records of medical examinations, and specification sheets or operating manuals pertaining to safety equipment or procedures to be followed while the policy is in force.

A premium note is a promissory note which the insurer accepts in lieu of cash payment of the premium. In most jurisdictions, the premium note and the insurance policy are considered to be separate obligations, each enforceable independently. In these jurisdictions, it is not important that the premium note be attached to the policy. However, in some jurisdictions, a premium note is not enforceable by the insurer unless incorporated into the policy for which the note constitutes payment, usually by attachment of a copy of the note.

An inspection report of an insured's premises is likely to contain highly relevant information for the underwriting of the property or liability insurance policy, just as a record of a medical examination may be part of the basis on which a life or health insurance underwriter decides to issue a policy. An inspection report or a record of a medical examination normally is not considered to be part of an insurance policy or an application, unless the report or record is physically attached to the other documents which make up the policy. Therefore, if an insurer wishes to have the opportunity to point to information in the inspection report or record of medical examination as a basis for showing that the policy was procured through misrepresentation or fraud by the applicant, this report or record must be physically attached to the policy. In some states, it must be referred to on the first page of the policy. Such a practice is the exception in property and liability insurance, but common in life insurance.

An insurer and an applicant may agree that the coverage provided by a particular property or liability insurance policy is conditioned upon the use of certain procedures or equipment in order to minimize losses. In such situations, a set of operating instructions or a manual of specifications may be incorporated by reference and used to define precisely and conveniently the loss prevention measures that must exist as a condition of the coverage promised in the policy.

PROCEDURES FOR COVERAGE ANALYSIS

Summaries of the general content and physical makeup of property-liability policies are helpful as descriptive introductions to the study of policy provisions. However, for the purpose of analyzing the coverage of a particular policy, even the best of broad summaries is no substitute for a systematic procedure. A person could simply read and study the policy provisions in the order in which they appear in the policy, but this can be more confusing than it is illuminating unless it is done within a logical framework that is external to the policy.

One logical framework consists of a series of specific questions which can be likened to the who-what-where-when-how questions a good newspaper reporter must answer in writing a news story. For example:

- Who is insured?
- What property or activities are insured?

- What perils are insured?
- When (during what time period) is coverage provided?
- What are the limitations, if any, on the amount of coverage?
- What conditions or other policy provisions may affect the coverage otherwise provided?

Such specific questions are then answered systematically (by studying the policy forms) as a procedure for coverage analysis.

The kinds of specific questions to be used in analyzing the coverage of a particular policy do not necessarily make good chapter or section headings for a textbook. For the latter purpose, the authors have selected the broader categories of insured entities, insured events, policy limits and loss valuation provisions, loss sharing provisions, multiple sources of recovery, and contract conditions. The first of these, insured entities, will be dealt with in the section that immediately follows.

INSURED ENTITIES

The *insured entities* under a property and/or liability insurance policy are the natural persons, corporations, or other entities who are entitled, as promisees to whom the insurer has made contractual promises, to receive benefits according to the terms and conditions of the contract. The insured entities do not have to be identified by name. They must be identified clearly, however, in order to answer the question of "who is insured" under a particular policy.

In examining the various means of identifying the insured entities, it will be assumed that the applicable insurable interest requirements have been satisfied. It will also be assumed that the losses are otherwise covered under the policy. These two assumptions will permit the discussion to focus on the entities a property-liability insurer intends to insure as a matter of contract.[4] Furthermore, although group life and health insurance is very widespread, the discussion will be limited solely to individually issued policies, since the true group approach is still quite rare in property and liability insurance.[5]

Under individual contracts of property and liability insurance, the insured entities most often are named insureds, "assignees," creditors, legal representatives of named insureds, family and household members, users or occupants of property, legal agents and principals in an agency relationship, and entities covered because of a representative insurable interest. These fall conveniently into one of two broad categories, (1) entities specifically identified by name and (2) entities identified by relationship to another insured.

Entities Specifically Identified By Name

Named insureds, assignees, and creditors are entities that may become insureds by being specifically identified by name in an insurance policy.

Named Insureds The declarations page of a typical policy has a blank space following the printed words, "named insured." An entity becomes a named insured by having its name inserted in the space provided. While the named insured is commonly just one person, partnership, corporation, political subdivision, or other entity with an ownership interest in property or an exposure to legal liability, virtually any combination of two or more entities could be listed as named insureds. Multiple named insureds are sometimes listed in the declarations as "Jones and Smith, as their interests may appear." The respective legal interests of Jones and Smith could be any of the property interests described in the previous chapter.

Assignees An *assignment* is a transfer of any property right from one entity to another. The entity that assigns (transfers) a property right is called an *assignor.* The entity to which a property right is assigned is called an *assignee.* Since an insurance policy is a contract that serves as evidence of valuable property rights, can such rights be assigned? If not, why not? If so, does the assignee become an insured under the particular policy that serves as evidence of the rights assigned? The answers to these questions depend primarily on whether the assignment seeks to transfer (1) only an entity's right to claim payment for a loss that has occurred or (2) some or all of an entity's ownership rights in the policy, before a loss occurs. The answers also depend, in the case of assignments before a loss occurs, on the type of insurance involved.

Assignment After a Loss Has Occurred. After a loss has occurred, the entity holding the right to collect any benefits payable under a property or life insurance policy may freely assign that right without the consent of the insurer. The holder of such a right, the assignor, is usually the *insured* (in property insurance) or the *beneficiary* (in life insurance). Regardless of which of these entities is the assignor, the assignee does not become an insured by virtue of the assignment. Nor does the assignee normally obtain any greater right than the assignor had at the time of assignment. The right assigned, after a loss occurs, is merely a claim for money. The insurer still might be able to deny payment to the assignee—perhaps on the grounds of fraud on the part of the insured, a breach of a policy condition by the insured, or the insured's lack of a valid insurable interest. Thus, in property and life insurance, an assignment of the post-loss right to claim any benefits payable is an assignment that may be made freely by the holder of that right. Such an assignment does not make the assignee a newly insured entity under the existing policy. It does not usually diminish any defenses the insurer may have had against the insured, and it poses no new hazards to the insurer. It is a type of assignment, therefore, that can be made without getting the insurer's consent.

Assignment Before a Loss Has Occurred. Before a loss occurs, an entity that has all the rights in an insurance policy may be thought of as the owner of the policy. The owner of a life insurance policy has valuable prematurity rights which normally include the rights to name or change the beneficiary, specify the manner in which the proceeds are to be paid, and (in cash value life insurance policies) to effect a policy loan or surrender the policy for cash. The most important pre-loss right in a property or liability insurance policy, on the other hand, is the right of its owner to protection against future losses. While the owner of a life insurance policy may assign all or a portion of the prematurity rights without obtaining the consent of the insurer, the owner of a property or liability insurance policy cannot validly assign the policy to another unless the written consent of the insurer is first obtained, as a general rule. Each of these two generalizations deserves a brief explanation.

After the death of the insured, the beneficiary of a life insurance policy is the entity who has both the right to claim the benefits payable and the power to assign that claim to another. Prior to the death of the insured, however, the *owner* is the only entity who may assign all or a portion of the policy rights to an assignee. All of the rights are permanently assigned when the purpose is to transfer the ownership of the policy to another person, normally for tax or other estate planning reasons, whereas only some of the rights are temporarily assigned when the purpose is to provide collateral security for a loan. In either event, life insurance assignments seldom pose problems when the assignee or the owner is also the beneficiary (as is not infrequently the case). Otherwise, there are potential conflicts between the rights of the assignee and the rights of the beneficiary with respect to who is entitled to receive the benefits payable under the policy. Although the various complexities of life insurance assignments lie well beyond the scope of this text, it should again be stressed that they may be made without the insurer's consent. Of course, it is highly advisable to send to the insurer a written notice of any assignment. If the insurer is not furnished with a written notice and the insured dies, the insurer has no other choice than to make payment to the designated beneficiary(ies). The assignee is left with no legal basis for collecting from the insurer any benefits to which it would have been entitled had proper notice been given to the insurer. Despite the practical advisability of furnishing notice to the insurer, it is not legally necessary to obtain the insurer's approval of the assignment, because the person insured continues to be the same person whose life was already insured before the assignment.

In contrast to assignments of life insurance policy rights, all pre-loss assignments of property and liability policies have the effect of changing the insured. For example, suppose the fee simple owner of a dwelling has given or sold the dwelling to another person, and the donor or seller also wants to assign its existing homeowners policy to the new owner of the dwelling. A legally valid assignment of the entire policy would effectively substitute the assignee (the new owner of the dwelling) for the assignor (the former owner of the dwelling) as the named insured under the existing homeowners policy. However, the new owner of the dwelling may not be a person with whom the insurer wishes to enter into a homeowners contract—perhaps because the new owner is known to be a convicted arsonist who was just released from prison. The physical characteristics of the dwelling itself may be perfectly acceptable to the underwriter, but the implications of potential moral and morale hazards are so significant that the insurance contract is ultimately "personal" in nature and legally recognized as such.[6] The insurer at least wants the opportunity to decide for itself whether to insure assignees, since the alternative would amount to relegating the underwriting function entirely to assignors whose own "underwriting standards" would not be controllable by the insurer. As a consequence, the general rule is that property or liability policies cannot be assigned without the insurer's written consent. This rule is expressed in the form of explicit policy provisions in most property-liability contracts.

Two exceptions to the general rule are well worth mentioning. First, the insurer's written consent is very seldom required for assignments of insurance policies providing property coverage on cargo in transit. Since cargo or other property in transit normally is not within the control of the insured cargo owner, a mere assignment of the policy to another party would seldom change the exposures to the insurer; moreover, the demands of commerce invariably would make it impractical to obtain the insurer's prior written consent to an assignment of the policy. Second, the insuring agreements of some property insurance policies are written to cover the interests of "for whom it may concern" (a common phrase in ocean marine cargo policies), or the interests of "the named insured or his assignees." Both phrases are broad enough to cover the assignee as an insured under the policy. Despite these exceptions, most property and liability policies contain a policy provision that the policy cannot be assigned unless the would-be assignor first secures the written consent of the insurer.

If the consent of the insurer is not obtained, the lack of consent does not invalidate the entire policy. However, the effect may be equally serious, because the insurer has no legal obligation to the would-be assignee. In fact, the insurer would have no legal obligation to the original named insured (assignor) of the policy, if such an insured does not have a valid insurable interest at the time of loss. Both the new owner and the former owner of property would be left with no insurance protection, for instance, when an invalid assignment of the policy is made to the buyer after the sale of the property. To avoid such consequences, an assignment of the policy should not be attempted without first securing the insurer's written approval of the policy assignment.

Assignments of property and liability policies are not very common. In practice, the somewhat limited use of assignments is partly due to the fact that most donees and buyers of property prefer to purchase new insurance policies from insurers and producers of their own choice. In addition, insurers typically are reluctant to give their written consent to policy assignments. This reluctance is based on court decisions which have held that the insurer's granting of written consent amounts to a waiver of defenses. That is to say, whatever defenses the insurer might have had against the former insured cannot be used against the assignee (the new insured), because they have been waived, in effect, by the insurer's approval of the assignment. There is little incentive for an insurer to weaken its legal position in this fashion, particularly since it would also involve the distinct possibility of *adverse selection*. (The assignees who could not qualify for new policies, according to the insurer's underwriting standards, would be the very ones most likely to seek approval of the assignment.)

Secured Creditors A creditor is said to be a "secured" creditor when the debtor has pledged specific property as collateral security for the repayment of the debt. A secured creditor has an insurable interest in such property, as explained in Chapter 8, because the courts recognize that damage or destruction of the property increases the likelihood of default and impairs the ability of the creditor to sell the property as a means of recovering any unpaid balance it is owed. In general, the secured creditor's insurable interest (in the property serving as collateral) is limited in amount to the remaining balance of the debt at the time of loss, including any unpaid interest that has accrued to the date of the loss. Property insurance to cover the creditor's interest may be arranged (1) by the creditor's direct purchase of its own policy and/or (2) by making the creditor an insured under a policy purchased and paid for by the debtor. The latter may be accomplished by means of an assignment, a loss payable clause, or a standard mortgage clause.

Creditor's Own Insurance. By the direct purchase of their own insurance, creditors are able to select the insurers and producers of their own choice. The managers of commercial lending institutions might justifiably feel that they will exercise greater care than many of their borrowers would exercise in selecting insurers and producers who are financially strong, competent, and reputable. They may also desire to buy the insurance from or through local firms that maintain deposits with the institutions they manage. Additionally, the direct purchase of insurance assures the creditor that its own insurance will not be invalidated by acts or omissions of its debtors. Under special types of insurance (discussed in CPCU 3), coverages are available for the unique needs of lending institutions and vendors involved in the extension of credit. Some of these special policies relieve the creditor of the administrative burden of filing debtors' insurance policies or otherwise checking to make sure they are kept in force.

From the viewpoint of the creditor, the chief disadvantage of purchasing its own insurance is that the creditor must pay the premiums. While the creditor may be able to "pass along" the insurance costs to the borrowers in the form of higher charges for the loans, the creditor must be mindful of any constraints imposed by regulations, statutes, or competitive considerations. In any event, it is common practice to require the *debtor* to insure the property pledged as collateral security for a loan, whether or not the creditor carries its own insurance as well.

CREDITOR INSURED BY DEBTOR'S POLICY. One possible way of insuring the secured creditor's interest in property would be to require the debtor to *assign* its insurance policy to the creditor, before any loss occurs, and stipulate that the debtor must continue paying the premiums. However, the mere assignment of a property insurance policy would not, by itself, provide adequate protection for either of the two parties.[7] The creditor would be insured to the extent of the unpaid balance of the debt, yet the debtor would no longer be an insured under the policy for which the debtor would be obligated to pay the premiums. In addition, the courts have generally held that a pre-loss assignment of a property insurance policy, if not accompanied by a related transfer of the property it insures, gives the assignee no greater rights than the assignor had in the policy at the time of the assignment. This means that the creditor (assignee) is subject to all the defenses the insurer may have had against the debtor (the former insured); consequently, the creditor may find its coverage jeopardized by the debtor's fraud or breach of a policy condition before the assignment became effective.

The fact that the insurer's legal position is not weakened by such an assignment would undoubtedly make it easier to get the insurer's written consent thereto, but the vast majority of creditors prefer, as an alternative to assignment of the debtor's policy, to buy their own insurance and/or to insist that every debtor buy and maintain a policy containing an appropriate loss payable clause or standard mortgage clause.

The *loss payable clause* is most commonly used to protect the creditor's interest in *personal* property, such as an auto that has been pledged as security for a debt. The typical loss payable clause names the creditor as the payee in a clause which stipulates that any covered "loss is payable to the named insured and (Big Bank and Trust Company), as their interests may appear." In the event of a covered loss, the insurer usually issues a check or draft payable jointly to the creditor and debtor. If the insurance payment is less than the amount of the outstanding debt, the creditor is entitled to keep the entire payment and reduce the debt accordingly. If the payment is more than the amount of the outstanding debt, the excess is payable to the debtor. In practice, however, the creditor often wants to keep the loan intact and have the property repaired or replaced, in which case the creditor merely withholds its signature on the check or draft until the repair or replacement is completed. (The creditor may also refuse to sign until the check or draft is endorsed over to the repair shop or vendor, to assure that the latter will be paid.) In any case, the loss payable clause protects both the debtor and creditor, to the extent that the coverage is both valid and adequate in amount and scope, while at the same time giving the creditor first priority to any amounts payable by the insurer.

As a device for protecting the creditor, the loss payable clause may not be reliable in all legal jurisdictions. Many courts have said that the loss payable clause does little more than make the creditor an appointee or representative of the debtor and, as such, the creditor is entitled to no greater rights than the debtor has under the policy. The creditor would not be entitled to collect any benefits otherwise payable under the policy, according to this interpretation, if any act or omission of the debtor serves to invalidate the coverage. A few courts interpret the loss payable clause as though it were a separate contract between the creditor and the insurer. The latter interpretation gives the creditor assurance that the creditor's rights under the policy cannot be jeopardized by an act or omission of the debtor.

The *standard mortgage clause* is most commonly used to protect the creditor's (mortgagee's) interest in *real* property which has been pledged as collateral security for a debt. The standard mortgage clause will be analyzed in detail in Chapter 15. The standard mortgage clause is uniformly interpreted as though it were a separate contract between the insurer and the mortgagee, as was apparently intended by the drafters of the clause. The mortgagee's rights under the policy cannot be impaired by an act or omission of the debtor (mortgagor). The only point of dispute seems to be that some courts hold the mortgagee "exempt" from the consequences of all the debtor's acts or omissions, whether they occur before or after the effective date of the mortgage clause, whereas other courts apply the exemption only with respect to acts or omissions which occur after the effective date of the mortgage clause.

Assuming the debtor never did anything to invalidate the coverage, the legal effect of a loss payable clause would seem to be about the same as that of a standard mortgage clause, in every legal jurisdiction. At least this is true in terms of the creditor's basic right to be compensated, up to the full extent of its insurable interest, before the debtor may receive any excess amount, payable under the policy. The two clauses are also similar in respect to the manner in which loss settlements are handled in practice.

The typical loss payable clause is very brief, sometimes no more than a single sentence in the declarations, or a simple endorsement. The standard mortgage clause is not really a "clause" at all; instead, it consists of several lengthy paragraphs that complement and supplement other policy provisions and set forth in detail the many rights and few duties of the mortgagee. For creditors who wish to rely to some degree on insurance purchased and paid for by the debtor, both the loss payable clause and the standard mortgage clause provide much better protection for the creditor, as well as the debtor, than a mere assignment of the debtor's property insurance policy.

Entities Identified By Relationship to Another Insured

In addition to the various entities that become insureds by being identified in the policy by name, most property and liability policies also cover, as insureds, one or more entities that are identified in terms of their relationship to the "named insured" (or in terms of their relationship to another insured, such as an assignee or a creditor). The entities insured by virtue of a relationship are not always separate insureds. For example, policies often define the term "insured" to include:

- *Legal representatives*—such as executors, administrators, and receivers in bankruptcy proceedings.
- *Personal representatives*—this term would include legal representatives and holders of a power of attorney.

- *Heirs and assigns*—the word "assigns" refers to assignees, and the word "heirs" refers to entities that will inherit the named insured's property, either by will or by operation of law.

Entities such as these are not truly separate insureds in a literal sense. They are instead acceptable legal *substitutes* for the named insured, empowered to act on behalf of the named insured (or a deceased named insured, in the case of executors and administrators). Since they have only the rights the named insured has or had while living, they can collect only for the named insured's covered losses, not for their own.

Unlike those who serve only as legal substitutes, many entities qualify as *separate* insureds by virtue of their relationship to the named insured. Perhaps the most obvious example is the husband or wife who is an insured under a policy, without being identified by name as such, because the policy definition of "insured" includes the "spouse" of the person who is listed in the declarations as the "named insured." However, the applicable policy definition may also confer automatic insured status on those who fall into other generic classifications, such as:

- family members,
- employees,
- users,
- legal agents,
- employers,
- household residents,
- officers, or
- other classifications stipulated in the policy and based upon personal or business relationships with the named insured.

When a policy consists of a package of several different types of coverages, as is often the case, the definition of an insured frequently varies by type of coverage. Different policy types may contain somewhat different definitions of an insured. Even the same basic type of policy may have definitions that differ from one state to another, to accommodate applicable regulations and statutes (such as no-fault auto insurance laws). What follows is no more than a sampling from a variety of policies, therefore, for illustrative purposes. Depending on the particular coverage and the kind of policy of which it is a part, the term "insured" may be defined to include the "named insured" plus:

(1) residents of the named insured's household who are either relatives under the age of twenty-one or in the care of an insured;

(2) any person or organization legally responsible for animals or watercraft owned by an insured;

(3) any person using a covered auto;
(4) any family member while occupying (or struck as a pedestrian by) a motor vehicle designed for use on public roads—and any other person while occupying a covered auto;
(5) the named insured, any partner or executive officer of the insured business, and any other person using an owned or hired automobile with the permission of the named insured; or
(6) for workers' compensation and employers' liability coverages, if the named insured is a partnership or joint venture, each partner or member thereof but only while acting within the scope of his or her duties as a partner or member.

The reader is certainly not expected to memorize the foregoing definitions (which have been edited and paraphrased, in some cases and may be subject to limitations not described here). They are simply for illustrative purposes. The important thing to remember is that property-liability policies frequently define the word "insured" to include all members of designated classifications, based on various relationships with the named insured, even though such members are not identified by name. Thus, the term *insured* is invariably a broad concept that may include most or all owners of property, operators or occupants of autos, employees or agents of a business firm, residents of a household, members of a family, persons who have custody or control of property, guests, or others who have a specified personal, business or even casual relationship to the named insured.

Summary of Insured Entities

Assuming the applicable insurable interest requirements have been met and the loss is otherwise covered, the entities insured under a property or liability insurance policy include all entities that have been identified in the policy as insureds, either by naming them or by specifying generic classifications based upon relationships to those who have been identified by name. Entities that are commonly identified by name are named insureds, assignees, and creditors. Entities that are commonly identified by generic classifications are either acceptable substitutes for the insured or separate insureds. Whereas the former serve merely as legal representatives of an insured, the latter have insured status that is independent of the rights of (and based upon formal or informal relationships with) the named insured. Since the definitions of an insured entity often differ by type of policy, by state, and by type of coverage within a policy, determining "who is insured" under a policy is necessarily a process of examining carefully those definitions applicable to each coverage included in that policy.

Chapter Notes

1. Some are inclined to say (or imply) that declarations, insuring agreements, exclusions, conditions, and miscellaneous provisions are five categories that are equally applicable to policies in *all* lines of insurance. In many cases this is just a loose usage of the word "all" when the writer or speaker really meant "most" insurance policies or all *property-liability* policies. The provisions of a life insurance policy can be forced into the aforementioned categories, but only by relegating some of the most important life insurance policy provisions to the miscellaneous or "catch-all" category. There are much better terms available to describe or classify the contents of a life insurance policy.

2. Some insurers use the heading "insuring agreement" to refer to a coverage part or a coverage form.

3. The discussion in this section omits consideration of the so-called "binder," a temporary and sometimes oral contract of insurance. Binders are thoroughly examined in CPCU 6.

4. The somewhat restricted scope of this discussion should be noted. The focus is on the various interests insurers intend to protect, not on the interests of any entities that may ultimately receive the loss payments made under any particular insurance contract. These two groups—the interests intended to be protected and the entities receiving insurance payments—largely overlap, but they need not exactly correspond. For example, an entity whose interest is not intended to be covered by an insurance policy may still receive payments under that policy in some unusual situations, such as when a buyer of property is able, through litigation, to claim proceeds under an insurance policy written to protect only the seller's interest, or when a remainderman brings suit against the life tenant to obtain a portion of the insurance payments under a policy issued solely in the name of the life tenant. The rights of these adverse claimants have been touched upon in the earlier discussion of insurable interest. Otherwise, they are beyond the scope of this course.

5. Group life and health insurance is studied briefly in CPCU 2. As a marketing technique, the "collective merchandising" of property and liability insurance is explained in CPCU 5. Though collectively merchandised auto and homeowners policies are often referred to as "group" insurance, they usually involve individually issued policies.

6. Though moral hazard is also significant in life insurance, especially in respect to the applicant who is to be named as a beneficiary on a policy that is to insure the life of another person, the physical or health characteristics of the insured are primary underwriting considerations, and the same can be said of health insurance. In this respect, life and health insurance contracts are clearly of a "personal" nature, as a matter of both law and common

sense. The personal nature of property and liability contracts is less obvious to the casual observer but formally recognized by the courts.

7. This is not true of collateral assignments in life insurance, where the standard assignments form (developed jointly by the life insurance industry and the American Bankers Association) works nicely to protect the interests of all parties concerned, as long as written notice is given to the life insurer. But such a collateral assignment does not change either the insured or the owner of the life insurance policy, as it would under a property insurance policy, because a collateral assignment of life insurance transfers only some of the rights to the assignee, not the ownership of the policy itself.

CHAPTER 10

Insured Events

INTRODUCTION

It was stressed in the preceding chapters that the question of "who is insured" under a given property or liability policy can be answered by identifying all entities that both (1) hold valid insurable interests in accordance with legal requirements, *and* (2) qualify as insureds, in accordance with the applicable policy definition(s). This chapter focuses on three additional questions of coverage, the "what, where, and when" aspects which collectively determine whether or not a policy covers a particular loss. The latter three questions are discussed under the general heading of "insured events," since property and liability policies are designed to cover only those losses that involve insured events or happenings.

An insured event may be broken down into six elements:

(1) covered properties or activities,
(2) covered causes,
(3) covered consequences,
(4) covered circumstances,
(5) covered locations, and
(6) covered time periods.

The first four elements pertain to *what* things are covered, while the last two pertain, respectively, to *where* and *when* they are covered. A particular loss will be an insured event only if all six elements are involved. If at least one element is missing, the loss will not constitute an insured event. For example, a loss that is not due to a covered cause is not an insured event, even if the loss involves a covered property, a covered circumstance, a covered consequence, a covered location, and a covered time period. If a loss involves all six elements, it is an "insured event." The insurer might have no obligation to pay for the loss if there is no insurable interest or if an important policy condition is breached, but it would not alter the fact that the *event* itself is insured. Similarly, limitations on the *amounts* of recovery do not alter the required elements of an insured *event*. Conditions and amount of limitations will be discussed in later chapters of this text. In the meantime, the six elements of an insured event may be thought of as necessary but not sufficient determinants of an insurer's contractual obligation to pay for a given loss.

This chapter will first use the six elements of an insured event to examine the events typically insured under *property* insurance policies. It will then use the six elements to examine the events typically insured under *liability* insurance policies. The numerous quotations of actual policy language are for the purpose of illustrating the basic principles involved. For this reason, most of the excerpts are not identified with specific policies, form numbers, or trade names.

INSURED EVENTS UNDER PROPERTY INSURANCE POLICIES

Covered Properties

An insured event under a property insurance policy must involve covered property. The legal concept of property refers to any right or bundle of rights that has an economic value. Although the legal concept of property is critical to an understanding of insurable interests, it does not offer a practical way of identifying the physical objects that are most commonly insured under property insurance policies.

Moreover, the language of insurance policies seldom corresponds precisely to the legal distinctions between real and personal property or intangible and tangible property. Intangible property is rarely insured by commercial insurers, with the exception of title defects and valuable records, and land as such is almost never insured. The remaining items of tangible property, those which are often insured, are usually referred to by descriptive terms like "buildings," "dwellings," "other structures," "personal effects," "business personal property," "unscheduled personal property," or simply "contents."

The typical property insurance policy (or property section of a policy that also provides liability coverage) first identifies the "building(s)" or "dwelling(s)" with a brief description in the declarations. The policy then goes on to stipulate what items are considered a part of the building or dwelling. An entire section of the policy is often devoted to describing covered property, real and personal, and a separate section is usually entitled "property not covered." However, these sections rarely contain all of the policy provisions relating to the properties covered. Specific types of property may be added or excluded, with respect to some or all of the perils insured against, by policy provisions that appear elsewhere in the policy forms or endorsements.

A similar pattern may be discerned in nearly all property insurance forms. The principal difference among commercial, residential, and auto physical damage forms lies in the types of property that each seeks to insure. Both the common pattern and the differing definitions are illustrated in the following examples.

Commercial Property One general property form, widely used to insure commercial property, stipulates that "insurance applies only to item(s) specifically described in this policy for which an amount of insurance is shown..." (in the declarations). The form goes on to say, under the heading of "property covered," that

> When the insurance under this policy covers "Buildings," "Personal Property of the Insured," or "Personal Property of Others" such insurance shall cover in accordance with the following description(s) of coverage.
>
> COVERAGE A-BUILDING(S): Building(s) or structure(s) shall include attached additions and extensions; fixtures, machinery and equipment constituting a permanent part of and pertaining to the service of the building; yard fixtures; personal property of the named insured used for the maintenance or service of the described building(s), including fire extinguishing apparatus, outdoor furniture, floor coverings and appliances for refrigerating, ventilating, cooking, dishwashing and laundering (but not including other personal property in apartments or rooms furnished by the named insured as landlord); all while at the described locations.
>
> COVERAGE B-PERSONAL PROPERTY OF THE INSURED: Personal property of the insured means only business personal property, owned by the named Insured usual to the occupancy of the named Insured, including bullion, manuscripts, furniture, fixtures, equipment and supplies, not otherwise covered under this policy, and shall also include the named Insured's interest in personal property owned by others to the extent of the value of labor, materials and charges furnished, performed or incurred by the named Insured; all while (1) in or on the described buildings, or (2) in the open (including within vehicles) on or within 100 feet of the described premises.
>
> This coverage shall also include Tenant's Improvements and Betterments, when not otherwise specifically covered. Tenant's Improvements and Betterments means the named Insured's use interest in fixtures, alterations, installations or additions comprising a part of the buildings occupied but not owned by the named Insured and made or acquired at the expense of the named Insured exclusive of rent paid by the named Insured, but which are not legally subject to removal by the named Insured.

COVERAGE C-PERSONAL PROPERTY OF OTHERS: The insurance shall cover for the account of the owner(s) (other than the named Insured) personal property belonging to others in the care, custody or control of the named Insured, while (1) in or on the described buildings, or (2) in the open (including within vehicles) on or within 100 feet of the described premises.

Loss shall be adjusted with the named Insured for the account of the owner(s) of the property, except the right to adjust such loss with the owner(s) is reserved to this Company and the receipt(s) of the owner(s) in satisfaction thereof shall be in full satisfaction of any claim by the named Insured for which payment(s) has been made. This coverage shall not otherwise benefit the named Insured nor any carrier or other bailee.

Under a section titled "Property Not Covered," the form eliminates coverage for injury or damage to animals and pets, aircraft, watercraft, growing crops and lawns, outdoor signs, outdoor swimming pools, fences, and several other types of property. However, under what are sometimes referred to as exceptions to the exclusions, coverage for some of the otherwise excluded property is effectively "added back" or restored, when the property is being held for sale. Under certain circumstances, limited amounts of coverage are also provided for newly acquired property, personal effects, valuable papers and records, and "trees, shrubs and plants." Then, under the heading of "perils insured against," one finds that certain types of property are not covered for damage or destruction from some of the perils that are otherwise insured against. To take just one example, the policy does not cover wind or hail damage to windmills, crop silos, metal smokestacks, or (when outside the building) trees, awnings, and television antennas.

The foregoing excerpts are typical of the language used by policy drafters to clarify the exact kinds of commercial property the insurer intends to cover under a particular form. Property excluded under one form can usually be insured by endorsement, or under another form, for an additional premium. This same general pattern can be found in policies designed to insure residential property.

Residential Property Coverage definitions for private dwellings, furniture, clothing and other property of a residential nature can be illustrated by the language of a modern homeowners policy, which uses the conversational words "you" and "your" to refer to the named insured (and his or her spouse), and the words "we," "us," and "our" to refer to the insurance company providing the insurance. The policy defines the *residence premises* as "the one or two family dwelling, other structures, and grounds or that part of any other building where you reside and which is shown as the 'residence premises' in the Declarations." Then, in a section entitled "coverages," the policy stipulates that:

COVERAGE A-DWELLING We cover:

a. the dwelling on the *residence premises* shown in the Declarations used principally as a private residence, including structures attached to the dwelling: and

b. materials and supplies located on or adjacent to the *residence premises* for use in the construction, alteration or repair of the dwelling or other structures on the *residence premises*.

COVERAGE B-OTHER STRUCTURES We cover other structures on the *residence premises*, separated from the dwelling by clear space. Structures connected to the dwelling by only a fence, utility line, or similar connection are considered to be other structures.

We do not cover other structures:

a. used in whole or in part for *business* purposes; or

b. rented or held for rental to any person not a tenant of the dwelling, unless used solely as a private garage.

COVERAGE C-PERSONAL PROPERTY We cover personal property owned or used by any *insured* while it is anywhere in the world. At your request, we will cover personal property owned by others while the property is on the part of the *residence premises* occupied by an *insured*. In addition, we will cover at your request, personal property owned by a guest or a *residence employee*, while the property is in any residence occupied by any *insured*. . . .

After specifying the maximum dollar amounts the insurer will pay for various classes of personal property, the homeowners policy goes on to exclude some types of property from any coverage. The excluded property takes the form of a list, as follows:

Property Not Covered. We do not cover:

1. articles separately described and specifically insured in this or any other insurance;

2. animals, birds or fish;

3. motorized land vehicles except those used to service an *insured's* residence which are not licensed for road use;

4. any device or instrument, including any accessories or antennas, for the transmitting, recording, receiving or reproduction of sound which is operated by power from the electrical system of a *motor vehicle*, or any tape, wire, record, disc or other medium for use with any such device or instrument while any of this property is in or upon a *motor vehicle;*

5. aircraft and parts;

6. property of roomers, boarders and other tenants, except property of roomers and boarders related to any *insured;*

7. property contained in an apartment regularly rented or held for rental to others by any *insured;*

8. property rented or held for rental to others away from the *residence premises;*

9. business property in storage or held as a sample or for sale or delivery after sale;

10. business property pertaining to a business actually conducted on the *residence premises;*

11. business property away from the *residence premises*.

In subsequent sections of the policy, additional policy provisions are used to limit the scope of coverage for otherwise covered property. For example, watercraft and outboard motors are not covered for theft that occurs away from the residence premises (covered locations); nor are they covered for wind and hail damage unless they are inside a fully enclosed building (covered causes). On the other hand, limited coverage is provided as an "additional coverage" for trees, shrubs, and plants damaged by certain covered causes such as theft, vandalism, fire, and lightning.

Like the general property form, the homeowners policy is one of many policies that cover personal property on an *unscheduled* basis. Such property is covered automatically, as long as it fits into the designated class of property and is not specifically excluded. It does not have to be specifically identified until a loss occurs. In contrast, personal property is said to be *scheduled* when the policy includes a list or schedule of particular items of property. Silver flatware is normally scheduled as a class, rather than piece by piece, while jewelry, furs, musical instruments, and other valuable articles usually are listed separately and identified precisely with descriptions, serial numbers, and other identifying marks or characteristics. Personal property may be scheduled by endorsement to the homeowners policy or under a separate personal articles floater. Business firms may also insure various items of movable property on a scheduled basis.

Autos Motor vehicles are items of personal property that do not fit neatly into the commercial or residential categories previously discussed. They may be used for either commercial or noncommercial purposes, and they are covered primarily under policies or forms designed specifically for cars, trucks, and other motor vehicles. Since most of these special policies may be used to insure against physical damage to motor vehicles, the covered vehicles are defined as carefully as covered properties are defined under other forms of property insurance.

For example, one widely used personal auto policy includes the following language:

> **"Your covered auto"** means:
> 1. Any vehicle shown in the Declarations:
> 2. Any of the following types of vehicles on the date you become the owner:
>   a. a private passenger auto; or
>   b. a pickup, panel truck or van, not used in any business or occupation other than farming or ranching.
>
> This provision applies only if you:
>   a. acquire the vehicle during the policy period; and

   b. ask us to insure it within 30 days after you become the
       owner.
   If the vehicle you acquire replaces one shown in the Declarations,
   it will have the same coverage as the vehicle it replaced. You must
   ask us to insure a replacement vehicle within 30 days only if you
   wish to add or continue Coverage for Damage to Your Auto. If
   the vehicle you acquire is in addition to any shown in the
   Declarations, it will have the broadest coverage we now provide
   for any vehicle shown in the Declarations.
   3. Any *trailer* you own.
   4. Any auto or *trailer* you do not own while used as a
       temporary substitute for any other vehicle described in this
       definition which is out of normal use because of its:
       a. breakdown;
       b. repair;
       c. servicing;
       d. loss; or
       e. destruction.

The meaning of "trailer" is clarified elsewhere in the policy. The
process of defining covered property is continued in the physical
damage section of the policy with language to the effect that the
insurer "will pay for direct and accidental loss to *your covered auto*,
including its equipment." Thus, equipment is also covered property.
The exclusions make it clear that the otherwise covered auto is not
covered for damage by causes such as routine wear and tear and
mechanical failure, and that tires are not covered for road damage.
Sound reproduction equipment is covered only if it is permanently
installed in the covered auto. Some items of property are not covered at
all. Examples of property items that are excluded entirely include
tapes, records, and sound receiving and transmitting equipment.
   The definitions of covered vehicles can be even more complicated in
policies providing physical damage insurance on commercial autos and
mobile equipment. The challenge faced by policy drafters is to clarify
the underwriting intent with regard to commonplace but specialized
items such as tractor-trailer rigs, refrigeration equipment, bulldozers,
power shovels, cranes, forklifts, and other mobile equipment and
machinery which may or may not be licensed for use on public streets
or highways.

   Other Property Physical damage insurance for motor boats,
tunnels, cargo, and similar items of property are considered in other
CPCU courses. The extent to which such items are insured is again
governed by the collection of policy provisions that are used in the
process of distinguishing among covered property, uncovered property,
and property that is only covered for some causes of loss.
   The foregoing illustrations will have served their purpose if they at
least convey the relationship between covered property and an insured

event. Remember that covered property definitions are only one element or determinant of whether a particular event is an insured event under the policy. The covered property must also be damaged, destroyed, or lost due to a covered cause.

Covered Causes

In order for a loss to be an insured event under a property insurance policy, an item of covered property must be lost, damaged, or destroyed *by a covered cause*. Analyzing this second element, the covered causes under a policy, requires a basic understanding of

(1) the "specified perils approach,"
(2) the "all-risks approach,"
(3) the "like perils approach," and
(4) the legal doctrine of proximate cause.

Specified Perils Approach The term "peril" refers to a cause of loss. When a policy specifically lists or names the perils it insures, it is said to be using the "specified perils approach" of identifying the covered causes of loss. For example, a policy might stipulate that it covers the perils of fire, lightning, windstorm, hail, vandalism, theft, and other perils that are specifically identified by name.

The mere listing of the perils does not mean that the policy intends to cover every loss associated with one or more of the named perils. To the contrary, policy definitions and/or exclusions invariably restrict the scope of the intended coverage by narrowing the meaning of some or all of the perils. For example, under most policies the windstorm and hail perils do not cover tidal wave or sleet damage, whether driven by wind or not. The peril of vandalism usually covers only willful damage *to* the property and not pilferage *of* it, and the theft peril is often defined to exclude theft from unattended and unlocked vehicles (circumstances).

Many specified perils are elaborately defined and clarified in the policy. Others are not defined at all in the policy itself, in which case their interpretation is ultimately in the hands of the courts. Fire is not defined in fire policies, oddly enough, but most courts have given the term fire a much narrower meaning than it has in ordinary conversation. Courts have said that fire is "oxidation rapid enough to produce flame or glow" and have held that the policy coverage does not extend to "friendly fires" which are deliberately set and remain in their normal confines (such as in a fireplace). However, court interpretations do not always have a narrowing effect. As will be explained later, in applying the doctrine of proximate cause to specific situations, the courts quite often require insurers to pay losses that most people would not regard as losses "caused by" a named peril.

In any case, the specified perils approach has the practical effect of placing the *burden of proof* on the insured. To obtain coverage, the *insured* must be able to prove the loss was caused by a covered peril. If such proof cannot be provided by the insured, the insurer is not legally obligated to pay the loss.

All-Risks Approach   Instead of enumerating the perils to be covered, many property insurance forms express the coverage by using the "all-risks" approach. (In this context, the term "risks" is synonymous with "perils.") The "all-risks" approach is to insure against all perils causing physical loss to the covered property *except those losses that are specifically excluded.* That is to say, if a loss is not excluded, it is covered. This approach is well illustrated in the language of a popular homeowners policy: "We insure for all risks of physical loss to the property described in Coverages A and B except:...." This phrase is then followed by a list of excluded perils.

Theoretically, a specified perils policy that contained a long list of covered perils and few exclusions could provide broader protection than an "all-risks" policy that had a long list of exclusions. In practice, however, the typical "all-risks" policy usually provides broader (and more expensive) coverage. Most insurance buyers actually have a wide range of choice among the progressively broader coverage options of

(1) a small number of specified perils on both buildings and contents,
(2) a longer list of specified perils on both buildings and contents,
(3) "all-risks" coverage on the buildings and specified perils coverage on the contents, or
(4) "all-risks" coverage on both buildings and contents.

To the extent that a policy provides "all-risks" coverage, the practical effect is to shift the burden of proof to the insurer in the event of a loss. If the *insurer* cannot prove that the loss is specifically excluded, it must be paid.

There is a subtlety here that should not pass unnoticed by the reader. When the drafters of "all-risks" coverage fail to anticipate all the various kinds of losses that might happen, insurers may end up paying for some losses they did not really intend to cover. This helps to account for the almost universal use of deductibles in "all-risks" forms.

For the consumer who can qualify and is willing to pay the higher premium, "all-risks" coverage is the broadest available. What is not universally agreed upon is whether "all-risks" coverage is a "better buy" for consumers than a form which covers a lengthy list of specified perils. Some analysts feel that the additional protection afforded by the "all-risks" approach is worth the additional premium. Others do not agree.

Like Perils Approach The like perils approach, used almost exclusively in ocean marine insurance, provides coverage for a group of specified perils *plus* "all other like perils." In other words, the policy covers all perils that are similar in nature to those listed by name, as well as the listed perils themselves. The approach is illustrated by the following language in an ocean marine cargo policy:

> The adventures and perils which the said Company [insurer] is content to bear and does take upon itself, are: of the seas, fire, rovers, assailing thieves, jettisons, criminal barratry of the master and mariners, and of all other like perils, losses and misfortunes, that have or shall come to the hurt, detriment, or damage of the aforesaid subject matter of this insurance or any part thereof except as may be otherwise provided for herein or endorsed hereon.

Particularly noteworthy is the cargo policy's use of the phrase "all other like perils." This phrase does not mean that *all* perils are covered, because the policy goes on to say "except as may be otherwise provided for herein, or endorsed hereon," thus forewarning of the inevitable exclusions that may be found in virtually every insurance policy. The phrase "all other like perils" is not even intended to provide "all-risks" coverage per se. Instead, it means that the insurer intends to cover, in addition to the perils identified by name, all other "perils of the seas" even those which have not been identified in the policy itself. A "peril of the seas" is a peril such as sinking, which would not have happened had the vessel been on dry land.

It follows from the foregoing that the like perils approach is a combination of specified perils and "perils of the seas." The latter is interpreted according to maritime law, which lies well beyond the scope of this text. However, further discussion of ocean marine insurance is included in CPCU 3.

Doctrine of Proximate Cause As noted at the beginning of this chapter, a loss is an insured event only if it involves, among other elements, a covered cause (just discussed) and a covered consequence (to be discussed in the next section). It is also legally required that there be a sufficiently close causal connection between the covered cause and the covered consequence. The required causal link is known as the *doctrine of proximate cause.*

According to the doctrine of proximate cause, a loss is insured under a policy only if a covered peril is the proximate cause of a covered consequence. A peril is a *covered peril* if it is either (1) specified and not excluded, in a specified perils policy or (2) not excluded, in an "all-risks" policy. A covered peril is the *proximate cause* if it is the cause that initiates an unbroken chain of events leading to a covered consequence. Or, as stated in one court decision:

> The proximate cause of any result is the active, efficient cause that sets in motion a train of events which brings about the result without the intervention of any force started and working actively from a new and independent source.[1]

In the case from which this quotation is taken, machinery in a factory was insured against loss by fire. A fire ignited an electrical tower on the insured's premises, some distance from the building in which the insured machinery was located. As a result of the fire, there was an electrical short circuit, which in turn caused a sudden increase in the pressure on a belt driving a flywheel. The flywheel disintegrated, its flying fragments damaging the machinery in question. By the standard given in the above quotation, the damage to the machinery was ruled to have been proximately caused by fire. Since the insurance policy covered direct damage (the covered consequences) by fire (the covered peril), the insurer had to pay for the damaged machinery, even though collision with flywheel fragments was not a covered peril. The fire unleashed an unbroken chain of events that resulted in the loss. Fire was the proximate cause of the loss, and fire was a covered peril.

Through the application of the proximate cause doctrine to specific sets of facts, the courts have significantly broadened the coverage scope of many property insurance policies. For example, when food stored under refrigeration was insured against "direct loss by windstorm," wind damage to power lines located off the insured's premises caused a failure of refrigeration and consequent spoilage of the food. This spoilage was ruled to be a covered loss proximately caused by windstorm.[2] Similarly, when cattle being transported by truck were insured against "direct loss by overturning of the vehicle," cattle tracks leading from the overturned truck went directly to a quicksand bog into which the cattle presumably wandered. The death of the cattle was ruled an insured event. Their carcasses were never found.[3] In this situation, the available evidence suggested an unbroken chain of events originating in the peril of overturning, a covered peril under the policy.

Application of the proximate cause requirement does not always expand the scope of coverage. It depends on whether the courts judge an actual loss to be (1) the proximate result of a covered peril, or (2) too remotely connected to a covered peril to be considered its result. For instance, suppose lightning struck a tree and the tree immediately fell on a house, thereby breaking a large plate glass window. Suppose the insured has a specified perils policy that covers direct damage from lightning but not from falling objects or glass breakage. Most courts would probably rule that the insurer must pay for the direct damage to the glass, because such damage was the proximate result of lightning (a covered peril). In contrast, suppose this same insured refused to have the window repaired for three months, perhaps because the insured was undecided about whether to add a room to the house where the window was located. To stretch a point for the sake of emphasis, suppose a passerby reached through the opening in the window and stole the insured's diamond wristwatch that had been left lying on a nearby table, and that the insured did not have theft coverage on personal property but only coverage for direct damage from fire and lightning. Most courts would not make the insurer pay for the theft, since such a theft would be too remotely connected to the covered peril, lightning, to be considered a proximate result thereof. The link between the lightning and the theft loss would be too weak to be deemed a causal connection, and there also would have been an intervening cause (the insured's negligence in both failing to have the window repaired and leaving the watch lying on the table). Likewise, in an actual case involving an insured whose auto was insured under "all-risks" coverage that excluded collision damage, the insured skidded into a tree and damaged the auto.[4] The insured's policy covered "any direct and accidental loss of or damage to the automobile, except loss caused by collision." The insured argued that "skidding" was the proximate cause and was, therefore, covered by the policy language. The court upheld the insurer's argument that collision was the proximate cause of loss, not skidding, and that the parties clearly did not intend to cover collision damage. Accordingly, the insurer was not required to pay for the loss.

In spite of the difficulty of forecasting how a court might interpret the proximate cause doctrine in the light of a given set of facts, understanding the requirement of proximate cause is important to insurance policy coverage analysis. An insured event must not only involve a covered cause; a covered cause must also be the proximate cause of a covered consequence.

Covered Consequences

In the context of property insurance policies, covered consequences may include (1) *direct losses* to or of the property, and (2) *indirect losses* resulting from the direct damage or taking of property. The term "direct losses" refers to the financial losses that nearly always result from the physical damage, destruction, or abstraction of the property itself causing a loss of intrinsic value. "Indirect losses" refers to other financial losses that *may* result as an indirect consequence of the physical damage, destruction, or abstraction of the property, causing a loss of economic value in use. Virtually all policies insuring tangible property are designed to cover direct losses from the perils insured against. Many property insurance policies cover only direct losses, in fact, unless indirect loss coverage has been added by the attachment of an endorsement or special policy form (for an additional premium).

Regardless of whether the coverage is written on a specified perils or an "all-risks" basis, *insurance for direct losses* is designed to produce funds to repair or replace property that has been physically damaged, destroyed, or abstracted as a direct result of such perils as fire, lightning, windstorm, or theft. However, it is important to remember that the courts interpret the phrase "direct result" to include both (1) the first result in an unbroken chain of causation and (2) any subsequent and "proximate" result in that unbroken chain. In the earlier example involving a policy that covered only direct damage from lightning, the lightning struck a tree, which in turn fell on the house and broke a window. The lightning set into motion an unbroken chain of causation. The first result was damage to the tree. The second and third results were damage to the house and breakage of the glass. All three results would be covered as "direct" losses from lightning.

Insurance for indirect losses may also be written on a specified perils or an "all-risks" basis. In either instance, insurance for indirect losses is designed to pay at least some of the financial losses, beyond the cost of repairing or replacing the property, that flow indirectly from a covered peril. For example, many indirect losses result from the inability to *use* the property during the period of time that is required to repair or replace the property after it has been damaged or destroyed. As explained in the Chapter 8 discussion of insurable interests, a fire that destroys a building may cause at least two kinds of financial loss of the building's intrinsic value. It may also cause an indirect loss of the building's economic value in use. The owner and/or the tenant may lose revenue (and/or incur additional expenses to secure substitute facilities) during the time it would take to restore the building, get it ready for occupancy, and resume a normal level of activity.

Insurance against the indirect losses that result from a deprivation of the property's use is sometimes referred to as *time element coverage*, because the required time for restoring the use value is a key element governing the amount of the loss. Business interruption and extra expense insurance, as well as other time element coverages, are readily available in the insurance marketplace. Certain types of time element coverage are included automatically in many policies. Whether purchased as an option or automatically provided, time element coverages are normally made a part of the policy that insures the direct losses to the property. The time element losses are usually covered for the same perils (or at least some of the perils) that apply to direct losses to or of the property itself.

Some indirect losses are not related to the loss of use of property, yet they are the indirect or consequential result of a covered peril. This kind of indirect loss is again rarely a *covered* consequence under policies that provide coverage for direct losses, unless the appropriate form of indirect loss coverage has been added to the basic policy. But the dividing line between direct and indirect losses is not always clear-cut. For example, the insuring agreement of a typical specified perils policy insures against "direct loss *to the property* covered by the following perils"; the comparable agreement in a typical "all-risks" policy insures against "all risks of physical loss *to the property*" (emphasis supplied). The words "direct," "physical," and "to the property" clearly show that the insurer does not intend to cover indirect losses from the loss of use of property. Nevertheless, what about other kinds of loss that appear to be indirect in nature? For instance, does the insurer intend to pay for the expenses of removing the debris before a damaged building can be rebuilt? Debris removal expenses could logically be considered a part of the overall replacement cost of the building. Likewise, debris removal expenses could be viewed as a proximate (direct) result of a covered peril. If so, what dollar limit applies to debris removal? To resolve these questions in advance, most property insurance forms covering buildings specifically state that the insurer will pay debris removal expenses, and that the insurer will pay no more (for debris removal *and* building damage combined) than the applicable limit of liability on the building.

In contrast, most property insurance policies specifically exclude certain kinds of indirect loss that might otherwise be interpreted by the courts as falling within the scope of the direct-loss wording of the insuring agreements. A prime example is the universal exclusion of both demolition costs and any increased costs of construction, following a fire or some other covered peril, as a consequence of building codes or ordinances. One such exclusion reads:

> This policy does not insure against loss: (1) occasioned directly or indirectly by enforcement of any local or state ordinance or law regulating the construction, repair, or demolition of building(s) or structure(s) unless such liability is otherwise specifically assumed by endorsement hereon. . . .

This exclusion refers to the various laws that require that a seriously damaged building be totally demolished before any new construction begins, as well as to building codes that impose higher (and more expensive) standards on new construction than were imposed at the time the building was originally built. While such losses are the direct result of laws and at most the *indirect* or consequential result of fire, a court might hold that the losses were the direct and proximate result of a covered peril like fire. Hence, the losses are specifically excluded to clarify the underwriting intent. If coverage is desired, it normally may be purchased by the payment of the required additional premium.

Numerous additional examples could be given of indirect losses that are specifically excluded or specifically listed as covered consequences, depending on the type of policy and the underwriting intent. However, the general rule is that property insurance policies are basically designed to cover direct losses to the property insured, including all losses that are the proximate (direct) result of a covered peril. Under most policies, direct losses are the primary or the only covered consequences of an insured event.

There are many different kinds of indirect loss and most of them are insurable. To be a covered consequence under a policy, a particular kind of indirect loss must be clearly identified in the policy as a covered consequence, and it must be an indirect result of a covered peril. In short, the covered consequences of property insurance policies *may* include both direct and indirect losses that are the proximate result of a covered cause of loss (peril).

Covered Locations

An insured event must not only involve a *covered property, a covered cause,* and a *covered consequence.* It must also involve a *covered location.* That is to say, the loss must happen within the geographical or territorial scope of the coverage provided under the particular policy in question. The territorial scope of property insurance coverages varies considerably among different types of policies and different types of property, ranging from one narrowly defined premises to anywhere in the world.

Since residential and commercial buildings are by nature situated at fixed locations, property coverage on them is restricted to the premises that is (are) specified and described in the policy declarations. However, the typical commercial form automatically provides limited and temporary coverage on newly acquired real property that is situated "within the fifty states of the United States of America and the District of Columbia." Homeowners and dwelling forms do not provide automatic real property coverage at newly acquired locations.

With the exception of the types of personal property that are not covered at all, the personal property coverage of homeowners policies extends to anywhere in the world. The same is true of separately purchased personal articles floaters. Worldwide coverage of (business) personal property is also available to business firms through the purchase of specialized inland marine floaters. Otherwise, most standard commercial property forms cover business personal property only while it is in the described building(s) or within 100 feet of the described premises. The coverage under many burglary and robbery forms is likewise restricted to the described premises, though some of the broader theft and crime coverages extend to "any of the fifty States of the United States of America, the District of Columbia, Puerto Rico, Canal Zone or Canada."

Under both the business auto policy and the personal auto policy, the designated autos are covered "in the United States of America, its territories or possessions, Puerto Rico or Canada; or while the covered auto is being transported between any of these places" ("between their ports," in the personal auto policy).

In ocean marine insurance, it is common to restrict coverage to the usual and customary routes connecting particular points between which an insured cargo is being shipped. Apart from any policy provision, there is an implied warranty of "no deviation." By this implied warranty, the insured agrees that all coverage shall be void if the vessel does not travel by the most direct route between the ports of departure and destination. Historically, deviations were permitted without voiding coverage only if required by events of nature (such as storms) or the need to save a human life. Modern policy provisions modify this common-law implied warranty and permit deviations made necessary for saving property, as well as lives. For cargo insurance, the modern provisions also excuse the shipper of the goods from this warranty, if the shipper promptly notifies the insurer of any deviation about which the shipper learns.

While broad generalizations are no substitute for carefully reviewing the language of any policy being considered, it is safe to say that the coverage of real property is confined mainly to the designated premises. Ocean marine coverage is normally confined to a somewhat restricted route, and physical damage coverage is confined to a territory that extends somewhat beyond the geographical boundaries of the U.S. and Canada. Otherwise, there appears to be a trend toward personal property coverage that is worldwide in its territorial scope.

Covered Circumstances

A loss will be an insured event under a policy only if the loss involves *covered circumstances*. Property insurance policies cover almost all of the ordinary circumstances surrounding a covered peril. They generally do not cover conditions or circumstances that are considered unusually hazardous in relation to the norm for most insureds covered by the type of policy in question. Circumstances that are not covered may take the form of (1) denials of coverage while the property is being used in a particular way (automatic suspensions of coverage during periods involving an increase in hazard), or (2) possible suspensions of coverage when dangerous conditions are discovered by the insurer.

Circumstances When Coverage Is Suspended Due to Increase in Hazard   In terms of the number of people who could be affected, perhaps the most important coverage suspension based on the *use* of property is found in the physical damage section of the personal auto policy. The insurer will not pay for "...loss to your covered auto which occurs while it is used to carry persons or property for a fee." This exclusion does not apply to a share-the-expense car pool. Ordinary car pools are not only consistent with public policy in an age of high gasoline prices; they also pose no unusual hazards for the insurers of the property coverages on the auto. The use of an auto as a taxi or public livery conveyance does involve extreme hazards that are material to the writing of physical damage coverage. Because such usage would require much higher rates, if indeed the insurer were willing to provide the coverage in the first place, the coverage is denied under the personal auto policy.

Many property insurance policies contain "increase-in-hazard provisions" which have the effect of automatically suspending coverage during periods when the hazards have increased above their normal levels. The classic example is embodied in the following language of the standard fire insurance policy:

> Unless otherwise provided in writing added hereto this Company shall not be liable for loss occurring (a) while the hazard is increased by any means within the control or knowledge of the insured; or (b) while a described building, whether intended for occupancy by owner or tenant, is vacant or unoccupied beyond a period of sixty consecutive days.

The quoted provision will be discussed in detail in Chapter 15. In the meantime, note that the removal of the hazardous circumstance will restore the coverage just as automatically as it was suspended. Coverage suspended on a building that was not occupied for sixty-five days, for example, would be restored automatically when the building again becomes occupied.

The homeowners form offers an additional example of an automatic coverage suspension based on an extraordinarily hazardous circumstance. The relevant provision says that the insurer will not cover the property for:

> ...vandalism and malicious mischief or breakage of glass and safety glazing materials if the dwelling has been vacant for more than 30

consecutive days immediately before the loss. A dwelling being constructed is not considered vacant.

The above provision suspends coverage when the dwelling has been vacant beyond thirty days, but only for the perils of glass breakage and vandalism and malicious mischief. Generally, a dwelling is considered "unoccupied" when it is not being used by persons as a residence. A dwelling is "vacant" when it is both unoccupied and devoid of furniture or contents.

Yet another example of an automatic coverage suspension can be found in a general property form that is widely used to insure the property of business firms. The provision reads:

> It is a condition of this insurance that the insured shall maintain so far as is within his control such protective safeguards as are set forth by endorsement hereto. Failure to maintain such protective safeguards shall suspend this insurance, only as respects the location or situation affected, for the time of such discontinuance.

The protective safeguards referred to include any fire or burglar alarm systems, sprinklers, locks, or other such devices that are described in an endorsement attached to the policy. It is not enough merely to have such protective devices. They must be maintained or kept in good working condition if they are truly to serve as safeguards. For a business property that is particularly vulnerable to fire, burglary, and/or some other peril(s), such safeguards may be deemed essential in order to keep the insurer's exposure commensurate with the premium charged and otherwise acceptable.

Circumstances Involving Possible Coverage Suspensions
Unlike the previous examples of coverage denials and automatic coverage suspensions, the second broad type of circumstantial restriction involves a *possible* suspension of coverage when dangerous conditions are discovered by the insurer. This type of provision is a part of the typical boiler and machinery policy, as follows:

> Upon the discovery of a dangerous condition with respect to any Object, any representative of the Company may immediately suspend the insurance with respect to an Accident to said object by written notice mailed or delivered to the insured.... Insurance so suspended may be reinstated by the Company but only by an Endorsement issued to form a part of this policy.... The insured shall be allowed the unearned portion of the premium paid for such suspended insurance, pro rata, for the period of suspension.

Unlike the provisions previously noted, this boiler and machinery clause does not result in an automatic suspension of coverage. Nor does it automatically restore coverage once the dangerous condition is rectified. The coverage suspension, if any, is discretionary on the part of the insurer's representative, and it is made effective by written notice to the insured. If suspended, the coverage can be reinstated only by endorsement (by written consent of the insurer, in other words). The boiler and machinery insured is entitled to a pro rata refund of any premiums paid for the period of the suspension, whereas the other illustrative suspension and denial provisions are silent on the subject.

Summary As stated at the outset, ordinary circumstances are nearly always covered by property insurance policies. Many hazardous circumstances are covered, as well, but commonly used policy provisions may totally deny coverage for specified uses of property and suspend coverage during periods of extreme hazards, regardless of whether the properties, causes, consequences, and locations are otherwise covered by the policy.

Covered Time Periods

A loss is an insured event only if a covered cause of loss falls within a time period covered by a legally enforceable agreement. In property insurance the so-called "policy period" is usually six months or one year.[5] However, the policy period is merely the intended initial duration of the written contract, not necessarily the *covered* time period of the enforceable agreement between the parties. The coverage may actually become effective before a policy is issued, by means of an oral or written "binder"—that is, a legally binding agreement that serves as a temporary contract until the policy is issued. After a policy is issued the coverage may be terminated by cancellation of the policy prior to the time it would otherwise expire, or by not renewing the policy beyond the time of its expiration, to the extent that such terminations are permitted by policy provisions and state laws. Alternatively, as long as both parties are willing and have the legal capacity to keep on renewing the policy for successive time periods, the coverage could be continued for many years. For all of the foregoing reasons, it is more accurate to think of the *covered time period* as the precise interval in time during which the coverage legally applies. This interval lies between the moment of coverage inception and the moment of coverage termination. It is the time interval within which a covered cause must fall if the loss is to be an insured event.

Inception and Termination Under an oral or written binder, the coverage becomes effective the very moment the applicant's offer is accepted by a person who has the legal capacity to enter into such contracts on behalf of the insurer, as when an authorized agent says, "You are covered as of 3:00 P.M. today for a period of thirty days." Such a binder could be renewed (or it could expire) thirty days thereafter at 3:00 P.M., but it normally would be replaced beforehand by the issuance of a policy.

Once the policy is issued, the inception of coverage is governed by an explicit provision in the policy declarations. The termination of coverage is a bit more complicated. The usual policy provision gives the insured the nearly unrestricted right to cancel the policy instantly by notifying the insurer (or agent). In the absence of a contrary statute, the usual policy provision also gives the insurer a right to cancel that is restricted only by the requirement that the insurer provide the insured with a written notice of its intention to cancel the policy a stipulated number of days after the notice is received. However, a number of state statutes now severely restrict the right of insurers to refuse to write, to refuse to renew, and/or to cancel auto and homeowners policies, except for a limited number of reasons (such as nonpayment of premium or revocation of a driver's license). The specifics of such statutes are beyond the scope of this text. Any permitted cancellation would usually take effect as of the day and time specified in the written notice provided by the insurer, and each renewal of coverage would simply extend the expiration date by one coverage period.

Most property insurance policies stipulate that the policy period is for "x" years, from one specified date to another at 12:01 A.M. standard time at some location, as in the following example:

> Policy Period: (one) Year From: (11-1-81) To: (11-1-82) 12:01 A.M. Standard Time at the residence premises.

The coverage inception is on November 1, 1981, 12:01 A.M. Standard Time at the residence premises, while the coverage termination is on November 1, 1982, 12:01 A.M. Standard Time at the residence premises (some policies say "at location of property involved" or "at the named insured's address stated above"). Thus, the interval between these two points in time is the period within which a covered cause must fall if the loss is to be an insured event.

Understandably, a different approach is used to define the covered periods in ocean and inland marine policies insuring ships, cargoes, and other property in transit. Rather than specifying a fixed policy period, such marine policies commonly provide coverage for whatever period of time it takes to complete a safe voyage or trip (including an allowed time for loading and unloading). Some policies are written on a per trip or per voyage basis, while others are written to cover all trips or voyages commencing within a one-year interval. Still others, called "open" policies, cover all voyages or trips that begin at or after midnight on the specified date of inception. Coverage is thereafter continued indefinitely until either the insured or the insurer sends a cancellation notice to the other, in which case voyages that started before the receipt of notice are covered until they are safely concluded.

Onset of Covered Causes   Once the covered period or interval is determined, when does a covered cause "fall within" that interval to make the loss an insured event? Generally, a covered cause falls within the prescribed interval of time if the onset or beginning of the loss causation lies within the interval. As long as the loss from a covered cause (peril) is a loss that *commences* during the policy period, it is not essential that the covered consequences lie entirely within the policy period. For example, suppose the policy period of a fire policy is from January 1, 1982 to January 1, 1983, 12:01 A.M. Standard Time at the location of the property. A fire destroys the property. The onset or beginning of the loss is the moment when the fire first begins to damage the property.[6] If a fire starts to damage the property ten minutes before the inception date, the loss *is not* an insured event, even if the fire continues to burn well into the policy period. If a fire starts to damage the property one hour before the policy's expiration date, the loss *is* an insured event, even if most of the damage occurs after the time of coverage expiration. The same general principles apply to windstorm, hail, riot, burglary, vandalism, collision, and any other perils that may be covered by a particular property insurance policy.[7]

In practice, nearly all property insurance claims are for causes and consequences of loss that lie clearly and entirely within one or more successive policy periods. But the comparatively few borderline situations can be disastrous to the insured entities involved, and they are at best problematical to insurers. The critical need for precision in defining covered time periods should therefore be obvious.

INSURED EVENTS UNDER
LIABILITY INSURANCE POLICIES

Liability policies do not provide coverage for direct damage to the *insured's* property. Otherwise, the previously discussed elements or determinants of an insured event also apply to liability insurance policies (and liability coverages in multi-peril policies), often in a manner quite similar to their corresponding applications in property insurance. Hence, to the extent that the basic nature of each element has already been explained, the following brief review will concentrate on the unique or distinctive aspects of events insured under liability policies.

Covered Activities

The first element of an insured event is that it must involve covered properties or activities. Liability policies cover *activities* of the insured entities, not direct damage to or loss of property owned by an insured. Indeed, most property damage *liability* coverages do not cover damage to "property that is owned by, rented to, or in the care, custody, or control of an insured." The very nature of liability insurance is to cover the legal liability which one might have to *others*—that is, to persons or entities who are "third parties," not as legal parties to the contract but as claimants who are not insureds per se. Because it would not make sense for a property owner to sue himself or herself for a "self-inflicted tort," a meaningless contradiction in terms, the owner's property should be insured under first-party property insurance covering the owner's interest in damage, destruction, or abstraction of the property rights.

What about property that is not owned by the insured? Is it not possible for a liability insured to be held legally liable for damage to nonowned property in the "care, custody, or control" of the insured? Yes, of course, it is possible. As noted in Chapter 8, an insurable interest may exist because of potential legal liability for damage to specific property of others. A common carrier, for example, has an insurable interest in its potential liability for damage to goods of others that the carrier has agreed to transport. An even broader insurable interest may exist based on factual expectations or representative status. These broad insurable interests in property owned by others, but in the care, custody, or control of the insured, can often be covered by some form of property or marine insurance. In fact, commercial and residential *property* coverages cited in the property insurance section of this chapter explicity provide coverage for loss to personal property of others.

Liability insurance policies sometimes provide limited care, custody, or control coverage. For example, the homeowners forms provide the following additional coverage under the liability section:

Damage to Property of Others. We will pay up to $250 per occurrence for *property damage* to property of others caused by any *insured*. We will not pay for property damage:
  a. to property covered under Section I of this policy;
  b. caused intentionally by any *insured* who is 13 years of age or older;
  c. to property owned by or rented to any *insured*, a tenant of *any insured*, or a resident in your household; or
  d. arising out of:
     (1) *business* pursuits

(2) any act or omission in connection with a premises owned, rented or controlled by any *insured* other than the *insured location,* or

(3) the ownership, maintenance, or use of a *motor vehicle,* aircraft or watercraft.

Careful study of this provision will reveal that the policy excludes property already covered under Section I of the policy; it partially restores coverage that would otherwise be deleted by the care, custody, or control exclusion; and, although it even covers losses not caused by negligence, it covers mostly property damage for which an insured might be held legally liable as a matter of negligence. However, since most liability policies do not provide such coverage at all, it can accurately be said that the subject matter of liability insurance is not various items of property. Instead, the subjects of liability insurance are the various activities of insureds that give rise to their legal liability to third parties. The term "activities" is used here as a short way of referring to natural or normal functions in the performance of which people may become liable for their acts or omissions. All insurable liability exposures fall into the general category of *covered activities* under liability insurance.

Many different activities are insurable for legal liability purposes. Some policies essentially cover only one type of activity. Others combine coverages for several different activities into a single policy. Examples of at least partially covered activities include those which are associated with:

(1) the ownership, maintenance, operation, use, loading, and unloading of autos;

(2) the ownership, maintenance, operation, use, loading, and unloading of aircraft;

(3) the ownership, maintenance, operation, use, loading, and unloading of watercraft;

(4) the ownership, maintenance, and use of premises, including operations necessary or incidental thereto;

(5) the manufacture or sale of products;

(6) completed operations;

(7) the manufacture, sale, distribution, or serving of alcoholic beverages;

(8) legal obligations assumed under contract;

(9) service rendered as a professional;

(10) service rendered as an officer or director of a corporation;

(11) services rendered as a common carrier, private carrier, or other bailee for hire; and,

(12) the obligation of an employer to provide safe working conditions for employees.

The above examples illustrate the general kinds of covered activities for which liability insurance is available. The broadest, most comprehensive liability policies combine a number of such activities into a single package of coverage. Other policies are designed as specialized coverage for only one or a few such activities.

The covered activities of a particular policy cannot be fully understood by a mere reference to the declarations, insuring agreements, and policy definitions. These provisions must be interpreted within the context of restrictions and exclusions on covered activities. For instance, any one of the above-listed activities may be covered in one liability insurance policy and excluded in another. Just as property insurance policies impose restrictions and exclusions by types of property, so also liability policies impose restrictions and exclusions by type of activity.

Covered Causes

Although property insurance policies routinely cover an insured's losses due to crimes committed *by others*, no insurance policy could legally insure against liability for criminal activities. To do so would make the contract unenforceable as contrary to the public interest. Hence, liability policies do not cover any criminal liabilities the insured may have to society as a whole. Nor do liability policies cover all causes of an insured's civil liability to other specific persons. The covered causes of liability insurance policies are the acts or omissions that serve as the legal grounds for the imposition of *tort* liability.

Generally, a "tort" may be thought of as a private or civil wrong, independent of contract, for which the law provides a remedy in the form of an action for money damages. The alleged "tortfeasor" (wrongdoer), the person who is believed to be guilty of a tortious act or omission, may become the defendant in legal action brought by the "plaintiff," the moving party or claimant who initiates the action in an effort to obtain compensation for his or her damage or injury. If the court so rules, the defendant is legally liable to the plaintiff for the dollar amount of damages stipulated by the court judgment. Liability insurance policies are designed to provide specified amounts of coverage for insureds who become defendants in tort actions, but most policies do not automatically cover all causes of tort liability.

Tort liability may be imposed on the basis of (1) negligent acts or omissions, (2) strict liability, or (3) intentional interference with the person or property of another. These three legal notions are thoroughly explained in other CPCU courses. For now, it is sufficient to know that *negligence* is the failure to exercise that degree of care which the law requires for the safety of others, as when a person negligently drives an automobile at sixty miles per hour on icy streets in heavy traffic. *Intentional interference* is a tort involving an intentional act, such as assault, battery, libel, slander, false arrest, or trespass. *Strict liability* refers to liability imposed, regardless of whether or not the defendant was guilty of negligence or intentional interference, as a matter of public policy. Sellers of defective products may be held strictly liable, for example, as may persons engaged in abnormally dangerous activities, such as the handling of highly dangerous explosives.

Negligence Liability arising out of negligence is covered by all liability policies, but the term itself is seldom found in the policy language. For example, the typical liability policy indicates that the insurer will "pay on behalf of the insured all sums which the insured shall become legally obligated to pay as damages because of bodily injury or property damage to which this insurance applies."

The liability sections of the more recent homeowners policies say essentially the same thing with the following language:

> If a claim is made or a suit is brought against any insured for damages because of bodily injury or property damage to which this coverage applies, we will pay up to our limit of liability for the damages for which the insured is legally liable.

Though no reference is made to negligence as such, it is a covered cause. It is a primary cause of legal liability for bodily injury or property damage, and it is not otherwise excluded; therefore, negligence is clearly a cause "to which this coverage applies."

Strict Liability Theoretically, all liability policies provide coverage for at least some *strict liability* situations. Such coverage is provided in two ways. First, in their real zeal to compensate injured parties, more than a few juries have ruled that an insured defendant was "negligent," despite compelling evidence to the contrary. Whenever this happens, all liability policies provide coverage for what amounts to a form of strict liability. The policies clearly cover negligence; the insured defendants are officially declared to be negligent; and the insurers must respond accordingly, even though the juries have *effectively* held the defendants strictly liable, by refusing to acknowledge that the defendants were not truly negligent by more objective standards.

Second, all liability policies provide at least some coverage when the claim or suit is brought as a strict liability action in the first place. The extent of coverage for an overt strict liability action depends on the particular policy. Liability policies generally cover legal liability for "bodily injury or property damage to which this insurance applies," a phrase that is broad enough to include acts or omissions for which an insured may be held strictly liable without regard to negligence or intent. However, the doctrine of strict liability is applied primarily to business firms, and then only to certain types of business activities. Since most *personal* liability policies specifically exclude coverage for business pursuits, the practical effect is to exclude coverage for the most common strict liability situations. The personal liability policy covers strict liability situations that do not arise from business pursuits, in other words, but such situations are comparatively rare (except in jurisdictions which often impose strict liability on the owner of a vicious dog for harm the dog does to persons who are not family members, or where a homeowner maintains a swimming pool or other "attractive nuisance" that harms a young child). Similarly, *professional* liability policies do not exclude strict liability per se, but physicians and other professionals are invariably sued in negligence actions. In contrast, both negligence and strict liability are common grounds for imposing tort liability on business firms. *Commercial* forms of liability insurance obviously do not exclude business pursuits entirely; nor do they exclude strict liability as a covered cause per se. However, as noted in the previous section on covered activities, most commercial liability policies exclude coverage for certain types of business activities. To the extent that a policy excludes coverage for the sale of products, the operation of aircraft, or other specific business activities for which strict liability may be imposed, the policy does not cover strict liability, as a practical matter. When an abnormally dangerous business activity (e.g., the use of explosives) causes bodily injury or property damage to others and the activity is a covered activity under the policy, the policy would provide coverage, whether the claim or suit was based upon negligence or strict liability.

Intentional Interference   Limited coverage for some intentional interference torts, such as libel and slander, may be obtained by endorsement to many basic liability policies. Specified types of *intentional interference* torts are covered automatically under most personal and commercial "umbrella" liability policies, that "sit on top of" underlying or basic policies. However, the general rule is that intentional interference torts are not covered at all by most liability policies. The typical liability policy covers only bodily injury and property damage. It does not cover human injury that does not involve physical harm to the body, as when a person's reputation is injured by libel or slander. Moreover, the typical policy covers only bodily injury or property damage that is "neither expected nor intended from the standpoint of the insured." Most personal policies also specifically exclude coverage for "any person who intentionally causes bodily injury or property damage." (One exception is the "damage to property of others" section of the homeowners policy, which provides up to $250 of coverage for property damage *intentionally* caused by an injured under thirteen years old.)

When intentional interference torts are covered at all, the so-called "personal injury coverage" broadens bodily injury coverage to encompass the particular torts specified in the policy. Depending upon the policy, the list of covered torts may include false arrest, false imprisonment, libel, slander, malicious prosecution, or wrongful eviction. Such torts are usually covered only to the extent that the injury or damage is neither expected nor intended from the standpoint of the insured. Where provided, assault and battery coverage is usually subject to the further restriction that it does not apply to assault or battery committed by or at the direction of the insured.

Generally speaking, then, negligence is a covered cause under all liability insurance policies. The acts or omissions that may lead to strict liability are also covered causes, to the extent that they are not specifically excluded under a policy, but the strict liability doctrine is applied mainly to business firms. Intentional interference torts are not covered causes under liability policies, unless coverage for them is purchased under special forms or endorsements (for an additional premium).

Proximate Cause The doctrine of "proximate cause" is universally applied in tort law and liability insurance, as well as in property insurance. A tortfeasor cannot be held legally liable for the harm done to the plaintiff unless the plaintiff can prove, to the satisfaction of the court, that the defendant's activities were the proximate cause of the plaintiff's harm. For example, suppose, due to his negligence, Eric's car collides with and damages the left rear of an auto owned by Fred. Fred (as plaintiff) sues Eric (as defendant) in a negligence action, and Fred demands $1,000 to repair the vehicle. It turns out that the $1,000 of claimed "damage" consists of $600 to repair and repaint the left rear of the auto, plus $400 to repair the old rust spots on the right front of the auto and to repaint the entire car. Fred could probably prove that Eric's negligence was the proximate cause of the $600 in damage to the left rear of the auto, but the rust damage was not the proximate result of Eric's negligence. Thus, Eric's liability insurer is required to pay Fred only $600. In any case, the plaintiff must first prove actual damages; otherwise, neither the defendant nor the defendant's liability insurer is liable for the tort committed.

Covered Consequences

Under liability insurance policies, the covered consequences are not limited to the payments the insurer may make to the claimant in an out-of-court settlement or a tort lawsuit. The financial consequences covered by all liability policies actually consist of

(1) damages legally owed by an insured,
(2) claims expenses, including the cost of defending an insured, and
(3) miscellaneous expenses incurred by the insured.

However, none of these consequences will be covered unless the wrong allegedly committed by the insured is a covered cause under the policy. The liability insurer obviously will not pay the costs of defending the insured in a criminal action. Less obviously, defense and other benefits will be provided only when an insured is accused of a covered kind of tort (arising from a covered activity, in covered circumstances, at a covered location, and falling within covered time periods). In short, there is no coverage for any financial consequences that do not meet all of the other tests of an insured event under the policy.

Damages Concerning the payment of damages, the insurer agrees to pay *on behalf of the insured*, up to the policy limits, *all sums the insured shall become legally obligated to pay as damages because of bodily injury or property damage* to which the insurance applies. In practice most liability claims are resolved in out-of-court settlements. Nonetheless, whether a claim is resolved by formal lawsuit or by informal settlement between the parties, the insurer is obligated to pay only the damages for which the insured is legally liable.

If intentional interference torts are covered by the policy, the wording of the insuring agreement is altered by substituting "personal injury" for "bodily injury" in the italicized phrase above. Personal injury is then defined to include both bodily injury and the covered types of intentional interference torts. Otherwise, the nature of the insurer's obligation to pay damages remains unchanged.

There are two broad types of damages that may be awarded in a tort lawsuit, compensatory damages and punitive damages. *Compensatory damages* are money payments that are made to compensate plaintiffs for the losses they sustain. The total amount awarded as compensatory damage may include reasonable medical expenses, the cost to repair or replace damaged property, the loss of a property's use value, lost wages, the loss of future wages, the imputed economic value of services lost in the past or in the future, and an amount arbitrarily determined by the jury to compensate for such intangibles as pain and suffering, bereavement, and the like, depending upon the kinds of losses suffered by the plaintiff (including the estate or the survivors of a deceased person, in a wrongful death action).

Punitive damages are arbitrary amounts determined by the court and awarded to the plaintiff to punish the defendant, teach the defendant a lesson, deter others from engaging in the same kind of conduct and serve as an example for others. Punitive damages are sometimes said to be "exemplary" in nature. Historically, punitive damages have seldom been awarded in ordinary negligence cases. Most courts have instead reserved punitive damages for cases involving "wanton and willful misconduct" by the defendant, "circumstances of outrage," or so-called "gross negligence" cases. More recently, the traditional view has been modified, in some jurisdictions, to favor awarding punitive damages in a wider range of tort cases. This development has prompted critics to charge that punitive damages are gradually becoming a disguised way of paying the fees of plaintiffs' attorneys, especially in cases where the defendant is insured and the defendant's conduct does not really deserve "punishment." Apart from such criticism, the insurability of punitive damages has posed extremely difficult questions of public policy.

The traditional wording of liability insurance contracts obligates the insurer to pay "all sums" which the insured shall become legally obligated to pay "as damages" because of bodily injury (or personal injury, in some contracts) or property damage. It may be that the drafters intended to cover both compensatory *and* punitive damages, if the insured is legally obligated to pay them. However, the laws or regulations of some states prohibit insurers from paying punitive damages on behalf of insureds, on the theory that such payments are contrary to public policy because they would defeat the purposes of punitive damages. This view, coupled with what appeared to be a trend toward awarding larger amounts of punitive damages in a wider range of cases, prompted insurers to seek approval of policy provisions designed to exclude coverage for punitive damages. The new exclusionary provisions were accepted by some state insurance regulators and rejected by others, and they remained highly controversial in every state.

Although the opponents of punitive damage exclusions acknowledged the merits of the public policy argument against allowing a third party (the insurer) to pay damages designed to punish the defendant, there were other important considerations. The insurers were effectively seeking to "take away" coverage previously provided, on the grounds that the punitive damage loss exposure had grown significantly larger than had been contemplated in the rate structure. But the insurers were not able to offer adequate statistical documentation to support their contention; they were not seeking a rate reduction to accompany the coverage elimination. A number of regulators felt that such a sudden exclusion of punitive damage coverage, with no corresponding rate reduction, would be a violation of their rating laws and tantamount to a rate increase without statistical justification. Opponents of the new punitive damage exclusion were also deeply concerned about its impact on the protection needed by responsible insureds, particularly in jurisdictions which may award punitive damages in ordinary negligence cases. It is one thing to deny insurance protection to insureds who are guilty of wanton and willful misconduct or outrageous behavior. It is quite another thing to deny insurance protection to insureds who just happen to make one unintentional mistake and are surprised to find that the punitive damages levied against them are not insured.

In the midst of the continuing controversy, the major insurance industry service organization eventually withdrew their filings of punitive damages exclusions. Today, virtually all current liability policies cover both compensatory and punitive damages. While insurers apparently will not be permitted to pay punitive damages in some jurisdictions, they are not excluded by the policy language.

Defense Costs and Other Claim Expenses Apart from the payment of damages on behalf of an insured, virtually all liability insurance policies also provide what are called "defense and supplementary payments benefits" (in the older forms) or "additional coverages" (in the easy-to-read forms). First and foremost, the insurer is obligated to defend the insured against any claim or suit involving an insured event, with counsel of the insurer's choice, and to pay all costs of the defense provided. For example, the pertinent language of the personal liability section of the homeowners policy reads as follows:

> If a claim is made or a suit is brought against any *insured* for damages because of *bodily injury* or property damage to which this coverage applies, we will: . . . .
>
> b. provide a defense at our expense by counsel of our choice. We may make any investigation and settle any claim or suit that we decide is appropriate. Our obligation to defend any claim or suit ends when the amount we pay for damages resulting from the occurrence equals our limit of liability.

These general insuring agreements are then made more specific in the additional coverages section of the policy, which states:

> We cover the following in addition to the limits of liability: . . . .
>
> *Claim Expenses.* We pay:
>
> a. expenses incurred by us and costs taxed against any *insured* in any suit we defend;

b. premiums on bonds required in a suit defended by us, but not for bond amounts greater than the limit of liability for coverage E. We are not obligated to apply for or furnish any bond;

c. reasonable expenses incurred by any *insured* at our request, including actual loss of earnings (but not loss of other income) up to $50 per day for assisting us in the investigation or defense of any claim or suit;

d. interest on the entire judgment which accrues after entry of the judgment and before we pay or render, or deposit in court that part of the judgment which does not exceed the limit of liability that applies.

Similar provisions are found in virtually every liability insurance policy. Especially noteworthy is the language that makes the defense costs and claim expenses payable *in addition to the limits of liability* that are applicable to damages. For example, suppose an insured's policy had a bodily injury limit of $25,000, a bodily injury judgment of $40,000 was entered against the insured, and the covered defense costs amounted to $8,000. Under a few types of policies covering special exposures, the insurer would pay only $25,000, because the defense costs are included in the specified limit of liability. However, under the vast majority of liability policies, the insurer is obligated to pay defense costs as an *additional* benefit, meaning that a total of $33,000 would be paid in the above case ($25,000 for damages plus $8,000 for defense). In fact, it is not uncommon for an insurer to pay more for investigation and defense than it does for damages.

While the amount an insurer might be required to pay for defense costs is theoretically unlimited, remember that the insuring agreements terminate the insurer's obligation to defend when the amount paid for damages equals the specified limit of liability. Thus, in the example above, suppose the actual costs of defense had been $18,000. If all these costs were incurred prior to the payment of the settlement or judgment, the insurer would have paid the entire $18,000 in defense costs, plus $25,000 for damages. Alternatively, if only $8,000 of the defense costs were incurred prior to the insurer's payment for damages, the insurer would have paid $8,000 for defense and $25,000 for damages. The remaining $10,000 of defense costs (probably due to an appeal) initiated by the defendant-insured would be paid by the defendant, who would also have to pay $15,000 in damages, the amount by which the initial court judgment exceeded the policy limit ($40,000−$25,000=$15,000). Except in unusual situations where the insurer is deemed negligent for failing to accept an offer to settle within the policy limits, the insurer's payment for damages will never exceed the policy limit. Yet, the combined total amount the insurer pays for damages *and* defense costs frequently exceeds the policy limit by many thousands of dollars.

Note also that the additional coverages obligate the insurer to pay premiums on litigation bonds, interest on the judgment, and other reasonable expenses incurred by the insured at the request of the insurer. These coverages are not insignificant. They can amount to large sums of money. Along with insurer payments for damages and defense costs, they are "covered consequences" of the events insured under all liability insurance policies.

Covered Locations

With very few exceptions, liability insurance policies invariably apply to any location within a broadly defined policy territory. In auto insurance, the policy territory is defined as "the United States of America, its territories or possessions, or Canada" or the accidents involving a "covered auto while being transported between their ports." A broader definition is found in the general liability policy jacket, as follows:

(1) the United States of America, its territories or possessions, or Canada, or

(2) international waters or air space, provided the bodily injury or property damage does not occur in the course of travel or transportation to or from any other country, state or nation, or

(3) anywhere in the world with respect to damages because of bodily injury or property damage arising out of a product which was sold for use or consumption within the territory described in paragraph (1) above, provided the original suit for such damages is brought within such territory. . . .

The broadest definitions of covered locations can be found in umbrella or excess liability policies. Whereas the covered territory of the typical commercial umbrella policy is "anywhere in the world," the covered territory of many personal umbrella liability policies is "anywhere." (Presumably the latter includes outer space.) Homeowners policies are not explicit as to the covered territory for purposes of the liability section. Though many claims are associated with the residence premises, one can infer from the policy language that the liability coverage, like the personal property coverage, applies to covered occurrences and covered insureds anywhere in the world.

Covered Circumstances

When analyzing property insurance policies, there is good reason to make the distinction between covered *properties* and covered circumstances. In the context of liability insurance policies, the distinction between covered *activities* and covered circumstances is less clear-cut. Liability policies are structured to cover all activities or "hazards" that are not excluded. When specific activities are excluded, the effect is to exclude the even larger number of circumstances which those activities may involve. By excluding business pursuits, for instance, personal liability policies effectively exclude virtually all circumstances directly associated with the conduct or operation of a business. Even so, once the covered activity(ies) is (are) defined, the concept of covered circumstances does have some meaning in liability insurance.

Consider first a business auto policy providing liability coverage. The insurer basically agrees to cover insured losses resulting from the ownership, maintenance, or use of a covered auto (covered activities). This does not mean the coverage will apply in all circumstances. The insurer does not cover "any obligation for which the insured (or his or her insurer) may be held liable under any workers' compensation or similar law," which is another way of saying that the insurer does not cover liability *to* an insured's injured employee under circumstances where an auto accident "arises out of and in the course of employment," even if the accident involved a covered auto. Virtually all liability policies have exclusions relating to the workers' compensation exposure (except the workers' compensation and employers' liability policy, of course).

The liability section of the personal auto policy excludes coverage under circumstances where an otherwise covered auto is being used to carry persons or property for a fee. Moreover, the policy makes it clear that the automatic liability coverage for a newly acquired vehicle does not apply unless it is either reported to the insurer within thirty days after ownership is acquired or it is a vehicle replacing one shown in the declarations.

As noted earlier, most liability policies do not provide property damage liability coverage for damage to property in the care, custody, or control of the insured. Liability policies cover the insured's *legal obligations* to others under such circumstances.

Once the insured activities have been designated, additional policy provisions are invariably used to exclude circumstances the insurer does not intend to cover. There is no need to belabor the point. Excluding activities or hazards also has the effect of excluding many circumstances that might otherwise be covered. In conclusion, covered circumstances are those which are implicit to the insured activities and not specifically excluded.

Covered Time Periods

A "covered time period" has been defined as the precise interval in time during which the coverage legally applies. This interval lies between the moment of coverage inception and the moment of coverage termination. It is the time interval within which a covered cause must fall if the loss is to be an insured event.

Since the principles that govern the covered time interval in liability insurance are the same principles that govern the covered time interval in property insurance, they will not be repeated here. What does need to be discussed briefly is the question of when a covered cause under a liability policy "falls within" the prescribed time interval. For simplicity, all examples will assume a covered time interval of one year.

Accidents Under policies like the old, basic automobile policies, no longer used in most states, the liability coverage applied to "accidents which occur during the policy period."

Nearly all auto accidents "occur" suddenly, in the sense that they start and end abruptly, often in a matter of seconds. Furthermore, the precise instant of the accident is not an important issue in the vast majority of cases, because the coverage was clearly in force long before and long after the accident is known or believed to have happened. Even when the coverage is terminated at 12:01 A.M. on the day of the accident, no particular problems are posed for the insured or claimant who can establish that the accident occurrred before 12:01 A.M. standard time at the named insured's address, as indicated in the declarations. Problems may arise when the coverage is terminated, if it cannot be established that the accident happened before coverage terminated.

When the insured's negligence causes an auto accident resulting in a claimant's bodily injury, the insured's *negligence* is actually the proximate cause of covered loss. But the policy coverage is defined in terms of *when the accident occurs*, rather than when the negligence occurs, because the time of the accident is easier to pinpoint than the time of the onset of the negligence. As long as the covered accident occurs during the policy period, all of the successful claimant's legal "damages" are covered, even if most of the damages are actually incurred long after the policy coverage is terminated, subject only to the requirement—external to the policy—that any suit must be brought within the time period of the applicable statute of limitations for tort claims. Medical expenses, lost income, loss of future income of a deceased person, and loss of a property's use value are examples of damages that might last well beyond a policy's termination date. An insured's liability for these were covered under the *liability* section of a policy written on an accident basis as long as they were the proximate result of a covered accident that occurred during a covered time period.

Occurrences Most liability policies are written on a so-called occurrence basis. An "occurrence" is often defined in such policies as "an accident, including continuous or repeated exposure to conditions, which results in bodily injury or property damage neither expected nor intended from the standpoint of the insured." This same definition also applies to "accidents" in modern policy forms. An occurrence does not necessarily have to be sudden. It could be "continuous or repeated exposure to conditions." However, policies written on an occurrence basis invariably go on to define "bodily injury" and "property damage" as follows:

> *Bodily injury* means bodily injury, sickness or disease sustained by any person which occurs during the policy period, including death at any time resulting therefrom.
>
> *Property damage* means (1) physical injury to or destruction of tangible property which occurs during the policy period, including the loss of use thereof at any time resulting therefrom, or (2) loss of use of tangible property which has not been physically injured or destroyed provided such loss of use is caused by an occurrence during the policy period.

Even in policies that do not define bodily injury or property damage, the insuring agreements obligate the insurer to pay for bodily injury or property damage "caused *by an occurrence*." The chain of causation, once again, is actually from the covered tort to the occurrence to the injury or damage to the ultimate financial consequences thereof. The occurrence approach could give the liability insured slightly broader coverage, because the insured's tort could cause "continuous or repeated exposure to conditions," in which case the resulting damages from either would be covered. However, since it might be extremely difficult to determine the onset of a continuous exposure, the coverage applies *if bodily injury or property damage occurs during the policy period.* This also avoids the linguistic awkwardness of determining "when an occurrence occurs." In other respects, the occurrence basis is the same as the accident basis. That is, as long as (1) the bodily injury or property damage is caused by an occurrence and (2) the bodily injury or property damage occurs during the policy period, all damages that are the proximate result of the insured tort are covered, even if most of the damages are incurred beyond a covered time period.

When "personal injury" liability coverage is provided—that is, when coverage is provided for specified types of intentional interference torts—the coverage is sometimes written on an occurrence basis.

In contrast, one widely used coverage part of personal injury liability simply lists the covered offenses. It then merely indicates that the coverage applies "if the offense is committed during the policy period." This approach is made necessary by the very nature of intentional torts such as libel, slander, or malicious prosecution. They do not involve bodily injury, and they do not result from an accident or repeated exposure to conditions. Therefore, *the date the tort is committed* governs the timing of coverage for these particular offenses.

Claims Made Policies written on an occurrence basis stipulate only that the bodily injury (or personal injury) or property damage must occur during the policy period. Many professional and products liability policies are now written on a claims-made basis, which means that the *claim must be reported during the policy period.* A claim reported during the policy period is covered, regardless of when the bodily injury or property damage occurs. However, to avoid duplicate coverage for an insured switching from an occurrence-basis policy to a claims-made policy, some claims-made policies provide coverage only for losses that occur after a stated *retroactive date,* which usually coincides with the date occurrence-basis coverage was discontinued.

As often as not, there is a delay between the time of injury or damage and the time a claim is made. For example, suppose a surgeon negligently leaves a foreign object in a patient during surgery. The object may not be discovered until some years later, the bodily injury it causes may not become apparent until later, or the claim simply may not be brought against the surgeon until long after the end of the policy period in which the surgery was performed. Delays such as this are rather common, especially in connection with the sale of products and the rendering of professional services. The longer the delay in reporting incurred losses, the longer it takes an occurrence-basis insurer to know what its losses really were in previous policy years. In the meantime, the rates and loss reserves are necessarily crude, and it is difficult for the insurer to forecast trends in loss frequency and severity.

The claims-made basis does not eliminate the delay problem entirely, because it still may take years to settle a claim after it is reported, but it does help minimize the problem by covering only claims reported during the policy period. Unless limited by a retroactive date provision, such a claim will be covered, even if the injury or damage occurs before the inception of the policy period. Conversely, if injury or damage occurs during the policy period and the claim is not made until after the termination date of the policy, no coverage applies (unless the policy has been renewed). This approach enables an insurer to determine its incurred losses at the end of each policy year.

The claims-made basis is explained more precisely in CPCU 4. However, there is one potential problem worth mentioning in the context of covered time periods. It can be dangerous for an insured to switch from a claims-made basis to an occurrence basis. For example, suppose an insured already has a claims-made policy with a coverage period corresponding to the calendar year 1981. The insured then purchases an occurrence policy with coverage commencing on the first day of 1982. A covered bodily injury occurs in 1981 but it is not reported until 1982. Neither policy would apply. The claims-made policy would not apply because the claim was not *made* in 1981, and the occurrence policy would not apply because the bodily injury did not *occur* in 1982. Special policies are sometimes available to resolve this problem.

Diseases   In nearly all liability insurance policies, "bodily injury" is defined to include *sickness or disease* which occurs during the policy period. Under policies written on an occurrence basis, determining whether a particular disease is covered can be problematical, especially when a latent disease does not become apparent until many years after its inception. If both the onset of the occurrence and the onset of the disease are clearly within a covered time period, the financial consequences of the disease are covered. However, what about the daughter who develops cancer many years after it is discovered that her mother had been taking prescription drugs, later determined to contribute to cancer in offspring, during or prior to the mother's pregnancy? Or, what about the worker who ultimately discovers a disease that may be attributed to "repeated or continuous exposure" to asbestos or other toxic substances? Some courts use the *manifestation theory* and take the position that the onset of such a disease, for liability insurance coverage purposes, is the time at which the disease becomes "manifest." Other courts use the *exposure theory* and hold that the onset of the disease is the time of the injured person's "exposure" to the harmful drug or toxic substance. According to the manifestation theory, the insurer at the time the disease became manifest would be obligated to provide coverage for the claim against its insured; according to the exposure theory, the insurer at the time of exposure would be obligated to provide coverage.

As to whether the manifestation or the exposure theory should prevail, there is a sharp difference of opinion among trial lawyers, liability insureds, the courts, consumer advocates, and liability insurers. Moreover, there appears to be at least some support for combining the exposure theory with a *pro rata theory* —the argument that the claims payments ought to be prorated among all insurers providing coverage during the period of exposure. For example, suppose a claimant discovers in 1980 a disease which is the proximate result of the claimant's exposure to asbestos during the previous ten years. Suppose three different insurers had provided occurrence-basis coverage at one time or another during the same ten-year period of exposure. One insurer had provided a bodily injury limit of $50,000 for eight years, while each of the other two insurers had provided bodily injury limits of $25,000 for one year each. The pro rata approach would require each of these three insurers to pay a percentage of the claimant's loss. It is possible that the insurers would be required to pay 50 percent, 25 percent, and 25 percent, respectively (based on the ratio of each insurer's limit to the total limits), or 80 percent, 10 percent, and 10 percent (based on the ratio of each insurer's years of coverage to the total number of years the claimant was exposed to the harmful substance). But suppose the three insurers had received premiums of $50,000, $6,000, and $4,000, or a total of $60,000 in premiums for the ten years of coverage. If the liability of each insurer is to be pro rata, it would seem more equitable to base the allocation on premiums, in which case the insurers in the example would respectively pay 50/60, 6/60, and 4/60 of the claimant's loss. Alternatively, suppose the insured did not have any applicable liability insurance during the first of the ten years of exposure. The manifestation theory would require the insurer providing coverage in the tenth year (the year the disease became manifest) to pay the entire loss. The initial exposure theory would require this insured to bear the entire loss out-of-pocket. And a combination of exposure and pro rata theory would require the insured to bear a small portion of the loss, while the bulk of the loss would be shared by all insurers providing coverage in the remaining nine years of the illustration. Such issues have not yet been resolved at the time of this writing. There appears to be an increase in the number of lawsuits involving latent diseases, but it is still too early to tell what will emerge as a majority view.

Presumably, the claims-made basis insurer avoids many of the difficulties posed by latent diseases. A latent disease is covered under such a policy if the claim is made and reported during a covered time period, irrespective of when the disease became manifest or when the claimant was exposed to the harmful agent. If the courts eventually adopt a pro rata interpretation of occurrence-basis policies, it is conceivable that claims-made policies may someday dominate liability insurance.

Chapter Notes

1. Lynn Gas & Electric Company v. Meriden Fire Insurance Company, 158 Mass. 570, 33 N.E. 690 (1893).
2. Fred Meyer, Inc. v. Central Mutual Insurance Company, 235 F. Supp. 540 (1964).
3. Providence Washington Insurance Company v. Weaver, 242 Miss. 141, 113 So. 2d 635 (1961).
4. Bruner v. Twin City Fire Insurance Company, 37 Wash. 2d 181, 222 P. 2d 833 (1950).
5. Though three- and five-year fire insurance policies were once quite common, they have been replaced, by most insurers, with shorter term policies that permit more frequent rate adjustments. Auto insurance is often written for policy periods of six months or less. Shorter term policies also make it easier for the insurer to discontinue coverage it no longer wants to provide, especially where state statutes impose more rigorous restrictions on cancellations by insurers than they do on nonrenewals by insurers.
6. Rochester German Insurance Company v. Peaslee-Gaulbert Company, 120 Ky. 752, 87 S.W. 1115 (1905).
7. There are a few unusual departures from these principles, especially the "discovery period" in fidelity bonds and the "lost or not lost" provision in ocean marine policies. Fidelity bonds and marine insurance are treated in CPCU 3.

CHAPTER 11

Policy Limits and Valuation Provisions

INTRODUCTION

In previous chapters the "who, what, where, and when" questions of coverage were considered under the headings of insurable interests, insured entities, and insured events. Assuming that a covered loss actually takes place, the next question to be addressed is the matter of "how much" is payable to or on behalf of the entity(ies) insured. Stated another way, what are the policy provisions and legal doctrines that determine the dollar amounts of recovery under property and liability insurance policies? These determinants include:

- policy limits,
- loss valuation provisions,
- insurance-to-value requirements,
- deductibles,
- other-insurance clauses,
- the legal doctrine of subrogation, and
- the principle of indemnity.

This chapter is devoted to policy limits and loss valuation provisions, the primary determinants of the *maximum* amounts payable for covered losses. Chapter 12 will deal with coinsurance provisions, deductibles, and other loss-sharing provisions that may reduce the amounts otherwise payable. Chapter 13 will be concerned with the amounts payable when there is more than one source of recovery for a particular loss. Since the implications of policy conditions are reserved for a thorough discussion in Chapter 14, all three chapters on amounts of recovery will presuppose that there has been no breach of policy condition or fraud which might release the insurer from its obligations to perform. In other words, in order to concentrate on the question of how much, it will be assumed that the insurer *will* pay some amount.

POLICY LIMITS

With some notable exceptions, property and liability insurance policies contain one or more dollar limits (or other stated limits) on the amounts of recovery. These so-called policy limits represent the *maximum* amounts the insurer will pay for the losses to which the limits apply. Though policy limits are quite often referred to as *"the* limits of liability," they are by no means the *only* limitations on the dollar amount that insurers are required to pay, and they are not unique to *liability* insurance. Policy limits merely serve as the *upper* limits on the amounts insurers are contractually obligated to pay to insureds (under property insurance policies) or on behalf of insureds (under liability insurance policies).

The most widely used types of policy limits will be described hereafter in separate sections on property and liability insurance coverages. These sections are prefaced by a brief discussion of the underlying rationale of policy limits generally.

The Rationale of Policy Limits

The focus of attention here will be restricted to the kinds of maximum policy limits which apply when one policy is the sole source of recovery for the insured. Such limits serve important functions related to (1) clarifying the insurer's obligations, (2) achieving actuarial goals, (3) enforcing the principle of indemnity, (4) giving consumers a range of choice, (5) confining the coverage to an insurer's capacity, and (6) complying with the requirements of excess insurance.

Clarification of the Insurer's Obligations Upper dollar limits, along with other policy provisions, offer *one* important means of clarifying the extent of an insurer's obligations under a policy. If the amount or extent of the insurer's obligation is not definite, the lack of clarity would create actuarial, legal, and other practical problems.

The nature of the actuarial problem should be fairly obvious. Since larger dollar losses are invariably less frequent than smaller losses, larger losses are more difficult to predict with confidence unless data are available on an extremely large number of exposure units. Without upper limits, potential losses under some insurance policies could have a range from zero to (theoretically) infinity. This possibly wide variation in potential losses would make it difficult for any actuary to forecast the insurer's future losses in the short run with an acceptable degree of accuracy.

The absence of any upper limit could also give rise to legal and other practical problems. For example, suppose a policy had no upper limit and stipulated that the insurer would pay "all reasonable medical expenses" resulting from an auto accident. Suppose an insured submits a claim for $1 million in medical expenses for a minor accident, including the cost of first class air travel to the Mayo Clinic, a private room with color television, private nurses, long distance telephone charges, and the travel, lodging, and meal expenses for a six-month "recovery period" at a plush resort in Australia. These expenses may not seem "reasonable" to the reader. The question is, what might a jury say? An upper dollar limit would have at least minimized the impact of court discretion by putting a lid on the insurer's obligation. However, dollar limits are only one of several important devices used by insurers to clarify the extent of their contractual obligations. Some policies do not contain any *dollar* limits, but the maximum amounts of recovery are normally limited in other ways.

Achievement of Actuarial Goals Though the specifics vary considerably from state to state, all insurance rating laws generally require property and liability rates to be adequate, reasonable, and equitable. The rates must be "adequate" or sufficient to pay losses and expenses and prevent insolvency, yet they must be "reasonable" or low enough to prevent "excessive" insurer profits or gains from operations, and they must not be inequitable or "unfairly discriminatory." Policy limits can help in achieving these goals.

To the extent that policy limits help in making loss predictions more accurate, they help prevent insurer insolvencies. Policy limits also tend to prevent "excessive" short run profits that might otherwise be made. An insurer faced with an open-ended obligation would quite naturally add to the rate structure substantial "margins for contingencies"—that is, extra margins of safety necessitated by the insurer's inability to predict losses with sufficient accuracy. Policy limits can serve to reduce the need for large contingency margins.

In addition, policy limits provide one of several means of achieving actuarial equity among policyholders. To illustrate, suppose fire insurance policies did not have a maximum dollar limit on the coverage for buildings. Within a particular rating class, two different building owners might be charged the same annual premium, despite the fact that one building had an insurable value of $100,000 and the other building had an insurable value of only $5,000. This obviously would discriminate unfairly against the owner of the smaller building. Policy limits help to correct such inequities by relating the amount of the premium to the amount exposed.

Enforcement of the Principle of Indemnity Policy limits can also assist in enforcing the principle of indemnity. As was explained in Chapter 8, the principle of indemnity is the universally accepted presupposition that the proper function of insurance is to do no more than to indemnify, make whole again financially, or put the insured back into the same financial position that he or she enjoyed before the occurrence of the insured event. Stated in the negative, the principle means that a person should not profit from an insured loss.

Property Insurance on an Indemnity Basis. Under property insurance policies written as contracts of indemnity in a legal sense, the insured cannot recover any greater amount than the loss sustained. When loss is less than (or equal to) the policy limit, the loss is the controlling maximum, not the policy limit. Thus, under property insurance policies that are legally contracts of indemnity, the principle of indemnity is preserved primarily by insurable interest requirements and provisions that limit the insurer's payment to the amount of the loss. The policy limits affect the amount of recovery only when the loss is greater than the policy limit.

Property Insurance on a Valued Basis. Under property insurance policies written on a valued basis, policy limits potentially have their most significant role as preservers of the principle of indemnity. For example, consider a painting that is insured for $10,000 on a valued basis. If the painting is destroyed by fire while the coverage is effective, the insurer would have to pay the agreed-upon amount of $10,000, regardless of the actual worth of the painting. But this is another way of saying that the policy limit can preserve the principle of indemnity under valued property insurance policies. In theory, the insurer could simply refuse to write a policy limit any greater than the insured's loss would be from the occurrence of a covered peril. To avoid profiteering over time, of course, the insurer would have to adjust the policy limits to correspond to any decrease in the property's insurable value. The various ways of making such adjustments will be dealt with later.

Accommodation of Consumer Preferences Policy limits also have the function of accommodating the differing consumer preferences with respect to coverage amounts and premium levels. This function partially overlaps with the achievement of actuarial goals, because questions of rating equity are necessarily involved when consumers are given a choice of coverage amounts. Nevertheless, the offering of optional coverage limits is dictated as much by competitive considerations as by questions of rating equity.

For instance, many owners of buildings elect to insure them for considerably less than their full insurable values—often for amounts equal to the unpaid balance of a mortgage, as required by a mortgagee. Also, many auto owners prefer to purchase the minimum liability limits that will satisfy the requirements of financial responsibility and compulsory auto insurance statutes. While competent insurance advisers attempt to convince consumers that such risk management decisions are irrational relative to the amount of the premium savings and the potential consequences of being underinsured, consumers do not always follow competent advice. The insurer that refuses to write the lower limits is then faced with the likelihood of losing a large volume of business to its competitors. The consumer's desire for the minimum required limits is entirely rational in some situations, such as where optionally higher limits for no-fault auto benefits would merely duplicate broader group health insurance coverage that is already provided, free of charge, by the consumer's employer. In any case, a choice of policy limits can help accommodate consumer needs and preferences, whether the latter are rationally or irrationally determined.

Insurer Capacity An insurer will sometimes impose an upper policy limit to keep the extent of its obligation within its financial capacity to absorb losses. For example, a fire insurer might refuse to write more than $100,000 of coverage on a $600,000 unprotected building, or a liability insurer might write a maximum of $1 million of products liability insurance for any one seller of products. The fire insurance example could simply reflect an underwriter's decision to avoid "putting too many eggs in one basket." However, either or both illustrations could reflect the fact that the insurer's reinsurance limits do not extend beyond the indicated amounts. The various meanings and measures of insurer capacity are explained in other CPCU courses. The point worth mentioning here is that policy limits sometimes have the function of confining the coverage to an amount which is considered safe in relation to the individual insurer's financial capacity to absorb losses (with its surplus and/or reinsurance recoveries).

Excess Insurance One final function of policy limits is elaborated in CPCU 2 and CPCU 4. In umbrella and excess liability insurance, it is common for the excess policy to stipulate that its insured must carry underlying (or primary) coverage with liability limits of at least "x" dollars. Exhibit 11-1 illustrates how this might apply in the case of a personal umbrella policy where the excess insurer—the insurer issuing the umbrella—requires the insured to carry $100,000 of comprehensive personal liability coverage, $300,000 of auto liability coverage, and $500,000 watercraft liability coverage on an owned yacht. The stipulated limits for the underlying coverages essentially serve as assurance that the excess layer will be over and above, not a substitute for, the primary or underlying layer of insurance. From the viewpoint of the underlying insurer, the limits it provides could be thought of as an example of accommodating the coverage needs of the insured. However, suppose the insured wants to purchase very large limits of liability. If the insured is to do so by purchasing an "excess layer" to sit on top of a "primary layer," the insured is not free to choose the minimum limits available from the primary insurer. Instead, the insured must buy at least the levels of primary limits that are prescribed in the excess policy—if there is to be no "gap" between the two layers of coverage. The prescribed limits accommodate the requirements of the excess insurer, therefore, more than they do the preferences of the insured.

Multiple Functions All policy limits have the effect of fixing the maximum amount of the insurer's obligation when one policy is the sole source of recovery for the insured. Policy limits serve at least six important functions. They may assist in (1) clarifying the insurer's obligation, (2) achieving actuarial goals, (3) enforcing the principle of indemnity, (4) giving consumers a choice of coverage levels, (5) confining losses to an insurer's financial capacity, and/or (6) complying with the requirements of excess insurance. Like exclusions, most policy limits simultaneously serve more than one function. And the multiple functions of policy limits help explain why they are regarded as an important part of most property and liability coverages.

Types of Policy Limits in Property Insurance

Numerous methods are used to express the upper limits that apply to property insurance policies (or the property coverages of multi-peril policies). Unusual or unique methods of expressing policy limits are reserved for study in CPCU courses dealing with the specific kinds of policies. Only the most widely used types of policy limits will be described in the following paragraphs, under headings that correspond more to common usage than they do to a rigorous system of classification.

Specific and Separate Limits A *specific limit* is a dollar amount which sets the upper limit on the amount the insurer will pay for each loss associated with a particular item or class of property. This is by far the most common type of limit in property insurance. Note that it is essentially a per-occurrence limit, whether applicable to a designated item of property—such as a described building, a designated class of property—such as business personal property, or a

Exhibit 11-1
Personal Umbrella Policy

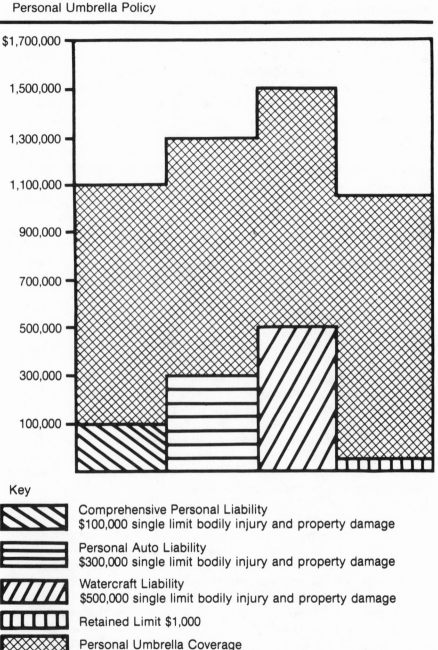

Key

 Comprehensive Personal Liability
$100,000 single limit bodily injury and property damage

Personal Auto Liability
$300,000 single limit bodily injury and property damage

Watercraft Liability
$500,000 single limit bodily injury and property damage

Retained Limit $1,000

Personal Umbrella Coverage

Uninsured Exposure

designated type of indirect loss—such as extra expenses incurred to maintain operations after damage from a covered peril.

Separate limits are merely specific limits found in one policy that apply separately to each of several locations, or to each of several items or classes of property. For example, a property insurance policy might provide a specific limit of $50,000 on the two-story brick veneer building situated at 114 Main Street, and a separate (specific) limit of $40,000 on the one-story frame building situated at 312 South Street. The same policy might also have a specific limit of $8,000 on the contents of the Main Street building and $6,000 on the contents of the South Street building. Note that these are truly separate limits. The limit on one building cannot be applied to the other building. Nor can the contents limits be applied to buildings '(or vice versa). If a covered windstorm destroyed all of the property in the foregoing illustration, the insurer would have to pay as much as $104,000 for that occurrence alone.

As an example of property insurance with separate limits applying to each of several classes of property, consider a homeowners policy providing $50,000 of coverage on a specified dwelling. Such a policy is commonly referred to as "a $50,000 policy." This is a useful convenience of language. However, $50,000 is not the overall maximum limit payable under this policy. A homeowners with $50,000 of coverage on the dwelling would normally provide, as additional amounts of insurance, a $10,000 separate limit on other structures (such as a detached garage), a $25,000 separate limit on personal property (the contents of the dwelling), and a $10,000 separate limit for additional living expense. If the dwelling and detached garage were completely destroyed by an insured event, the insurer might have to pay as much as $95,000 for that occurrence.

Specific limits entered in the declarations are not the only limits which may apply to a covered occurrence. Most property insurance policies also include various *sublimits*, as well as limits on so-called coverage extensions and coverage additions.

Scheduled Limits   As mentioned briefly in Chapter 10, property is said to be "scheduled" when the policy covers a schedule of particular items of property that are listed separately and identified precisely with descriptions, serial numbers, or other identifying marks or characteristics. This is in contrast to "unscheduled" property, which does not have to be specifically identified until a loss occurs. Unscheduled property is covered automatically, as part of the designated class of property, unless it is excluded.

Although the term "scheduled property" is broad enough to include buildings that are identified and described in the declarations prior to loss, the term is most commonly applied to personal property items identified on an endorsement or policy covering only personal property. Specific limits are indicated separately for each covered item or class of property. For example, a personal articles floater or endorsement might have scheduled limits of $7,000 on one painting, $3,000 on a particular diamond ring, and $12,000 on silverware (as a class). Scheduled limits are just a more elaborate and detailed form of specific limits. However, unlike other specific limits, scheduled limits are seldom limited to property at one location. Coverage usually applies to any location in the world, and it is usually not subject to sublimits. Some scheduled limits are also valued (rather than indemnity) limits, which means that no lesser limit will be imposed by policy valuation provisions, in the event of a total loss. In short, scheduled limits are types of separate limits used to provide broad coverage on valuable items of movable personal property, wherever they may be located.

Blanket Limits A *blanket limit* is a policy limit which applies to two or more items or classes of property and/or to property at two or more locations. Blanket limits, which are often used to insure movable property of business firms, are helpful when the aggregate value of property is fairly constant but the values may shift between or among several locations. For example, suppose a furniture merchant has two warehouses and a retail store located in three different cities. Though the aggregate value of furniture remains relatively constant at $100,000, it is seldom equally distributed among the three buildings. The furniture is shifted from one building to another, as needed, and the main retail store may have as much as $70,000 of furniture at any one time. If the merchant buys a separate limit of property insurance for the contents of each location, the merchant will likely be underinsured or overinsured at the time of loss, because of the shifting values. A blanket limit can help solve this problem. The merchant could simply buy a $100,000 blanket limit and designate all three building locations in the policy declarations. Such a limit would apply, as needed at the time of loss, to any one (or all three) of the locations.

A blanket limit differs from a scheduled limit in several important respects. Whereas a blanket limit applies to property at any one of several designated locations, a scheduled limit applies to a designated item or narrowly defined class of scheduled property at any location in the policy territory. A blanket limit is an aggregate limit for all covered property; a scheduled limit is one of several separate limits for each item or class of covered property. Finally, blanket limits are by nature suited to indemnity coverages, while scheduled limits are appropriate for either indemnity or valued coverages.

Sublimits All of the preceding types of limits, which are usually selected by the insured and entered in the declarations, are *upper* limits on the amount of recovery. In addition to upper limits, most policies covering buildings and/or unscheduled personal property also contain one or more "sublimits." A *sublimit* is a limit within an upper limit; it is a part of the upper limit, not an addition to the upper limit. While sublimits are much smaller amounts than the upper or maximum limits, sublimits usually apply only to specific kinds of property, and they sometimes apply only to specific perils or specific locations otherwise covered.

For example, under some homeowners forms, the sublimits on personal property are referred to as "special limits of liability." These special limits include:

(1) $100 on money, bank notes, bullion, gold other than goldware, silver other than silverware, platinum, coins, and medals

(2) $500 on securities, accounts, deeds, evidences of debt, letters of credit, notes other than bank notes, manuscripts, passports, tickets, and stamps

(3) $500 on watercraft, including their trailers, furnishings, equipment, and outboard motors

(4) $500 on trailers not used with watercraft

(5) $500 on grave markers

(6) $500 for loss by theft of jewelry, watches, furs, precious and semi-precious stones

(7) $1,000 for loss by theft of silverware, silver-plated ware, goldware, gold-plated ware, and pewterware

(8) $1,000 for loss by theft of guns

These sublimits do not increase the maximum overall limit applicable to unscheduled personal property. Instead, they impose smaller limits for the listed types of personal property, and the last three sublimits apply only to loss by theft. To illustrate these points, suppose a homeowners insured has a $20,000 upper limit on unscheduled personal property and a fire totally destroys all the insured's personal property. Suppose the fire destroyed $250 of money, $400 of securities, a $500 boat, a $300 outboard motor, and a $4,000 fur coat, plus additional clothing, furniture, and appliances. In determining the total amount of recovery (ignoring deductibles, for the sake of discussion), the insured could count $100 of money (see limit 1 above), $400 of securities (the actual loss, if less than limit 2), $500 for watercraft, including the motor (see limit 3), and $4,000 for the coat (limit 6 applies to theft, not fire). This totals $5,000 for the property subject to the sublimits. If the loss of the remaining property amounted to $15,000 or less, the insured would be compensated in full for the remaining property. If the remaining loss amounted to more than $15,000, the insured could only recover a total of $20,000 ($5,000 for property subject to sublimits, plus $15,000 for the other property), and the excess above the overall upper limit would have to be borne by the insured.

Some sublimits take the form of specific limits for so-called "extensions of coverage" that are included automatically in the policy for no (identifiable) extra premium charge. For example, the general property form stipulates that the named insured may apply up to 5 percent of the limit for Coverage B (Personal Property of the Insured), but not exceeding $500, to valuable papers and records. Thus, if the insured has a $20,000 limit on Coverage B, up to $500 of that limit could be applied to valuable papers and records. This kind of extension does not operate to increase the $20,000 limit to $20,500. Rather, if the insured elects to apply $500 to valuable papers after a serious fire, only $19,500 would be available to cover other personal property of the insured. In that sense the $500 is just a sublimit of the upper limit for Coverage B. Similar extensions of coverage may be found in many property insurance forms, but not all "extensions of coverage" are sublimits. Some are automatic coverage *additions*, discussed in the next section.

Limits for Automatic Coverage Additions It is common for property insurance policies to provide various coverages, automatically, under sections entitled "additional coverages," "supplementary coverages," or words to that effect. Unlike sublimits, the specific limits for coverage additions are not a part of the upper limits entered in the declarations. They are amounts of insurance payable *in addition to* the maximum limits that apply to the basic coverages.

Examples can again be found in the homeowners policy, which pays up to $250 for a fire department service charge, plus up to 5 percent of the dwelling limit for trees, shrubs, and plants (subject to a maximum of $500 for any one tree, shrub, or plant), *in addition to* the applicable limits for the dwelling and its contents. Similarly, the SMP general building form stipulates that the insured may apply up to 25 percent of the building limit (but not more than $100,000) as an *additional* amount of insurance to cover newly acquired property.

Unfortunately, such additional limits are often found in a section of the policy called "extensions of coverage." Other than the fact that the limits for both coverage extensions and coverage additions are frequently expressed as a percentage of an upper limit for a basic coverage, a true coverage "extension" is not the same thing as a coverage "addition." A true coverage extension merely extends a portion of the upper limit (i.e., a sublimit) so that it may be applied, if desired by the insured, to a type of property or loss that would not otherwise be covered. A coverage addition, on the other hand, is an additional amount of insurance, not a sublimit, and it is a *separate* amount which is payable over and above any other limits in the policy.

Other Limits   Not all property insurance limits are expressed in dollars. This is true, for example, with auto physical damage coverage where the limit of liability is expressed as "the lesser of the (1) actual cash value of the stolen property or (2) amount necessary to replace the property." While these limits can be translated into dollars after a loss occurs, there are no maximum dollar limits as such.

Coverages with virtually no upper limits may be found in some types of insurance. Until recently, they were almost unheard of in fire and allied lines insurance, where upper limits, sublimits, and limits on coverage additions have been the rule. True aggregate limits are seldom used in property insurance (with the notable exception of reinsurance arrangements). The vast majority of property insurance limits take the form of per-loss limits which are applied to each occurrence of a fire or other covered peril. This is generally true of all property insurance limits, whether they are specific upper limits, blanket upper limits, scheduled upper limits, sublimits, or limits on coverage additions.

Restoration of Policy Limits   If an insured has a limit of $60,000 and incurs a covered loss of $20,000 at some point during the policy year, does the $20,000 loss reduce to $40,000 the applicable limit for additional losses that may occur in the remainder of the policy year? If so, can the insured pay an extra premium, following each loss, to restore the original $60,000 limit? In the absence of an explicit policy provision, the courts have generally answered "yes" to both questions. However, many property insurance policies contain an express provision which automatically reinstates the original limit following each and every loss, without any additional premium charge.

The usual policy provision, commonly known as a *loss clause*, makes it clear that a loss payment shall not reduce the amount of insurance applicable to future losses. For example, the homeowners policy states: "Loss hereunder shall not reduce the applicable limit of liability under this policy." The general property form for commercial properties similarly states: "Any loss hereunder shall not reduce the amount of this policy." Policies covering loss of use of property, such as business interruption insurance, typically have a loss clause like that of the general property form. Some policies (e.g., the jewelers' block policy), while providing that loss *does* reduce the amount of insurance, also grant automatic reinstatement of the original limit of liability and stipulate a proportionate additional premium for the balance of the policy period. The latter type of provision is comparatively rare. Most property insurance policies do not require any additional premium for the automatic restoration of policy limits.

Insurers' reasons for not reducing the amount of insurance by the amount of past losses are largely practical. In the wake of a loss, many insureds would not understand why they would be asked to pay an additional premium to reinstate their initial amount of insurance. If insurance is designed to compensate for loss, they would ask: Why is the insurer now asking us to return part of that compensation as a premium to restore the amount of coverage initially purchased? Furthermore, in many cases, the extra administrative cost of collecting the additional premium would be substantial. These factors help account for the widespread "automatic reinstatement" of original policy limits for those lines of coverage with respect to which common-law rules would otherwise reduce the remaining amount of insurance. Several deviations from "automatic reinstatement," particularly in ocean and inland marine insurance, are examined in other CPCU courses. Noted here, however, is one interesting deviation, found in the mercantile open stock burglary policy:

> The occurrence of any loss shall reduce the applicable limit of insurance by the extent of the company's liability for such loss until the premises are restored to at least the same condition of safety as immediately prior to the loss; but such reduction shall not occur with respect to loss occurring subsequent to the receipt by the company of notice of loss for which the company is liable under this policy, if the insured shall maintain within the premises at least one watchman while the premises are not open for business.

This policy provision is designed to encourage the insured to act promptly to safeguard remaining insured property following an insured loss.

Variable Limits   In recent years, the seemingly endless phenomenon of economic inflation has been so severe that it has reached "double-digit" rates. This raises serious questions about the adequacy of property insurance limits expressed in a fixed number of dollars. Some insurers have addressed the problem by automatically increasing property insurance limits and premiums at each annual renewal date, unless such increases are rejected by the insured. The amount of the coverage increase is typically based upon an average annual inflation rate, as measured by one or more price level indices. While this approach is not without merit, it does not guarantee adequate coverage limits for the policyholder. First, the policyholder who is underinsured at the beginning of the policy period will still be underinsured after renewal. Second, even if the coverage is adequate at the beginning of each policy period, the coverage is likely to be inadequate at the time of loss, especially if a total loss occurs just prior to renewal, since the coverage limits are not increased between renewal dates.

Property insurers have been experimenting with *variable limits* that increase automatically according to a predetermined method. Such limits are provided by the terms of an optional endorsement to a basic property insurance form. Of the several types of endorsements which are now available, most utilize either the "inflation guard" or the "indexed limits" approach.

The *inflation guard* type of endorsement, often called an "automatic increase in insurance endorsement," was originally designed for use with homeowners policies. For homeowners policies, the separate property limits are automatically increased at a fixed percentage rate per quarter. The percentage increase at the end of each three-month interval is applied to the original policy limits. Accordingly, if a three-year policy has an initial dwelling limit of $25,000, and a 1 percent endorsement is involved, the limit will be increased to $25,250 at the end of the first three months. The limits are thereafter increased at the end of each quarter at the rate of 1 percent of the original limits, so that the limit becomes $27,750 for the final three months of the policy. However, the premium does not increase with each increase in limits. An additional premium for the endorsement, based upon a percentage of the three-year premium is applied at the policy inception.

In many cases, the insured has a choice among a 1 percent, 1.5 percent, 2 percent, 2.5 percent, or 3 percent quarterly increase in the initial policy limits. While substantially similar endorsements are now available for commercial property forms covering buildings (including their contents, in some territories), they generally may not be used with time element coverages.

The inflation guard type of endorsement at least partially overcomes the deficiencies of fixed-dollar limits. Nonetheless, if an inflation guard endorsement is relied upon as the sole method of maintaining adequate coverage limits, it suffers from three major defects:

(1) If the policyholder is underinsured at the outset, the endorsement does not correct the basic coverage inadequacy relative to large losses.
(2) The coverage increments may bear little or no relationship to the actual rates of inflation.
(3) Though quarterly increases in limits are obviously more responsive to inflation than increases effected only on renewal dates, quarterly adjustments may still leave the policyholder significantly underinsured *between* the dates of automatic coverage increases.

The second type of endorsement has the effect of providing indexed limits for the property insurance coverages. Generally, an *indexed limit* is a policy limit that is linked, in a predetermined manner, to a price level index. Under the approach used by one insurer for homeowners policies, the process begins with an elaborate program to ensure adequate initial coverage amounts. Once adequate initial limits are established, the subsequent limits for dwellings and other structures are tied to the U.S. Department of Commerce's Construction Cost Index, and the subsequent limits for contents are tied to the U.S. Department of Labor's Consumer Price Index. Whenever there is a 1 percent increase in the relevant price index, the policy limits are automatically increased by 1 percent. The additional premium charge for indexed limits is fixed at the inception of the policy; it is not recalculated until the date of renewal. The recalculated premium applies to the next policy period, and no retroactive premium adjustments are made.

Assuming the insured has adequate amounts of initial coverage, indexing can be more accurate than the inflation guard approach as a means of maintaining adequate limits. Yet, indexed limits are not without shortcomings. Government indexes are used primarily because they are already published for other purposes and are readily available, at little if any cost, on a timely basis. However, price level indexes are at best crude measures of *average* price level changes. They do not provide precise measures of increases in the labor and materials costs of repairing or replacing a particular insured's property at the time and location of the loss. Consequently, indexing should be viewed as a helpful supplement to more personalized approaches for maintaining adequate limits.

Under both the inflation guard and indexing approaches, there is one additional defect that should be noted. As the approaches are currently being implemented, the automatic coverage increases normally do not apply to the sublimits that are expressed in fixed dollars. For example, an automatic increase in the dwelling limit of a homeowners policy would automatically increase the overall limit on personal property, because the latter is based upon a percentage of the dwelling limit, but the sublimits on jewelry, watercraft, silverware, and the like would remain unchanged. The insured who wishes to increase any of the fixed-dollar sublimits must do so by means of a separate endorsement.

To the extent that the inflation guard and indexing approaches operate to maintain adequate limits, they also help to avoid the penalties that might otherwise be imposed in situations involving coinsurance clauses or similar loss-sharing provisions. Such provisions will be discussed in the next chapter.

Types of Policy Limits in Liability Insurance

In liability insurance policies, considerably different types of upper limits are used for different types of coverages, and most policies contain multiple coverages. The following discussion will concentrate on the types of policy limits which usually apply to each of several major coverage categories.

Liability Coverage Limits Liability policies often contain medical payments and other coverages that are not tort "liability" coverages in a strict sense of the term. This discussion deals only with the liability coverages of a "liability policy." The primary liability coverage is in the form of the insurer's agreement to pay on behalf of the insured, up to the policy limits, all sums which the insured shall become legally obligated to pay as damages for bodily injury or property damage. The maximum coverage limits for bodily injury and property damage are invariably *specific* dollar limits, but they may be expressed as "split limits," or "single limits." In addition to "per occurrence" limits, many liability policies also use "aggregate limits."

Split Limits. Split limits of liability, sometimes called divided limits, are separate limits for bodily injury and property damage claims. Many split-limit liability policies contain three separate limits—a bodily injury limit applicable to each injured person, a larger bodily injury limit applicable to two or more injured persons, and a property damage limit. For example, the split liability limits endorsement to the personal auto policy explains how the limits apply:

> The limit of liability shown in the Declarations or in this endorsement for "each person" for Bodily Injury Liability is our maximum limit of liability for all damages for bodily injury sustained by any one person in any one auto accident. Subject to this limit for "each person", the limit of liability shown in the Declarations or in this endorsement for "each accident" for Bodily Injury Liability is our maximum limit of liability for all damages for bodily injury resulting from any one auto accident. The limit of liability shown in the Declarations or in this endorsement for "each accident" for property damage liability is our maximum limit of liability for all damages to all property resulting from any one auto accident.

> This is the most we will pay regardless of the number of **covered persons,** claims made, vehicles or premiums shown in the declarations, or vehicles involved in the auto accident.

Schedule

Bodily Injury Liability	$_____	each person
	$_____	each accident
Property Damage Liability	$_____	each accident

Split limits are universally referred to by the useful expedient of a short-cut expression. For example, the abbreviation "10/20/5" is intended to mean a $10,000 maximum bodily injury limit per person, a $20,000 maximum bodily injury limit for two or more persons (subject to the $10,000 maximum for any one person), and a $5,000 maximum property damage limit. Thus, in this case, the first two limits pertain to bodily injury claims, while the third pertains to property damage claims.

Split limits are truly separate limits. To illustrate, suppose an insured who has 25/50/10 limits negligently causes $15,000 in damage to the property of a third-party claimant. The insurer would pay no more than $10,000 for such damage; the insured could not use either of the bodily injury limits for property damage liability. Likewise, if the same insured negligently caused $27,000 in bodily injury to Mrs. Smith and $4,000 to Mr. Smith, the insurer would at most pay $25,000 to Mrs. Smith and $4,000 to Mr. Smith. Or, if the insured had negligently caused $134,000 in bodily injury to all five members of the Smith family, as well as $18,000 in property damage, the insurer would pay the claimants no more than $60,000, the maximum total amount payable under 25/50/10 policy limits.

Single Limits. While the traditional split-limit approach is still in use, many liability policies are now commonly written with a *single limit* of liability. That is, the split limits have been replaced by one specific dollar limit that applies to bodily injury and property damage, or a combination of both, regardless of the number of claimants involved. For instance, if an insured has a single limit of $100,000, the insurer might pay the entire $100,000 for bodily injury to one person, or for damage to the property of one person, or for some other combination of bodily injury and property damage sustained by one or several persons.

Whether the policy is written with a single limit or with split limits of liability, the relevant maximum limit applies to each and every separate insured event that happens during a covered time period. Stated another way, the limit(s) is (are) applied per accident or per occurrence, depending upon which basis is used by the policy. However, in addition to the per-event limit(s), many policies also contain "annual aggregate limits."

Aggregate Limits. An *aggregate limit* is a specific upper limit on the amount an insurer will pay for the cumulative total of damages from all covered events during the covered period (or for the total of all claims made, in claims-made policies). For example, assume that a policy has a single limit of $100,000 per occurrence, as well as an annual aggregate limit of $250,000. During the first six months of the policy year, one covered occurrence results in damages of $120,000, and a separate occurrence results in damages of $150,000. The insurer would pay $100,000 for the first occurrence and $100,000 for the second occurrence, or a cumulative total of $200,000 during the first six months. But the insured would only have $50,000 of coverage for the remaining six months of the policy period. If, in the seventh month, another separate occurrence results in damages of $60,000, the insurer's payment of $50,000 would exhaust the $250,000 annual aggregate limit, because it was the most the insurer had agreed to pay for the cumulative total of all separate occurrences during the entire policy year. The insured would be forced to retain the exposure or to buy new coverage for the remaining five months. Otherwise, the annual aggregate limit would not be reinstated until the beginning of the next policy year (if the policy is renewed).

Annual aggregate limits are seldom applied to the liability coverages of homeowners, personal auto, and other policies covering personal and family exposures. However, aggregate limits are quite common in the writing of products, personal injury, professional liability, and some other commercial and liability coverages.

Defense and Supplementary Payments Limits As noted in the previous chapter, there are a few specialized liability policies that include the defense costs in the limit specified for the payment of damages. For instance, if such a policy had a single limit of $100,000 per occurrence, the insurer would pay a maximum of $100,000 per occurrence for the combined total of damages *and* defense costs. If the policy also contained an aggregate annual limit, the aggregate limit would be applied to the cumulative total of damages and defense costs from all occurrences during the policy period.

Under the vast majority of liability insurance policies, the defense costs are paid *in addition to* the maximum amount payable for damages, and there is theoretically no dollar limit on the amount the insurer might be required 'to pay for defense costs and other supplementary benefits. However, this statement is true, strictly speaking, only with respect to defense costs and claims expenses incurred *prior to* the payment for a negotiated settlement or a court judgment. The insuring agreement stipulates that the insurer's obligation to defend a claim or suit terminates when the amount it pays for damages equals the specified limit(s) of liability.

Again using a $100,000 single limit for illustrative purposes, suppose the insurer incurred investigation and defense costs of $470,000 in a malpractice suit in which the insured physician is initially held liable for $90,000 in damages. The example might seem unrealistic to the reader, because it would appear that an insurer would settle with the claimant long before incurring defense and claims costs of this magnitude. The example is quite realistic, however, for at least two reasons. First, some malpractice policies require the insured physician's permission before the insurer can make an out-of-court settlement with the claimant. It is not at all unusual for the physician to refuse such permission and insist on a trial, for fear that a settlement would be construed as an admission of guilt or otherwise ruin the physician's reputation. Second, the claimant might well have refused an offer to settle for the policy limit, hoping to get more from a jury. In any event, the insurer in the above example would be required to pay all the defense costs of the initial trial, whether they were $470,000 or $4 million, because the $90,000 judgment was less than the insurer's maximum liability for damages. Suppose the plaintiff then appealed the case in a higher court. The insurer would probably end up paying all costs of defending the appeal. But the insurer's defense obligation would end the moment its total payment for *damages* reached its limit of $100,000.

The theoretically unlimited nature of the liability insurer's obligation to pay defense costs should also be qualified in several other practical respects. First, while the insurer agrees to pay the premiums on litigation bonds and certain first-aid expenses incurred by the insured, these particular items seldom amount to large sums of money. Second, in many policies the insurer agrees to pay the insured for any loss of earnings necessitated by the insured's involvement in the investigation or defense of a claim (usually as a witness in a trial), but the payment is limited to $50 per day ($25 per day, in some contracts), and the involvement giving rise to the loss of earnings must be at the request of the insurer. This brings up a third and more important qualification on the otherwise unlimited defense obligation of the insurer; namely, the usual contract gives the insurer the exclusive right to control the defense. Of course, the insurer may not be able to "control" the claimant or the claimant's attorney. Yet, the insurer can select defense counsel of its choice and monitor the case from beginning to end. The insurer can keep tabs on the defense costs, and attempt settlement if they become disproportionally high. Insurers are not infrequently required to pay out, for defense costs and damages combined, amounts well in excess of the limit of liability for damages. But the notion that the liability insurer's defense obligation is literally "unlimited" in amount is more theoretical than practical.

Medical Payments and Damage to the Property of Others Limits

Section II of the homeowners policy automatically includes coverages for (1) "medical payments to others" and (2) "damage to property of others." These coverages are analyzed in CPCU 2. Here, it will suffice to know that both kinds of payments are provided by the insurer without regard to whether the insured was or would be legally obligated to pay them.

In homeowners forms, the upper limit for *damage to the property of others* is a specific limit of $250 per occurrence. Most insurers will not increase this limit, even if the insured is willing to pay an additional premium charge, in part because the insured already has a single limit of at least $25,000 to cover all damages, including property damage, for which the insured *is* legally liable. There is also the feeling that property owned by another should be insured by its owner for most perils. And there is always the possibility that the homeowners insured who has more than $250 of coverage for the property of others might be less careful in handling others' property, or might even conspire with close friends to cover their otherwise uninsured property losses. For similar reasons, the homeowners policy, and other policies providing comprehensive personal liability coverage, are about the only forms that provide so-called "voluntary" property damage coverage. Nearly all other liability coverages specifically exclude liability for damage to property which is in the care, custody, or control of the insured. Some business firms are able to have the exclusion removed from their commercial liability policies, but the additional premium for doing so is often quite substantial.

Under the homeowners forms, the limit for *medical payments to others* is normally $500 per person. However, most insurers will, for a small additional premium, increase this limit to at least $1,000 or $2,000 per person (or more). The coverage may also be deleted, at the insured's option. The older homeowners forms also contained, in addition to the per person limit, an aggregate limit of $25,000 per accident, regardless of the number of persons involved. The aggregate per accident limit has been removed from most modern homeowners forms. Subject to the policy limit(s), the insurer agrees to pay "the necessary medical expenses incurred *or medically ascertained* within *three years* from the date of an accident."

Under commercial liability policies, coverage for medical payments to others is usually optional, with available per person limits of from $250 to $1,000, and per accident limits of from $10,000 to $50,000. The coverage generally applies, up to the per person and per accident limits selected, to reasonable and necessary medical expenses incurred within one year from the date of the accident. Like the medical expenses covered by homeowners policies, the medical expenses covered by commercial forms are only those due to an *accident* on the insured's premises or arising out of an insured's covered activity, even if the liability policy is written on an occurrence basis.

The once-popular option of medical payments coverage on auto policies has been replaced, in many states, by mandatory or optional "no-fault" benefits, described below. Where available, auto medical payments coverage limits are similar to those that are applicable to the medical payments section of homeowners policies. However, auto medical payments coverage differs sharply from the medical payments coverages of homeowners and general liability policies. While the medical payments of homeowners and general liability policies apply only to persons *other than the insureds*, auto medical payments apply *only to insureds*.

Auto No-Fault Limits At the time of this writing, roughly one-half of the states have enacted statutes which apply the no-fault concept to the bodily injury aspects of auto insurance. The effects of such laws on personal and commercial auto coverages are analyzed in CPCU 2 and 4. Even in a narrow discussion confined to policy limits, generalizations are made difficult by the substantial variations among state laws.

The "no-fault" benefits are set forth in a *personal injury protection endorsement*, referred to as PIP. The PIP endorsements contain specific features that differ significantly from state to state, in accordance with the applicable state statutes. Many states require the attachment of a designated PIP endorsement to business and/or personal auto liability policies. In other states, a PIP type of endorsement is an option that may be attached to an auto liability policy for an additional premium. Whether the basic PIP endorsement is compulsory or optional, its coverage limits usually may be increased by any insured who is willing to pay a higher premium.

Generally speaking, nearly all PIP endorsements provide specified amounts of what are essentially life and health insurance coverages restricted solely to losses arising out of motor vehicle accidents, irrespective of who may be negligent. More precisely, the usual endorsement provides at least some coverage for medical expenses, funeral expenses, survivor benefits, loss of income, and the replacement of essential services.

In some states the medical expense benefits of the PIP endorsement are unlimited in amount, provided that the expenses are "reasonable and necessary," and they are the proximate result of a motor vehicle accident. In other states the payment of medical expenses is subject to a specific, per person dollar limit of, say, $5,000 (or more); or, there may be an overall dollar limit, such as $7,500 or $10,000, on several benefits combined, including medical expense benefits.

Funeral and burial expenses are usually paid subject to a specific dollar limit, such as $1,000 per person. Survivors of a deceased insured are paid a continuing income of up to "x" dollars per week for up to "y" number of weeks (or up to an overall dollar maximum). Loss of income benefits, as well as the costs of hiring a substitute to perform services that otherwise would have been performed by a disabled insured, are likewise payable up to the daily, weekly, and/or overall maximums specified in the endorsement (and in the applicable state statute, if any).

The diversity of state auto insurance laws creates a potential problem for the person who is involved in an auto accident in a state which requires coverages (or coverage limits) that are not required in the person's state of residence. Auto policies have resolved this potential problem with a specific provision for *out-of-state coverage*. If an insured is involved in an accident in another state which requires a nonresident to maintain minimum levels of coverage while using a vehicle in that state, the insured's policy is automatically interpreted as though it provided the required coverage and limits—unless, of course, the insured already has higher limits for the required types of coverage. The automatic adjustments are made to liability coverages, PIP coverage, or both, as necessary, and they also apply to whatever minimum coverages are mandated by the various provinces in Canada. However, some auto policies require the insured to repay the insurer for any payment that the insurer would not have made in the absence of the out-of-state coverage provision.

Workers' Compensation and Employers' Liability Limits

The laws and insurance coverages for job-connected injuries and diseases are analyzed in CPCU 4. Before describing the policy limits, it is necessary to explain that the standard workers' compensation and employers' liability policy provides the insured employer with two broad kinds of coverage. Coverage A pertains to the workers' compensation benefits that are embodied in the applicable statute(s). Coverage B pertains to the employers' liability exposure under common law. The two coverages are governed by separate and distinct types of upper limits.

The insuring agreement for Coverage A is quite simple: "To pay promptly when due all compensation and other benefits required of the insured by the workmen's [sic] compensation law." Then, in the definitions section of the policy, "the workmen's compensation law" is defined to include the workers' compensation and occupational disease law of *any* state or other jurisdiction *that is specifically designated in the declarations.* A small employer operating solely within one state might list only one particular state in the declarations, while a large interstate firm might list many states, territories, and federal jurisdictions or obtain country-wide coverage by endorsement. Once the statutory jurisdiction(s) is (are) designated in the policy, it is not necessary to spell out the limits for Coverage A, since all the statutory limits have been incorporated by reference in the above-quoted language of the insuring agreement. Generally speaking, all the statutes require covered employers to pay medical expenses and compensation for disability or death due to the job-connected injuries and diseases of their covered employees. The greater number of states now require the payment of medical expenses without any upper dollar limit. However, the amounts payable as compensation for death, disability, dismemberment and related benefits are invariably governed by specific limits which are set forth in the relevant statute.

The insuring agreement for Coverage B, Employers' Liability, says that the insurer "will pay on behalf of the insured all sums which the insured shall become legally obligated to pay as damages. . . ." Except for its restriction to tort actions brought by employees for employment-related injury and disease, the insuring agreement of Coverage B contains the familiar wording of most liability coverages. The policy automatically provides a $100,000 single limit of liability for Coverage B, but this basic limit may be increased to as much as $1 million or more. As to bodily injury, the limit applies to *each accident*, regardless of the number of persons involved. As to disease, the same limit serves as an *aggregate annual limit per covered jurisdiction* for all diseases caused or aggravated by exposures to conditions of employment, where the last day of exposure occurs during the policy period, if a written claim or suit is brought within thirty-six months after the end of the policy period.

In the workers' compensation and employers' liability policy, the insurer does not reimburse the insured for any loss of earnings, even if incurred at the request of the insurer. The insured is the employer, of course, which means a corporation or self-employed proprietor or partner who would normally not lose earnings as such by testifying or otherwise assisting with a claim. (Furthermore, an officer, proprietor, or partner would seldom be called on to assist in most compensation cases, which are either routine or at least can be handled entirely by the insurer). To those who are not familiar with compensation claims, the payment of claims expenses and defense costs for Coverage A may not seem very significant, since these benefits are required by statute. However, each state has an administrative agency or board which is given broad discretionary powers in the daily administration of the statute. The decisions of the administrative agency are binding, unless overruled by a court of competent jurisdiction. Rather than eliminating litigation and simplifying claims procedures, as orginally intended by the statutes, the volume of litigation and paperwork has actually increased in many states, so much so that the expenses of handling claims have become a significant part of the premiums paid by employers for worker's compensation coverage.

Defense and supplementary benefits are payable *in addition to* the amounts payable under Coverage A or the applicable limit of liability under Coverage B. Unlike other liability policies, the compensation policy's obligation for defense and claims expenses is literally unlimited in amount. The insurer's obligation to defend does *not* cease when the insurer has paid the amounts required by statute. Nor does it end when the insurer has paid an amount for common-law damages equal to the Coverage B limit of liability.

Restoration of Policy Limits A *per person* liability limit is restored automatically for future losses, because such a limit is applied per accident or per occurrence. Clearly, the intention is to make a per person limit available to *each* separate accident or occurrence covered during the policy term. If the policy *also* contains an aggregate annual limit, it may come into play to limit coverage available for future claims.

A limit per event, per accident, per occurrence, or per claim, is designed to put a lid on the insurer's total payment when two or more persons are claimants. Once exhausted, it cannot be restored *for that particular accident.* Yet, the full limit is automatically restored for future losses, in effect, by its application to each separate accident (unless coverage is reduced by an aggregate limit).

As explained earlier, some liability policies contain an *annual* aggregate limit on the amount the insurer will pay for the cumulative total of all separate accidents or occurrences during the policy period. Once exhausted, an annual aggregate limit is not automatically reinstated until the beginning of the next policy year, assuming the policy is renewed. In the meantime, a partially or fully exhausted aggregate annual limit can be restored to the original amount only by the payment of an additional premium.

When the coverage is not subject to an upper dollar limit, such as the medical expense coverages mandated by workers' compensation and some no-fault auto statutes, there is obviously no need for the restoration of policy limits. Nor is there any reason to restore what are already unlimited defense benefits under the standard workers' compensation and employers' liability policy. Concerning other liability policies, the insurer's duty to defend ceases as soon as it has paid its limit of liability for damages. The policies are silent on the matter of whether exhausted defense coverage is or can be restored, but the clear implication is that defense coverage is automatically restored, along with the limit of liability for damages, in respect to all separate accidents (or occurrences, depending upon the basis on which the policy is written). On the other hand, it is highly unlikely that an insurer would be willing to restore defense coverage for the same accident that exhausted the limit of liability for damages; to do so would again be the equivalent of backdating coverage for an event that has already occurred.

Variable Policy Limits   The "inflation guard" type of endorsement is not available for use with liability coverages. However, there are some ways in which liability coverages adjust for the effects of inflation. For example, a crude form of indexing is used in workers' compensation statutes, where the weekly income benefits are partially linked to a periodic recomputation of the state's average wage. However, the income benefits are based on the latest average wage figure available at the time the benefits *begin*. Most states do not thereafter require upward adjustments of income benefits, through indexing or otherwise, over the duration for which they are payable (which could be many years). When benefit amounts are increased by amendments to the statutes, the higher benefits are very seldom applied retroactively to persons disabled prior to the effective date of the amendment. Once the legislators effect an increase in any of the compensation benefits or maximums, future claimants will receive them automatically, the amendments having been incorporated by implied reference in the insuring agreements of the policy.

To the extent workers' compensation and no-fault auto laws require unlimited medical expense benefits, there is no need for variable policy limits. This is likewise true of unlimited payments for defense costs in liability policies generally.

With respect to single or split limits of liability for damages due to bodily injury, personal injury, and property damage, the lack of variable policy limits is of little practical significance. It is certainly true that inflation is among the major reasons for noticeable increases over time in the *average* amounts paid for informal settlements and court judgments, if only because inflation has involved sharp increases in medical expenses, auto repair costs, and the dollar levels of income lost due to death or disability, all of which are important components of tort damages. It is also true that a $25,000 single limit is even less adequate today than it was ten years ago. Nevertheless, it can be a disastrous mistake to measure the adequacy of liability insurance policy limits solely in terms of average or maximum loss amounts in the past. In deciding the cases of tomorrow, the courts are not bound by either the average or the largest losses in the historical record. Nor are the courts necessarily constrained by the amount of the liability limit(s) carried by the policyholder. The crucial question, therefore, is what limit will be large enough to cover the damages levied against a particular insured in a tort lawsuit tomorrow? That question is ultimately like asking "how high is up?" Accordingly, if an insured had a single limit of

$100,000 ten years ago and an inflation guard endorsement or the insured's initiatives had increased the limit to $200,000 today, the insured would be better off, but would today's limit be adequate for tomorrow's loss? The question is well worth pondering. It could be that some insurers will be venturesome enough to offer liability insurance with no upper dollar limits, as is beginning to be the case in major medical expense insurance. However, liability insurers find themselves on the horns of a rather unique dilemma. Smaller liability limits leave insureds with inadequate protection; larger liability limits may tend to foster larger court judgments. The writing of unlimited liability insurance would be somewhat like giving juries a blank check on somebody else's account (the insurer's, and ultimately its stockholders and/or policyholders, as well as all buyers of products and services for which the prices include the cost of liability insurance).

Types of Policy Limits in Multiple-Line Insurance

Homeowners, businessowners, special multi-peril, and many other popular insurance policies are packages or combinations of property, liability, and related coverages in a single policy. Such policies are generally divided into distinct sections, with separate limits for each section or coverage within a section. Therefore, the governing policy limits already have been discussed under the previous headings. There is little else to be said about the limits of package policies.

LOSS VALUATION PROVISIONS AND LIMITS

Specified policy limits and insurable interest requirements are not the only determinants of the maximum amounts payable for insured events. Under property and liability insurance contracts, a third such determinant is the compensable amount of the loss, as prescribed in the relevant policy provisions, statutes, and/or common law principles. As a general rule, the maximum amount an insured under a property policy may recover is *the smallest of*

(1) the amount of the insured's legal interest in the property,
(2) the applicable policy limit, *or*
(3) the compensable amount of the loss.

The maximum amount a third-party liability claimant may be paid by the insurer is *the lesser of*

(1) the applicable policy limit *or*
(2) the compensable amount of the loss.

Before refining these general rules, it is first necessary to explain the primary valuation methods which are used to arrive at the *compensable amount of the loss.*

Loss Valuation Methods in Property Insurance

Under all property insurance coverages, the compensable amount of the loss is not determined until after the occurrence of the insured event. To arrive at the compensable amount of direct loss due to damaged, destroyed, or stolen property, most indemnity policies stipulate valuation methods based on the notions of "actual cash value," "replacement cost," "repair cost," or the smallest of the three figures, at the time of loss. A few indemnity policies use "reproduction cost," "selling price," or other methods of loss valuation. Under property insurance coverages written on a valued basis, an agreed-upon value is paid to the insured, if the property is stolen or totally destroyed.

Under time element coverages, the compensable loss is generally computed on the basis of the decrease in revenue or increase in expenses (or both) during the period of time required to repair or replace the damaged or destroyed property involved. However, time element coverage is sometimes also written on a valued basis.

Actual Cash Value The concept of "actual cash value" is seldom defined in property insurance policies, and many court definitions of the concept are lacking in precision and/or consistency. Even so, it is generally agreed that the *actual cash value* of property, at the time of loss, is the then current cost of replacing it with new property of like kind, less the dollar equivalent of any physical depreciation and economic obsolescence that had accumulated immediately prior to the property's destruction or abstraction. Expressed in terms of an algebraic formula, the actual cash value is:

$$ACV = RCN - D \pm O$$

where ACV is the actual cash value of the property at the time of loss; RCN is the replacement cost, at the time of loss, of new property of like kind; D is the amount of physical depreciation, if any, that had accumulated with respect to the destroyed or stolen property immediately prior to the loss; and O is the amount of economic obsolescence, if any, that had accumulated with respect to the destroyed or stolen property immediately prior to the loss. As respects new property in perfect condition, there is no depreciation and normally no obsolescence to subtract in the above equation. It follows that the actual cash value of new property is equal to the replacement cost of new and comparable property. As time goes by, the amount of the aging property's actual cash value will depend on the net effect of changes in the relationship between replacement cost and the total amount of accumulated depreciation and obsolescence.

The replacement costs of buildings and personal property are determined by all of the many factors that determine construction costs and product prices in our highly complex economic system. Construction costs and the prices of clothing, furniture, appliances, and most other items of personal property have been increasing over the years, and this general trend is expected to continue into the foreseeable future. Consequently, the replacement cost component of the ACV formula will likewise continue to increase, with the exception of the few items of new property whose prices will decline. This does not necessarily mean that a property's ACV will increase over time. The ACV could increase or decrease over time, depending on the rate of increase in the amount of accumulated depreciation and obsolescence.

The depreciation component of the ACV formula does not refer to the artificial depreciation schedules prescribed or permitted for taxation or other accounting purposes. Instead, it refers to the *physical* depreciation of property— or, in other words, to any decline in the property's value due to such factors as use, normal wear and tear, deterioration, and/or age of the property.

The economic obsolescence component acknowledges the possibility that old property, even if it is in good condition, may become less useful or outmoded by a new style, model, or kind of property that is of better quality (or is otherwise more desirable).

If the old property is not obsolete, the obsolescence component of the formula is zero, and the actual cash value of the property is simply its replacement cost, less accumulated depreciation. Even if the old property is obsolete, no explicit adjustment for obsolescence is required in situations where the old property is easily replaced by *used* property of the same kind and *quality*, since the obsolescence adjustment has already been made, implicitly, in the market price for used property of the same quality. However, it is sometimes difficult or impossible to obtain used property of the same quality as the obsolete property being replaced, in which case the only practical alternative is to find the replacement cost of new property and adjust it to reflect the qualitative differences in the new property. Because there is some truth in the notion that "they don't make things like they used to," the required adjustment conceivably could take the form of an increase in the ACV of the old property, to reflect the fact that its quality was superior to anything now available. More commonly, the adjustment for obsolescence is a deduction from the replacement cost of new property, with the net effect of reducing the ACV of the old property, to reflect the superior quality of the new property.

The preceding discussion has identified five possibilities; namely, the destroyed or stolen property can be

(1) new property,
(2) old property which is not obsolete,
(3) old property which is obsolete but easily replaced with used property of the same quality,
(4) old property which is obsolete and replaceable only with new property of inferior quality, and
(5) old property which is obsolete and replaceable only with new property of superior quality.

All five possibilities are taken into account in the following, simplified version of the formula for computing the actual cash value:

$$ACV = RCQ - D$$

As before, ACV refers to the actual cash value at the time of loss, and D refers to the accumulated amount of physical depreciation, if any, just prior to loss. But the earlier formula utilized the letters "RCN" to refer to the replacement cost of new property of like kind, thereby requiring a subsequent deduction or addition for "O," the amount of accumulated obsolescence, in appropriate situations. The simplified formula accomplishes the same result by the expedient of assuming that "RCQ" is the replacement cost of property of like kind and *Quality*, whether new or used. No further adjustments for obsolescence are needed, therefore; they are made, as and when appropriate, as an adjustment to the replacement cost amount. While the two formulas are equivalent, the simplified version has the advantages of (1) focusing attention on the physical depreciation of property, which is much more common than obsolescence, and (2) remaining sufficiently flexible to apply in unusual situations.

Some types of *personal* property do not actually decline in market value over time. Recent examples include used goldware, silverware, and diamonds, which have skyrocketed in value in response to worldwide demand for precious metals and gems. Furthermore, owing to their almost infinite useful lifetimes, such items are subject to little or no physical depreciation each year. Their actual cash value is essentially the same as the market value for *new* items of like kind and quality (if they are new at the time of loss), or the market value for *used or old* items of like kind and quality (if they are used or old at the time of loss). In fact, with respect to any item of *personal* property that is easily replaced with an item of like kind, quality, and *condition*, the actual cash value is essentially the market value of the substitute item. Deductions for physical depreciation are normally made only when the readily available market prices are for items in better condition than those to be replaced. The market value for *real* property is another matter entirely.

In applying the actual cash value concept to dwellings and other buildings, the market value is often irrelevant (though some courts disagree). First, the market value of real property includes the value of the land upon which the building is situated, but the land itself is virtually never insured. Second, the *market value* is merely the price for which the real estate would exchange hands between a willing and informed buyer and a willing and informed seller, given the prevailing economic conditions at the time. Third, since the value of the land usually increases faster than the building depreciates, so also does the total market value of the real estate usually increase over time; hence, the total market value of the real estate is not an appropriate starting point for computing the actual cash value of the building, because the "ACV" of the building declines, by definition, to the extent of increases in the total amount of accumulated physical depreciation over time. It is sometimes suggested that a rough estimate of a building's ACV may be obtained by subtracting the appraised market value of the land from the appraised market value of the real estate (i.e., the total value of the building and land combined). However, appraised market values are at best matters of informed opinion. Even if the appraised market value of the real estate turns out to be accurate, there is no necessary reason to suppose that the buyer attaches the same value to the building as the appraiser. Nor does the buyer's assessment of the building's worth have any necessary relationship to its actual cash value. Indeed, the buyer might tear down the building immediately after its purchase, thus indicating the buyer's willingness to invest the entire purchase price to obtain the land alone. For insurance purposes, therefore, determining the market value is not particularly helpful, as a means of arriving at the building's insurable value. The ACV is more accurately computed by deducting physical depreciation from the RCQ.

As might be expected, most of the disputes in determining ACV arise in connection with the amount of any deduction for accumulated depreciation and obsolescence. Recognizing that insureds are inclined to think of such a deduction as taking something away from them, many claims representatives prefer to explain the deduction as what the insured must "pay" for "betterment"—that is, for the increased lifetime and enhanced value that the insured would receive from the purchase of new property to replace old property. The positive approach does not eliminate all the disputes concerning the amount of the deduction, but it does help convey the intention of putting the insured in the same post-loss financial position that he or she enjoyed immediately before the loss.

In property insurance coverages written on an actual cash value basis, the ACV is not the only method an insurer uses to value the loss. Most coverages reserve to the insurer the right to minimize its outlay by paying the cost to repair or replace property, if either is smaller than the ACV at the time of loss. The implications of such alternatives will be discussed under the subsequent heading of insurer options.

Replacement Cost Under property insurance coverages written on a replacement cost basis, there is no deduction for physical depreciation. The insurer's payment is based on the current cost, at the time of loss, of replacing the damaged or stolen property with *new* property of like kind and quality. The insurer's payment is subject to the applicable policy limits, of course, as well as to other policy provisions which may affect the amount of recovery.

For many years the actual cash value basis was the only method used by property insurers to value the maximum amount of compensable loss. It is still the primary method in many property insurance policies. Initially, replacement cost coverage was available only for nonprofit institutions and the owners of some commercial buildings with superior physical characteristics. Applicants were screened carefully for possible moral hazards, and those who became policyholders were required to insure the buildings for 100 percent of their then current replacement costs. In practice, some insurers had always settled small losses without any deductions for physical depreciation, if only to maintain good public relations in a relatively inexpensive way. But the newer policies made replacement cost coverage an explicit contractual obligation which also applied to large and total losses.

As insurers gained more experience with replacement cost coverage, it was gradually made available for: dwellings; business tenants' improvements and betterments to commercial buildings; personal property of governmental agencies and educational, charitable, and religious institutions; and furniture, fixtures, equipment, and supplies of business firms. Underwriting restrictions were gradually relaxed, and insurance-to-value requirements were reduced to as low as 80% of the property's replacement cost. More recently, replacement cost coverage has become readily available for household goods and other residential contents, as an optional endorsement to homeowners policies.

For a period of several decades *all* homeowners forms with building coverage provided replacement cost coverage (up to the policy limits) on dwellings and their appurtenant structures, as long as the amount of insurance carried on the damaged building was equal to at least 80 percent of its replacement cost. While this is still true of most homeowners forms in use today, some insurers have introduced an actual cash value form intended for use on older homes where there is a substantial difference between the actual cash value and replacement cost. It is no longer unusual for an older dwelling with a market value of $30,000 to have a replacement cost of $200,000 or more. In this situation, an insured seldom desires to pay the premium for $200,000 of coverage. Moreover, underwriters are unwilling to provide $200,000 of coverage because of the moral hazard. An actual cash value homeowners form provides a tool for resolving this problem without requiring the insured to forgo the advantages of a homeowners policy.

Repair Cost A number of insurers are now offering new types of homeowners policies with sublimits, deductibles, covered perils, and other policy provisions significantly different from those contained in standardized forms. Although the new policies are not uniform from insurer to insurer, they are all similar in two respects that are relevant to this discussion. Generally, all the new policies (1) have eligibility requirements tied to the market value of the dwelling, and they all (2) use a modified version of repair or replacement cost as the stipulated valuation method for building losses.

The new policies are referred to as "market value" homeowners policies, but only because the eligibility rules require the applicant's dwelling to have a market value of between 40 percent and 80 percent of its replacement cost. If so, the policyholder must then insure the dwelling for an amount equal to or greater than its market value. All personal property losses are valued on an actual cash value basis. All dwelling losses are valued on the basis of the cost to repair or replace the property using *accepted repair practices, building materials, and construction techniques currently in common use.* The latter provision applies both to the repair of damaged real property and the replacement of destroyed real property; yet it is called the "repair cost approach," to distinguish it from the traditional replacement cost provision. The traditional provision obligates the insurer to pay on the basis of the cost to repair or replace with new property of like quality; the new approach permits the insurer to use "modern" materials and construction techniques, which often involve materials and skills of a lesser quality than were used in the original construction of the dwelling. For example, plaster walls could be replaced with drywall, hardwood floors with plywood subfloors and inexpensive floor coverings, tile roofs with asphalt shingles, two-by-ten lumber with two-by-fours, solid wood paneling with veneer paneling, and so on. At least one large insurer limits the payment for a total loss to the dwelling's "value on the open market at the time of loss," while limiting the payment for a partial loss to the cost of repair "with commonly used building materials to put the property in a livable condition." The latter phrase obviously gives the insurer considerable latitude, if interpreted literally.

Many of the market value homeowners policies settle roof damage on an actual cash value basis, unless the damage was caused by fire; otherwise, settlements of dwelling losses do not require deductions for physical depreciation as such. Thus, the so-called market value or repair cost policy involves a hybrid or combination of loss valuation provisions—actual cash value and repair or replacement according to construction standards that are substantially less rigid than the traditional notion of like kind and quality. Some policies also impose a new kind of policy limit equal to the market value of the dwelling. The intention of the repair cost type of policy is to provide owners of older homes with a choice. Unable to obtain traditional replacement cost coverage, the owner of an older home could only purchase actual cash value coverage on the dwelling. Repair cost dwelling coverage offers such an owner a somewhat better alternative.

Clauses to Modify or Clarify Basic Loss Valuation Methods Various policy provisions or endorsements are sometimes used to modify or clarify the basic loss valuation methods of indemnity-type property coverages. Three such clauses are the "selling price clause," the "cost of reproduction clause," and the "pair and set clause." All three pertain to the direct damage or destruction of personal property. The first is a modification of primary valuation methods, while the second and third are in the nature of clarifications.

The *selling price clause or endorsement* may be provided in a commercial fire or commercial multi-peril policy covering the merchandise inventory of a wholesaler or retailer or the finished goods inventory of a manufacturer. Such property is generally not subject to physical depreciation (unless it is "shopworn"), but the usual basis of recovery is its replacement cost *to the merchant or manufacturer*, less any salvage value, rather than the price for which the merchandise is expected to be sold. The selling price clause for retailers and wholesalers converts the loss valuation method from actual cash value to "selling price less discounts and unincurred expenses." This particular clause applies only to merchandise which has been sold but not yet delivered. Manufacturers, on the other hand, can obtain coverage on a market value basis. The manufacturer's selling price endorsement provides, "...the actual cash value of finished stock manufactured by the insured shall be that price, less all discounts and unincurred expenses, for which said stock would have been sold had no loss occurred."

The *cost of reproduction* is a commonly used basis for insuring valuable papers and records. Papers and records that cannot be restored are sometimes insured on a valued basis. For papers and records that can be restored, the amount of recovery is limited to research and other expenses necessarily incurred to reproduce the valuable papers and records.

In policies covering personal property, *pair and set clauses* are used to clarify the insurer's obligation in situations involving the loss of property which is part of a matched pair or set, such as a pair of earrings, a pair of candle holders, a set of fireplace tools, or a set of silverware. Suppose one earring is destroyed or stolen. Surely the remaining earring is now worth less than one-half of the value of the original pair. In fact, in the absence of a policy provision to the contrary, the insured could argue that the remaining earring no longer has any value. The older homeowners forms dealt with the matter in the following way:

> PAIR AND SET CLAUSE: If there is loss of an article which is part of a pair or set, the measure of the loss shall be a reasonable and fair proportion of the total value of the pair or set, giving consideration to the importance of said article, but such loss shall not be construed to mean total loss of the pair or set.

The quoted provision leaves considerable room for negotiation between the insurer and the insured, especially in regard to the meaning of "reasonable and fair proportion of the total value." Some newer forms are a bit more explicit in saying:

> *Loss to a Pair or Set.* In case of loss to a pair or set we may elect to:
> a. repair or replace any part to restore the pair or set to its value before the loss; or
> b. pay the difference between actual cash value of the property before and after the loss.

While the newer language still leaves some room for negotiation, it at least specifies the differential actual cash value notion as the basis for computing what was formerly called a reasonable and fair proportion, and it explicitly acknowledges the insurer's right to repair or replace any part of a pair or set.

Loss Settlement Options   To repeat the general rule, the maximum amount a property insured may recover is *the smallest of*

(1) the amount of the insured's legal interest in the property,
(2) the applicable policy limit, or
(3) the compensable amount of the loss.

In the case of indemnity coverages, the *maximum* compensable amount of loss is most commonly determined by one of three primary methods: actual cash value, replacement cost, or repair cost. However, all three of these methods serve as *optional* modes of settlement under the usual property insurance coverage. The *insurer* retains the right to settle covered loss on the basis of the *least* costly of the loss valuation alternatives that are set forth in the policy. The actual cash value, replacement cost, and repair cost methods are usually among the stipulated alternatives.

For example, the personal and business auto policies give the insurer several options in determining the compensable amount of a physical damage loss. First, the insurer's upper limit of liability is the *lesser of* (1) the actual cash value of the stolen or damaged property or (2) the amount necessary to repair or replace the property. Second, the insurer has the option of (1) paying the loss in money, or (2) repairing, or (3) replacing the property. Third, the insurer may keep all or part of the property, if it so desires, at an agreed or appraised value. Damage to an auto frequently would involve repair costs that exceed the value of the auto. If so, the damage is treated as a "constructive total loss," because the effect on the insurer's liability is the same as if the auto had been totally destroyed; the insurer is obligated to pay the smaller of the actual cash value or the replacement cost of the auto. The insurer may pay the smaller of these two amounts in full, keep the damaged auto, and sell it for its salvage value. Or, the insurer may reduce its payment to the insured by the salvage value, and allow the insured to keep the damaged vehicle.

The loss settlement options of modern replacement-cost homeowners forms are much more elaborate. The relevant provisions are reproduced below.

> *Loss Settlement.* Covered property losses are settled as follows:
> a. Personal property and structures that are not buildings at actual cash value at the time of loss but not exceeding the amount necessary to repair or replace;
> b. Carpeting, domestic appliances, awnings, outdoor antennas and outdoor equipment, whether or not attached to buildings, at actual cash value at the time of loss but not exceeding the amount necessary to repair or replace;
> c. Buildings under Coverage A or B at replacement cost without deduction for depreciation, subject to the following:
>
> > (1) If at the time of loss the amount of insurance in this policy on the damaged building is 80% or more of the full replacement cost of the building immediately prior to the loss, we will pay the cost of repair or replacement, without deduction for depreciation, but not exceeding the smallest of the following amounts:

(a) the limit of liability under this policy applying to the building:

(b) the replacement cost of that part of the building damaged for equivalent construction and use on the same premises; or

(c) the amount actually and necessarily spent to repair or replace the damaged building.

(2) If at the time of loss the amount of insurance in this policy on the damaged building is less than 80% of the full replacement cost of the building immediately prior to the loss, we will pay the larger of the following amounts, but not exceeding the limit of liability under this policy applying to the building:

(a) the actual cash value of that part of the building damaged; or

(b) that proportion of the cost to repair or replace, without deduction for depreciation, of that part of the building damaged, which the total amount of insurance in this policy on the damaged building bears to 80% of the replacement cost of the building.

(3) In determining the amount of insurance required to equal 80% of the full replacement cost of the building immediately prior to the loss, you shall disregard the value of excavations, foundation, piers and other supports which are below the undersurface of the lowest basement floor or, where there is no basement, which are below the surface of the ground inside the foundation walls, and underground flues, pipes, wiring and drains.

(4) When the cost to repair or replace the damage is more than $1000 or more than 5% of the amount of insurance in this policy on the building, whichever is less, we will pay no more than the actual cash value of the damage until actual repair or replacement is completed.

(5) You may disregard the replacement cost loss settlement provisions and make claim under this policy for loss or damage to buildings on an actual cash value basis and then make claim within 180 days after loss for any additional liability on a replacement cost basis.

These provisions are worth careful scrutiny. Items "a." and "b." represent the typical settlement options for actual cash value coverage (though it may be endorsed to provide replacement cost coverage, as explained earlier). Item "c." represents the typical settlement options for replacement cost coverage on buildings, but adds some loss-sharing provisions that will be examined more carefully in Chapter 12.

Historically, property insurance coverages written on an indemnity basis have applied the optional loss settlement methods as of *the date of loss or damage,* and the settlement options usually have been options of the *insurer,* not the insured. This statement is still largely true today. But a few large insurers have recently started experimenting with a different approach. The traditional time-of-loss method can penalize the insured when there is a time lag between the date of loss and the date of completing a building's repair or replacement, especially when there is rapid inflation in the interim. In view of this problem, the dwelling forms of one insurer have been changed to read:

> At your option the cost to repair or replace can be determined at: a) date of loss; or b) date that repair or replacement is complete, provided it was completed with due diligence and dispatch.

This same policy is written without any upper dollar limit on the dwelling. Reportedly, a few other insurers are now writing coverage with no maximum dollar limit on commercial buildings. With the exception of auto physical damage coverages, where the absence of upper dollar limits has long been common, property insurance coverages without dollar limits are quite rare, yet they would have obvious advantages to the insured as an automatic inflation correction mechanism. Settlement options such as the one quoted above may also supplement other approaches for maintaining coverage adequacy in periods of sharply increasing construction costs.

Valued Coverage The general nature of "valued" property insurance coverage has already been explained. Briefly, under a valued coverage, an agreed-upon value for the insured property is established prior to loss and entered in the policy declarations. In the event of a total loss, the agreed-upon value is paid to the insured. For a partial loss, the amount payable is governed by policy provisions, if any, or the terms of a so-called "valued policy statute" (in the few states where valued policy statutes apply to a partial loss).

By Policy Provisions. Valued property insurance coverage may be obtained on personal property such as antique cars, fine arts, and cargos in transit, apart from any statutory requirements. The amount payable for a total loss is the agreed value, while the amount payable for a partial loss is determined by policy provisions and/or court interpretations. For example, one open cargo policy prescribes the following procedure for the valuation of a partial loss:

> In case of partial loss by perils insured against, the proportion of loss shall be determined by a separation of the damaged portion of the insured property from the sound and by an agreed estimate (by survey) of the percentage of damage on such portion; or if such agreement is not practicable, then by public sale of such damaged portion for the account of the owner of the property.

In application, if this procedure revealed that the insured cargo suffered a 30 percent decline in value, the insured would receive 30 percent of the agreed full value of the cargo (assuming, as is typically the case, that the cargo was insured to full value).

When a valued property insurance policy does not specify a procedure for determining the amount of recovery for a partial loss, some uncertainty exists in the law.[1] Some courts have based the valuation of partial losses on a percentage of the agreed value for total losses, following the same sort of procedure that is used for open cargo losses, on the theory that the reason for agreeing upon a value is to minimize disputes on both partial and total losses. Other courts view the agreed value as solely a device for setting an upper limit on the insurer's liability, and feel that partial losses should be paid on the basis of actual cash value, repair cost, or replacement cost, depending upon the valuation standard of the policy.[2]

By Statute. Over twenty states have so-called "valued policy statutes" which require a property insurer to pay the full amount of the policy if the insured property is totally destroyed by a peril specified in the statute and covered by the policy. Many such statutes apply only to dwellings and other buildings, and then only to the perils of fire and lightning. While enactment of the statutes was motivated by a desire to reduce the number of disputes and abuses associated with arbitrary depreciation applications, there is little evidence to confirm whether the statutes have had any such effect.

In a state with a valued policy statute, when a building is *totally* destroyed by fire, the insurer usually must pay the policy limit. Depreciation cannot be taken into account, and the insurer seldom has the option of rebuilding the destroyed property.[3]

However, most valued policy laws permit the insurer to settle *partial* losses on the basis of their actual cash value at the time of loss—or, if smaller, the costs of repairing or replacing the damaged property with like kind and quality. Some of the laws stipulate that payments for partial losses are to be a percentage of the agreed value, with the percentage corresponding to the degree of damage to the property. For partial fire losses, some laws even bar the insurer from applying deductibles or coinsurance provisions.

General Effect of Valued Coverage. Even if valued coverage were to be more widespread, it would not alter the general rule for determining the maximum amount of recovery under property insurance policies. Whether the coverage is of the valued or the indemnity type, the maximum amount a property insured may recover is *the smallest of* (1) the amount of the insured's legal interest in the property, (2) the applicable policy limit, if any, or (3) the compensable amount of the loss. The distinguishing feature of valued property coverage is that the agreed value is both the applicable policy limit *and* the compensable amount of the loss, in the case of a total loss which is due to a covered peril. For partial losses, the recovery depends on the statute in question.

Time Element Loss Valuation Methods A more complete discussion of business interruption, extra expense, and other time element coverages is reserved for other CPCU courses. What should be noted here is that several time element coverages can be written on either an indemnity or a valued basis. Indemnity coverages use loss valuation methods which are governed largely by decreases in revenue, increases in expenses (or both) during the period of time required, with the exercise of due diligence and dispatch, to repair or replace the damaged or destroyed property and resume normal operations. Since valued coverages involve agreed policy limits or values which replace, to a degree, more exact measures of the actual loss sustained, insurer underwriting standards are generally higher for valued time element coverages than they are for indemnity coverages. Nonetheless, the general rule concerning the maximum amount of recovery is the same for all indirect and direct loss property coverages.

Loss Valuation Methods in Liability Insurance

The methods of determining defense costs, supplementary payments, punitive damages, and compensatory damages were explained earlier under the headings of covered consequences and policy limits. Accordingly, only a few additional observations are necessary at this juncture.

The maximum amount an insurer will pay under a particular liability insurance policy is *the lesser of* (1) the applicable policy limit or (2) the compensable amount of the loss. Perhaps the most important exception to this general rule takes place when the insurer is held liable for an amount in excess of the policy limit, due to its negligence or bad faith in failing to settle the claim for less than the policy limit. Such situations, while not everyday occurrences, are explained in other CPCU courses.

The maximum amount a third-party liability claimant may recover under a given liability policy is not limited by any requirement that the claimant have an insurable interest, since a third-party claimant is not a legal party to the insurance contract in question. In fact, the legal remedy of such a claimant does not necessarily rest upon *any* express or implied contract with the insured. The claimant's remedy could arise from an enforceable contract which obligates the insured to assume, contractually, certain tort damages caused to others by the claimant. Even so, in the more common case, the third-party claimant's cause of action for damages is founded in tort law principles which are independent of any contractual relationship with the alleged tortfeasor.

In a jury trial, the compensable amount of the loss takes the form of whatever amount the jurors decide to award to the plaintiff as damages. That amount is what the insurer will pay on behalf of the insured, subject to the policy limits. Though the judge has the power to reduce the award (or set it aside) if it "shocks the conscience of the court," this is not done very often; moreover, neither the judge nor the jury are bound by the applicable policy limit. In the usual case involving a judgment in excess of the policy limit, the liability insurer is not obligated to pay the excess. The excess portion falls upon the shoulders of the insured/defendant.

In the absence of a formal trial, the compensable amount of the loss is determined by informal negotiations between the liability insurer and the claimant (or the claimant's attorney). Generally, both parties to the negotiations are trying to anticipate what a court of law would do if presented with the same facts. The insurer wants to minimize the amount of the settlement; the plaintiff's attorney wants to maximize the amount of the settlement. Both parties are conscious of the time and expense of a formal trial. Just as the plaintiff might knowingly settle for less than a court would award, the insurer might knowingly settle for more than a court would award. The insured/defendant has no right to prohibit a settlement or influence its amount (except where professional liability policies require the insured's permission before settling out of court). The liability insurer usually has control over the defense costs and amounts it wishes to offer as settlements. It may not have any appreciable "control" over the plaintiff, the plaintiff's attorney, or the court. Thus, there is a primary sense in which the loss valuation methods in liability insurance are not governed by policy provisions. The policy limit normally serves as a lid on the maximum amount an insurer will or must pay for damages, of course. Otherwise, the liability insurer has much less to say about the maximum amount of recovery than the property insurer does for its insureds. Unless current tort law principles governing damage amounts are altered significantly, it is unlikely that insurers and reinsurers will be willing to offer liability coverages without dollar limits.

Chapter Notes

1. Walter Williams, "The Valued Policy and Value Determination," *Insurance Law Journal* (no. 457, Feb. 1961), pp. 71-78.
2. For a discussion of these conflicting cases, see Robert E. Keeton, *Basic Text on Insurance Law* (St. Paul: West Publishing Co., 1971), pp. 140-142; and Edwin W. Patterson, *Essentials of Insurance Law*, 2nd ed. (New York: McGraw-Hill Book Company, 1957), pp. 146/147.
3. Those interested in the details of how particular states' valued policy laws affect the adjustment of losses may wish to consult Philip Gordis, *Property and Casualty Insurance*, 23rd ed. (Cincinnati: The Rough Notes Company, 1976), pp. 66-68.

CHAPTER 12

Loss Sharing Provisions

INTRODUCTION

The insurable interest doctrine, policy limits, and loss valuation provisions—discussed in previous chapters—govern the *maximum* amounts that insurers might be required to pay for the losses covered by a particular policy. However, when insured entities are permitted or required to retain a portion of the losses they incur, they actually recover less than the maximum amounts that would otherwise be payable. They participate, in effect, in "loss-sharing" arrangements with the insurer.

Loss sharing is involved when retention is combined with insurance. As noted in Chapter 3, combining retention with insurance may take the form of (1) coverage limitations, (2) inadequate insurance, and (3) deductible or excess insurance. The first type of partial retention—coverage limitations—is a subject dealt with elsewhere in this volume. In this chapter, emphasis is on the latter two ways in which retention and insurance are combined.

Inadequate insurance was briefly described in Chapter 3 as purchasing insurance that is less than the maximum possible loss. This variety of partial retention, it was noted, may occur because the insurer refuses to issue higher limits, because the insured does not want to pay the premium for higher limits, or because either party did not properly estimate the maximum possible loss exposure. It was noted that most liability insurance must be considered "inadequate," because it is usually impossible to determine the maximum possible liability loss.

Many ramifications of inadequate insurance were not addressed in Chapter 3. The first part of this chapter will expand on insurance policy provisions that come into play when inadequate insurance is involved.

159

Deductible insurance was described in Chapter 3 as an approach in which the insured retains a "relatively small" part of the maximum possible loss. *Excess insurance*, it was noted, differs slightly in that the insured is retaining a "relatively large part" of the maximum possible loss. It was also noted that the terms "deductible" and "excess" are sometimes used interchangeably, and that the portion that is retained can be referred to as a "deductible," regardless of whether deductible or excess insurance is involved. Deductibles are the second major subject to be examined in this chapter.

Note the shift in emphasis between Chapter 3 and this chapter. When partial retention was introduced, it was examined in a risk management context. Discussion was from the perspective of a risk manager attempting to select the most desirable combination of financing techniques for treating loss exposures. Here, the context is one of examining the various provisions found in insurance policies to determine why they are used and how they address the needs of both insurers and insurance buyers. The first major section of this chapter, "insurance-to-value requirements," will address insurance policy provisions intended to discourage inadequate insurance and how insurance contracts handle inadequate insurance when it exists.

INSURANCE-TO-VALUE REQUIREMENTS

As the phrase implies, "insurance-to-value requirement" generally refers to a relationship between the *minimum amount of insurance required* and the *insurable value* of the property. Though "insurance to value" is frequently required by underwriters at the inception and renewal dates of property insurance policies, underwriting practices are not under examination in this text. This section is concerned solely with *policy provisions* (and ocean marine insurance customs which have the effect of policy provisions) that become operative as insurance-to-value requirements *at the time of loss*. To be considered here are coinsurance clauses, replacement cost coverage requirements, and agreed amount clauses—all of which are used with property insurance coverages but not with liability coverages, for reasons to be discussed.

Coinsurance Clauses

With respect to property insurance coverage written on an indemnity basis, the most common type of insurance-to-value requirement is a *coinsurance clause*, in which the *minimum amount of insurance required* is expressed as a *percentage of the property's insurable value at the time of loss*. If the insured carries insurance limits that fail to meet the requirement, the insured will suffer a "penalty" for underinsurance by partially retaining the financial consequences of an insured loss. In exchange for making the coinsurance clause a part of the policy, the insured is granted a reduction in the rate for each unit of coverage.

(The term "coinsurance" is also used in health insurance, but *in an entirely different sense*. Readers should be alert to this fact. Likewise, coinsurance clauses should *not* be confused with the replacement cost clause in residential building insurance, which was briefly introduced in Chapter 11.)

Objectives of Coinsurance Clauses   Coinsurance clauses are intended to encourage insurance to value, achieve a degree of equity among policyholders, and maintain premium adequacy for insurers.

Encouraging Insurance to Value.   Property insurers have always been plagued by the problems associated with "underinsurance." It is a well-known fact that many properties are insured for considerably less than 100 percent of their insurable values. The problems of underinsurance become belatedly obvious to the comparatively few policyholders who suffer large or total losses, as well as to claims representatives, producers, regulators, and others who deal directly with the insuring public. Insurers and their representatives have made concerted efforts to appraise properties where feasible and to recommend appropriate coverage amounts. The trouble is, many consumers do not follow the advice; the appraisals become outdated quickly; and appraisals are often so expensive as to be impractical, especially when relatively small dollar values are involved. In any event, many property owners maintain inadequate amounts of coverage.

Achieving a Degree of Rate Equity.   A second and closely related problem has to do with the matter of rate equity. Different insureds purchase sharply different amounts of insurance for similar property. Some policyholders buy coverage amounts equal to 100 percent of their property's insurable value, while others buy amounts equal to 80 percent, 60 percent, 40 percent, or even smaller percentages of insurable value. Because small losses occur much more frequently than large losses, any significant differences among insurance-to-value ratios could be unfair to those who purchase high percentages of insurance to value.

The following illustration will demonstrate why differing insurance-to-value ratios among insureds might be unfair. Consider two identical sprinklered fire-resistive office buildings, Building A and Building B, each with an insurable value of $500,000. Although the maximum possible loss to each building is $500,000, the maximum probable loss by fire might be as low as $150,000. Assume the owner of

Building A insures it for $400,000, while the owner of Building B insures it for $200,000. If both building owners were charged the same annual rate of $.40 per $100 of coverage, one would pay a premium of $1,600 per year, and the other would pay $800 per year. This premium structure would not be fair to the owner who insured Building A for $400,000. Small losses are much more frequent than large losses. For $800, the owner of Building B would be able to purchase insurance that would pay in full for all probable losses. The owner of Building A is very unlikely to use the additional protection obtained by doubling his or her insurance premium. Coinsurance clauses help overcome this inequity.

Maintaining Premium Adequacy. A coinsurance clause is one convenient method of simultaneously addressing the problems of coverage adequacy and rate equity without sacrificing premium adequacy. As an inducement to insure property for a higher ratio of insurance to value, a policyholder who is willing to accept the terms of a coinsurance clause is charged a lower rate per unit of coverage. The lower rate per unit of coverage then results in a premium that is substantially less than the same amount of coverge would cost without a coinsurance clause. In exchange for the bargain rate, however, the policyholder agrees to the terms of the coinsurance clause. If the policyholder is carrying less than the *minimum amount of insurance required* at the time of loss, the policyholder will be a "coinsurer" of the loss and will pay a "coinsurance penalty" by retaining a portion of the loss. This "penalty" keeps the insurance recovery in line with the premium, and thus serves the objective of premium adequacy.

The Coinsurance Formula When a coinsurance clause is in effect, losses are paid in accordance with the following general formula:

$$\text{Maximum amount payable by the insurer} = \frac{\text{Amount of insurance carried at the time of loss}}{\text{Minimum amount of insurance required at time of loss}} \times \text{Amount of the loss}$$

Note carefully the following key points:

- The *minimum amount of insurance required at the time of loss* = the stipulated coinsurance percentage × the property's insurable value at the time of loss.

- The property's *insurable value at the time of loss* = (1) the actual cash value of the property (if ACV coverage), or (2) the replacement cost of the property (if RC coverage).

- The *amount of the loss* = (1) the ACV of the damaged property (if ACV coverage), or (2) the cost, at the time of loss, of repairing or replacing the damaged or destroyed property (if RC coverage).

- The *maximum amount payable by the insurer* will never be more than (1) the amount of the loss or (2) the applicable policy limit, whichever is *less*.

To illustrate, suppose a building's actual cash value is $100,000 just before a loss. It is insured in a policy that agrees to pay losses on an actual cash value basis and contains an 80 percent coinsurance clause. In this case:

- the *insurable value at the time of loss* of the building is $100,000 (its actual cash value at the time of loss), and

- the *minimum amount of insurance required at the time of loss* is $80,000 (the stipulated coinsurance percentage times the building's actual cash value at the time of loss = 80 percent times $100,000 = $80,000).

If the insured has a covered loss, the amount paid by the insurer will depend on the *amount of insurance carried at the time of loss*. For example, if the amount of loss was $1,000 and the insured carried $60,000 of coverage, the insurer would pay $750, determined as follows:

$$\frac{\$60,000 \text{ (amount of insurance carried)}}{\$80,000 \text{ (minimum amount of insurance required)}} \times \$1,000 \text{ (loss)} = \begin{array}{c} \$750 \text{ (the amount} \\ \text{payable by} \\ \text{the insurer)} \end{array}$$

Not having carried the *minimum amount of insurance required* by the coinsurance clause, the policyholder must bear $250 of the loss, thus becoming a "coinsurer." If the insured had met the minimum requirement by carrying $80,000 of coverage, the insurer would pay the full $1,000 of the loss, determined as follows:

$$\frac{\$80,000 \text{ (amount of insurance carried)}}{\$80,000 \text{ (minimum amount of insurance required)}} \times \$1,000 = \$1,000$$

The latter situation illustrates another key point:

- *The insured who carries at least the required minimum amount of coverage is never penalized with respect to any loss that is equal to or less than the policy limit.*

However, the insured who merely complies with an 80 percent minimum requirement will not be adequately protected against losses that exceed the policy limit. To illustrate, again assume that the owner of a $100,000 building has insured it for the required minimum amount of $80,000, but this time a fire totally destroys the building. The result would be:

$$\frac{\$80,000}{\$80,000} \times \$100,000 = \$100,000$$

but the *maximum amount payable by the insurer* will not be more than the policy limit of $80,000.

While not penalized *by the coinsurance clause* itself, the policyholder in the above example is still *underinsured* by $20,000, since the $80,000 of coverage merely complied with the prescribed *minimum* of 80 percent of the building's full actual cash value; it did not provide adequate protection for a total loss.

If the policyholder had carried $100,000 of coverage at the time of loss, the insurer would have paid $100,000 in the event of the building's total destruction, determined as follows:

$$\frac{\$100,000}{\$80,000} \times \$100,000 = \$125,000$$

but the insurer would not pay more than the policy limit of $100,000.

Because of the application of the policy limit, if the policyholder had carried $60,000 of coverage at the time of loss, the insurer would have paid only $60,000 for a total loss, determined as follows:

$$\frac{\$60,000}{\$80,000} \times \$100,000 = \$75,000$$

but the insurer would not pay more than the policy limit of $60,000.

The effects of the coinsurance formula are summarized in Exhibit 12-1. Careful study of this exhibit will reveal that:

- Any insured will be penalized (underinsured) whenever the *policy limit* is less than the *insurable value of a loss*, whether or not a coinsurance clause applies.
- The coinsurance clause merely imposes an additional penalty when both the *loss* and the *amount of insurance carried at the time of loss* are less than the *minimum amount of insurance required*.

Exhibit 12-1
Effects of an 80 Percent Coinsurance Clause on Actual Cash Value Coverage of a Policy with No Deductible

(a) Amount of Insurance Carried at the Time of Loss	(b) Amount of Insurance Required at Time of Loss	(c) Loss Situation	(d) Coinsurance Penalty Applies?	(e) Maximum Amount Payable by the Insurer[1]
100% of ACV	80% of ACV	Partial loss of any size	No	The ACV of the loss
100% of ACV	80% of ACV	Total loss	No	The ACV of the loss
More than 80% but less than 100% of ACV	80% of ACV	Partial loss equal to or less than the policy limit	No	The ACV of the loss
More than 80% but less than 100% of ACV	80% of ACV	Any loss greater than the policy limit, including a total loss	No	The policy limit
80% of ACV	80% of ACV	Partial loss equal to or less than the policy limit	No	The ACV of the loss
80% of ACV	80% of ACV	Any loss greater than the policy limit, including a total loss	No	The policy limit
Less than 80% of ACV	80% of ACV	Partial loss that is less than the amount required	Yes	$\dfrac{\text{Amt. carried}}{\text{Amt. required}}$ X Amt. of loss
Less than 80% of ACV	80% of ACV	Partial loss equal to the amount required	Yes, but formula yields same amount as the policy limit	The policy limit
Less than 80% of ACV	80% of ACV	Any loss greater than the amount required, including a total loss	Yes, but formula yields an amount larger than the policy limit	The policy limit
Any amount	80% of ACV	No loss	No	Zero (no loss)
Any amount	No coinsurance requirement	Any size of loss	N/A	The ACV of the loss or the policy limit, whichever is less

1. Note that all entries in column (e) refer to the *maximum* amount payable by the insurer. Remember, most actual cash value coverages give the insurer the option to settle on the basis of repair or replacement cost if either would be smaller than the ACV or the policy limit. But settlement options do not alter the effects of a coinsurance clause per se.

- The coinsurance clause has absolutely no effect on recovery for any size of loss, even a total loss, as long as the property remains insured for its full *insurable value.*

Relation to Valued Policy Forms   Coinsurance clauses are not normally found in valued policy forms. As explained in the previous chapter, valued coverages may be purchased for certain types of personal property, and they are required for some buildings by the valued policy laws of a number of states. In either case, the amount paid for a *total* loss is the amount of insurance that was entered in the declarations or schedule.

In valued policies, *partial* losses of personal property are usually governed by policy provisions that base the settlements on a percentage of the amount of insurance, depending on the degree of damage. Since insured items of personal property are presumably insured for their full value, coinsurance clauses are not considered necessary. Furthermore, where valued policies are required for commercial buildings, some of the state laws would bar an insurer from enforcing any coinsurance clause in the policy.

In short, the prevailing view is that valued coverages effectively provide insurance to value and are a substitute for coinsurance clauses. It follows that coinsurance clauses are used almost entirely in connection with indemnity-type property insurance coverages.

Coinsurance Percentage Used   An 80 percent coinsurance clause was assumed in the earlier illustrations because it is probably the most popular of all the percentage-of-value clauses. Nonetheless, the insured often has a choice of several options in selecting a coinsurance percentage. The coinsurance percentage may vary from 10 percent to 100 percent, depending largely on the nature of the coverages, the types of property, the insured perils, and the underwriting rules that are involved. For example, the coinsurance percentages used with burglary and sprinkler leakage coverages are typically at the lower end of the range, for reasons to be explained later, while business interruption is near the middle, and 80 percent, 90 percent, and 100 percent are the most commonly used coinsurance percentages with direct damage coverages on commercial buildings and their contents. Regardless of which particular percentage is stipulated, the principles are essentially the same. As shown in the basic formulas presented at the beginning of this chapter, the minimum amount of insurance required is computed by multiplying the property's insurable value by "the stipulated coinsurance percentage." Inserting any given percentage for the quoted phrase will not otherwise alter the rest of the coinsurance calculations. If the stipulated coinsurance percentage is, say, 90 percent, Exhibit 12-1 may be revised simply by substituting 90 percent wherever 80 percent now appears in columns (a) and (b); the general effects of a 90 percent clause are already accommodated by the Exhibit, because the effects are not expressed in dollars. However, Exhibit 12-1 presupposes actual cash value coverage. Coinsurance clauses are also used with replacement cost coverage.

Relation to Replacement Cost Coverage When *replacement cost* coverage is written, the coinsurance formula itself remains unchanged. However, the property's "insurable value at the time of loss" is the cost of replacing the property, at the time of loss, with *new* property of like kind and quality. And "the amount of the loss," for formula purposes, is the cost of repairing or replacing the damaged or destroyed property with new materials or property of like kind and quality at the time of loss. These two definitions were shown as alternatives to the actual cash value definitions in the earlier listing of the basic formula. If replacement cost coverage is written subject to an 80 percent coinsurance clause, as is sometimes the case, Exhibit 12-1 is easily corrected by substituting the letters "RC" (replacement cost) for "ACV" (actual cash value) wherever the letters ACV now appear in the exhibit. The general effects of coinsurance would then be accurate for replacement cost coverage.

In summary, while actual cash value and replacement cost coverages involve the same fundamental coinsurance principles, their application to replacement cost coverage differs in at least two respects:

- In determining the *minimum amount of insurance required* by coinsurance clauses, the coinsurance percentage is applied to the replacement cost of the property.
- The replacement cost valuation method is used to determine the *amount of the loss*.

Other aspects of coinsurance clauses are unique to insurance on certain specific types of property or perils. These will be described later.

Evaluation of Coinsurance Clauses

By means of minimum coverage requirements, rate incentives, and penalties for noncompliance, coinsurance clauses seek to encourage insurance to value, maintain premium adequacy for the insurer, and achieve a degree of equity among policyholders. In practice, the coinsurance concept does not completely meet all these objectives. Critics are quick to point out that coinsurance clauses suffer from the following disadvantages:

(1) *Coinsurance clauses are among the least understood property insurance coverage provisions.*

(2) *Coinsurance clauses penalize only the underinsureds who have losses, yet other underinsureds who are subject to coinsurance clauses will also enjoy lower rates, without penalty, for the entire duration of each loss-free time period.* In those lines of insurance dominated by partial losses, it was shown that rates should be a function of the ratio of insurance carried to insurable value. Coinsurance clauses do nothing to penalize those loss-free insureds who enjoy the lower "coinsurance rate" but do not comply with the requirements of the clause.

(3) *Coinsurance clauses discriminate against those who carry more insurance than required by the stipulated coinsurance percentage.* For example, suppose an insured who is subject to a 90 percent coinsurance clause elects to insure the property for 100 percent of its insurable value. Such an insured will receive only the 90 percent coinsurance rate credit. True, the insured could insist on a 100 percent coinsurance clause (and the correspondingly lower rate), but to do so is to take the chance of being penalized for even a slight increase in the property's insurable value.

(4) *Coinsurance clauses give rise to numerous disputes in the loss settlement process.* Inevitably, there are some arguments concerning the valuation of losses, apart from whether coinsurance clauses are applicable. But coinsurance clauses also result in disputes over the insurable value of all of the property, damaged and undamaged, at the time of loss—the basis to which the coinsurance percentage is applied in determining the required amount of insurance.

(5) *The policyholder who suffers a loss near the end of the policy period is penalized more severely by coinsurance than the policyholder who suffers a loss near the beginning of the policy period.* When a coinsurance penalty is imposed, it is customarily based on the relationship between the amount of insurance carried and the insurable value of the property *at the time of loss.* Most property insurance policies have dollar limits that are fixed or constant during the policy year, during which inflation can sharply increase the insurable value of the property. Although these statements are correct, the criticism itself is not very accurate. As respects the partial losses of underinsured policyholders, the criticism is not altogether valid; as respects total losses, the criticism should be leveled at fixed-dollar limits, not coinsurance.

To take a simple example, suppose a building has an insurable value of $100,000 at the beginning of the year and a $110,000 insurable value at the end of the year. It is insured for $60,000, throughout the year, in spite of an 80 percent coinsurance clause in the policy. This means that the policyholder was only insured for 75 percent of the required minimum at the beginning of the year ($60,000/$80,000 = 75%) and 68.2 percent of the required minimum at the end of the year ($60,000/$88,000 = 68.2%). Accordingly, this underinsured policyholder would be paid $750 of a $1,000 partial loss that happened near the start of the year, but only $682 of a $1,000 partial loss that happened near the end of the year. Right? Not necessarily. The example was "rigged"—to underscore an assumption that critics of coinsurance do not always make explicit—by expressing the loss amount in fixed dollars, rather than the degree of damage. However, a given degree of damage will normally cost more to repair or replace at a later date. Under *replacement cost coverage*, the $1,000 dollar loss would have increased to $1,100 by the end of the year, using the same rate of increase as the insurable value of the building. Hence, the insurer would have paid $750 for the same degree of damage, whether it happened at the start or the end of the year (75% × $1,000 = $750 = 68.2% × $1,100).

Under *actual cash value coverage*, the amount paid by the insurer would depend on the relationship between the rate of depreciation and the rate of inflation. In the most likely case, the $100 increase in repair or replacement would be reduced by, say, $50 of depreciation, thus resulting in a $714 payment by the insurer ($1,050 × 68%) for a year-end loss, which is less than the $750 that would have been paid had the same degree of damage happened at the first of the year. The critics of coinsurance have a valid point, then, but only with respect to partial losses under *actual cash value coverage* where the fixed-limits policyholder is not in compliance with the coinsurance clause throughout the year.

As respects total losses, the underinsured policyholder will be penalized by a fixed dollar limit, not the coinsurance clause per se, whether the loss happens at the start or the end of the year. This is equally true under both actual cash value and replacement cost coverages. In the earlier example, the policyholder would have a $100,000 or a $110,000 *total* loss, depending on whether it happened near the start or the end of the year. But the insurer would only pay the maximum policy limit of $60,000 in either case.

Perhaps because it is natural to be more concerned about

policyholders who attempt to comply with policy provisions, the most common variation of the time-of-loss criticism is that coinsurance imposes on conscientious policyholders (and their advisers) the burden of *maintaining* the required minimum ratio of insurance to value, a particularly troublesome burden in periods of rapid inflation. For example, if the owner of a $100,000 building initially complied with an 80 percent coinsurance clause by insuring the building for $80,000 at the outset, partial losses would at first be paid in full by the insurer. By year end, when the insurable value has jumped to $110,000, it would then require a minimum of $88,000 of coverage, just to get partial losses paid in full, and the policyholder would still be $22,000 underinsured for a total loss (as opposed to $20,000 underinsured for a total loss at the beginning of the year). However, this is once again primarily the fault of fixed dollar policy limits, not of the coinsurance concept. A policy with *variable* limits, as discussed in the previous chapter, would alleviate this criticism.

(6) *The size of the rate credits given for some of the coinsurance percentages are based on incomplete statistical data.*

(7) *Coinsurance clauses with stipulated percentages of 90 percent or less tend to perpetuate irrational purchasing decisions by implying that the experts recommend or condone the insuring of property for less than its full insurable value.* This is especially true of the popular 80 percent clause and the even smaller coinsurance percentages allowed in some lines of insurance.

Coinsurance was invented partly to encourage more people to purchase higher ratios of insurance to value. However, the widespread existence of underinsurance attests to the fact that, while many people are willing to attach the clause (and get the lower rate), fewer are willing to maintain the required amount of insurance. Equally important, all those who carry coverage amounts of less than 100 percent of value are underinsured for *total* losses. The familiar situation is a policyholder who insures for 80 percent of value on the theory that, since "total losses do not happen very often," full coverage "is not worth the additional premium it requires." Such a decision could be dismissed as a mere willingness to gamble, if the policyholder truly understood the implications of the decision, but all too many policyholders base such decisions on a misinterpretation of probability. True, "total losses do not happen very often." Nonetheless, *any one* of the policyholders could be among the unfortunate few who experience a total loss, and probability computations do *not* tell us who they will be. If a $100,000 building, insured for $80,000, is totally destroyed, it will be very little consolation for the owner to be told, at that point, that "$100,000 building losses do not happen very often." The typical owner would be unwilling to bear $20,000 of the loss, given the choice between a $20,000 immediate loss and the additional premium for full coverage. Indeed, this very same policyholder would typically reject a *deductible* of 20 percent of the building's insurable value, even though the premium savings would be greater than the additional premium to insure to full insurable value.

In any case, the critics of coinsurance do have a point. For whatever reasons, rational or irrational, many policyholders and producers are inclined to insure their property for less than its full insurable value. The use of smaller coinsurance percentages does tend to perpetuate the practice. Presumably, these critics would be better satisfied if there were only two choices, a 100 percent coinsurance clause or no coinsurance clause.

All seven of the foregoing criticisms have merits worth pondering. They would be more compelling if coinsurance clauses were always mandatory. However, a number of alternatives to coinsurance are now available in the marketplace, and coinsurance clauses are not used at all with some types of property insurance. The extent of their use, as well as the major alternatives, will now be summarized under appropriate headings.

Uses of Coinsurance Clauses

Use in Direct Damage Coverage on Residential Property   In the vast majority of states, coinsurance clauses are *not* used at all in fire and related direct damage coverages on dwellings and household goods. A different kind of insurance-to-value requirement is imposed by policy provisions, as a condition of receiving *replacement cost coverage* on residential property. These replacement cost provisions will be described later in this chapter.

Use in Direct Damage Coverage on Commercial Property Coinsurance clauses have been used for many years in the writing of indemnity-type direct damage fire and allied lines insurance for business firms to cover their real and personal property. Generally, actual cash value coverage may be written:

(1) without a coinsurance clause, but subject to a higher rate per $100 of coverage, or

(2) with an 80 percent, 90 percent, or 100 percent coinsurance clause, which entitles the policyholder to a rate credit corresponding to the coinsurance percentage selected—the higher the percentage, the lower the rate per $100 of coverage.

A coinsurance clause is mandatory in many instances.

When used in connection with direct damage coverages on commercial property, coinsurance clauses utilize the same percentage-of-value requirements and penalties that have already been discussed in detail. A few additional aspects are of importance in applying the coinsurance concept to buildings, movable property (while on land), and ships and their cargoes.

Buildings. Whether direct damage insurance is written on a replacement cost or an actual cash value form, the *building* coverage is usually adjusted to exclude a portion of the realty, whenever a coinsurance clause applies. The typical exclusion reads as follows:

THIS POLICY DOES NOT COVER THE FOLLOWING PROPERTY WHEN SECTION IV—COINSURANCE CLAUSE APPLIES, UNLESS ADDED BY ENDORSEMENT:

1. Cost of excavations, grading or filling;
2. Foundations of buildings, machinery, boilers or engines which foundations are below the undersurface of the lowest basement floor, or where there is no basement, below the surface of the ground;
3. Pilings, piers, pipes, flues, and drains which are underground;
4. Pilings which are below the low water mark.

Note that the above-listed property is excluded only when a coinsurance clause applies to the building coverage. The intention is to exclude property which is seldom damaged by fire, windstorm, hail, and most other perils. Excluding such property has the effect of substantially reducing the required amount of insurance, because it reduces the insurable value of the building for coinsurance purposes. Even so, underground property is not entirely immune from damage by the perils typically covered, especially explosion. If desired by the insured, the excluded property may be "added back" to the policy by endorsement. Then, the required amount of insurance would increase for coinsurance purposes, since the value of the underground property and the cost of excavations would be considered a part of the insurable value of the building.

Earthquake damage is either not covered or else specifically excluded from coverage in virtually all standard building insurance forms. The coverage may be obtained by the purchase of an "earthquake extension endorsement." The endorsement requires a coinsurance clause with an 80 percent minimum coinsurance percentage. It also covers, automatically, "direct loss by earthquake to foundations, excavations and all other portions of the building." Thus, if a policyholder wants earthquake coverage on a building, (1) a coinsurance clause is mandatory and (2) the value of underground property and excavations must be included in the total insurable value of the building to determine the minimum amount of insurance that is required by the coinsurance clause.

Movable Property. Many items of movable commercial property are insured on inland marine ACV forms or valued policy floaters that provide direct damage coverage without a coinsurance requirement. On the other hand, coinsurance clauses are usually found in property policies covering the contents of a specified building. In general, coinsurance clauses are not used as often with personal property coverages as they are with building coverages.

Ships and Their Cargoes. In some lines of insurance, it has long been the understood custom that the insured will purchase coverage equal to 100 percent of value. Where this custom exists, it is the usual practice—without any specific provision in the applicable insurance contract—for the insured's recovery to be reduced by the same proportion that the applicable insurance falls short of the full value of the insured property at the time of any loss. In essence, this practice creates a 100 percent insurance-to-value requirement.

This custom has been most prevalent in ocean marine insurance covering cargoes and hulls. Many United States ocean marine insurance practices originated in English custom and common and statutory law. With respect to insurance to value, the English (and, by importation, the American) custom, as subsequently stated in the 1906 Marine Insurance Act of Great Britain, is:

> Where the assured is insured for an amount less than the insurable value or, in the case of a valued policy, for an amount less than the policy valuation, he is deemed to be his own insurer in respect of the uninsured balance.

Beyond ocean marine insurance, insurance-to-value requirements implied by custom have not found judicial favor in the United States, where the courts generally rely on the principle that the entire agreement between the insurer and the insured must be stated in a written contract. This principle may have its origin in concern for the insurance consumer, uninitiated in the seemingly arcane rules and procedures of insurance. Throughout Europe, however, an implicit 100 percent insurance-to-value requirement, comparable to that in the

British statute just cited, is read into nearly all property insurance contracts, whether issued to business firms or to private individuals.

Use in Sprinkler Leakage Coverage Since specified peril, fixed location property insurance policies do not usually cover most types of water damage, the insured who wants to insure against the peril of damage caused by *accidental* discharge of an automatic sprinkler system must purchase a special endorsement. Sprinkler leakage coverage is available for buildings, specific types of contents, or all contents. The coverage may be written with or without a coinsurance clause. If no coinsurance clause is desired, a *minimum* dollar amount of coverage (often $25,000) must be purchased. If a coinsurance clause is desired, the insured is given a choice of coinsurance percentages, ranging from 100 percent to as low as 10 percent of the property's value. Most buyers opt for lower coinsurance percentages, such as 10 percent or 25 percent. With regard to sprinkler leakage damage, the smaller percentages correspond roughly to the probable loss severity.

If the insured so desires, different coinsurance percentages may be used for different categories of property. For example, an insured could have a 25 percent coinsurance clause on the contents and a 10 percent coinsurance clause on the building. When a coinsurance clause applies to buildings, there is the usual exclusion pertaining to underground property and excavations, as well as the usual opportunity to eliminate the exclusion by endorsement.

The coinsurance arrangements for sprinkler leakage coverage are a good bit more flexible than they are for other coverages. Otherwise, their general effects are the same as the percentage-of-value clauses previously discussed.

Use in Mercantile Open Stock Burglary Coverage One unique application of coinsurance is customary in connection with "mercantile open stock burglary coverage," which is designed to protect businesses against the stealing of merchandise, furniture, fixtures, and equipment during the hours when the premises are closed.

The coinsurance clause of "MOS" burglary coverage is unusual in two respects. First, the coinsurance percentage varies by *territory*, in recognition of the fact that larger burglary losses are more likely in some geographical areas than they are in others. Second, in addition to the stipulated coinsurance percentage, a dollar "coinsurance limit" is specified. This coinsurance limit represents the dollar amount of insurance that will always satisfy the minimum coinsurance coverage requirement, regardless of the coinsurance percentage. Within any given territory, the coinsurance limit varies by *type of property* insured. Higher coinsurance limits are set for valuable property that is relatively easy to steal in large quantities. Lower coinsurance limits are set for bulky property that has less value. Thus, a $30,000 limit might be set for jewelry stores, while a $7,500 limit might be set for a manufacturer of heavy machinery, or an even smaller limit, such as $2,000, might be set for a bakery.

In applying the coinsurance formula to a mercantile open stock loss, the *minimum amount of insurance required at the time of loss* is either:

(1) the dollar *coinsurance limit,* or
(2) the *coinsurance percentage* times the property's *insurable value at the time of loss,*

whichever is *less.*

To illustrate, assume that a given territory has an 80 percent *coinsurance percentage.* The type of merchandise in question has a required *coinsurance limit* of $15,000. As long as the insured carries at least $15,000 of open stock insurance, there will be no coinsurance penalty, and the *coinsurance percentage* is irrelevant. For instance, if the actual cash value of the insured merchandise is $30,000 at the time of loss, the *coinsurance percentage* would seem to require at least $24,000 of coverage ($30,000 × 80% = $24,000), but the *coinsurance limit* of $15,000 is less. If the insured is carrying $15,000 of coverage at the time of loss, the insured will not be penalized by the coinsurance clause, because a coverage amount equal to or greater than the dollar *coinsurance limit* will always satisfy the requirement.

On the other hand, if the insured is carrying less than the specified *coinsurance limit,* the *coinsurance percentage* becomes operative, and the insured may or may not be penalized, depending on the relationship between the amount of insurance carried and the actual cash value of the property. A penalty would be imposed, for example, when $17,500 of merchandise is insured for $7,000 on a policy that has an 80 percent *coinsurance percentage* and a $15,000 *coinsurance limit.* In this case:

(1) the *coinsurance limit* = $15,000, and
(2) the *coinsurance percentage* times the property's insurable value at the time of loss (80% × $17,500) = $14,000.

Because $14,000 is *less* than $15,000, the *minimum amount of insurance required at the time of the loss* is $14,000. Thus, the maximum amount payable by the insurer would be determined by the *coinsurance percentage.* The maximum amount payable would be $7,000/$14,000, or 50 percent of any loss (subject, of course, to the $7,000 policy limits).

As the foregoing examples illustrate, insureds with a larger exposure are not required to carry any more burglary coverage than the dollar coinsurance limit for the type of property in question; smaller insureds are not penalized merely because the value of their merchandise is less than the dollar coinsurance limit. The *coinsurance percentage* reflects the burglary loss exposures of a particular territory. The *coinsurance limit* reflects the burglary loss exposure of a particular type of merchandise. Once these are established for, say, jewelry merchants in Chicago, the percentage requirement and the dollar limit are applied in a fashion that achieves a degree of equity among smaller and larger jewelers in Chicago.

In summary, the insured who complies with either the requirements imposed by the *coinsurance percentage* or those imposed by the *coinsurance limit*—whichever is *less*—will not be penalized by coinsurance (though the insured's policy limits may be inadequate for larger losses). The insured whose coverage falls below both minimums becomes a "coinsurer" of the burglary loss, according to the same basic coinsurance formula used in fire insurance.

Use in Business Interruption Coverage The use of coinsurance is not limited to direct damage and burglary coverages. Coinsurance clauses also may be found in some policies covering *indirect* losses, i.e., losses which are the indirect result of fire or some other covered peril. Business interruption coverage is among the most popular of the "time element" forms of indirect loss insurance.

Business interruption insurance is designed for the business firm that would cease to operate or whose operations would be reduced in the event of damage to insured property. Generally, the insurable value of the loss is measured by the decline in earnings, less noncontinuing expenses, during the period of shutdown.

The coverage is sometimes written on a valued policy form, in which case there is no coinsurance clause. In the event of a total shutdown, the policyholder is paid the agreed amount per day, per week, or per month of shutdown, subject to a stipulated maximum number of days or weeks, depending on the form used. In the event of a partial shutdown where the policyholder is operating at, say, 50 percent of capacity, the policyholder would be paid 50 percent of the benefit amount agreed upon for a total shutdown.

More often, business interruption insurance is written on an indemnity form which provides reimbursement on the basis of the actual loss sustained. Some of the forms do not contain a coinsurance clause. Under the forms that do contain the usual percentage-of-value coinsurance clause, the insured may choose a 50, 60, 70, or 80 percent coinsurance percentage. In determining the minimum amount of insurance required at the time of loss, the stipulated coinsurance percentage is multiplied by the *gross* earnings that probably would have been earned (had there been no shutdown) during the *twelve-month period* beginning with the day of shutdown. The coinsurance percentage then should reflect that portion of twelve months which it would take for the business to reconstruct after a total loss (assuming earnings are uniformly spread across the year). For example, a possible six-month interruption would suggest the use of a 50 percent coinsurance clause.

Insurance-to-Value Requirements in Extra Expense Insurance

Extra expense coverage is designed to reimburse a business firm for the extraordinary expenses of continuing to operate when its property has been damaged by a covered peril. Generally, the relevant insurable value is the potential amount of the loss—the extra expense of continuing to operate the business as normally as possible during the period of time required, with the exercise of due diligence and dispatch, to repair or replace the damaged property—which necessarily must be an estimate until a loss actually occurs. Making such an estimate is much more subjective and difficult than determining potential amount of a direct loss to a building or an item of personal property. Therefore, coinsurance clauses are not used with extra expense coverage, because it would be unfair to penalize policyholders for underinsurance when the maximum possible loss is so difficult to estimate.

This does not mean that the notion of insurance to value is ignored altogether. Extra expense insurance resembles direct damage insurance in that small losses (say, one month or less) occur much more frequently than large losses. Likewise, it is considered desirable to encourage insurance to value. The extra expense policy contains month-by-month limits which are expressed as a percent of the amount of coverage carried. For instance, one popular form is written with the following limits of liability:

(1) 40 percent of the amount of the policy when the period of restoration is not in excess of one month;
(2) 80 percent when the period of restoration is in excess of one month, but not in excess of two months; or
(3) 100 percent when the period of restoration is in excess of two months.

These limits of recovery are cumulative. The policy does not contain any type of coinsurance clause, as recovery is limited to a stipulated amount per month as indicated above.

With coverage on this basis, a policyholder would need a $20,000 policy limit just to have adequate coverage for an expected first-month extra expense loss of $8,000 ($20,000 × 40% = $8,000). By this method, the policyholder is given the incentive to maintain coverage amounts that will be adequate for larger losses. To the extent that policyholders do so, insurance to value is achieved.

Insurance-to-Value Requirements in Homeowners Insurance

In most states, homeowners policies provide coverages that are not subject to coinsurance clauses. The Section I or property insurance coverages are designated as:

Coverage A	Dwelling
Coverage B	Other Structures
Coverage C	Personal Property
Coverage D	Loss of Use

Since the insurance-to-value requirements vary by type of coverage, they will be analyzed under separate headings.

Dwelling Buildings It should be noted at the outset that the amount of insurance on a dwelling usually must meet the minimum requirements imposed by insurers and mortgagees. To qualify for homeowners insurance, the policyholder must insure the dwelling for at least the minimum dollar amount that is prescribed for a particular form by the underwriting rules of the insurer. Furthermore, most dwellings are purchased subject to the terms of a mortgage loan, and the commercial lending institution (mortgagee) invariably requires the mortgagor to insure the dwelling for an amount that is at least equal to the unpaid balance of the loan. This practice often results in "overinsurance" when a dwelling is purchased with only a 10 percent down payment (as is often permitted under FHA and VA guaranteed loans).

For example, if a new dwelling is bought for $90,000 with a $9,000 down payment and an $81,000 mortgage loan, the dwelling must be insured for at least $81,000. However, the land may be worth $15,000, in which case the dwelling itself may have a replacement cost value of only $75,000.

In contrast, consider the homeowner who purchased a dwelling ten years ago for $30,000. Because of inflation, the replacement cost value of the building may have increased to $75,000 while the unpaid mortgage balance has decreased to $20,000. If this homeowner bought only enough coverage to equal the unpaid mortgage balance, the coverage would be considerably less than the insurable value of the dwelling. The policyholder would be seriously underinsured.

With respect to the insured dwelling (Coverage A) and other

structures (Coverage B), the relevant policy provisions are reproduced below.

Loss settlement. Covered property losses are settled as follows:

Buildings under Coverage A or B at replacement cost without deduction for depreciation, subject to the following:

(1) If at the time of loss the amount of insurance in this policy on the damaged building is 80% or more of the full replacement cost of the building immediately prior to the loss, we will pay the cost of repair or replacement, without deduction for depreciation, but not exceeding the smallest of the following amounts:
   (a) the limit of liability under this policy applying to the building;
   (b) the replacement cost of that part of the building damaged for equivalent construction and use on the same premises; or
   (c) the amount actually and necessarily spent to repair or replace the damaged building.

(2) If at the time of loss the amount of insurance in this policy on the damaged building is less than 80% of the full replacement cost of the building immediately prior to the loss, we will pay the larger of the following amounts, but not exceeding the limit of liability under this policy applying to the building:
   (a) the actual cash value of that part of the building damaged; or
   (b) that proportion of the cost to repair or replace, without deduction for depreciation, of that part of the building damaged, which the total amount of insurance in this policy on the damaged building bears to 80% of the replacement cost of the building.

(3) In determining the amount of insurance required to equal 80% of the full replacement cost of the building immediately prior to the loss, you shall disregard the value of excavations, foundations, piers and other supports which are below the undersurface of the lowest basement floor or, where there is no basement, which are below the surface of the ground inside the foundation walls, and underground flues, pipes, wiring and drains.

(4) When the cost to repair or replace the damage is more than $1,000 or more than 5% of the amount of insurance in this policy on the building, whichever is less, we will pay no more than the actual cash value of the damage until actual repair or replacement is completed.

(5) You may disregard the replacement cost loss settlement provisions and make claim under this policy for loss or damage to buildings on an actual cash value basis and then make claim within 180 days after loss for any additional liability on a replacement cost basis.

The policyholder who is aware of these provisions has a strong incentive to maintain an adequate amount of insurance on the dwelling. Subject to the policy limits, and assuming repairs or replacement are actually completed, all building losses—whether small, large, or total—

will be settled on a *replacement cost basis,* provided that the damaged building is insured, at the time of loss, for *at least 80 percent of its full replacement cost.* If this condition is *not* met, the insured will *not* receive full replacement cost coverage; instead, all building losses will be settled on the basis of

(1) the actual cash value of the loss, or, *if larger,*
(2) a proportion of the repair or replacement cost, based upon the ratio of insurance to 80 percent of replacement value.

In determining the replacement cost of the building for the purpose of applying the aforementioned provisions, the value of excavations and property such as underground pipes is ignored.

For example, assume that a dwelling has a replacement cost of $100,000 (not including underground pipes, excavations, and so forth valued at $6,000). The owner insures the dwelling for $100,000 under a homeowners form containing the loss settlement provisions referred to above. Whether the owner sustained a covered dwelling loss of $10,000, $50,000, or $100,000, the loss would be settled on the basis of its full repair or replacement cost (disregarding deductibles).

Suppose the owner also has a detached garage with a replacement cost of $8,000. The homeowners policy usually provides a Coverage B or "other structures" limit of 10 percent of the amount of insurance on the dwelling. Therefore, in this case assume the declarations show a $10,000 separate limit on the detached garage. Since the owner has insured the garage for at least 80 percent of its replacement cost, all garage losses would also be settled on the basis of their full repair or replacement cost.

In the case of losses in excess of $1,000 (repair or replacement cost) or 5 percent of the amount of insurance on the covered building, replacement cost coverage is not provided "until actual repair or replacement is completed." This latter condition would apply here to any dwelling loss in excess of $1,000 (since 5% × $100,000 = $5,000) or to any garage loss in excess of $500 (since 5% × $10,000 = $500, which is less than the $1,000 alternative). Alternatively, suppose the owner had insured the dwelling building for $80,000, and had a limit of $8,000 on the detached garage. The owner's building losses would still be settled on a replacement cost basis, but

(1) completion of repair or replacement would be required in order to get replacement cost for any garage loss in excess of $400 (5% × $8,000);
(2) the insurer would pay no more than $8,000, the applicable limit, for any loss to the garage;

(3) completion of repair or replacement would be required in order to get replacement cost for any dwelling loss in excess of $1,000; and

(4) the insurer would not pay more than $80,000, the applicable policy limit, for any loss to the dwelling building.

In contrast, suppose the above owner had insured the same dwelling for $60,000, and the garage for $6,000, and the dwelling had an actual cash value of $40,000 at the time of loss. A tornado totally destroys both the dwelling and the detached garage. Since the owner is carrying dwelling insurance of *less than* 80 percent of the dwelling's replacement cost, all dwelling building losses will be settled, up to the policy limit, on the basis of the *larger of* (1) the ACV of the loss or (2) that proportion of the repair or replacement cost which the limit on that building is to 80 percent of that building's total replacement cost. Therefore, as to the destroyed dwelling, the insurer would pay $60,000, determined as follows. The ACV of the dwelling = $40,000 or, if larger,

$$\frac{\text{Dwelling limit}}{80\% \text{ of the dwelling's replacement cost}} \times \begin{array}{c} \text{The repair or} \\ \text{replacement cost} \\ \text{of the loss} \end{array}$$

$$= \frac{\$60,000}{\$80,000} \times \$100,000 = \$75,000$$

but in no event more than the amount of insurance carried on the dwelling or $60,000.

As to the destroyed garage, assume that it had an actual cash value of $4,000 at the time of loss. The insurer would pay the ACV of the garage, $4,000, or, if larger,

$$\frac{\text{Garage limit}}{80\% \text{ of the garage's replacement cost}} \times \begin{array}{c} \text{The repair or} \\ \text{replacement cost} \\ \text{of the loss} \end{array}$$

$$= \frac{\$6,000}{(80\% \times \$8,000)} \times \$8,000 = \$7,500$$

but in no event more than the amount of insurance carried on the garage or $6,000.

Now, suppose the tornado had not totally destroyed the garage but had severely damaged its roof. Though the damaged portion of the roof had a depreciated or actual cash value of $500, it would cost $1,000 to repair the damage, in which case the insurer would pay the ACV of the loss, $500, or, if larger,

$$\frac{\text{Garage limit}}{80\% \text{ of the garage's replacement cost}} \times \begin{array}{c}\text{The cost of}\\\text{repairing}\\\text{the damage}\end{array}$$

$$= \frac{\$6,000}{\$6,400} \times \$1,000 = \$937.50$$

In this case, the insurer would pay $937.50, which is more than the ACV of the roof damage but less than the full cost of repair.

Note that *the building loss settlement provision of a home-owners policy is not really a coinsurance clause*. When the amount of insurance carried on a covered building is *equal to* 80 percent or more of its replacement cost, all losses up to the policy limit are settled on the basis of the cost to repair or replace, without any deduction for physical depreciation of the building. When a building is insured for *less than* 80 percent of its replacement cost, though underinsured, the policyholder will *at the least* have actual cash value coverage. The ratio alternative of the loss settlement provision cannot penalize the insured by providing coverage for less than actual cash value. It can only *increase* the amount that would otherwise be payable. Furthermore, the ratio notion becomes applicable only in the case of a *partial* loss which has a repair or replacement cost of less than the total amount of insurance carried on the building. In all uses, the policy limit governs the maximum amount payable by the insurer.

The previously described loss settlement provisions are contained in most homeowners forms covering dwelling buildings. When the policy contains an "inflation guard endorsement" or "indexed policy limits," the automatic increases in policy limits help to maintain replacement cost coverage to the extent that they keep pace with rising construction costs.

In the so-called "repair cost" forms now offered by some insurers, the notion of repair or replacement with like kind and quality is redefined to permit "repair or replacement with accepted materials and construction techniques currently in common use." This revised definition serves as the basis for the settlement of all building losses that do not exceed the policy limits, regardless of the ratio of insurance carried to the insurable value of the building. Although there are no insurance-to-value provisions in the policy itself, a crude relationship is usually obtained, at the policy inception date, by the underwriting rule that the dwelling must be insured for an amount equal to at least the market value of the realty. Repair cost homeowners forms are neither as standardized nor as widely used as the traditional replacement cost forms.

For the reasons explained in Chapter 11, some homeowners cannot obtain replacement cost coverage on their dwellings and related buildings. Such homeowners usually purchase an actual cash value form. The standardized actual cash value form does not condition replacement cost coverage on a minimum ratio of insurance-to-value, since it does not provide replacement cost coverage on the building. Nor does the ACV homeowners form contain a coinsurance clause (in most states). In fact, the usual ACV homeowners form does not contain an insurance-to-value policy provision of any kind. The policyholder is free to insure the dwelling for any amount that will satisfy the insurer.

All of the foregoing comments pertain to the insurance-to-value provisions, if any, in policies which contain upper *dollar* limits on the amounts of recovery. Maximum dollar limits have long been universal in both ACV and replacement cost homeowners forms, including those which have been endorsed to provide dollar limits that automatically increase during the policy period. However, as mentioned in the previous chapter, a few insurers are now experimenting with replacement cost homeowners forms that contain no upper *dollar* limit on the dwelling coverage. All dwelling losses are settled on the basis of their repair or replacement costs without a dollar limitation as such. Any kind of insurance-to-value provision would be pointless, therefore, since all policyholders are instantly and continuously insured for 100 percent of the replacement costs of their respective dwellings.

Personal Property Most homeowners forms automatically provide coverage for unscheduled personal property (Coverage C) on an actual cash value basis. The applicable loss settlement provisions do not make any reference to insurance-to-value requirements. Under homeowners policy rules the usual limit for personal property on the premises is 50 percent of the dollar limit on the dwelling building, although it may be reduced to as low as 40 percent. This fixed relationship affords no guarantee that the policy limits on household goods will be sufficient to cover the large or total losses of a particular policyholder, especially when the policyholder does not maintain an adequate amount of coverage on the dwelling; nonetheless, the dwelling replacement cost conditions give the policyholder a rather strong incentive to keep the dwelling insured for at least 80 percent of its replacement cost, and this helps to keep the personal property limits in line with the actual cash value of the property.

In summary, the replacement cost conditions in standard homeowners forms apply only to buildings. With respect to personal property, homeowners rules mandate a fixed relationship between the *minimum* personal property dollar limit(s) and whatever dollar limit is carried on the dwelling. Regardless of the dollar limit actually carried on personal property or its relationship to the dwelling limit, the maximum amount payable for any personal property loss is the ACV of the loss or the applicable policy limit, whichever is the smaller of the two.

Many insurers now offer a homeowners endorsement that converts the unscheduled personal property coverage from an ACV to a replacement cost basis. These endorsements are not standardized, but most of them do not contain any explicit insurance-to-value conditions. Yet, a high ratio of insurance to value is normally achieved by strict underwriting requirements. The typical insurer will insist that the policyholder insure personal property for at least 70 percent of the amount of insurance carried on the dwelling. This is a more stringent requirement than it might appear to be on the surface. First, the insurer may refuse to attach a replacement cost endorsement unless the policyholder also insures the dwelling for at least 80 percent of its replacement cost. Second, the typical replacement cost endorsement does not apply to antiques, fine arts, paintings, and similar articles which, by their nature, cannot be replaced with new articles. Nor does the typical endorsement apply to articles "whose age or history contribute substantially to their value," nor to *any property* which has not been "maintained in good and workable condition." Therefore, the excluded items of personal property are covered on an actual cash value basis, just as they are without the replacement cost contents endorsement.

The underwriting requirements for contents replacement cost endorsements generally require higher personal property coverage limits than are required for ACV coverage. Such requirements, however, merely set the minimum contents-insurance-to-building-value ratios that are acceptable to insurers. The required minimum limit on unscheduled personal property may or may not be sufficient to cover the large or total losses of a particular policyholder on a replacement cost basis.

Loss of Use Under Coverage D, loss of use, the standard homeowners forms provide two types of indirect loss coverage, "additional living expense" and "fair rental value." Either or both coverages may apply when the occurrence of a covered peril renders the dwelling uninhabitable. The insurer then pays any necessary increase in living expenses incurred by an insured to maintain the household's normal standard of living. The insurer also would pay the fair rental value of any portion of the dwelling that is rented to others (or held for rental to others). Such payments are made for the shortest time required to repair or replace the damaged or destroyed building. Thus, the homeowners' loss of use coverages are roughly comparable to the extra expense and business interruption coverages which are available to commercial enterprises.

The homeowners' loss of use coverages do not contain anything even resembling a coinsurance clause. As with extra expense insurance for a business, the notion of insurable value would be difficult to apply in this context. Thus, the only homeowners insurance-to-value requirement is the minimum loss-of-use coverage limit that is required by the rules of the policy program. Depending on the particular form purchased, the automatic limit on loss-of-use coverage is either 10 percent or 20 percent of the amount of insurance carried on the dwelling. Like the minimum Coverage B and C limits, which are also expressed as a percentage of the dwelling limit, insurance-to-value is encouraged because the loss-of-use limit is closely tied to the amount of insurance carried on the dwelling.

Insurance-to-Value Requirements in Liability Insurance

The concept of "underinsurance" is virtually meaningless in the context of the coverages typically provided by liability insurance. Consequently, the various insurance-to-value requirements that are so commonly found in property insurance coverages have very few counterparts in legal liability coverages.

Since there is no theoretical upper limit on the dollar amount of damages that *might* be levied against an insured, the maximum amount of potential loss cannot be determined. *After* a loss has occurred, a policyholder may truly be "underinsured" relative to the *actual* size of a liability loss. *Before* the fact, a policyholder is merely thought to be "underinsured" relative to the *potential* size of a liability loss. Indeed, in the sense that the potential loss is unlimited in amount, every liability policyholder is underinsured.

To say that the amount carried at the time of loss must be some percentage of an amount that cannot be determined until after loss would be outrageously unfair. Therefore, policy provisions requiring a ratio of insurance-to-value are not used in most types of third-party liability insurance. Some exceptions arise with respect to liability insurance covering liability arising out of damage to specific property. Some of the purposes of insurance-to-value requirements are also served by minimum amount of insurance requirements. Finally, it is necessary to note that some liability insurance coverages contain no policy limits and thus do provide full insurance to value. Other features of these types of insurance eliminate the problems that might be expected to arise with a no-limit policy.

Liability Insurance Covering Damage to Specific Property
There are many instances of insurance being issued to an entity that
has an insurable interest based only on potential legal liability for
damage to *specific* property of others. A bailee (such as a dry cleaner)
may insure its liability for damage to the property of others left in its
custody for storage or repair. A common carrier has an insurable
interest in its liability for damage to goods of others which the carrier
has agreed to transport. A contractor has an insurable interest in legal
liability for damages to a building under construction. A garagekeeper
has an insurable interest in legal liability for damages to customers'
cars in the garagekeeper's custody. A tenant has an insurable interest
in legal liability for damages *to* a rented building.

Some of the above exposures may be insured using property
insurance or inland marine forms that closely resemble first-party
property insurance. Discussion of specific coverages is deferred to
other CPCU courses, but it can be said in general that coinsurance
clauses and other property insurance-to-value provisions are found in
insurance policies for some of these exposures covering liability for
damage to specific property.

Minimum Amounts of Insurance Requirements Requirements that a certain minimum amount of insurance be purchased are
not insurance policy provisions, but rather underwriting practices that
support the concept of insurance to value. Minimum dollar limits are
required in property insurance, in situations where minimum policy
limits are considered equitable to the majority of the insureds. It
obviously would not be fair to require all building owners to insure
their buildings to a minimum of $25,000. Any rate predicated on this
assumption would be inequitable if applied to the owners of $5,000
buildings and $200,000 buildings. Both the probable and the possible
size of loss are obviously functions of the respective values of the
buildings. However, a flat dollar minimum limit is a fairer approach in
liability insurance. Although one firm may own a $5,000 building and
another a $200,000 building, *either* firm could be held legally liable for
$1 million in damages resulting from the sale of a defective product
that cause serious injury to the buyer or user of the product. Each firm
also faces the possibility of an even larger liability loss. To require each
firm to purchase at least $25,000 of liability insurance would not be
unfair.

In many cases, minimum amounts of insurance are required by
law. For example, compulsory auto insurance laws in many states
require each auto owner to purchase liability insurance that meets the
state "financial responsibility" limits.

Coverages with No Dollar Policy Limits All workers' compensation policyholders are "fully insured" for losses that fall within the scope of coverage. The coverages automatically comply with legislative changes. Especially where statutes already require unlimited medical expense benefits, an insurance-to-value requirement would be pointless. Similar considerations apply to no-fault auto insurance in states that require coverage for unlimited medical expenses. While extremely large amounts may occasionally be paid under such coverages, there are practical limitations on the amount of *medical expenses* that may be incurred during a claimant's lifetime.

There is also no need to require a minimum ratio of insurance to value in connection with the defense and supplementary payments benefits of liability insurance policies. In most contracts, the insurer's obligation to pay defense costs is theoretically unlimited in amount. However, by contract, insurers generally have the option to settle with a claimant, and the insurer's obligation to provide defense benefits ends when the policy limits have been exhausted. Therefore, an insurer can, in practice, limit its defense payments by arriving at a settlement or (in the case of a large claim) paying the policy limits and ceasing to incur further expenses for defense.

DEDUCTIBLES

Broadly speaking, a deductible is a policy provision that calls for the *deduction* of a specified or determinable amount from the recovery which would otherwise be due the insured. The amount to be deducted may be "designated" (as with a $100 deductible), or it may be "determinable" (as when it is a certain percentage of the loss or of the policy limit).

The rationale for deductibles relates to the objectives of premium rate adequacy and equity. In computing its premium charges, an insurer must make several assumptions regarding the losses an insured may suffer and the extent of the insurer's liability for these losses. Taken together, these assumptions yield the expected value of the loss payments an insurer will make—losses for which the insurer must have collected premiums from insureds.

Deductibles reduce the expected value of an insurer's loss payments. Deductibles relieve the insurer of liability for:

(1) the full amount of all losses that are less than the deductible, and

(2) under most deductibles, some portion of those losses that exceed the deductible.

In return, the insured receives a rate credit.

Aside from any impact on rate adequacy and equity, deductibles are said to have other positive effects:

(1) Having to participate in any future loss is said to induce insureds to take greater care to prevent or reduce losses.

(2) Because insuring small, regular losses generates administrative costs that are relatively high in comparison with the insurance recovery, deductibles save insureds premium dollars. Deductibles simultaneously relieve insurers of administrative costs for many small losses, thus improving their efficiency. This increased efficiency tends to protect the adequacy of the insurer's premium income while, at the same time, keeping insured's costs of protection below what they might otherwise be.

(3) In addition, the judicious use of deductibles enables insureds and risk managers to use partial retention to obtain the mix of loss financing techniques that best serves the firm's pre-loss and post-loss risk management objectives.

Deductibles are not, however, without their disadvantages. One alleged disadvantage is the insured's disappointment on finding that a deductible provision has deprived it of full compensation. Another disadvantage is that deductions from the insurance recovery also may cause dissatisfaction among insurance producers. It is sometimes felt that a fully compensated loss is the best advertisement in competing for and retaining business. A third possible disadvantage is that insureds are sometimes said to inflate the amounts of losses reported to insurers in order to collect a recovery, after subtracting the deductible, that approximates the insured's true loss. This practice, which defeats the purpose of the deductible, would threaten the adequacy of the insurer's premium income and discriminate against those insureds who report and document their losses fairly.

The next three sections (1) describe and illustrate some of the most common types of deductible provisions, (2) explain the general rationale of the deductible concept, and (3) summarize the extent to which deductibles are used in property and liability insurance. Additional aspects of deductibles are discussed in other CPCU texts in connection with specific insurance coverages.

Types of Deductible

Fixed Dollar Amount Per Loss Perhaps the most common

Exhibit 12-2
Straight Deductibles Illustrated

(a) Amount of Loss	(b) Deductible Amount	(c) Excess of (a) over (b)	(d) Policy Limit	(e) Amount Paid by Insurer	(f) Amount Retained by Policy- holder
$ 400	$500	0	$10,000	0	$ 400
500	500	0	10,000	0	500
2,000	500	$ 1,500	10,000	$ 1,500	500
10,000	500	9,500	10,000	9,500	500
12,000	500	11,500	10,000	10,000	2,000

type of insurance deductible is that which involves the deduction of a fixed dollar amount per loss. This type of deductible is often called *"straight deductible."* A fixed dollar amount is subtracted from each loss, and the insurer is obligated to pay the remainder, i.e., the amount by which the loss exceeds the deductible, up to the applicable policy limit. One such deductible provision reads as follows:

> The first $_____ of any one loss is not insured hereunder, and this insurer is liable only for loss in excess thereof, subject to all other applicable limits of liability.

The deductible amount is preprinted or is inserted in the blank space of the clause, and the insured is granted a corresponding premium reduction. Generally, the greater the amount of the deductible, the greater the premium reduction.

To illustrate the application of a straight deductible provision, assume a policy limit of $10,000 and a deductible amount of $500 per loss. No coinsurance clause applies. No other policy is in force. The results for various amounts of loss would be as shown in Exhibit 12-2.

This type of deductible applies to each separate loss, as "a loss" is defined in the relevant coverage. Depending upon the coverage, the deductible could apply to each fire, windstorm, theft, collision, accident, or occurrence, to cite a few examples. Consequently, a per-loss deductible can be deducted as many times as separate losses occur during a policy period. In the illustration shown in Exhibit 12-2, if the insured had three different windstorm losses during the period, each amounting to more than $500 in damage, the insured would be out-of-pocket for at least $1,500.

Exhibit 12-3
Examples Comparing Percentage Deductibles

	ACV of Property	Amount of Loss	Deductible Percentage	Percentage-of-Loss Deductible Amount	Percentage-of-Value Deductible Amount
(1)	$10,000	$ 1,000	5%	$ 50	$ 500
(2)	20,000	5,000	5%	250	1,000
(3)	30,000	10,000	5%	500	1,500
(4)	50,000	30,000	5%	1,500	2,500
(5)	50,000	50,000	5%	2,500	2,500

Fixed Percentage Per Loss   With a second type of deductible, the deduction takes the form of a fixed percentage per loss. While the stated percentage is usually applied to the amount of the loss, it is sometimes applied to the insurable value of the covered property. In either case the deductible affects each insured event or loss. The percentage-of-loss and percentage-of-insurable value deductibles are both illustrated in Exhibit 12-3.

For any partial loss, note that a percentage-of-value deductible will result in a larger deduction than the same percentage-of-loss deductible, as shown in examples (1) to (4) of Exhibit 12-3. For any total loss as shown in example (5), these two types of percentage deductibles will result in the same amount of deduction, because the amount of a total loss is the ACV of the property, by definition (assuming an ACV basis of loss settlement). However, for any partial or total loss, the policy limit will be the maximum amount of recovery. For instance, if an insured has a $15,000 loss, a $10,000 policy limit, and a percentage deductible that is equivalent to $500 (or a straight deductible of this amount), the insured will recover only $10,000, regardless of whether the loss is partial or total.

In the above illustrations of a percentage-of-value deductible, the insurable value of the property was assumed to be its actual cash value. In a replacement cost form, the insurable value would be the replacement cost of the property. Likewise, the amount of the loss is determined on an ACV or an RC basis, depending upon the form.

Comparing Fixed and Percentage Deductibles   If the insurable value of property would remain constant, the percentage-of-*value* deductible would yield a deductible amount that remained constant for any size of loss. In practice, this deductible amount grows larger in periods of inflation, but so does the dollar size of the loss and the amount of recovery, assuming adequate policy limits, because the deductible has a fixed-percentage relationship to the value of the property insured.

The percentage-of-*loss* deductible yields a deductible amount that varies by dollar size of loss, but is not affected by the total dollar value of the property. This deductible amount also grows larger in periods of inflation, because a given degree of damage results in a larger dollar loss. On the other hand, a percentage-of-loss deductible by itself inherently requires the insurer to pay *nearly all* of even a very small loss. A 5 percent of loss deductible, for example, would require the insurer to pay $19 of a $20 loss. The payment of such losses would not enable the deductible to function as intended. To avoid payment for minor losses, as well as to reduce the impact of large losses on the policyholder, a percentage-of-loss deductible is frequently subject to both a dollar minimum and a dollar maximum. An illustration is a policy which contains a 5 percent of loss deductible, subject to a minimum deductible of $250 per loss and a maximum deductible of $2,000 per loss. Such a deductible would never be less than $250 per loss nor more than $2,000 per loss; otherwise, the deductible would be 5 percent of the loss. Deductibles expressed as either a percentage of loss or as a percentage of value automatically adjust for inflation. Deductibles expressed as a fixed dollar amount per loss do not so adjust. Therefore, there is a tendency for fixed dollar deductibles to become larger during inflationary periods. For example, $50 deductible auto collision insurance used to be fairly common. Today, a $250 collision deductible is not at all uncommon.

Franchise Deductible A "franchise" deductible is a deductible provision that applies only to losses that are less than a stipulated "franchise amount." Any loss that equals or exceeds the franchise amount is paid in full, up to the applicable policy limit. This type of deductible gets its name from the noun "franchise," meaning "freedom from a restriction or burden vested in a person or group." Those who sustain losses smaller than the franchise amount must bear the burden themselves; those who suffer losses equal to or larger than the franchise amount are relieved of the burden which a straight or percentage deductible would otherwise impose upon them.

A franchise deductible may be expressed in terms of a fixed number of dollars. A flat dollar figure, such as $500, is inserted in the deductible clause to serve as the franchise amount. No payment is made by the insurer for any loss of $499 or less, but any loss of $500 or more is paid in full (subject to policy limits).

The stipulated franchise amount is more often expressed as a percentage of the insurable value of the property. To illustrate, suppose a small aircraft is insured subject to a franchise deductible of 3 percent of its actual cash value. If the aircraft has an ACV of $40,000 at the time of loss, the franchise amount is $1,200 (3% × $40,000). Any loss of $1,200 or more would be paid in full, up to the policy limit, without deducting the $1,200 franchise amount. Or, if the ACV of the aircraft had been $50,000 at the time of loss, the deductible or franchise amount could have been $1,500 (3% × $50,000).

The flat-dollar franchise is fixed or constant throughout the policy period, in spite of any change in the insurable value of the property. The dollar amount of the percentage of value franchise reflects changing property values.

Prior to 1970, percentage-of-value and fixed-dollar franchise deductibles were the prevailing custom in ocean marine insurance. They are still used, to some extent, in both hull and cargo coverages. However, the franchise deductibles have not been as widespread since 1970, when the hull insurance forms were changed to leave a blank space for the insertion of a straight deductible amount. Though it is called a straight deductible, it is only applied to partial losses if, as is frequently the case, the insurer includes a clause requiring the waiver of the deductible in the event of a total loss.

Disappearing Deductible   Some insurance practitioners refer to a franchise deductible as a "disappearing deductible" because it, in effect, disappears (that is, it is not applied) when a loss reaches the stipulated threshold. Most people reserve the term *disappearing deductible* for a deductible that gradually diminishes to zero as the size of loss increases within a given dollar range. For example, the insurer might apply a straight $50 deductible to a loss of $50 or less, and a franchise deductible to a loss of $500 or more. For any loss between $51 and $499, the insurer would then pay 111 percent of the amount by which the loss exceeds the $50 straight deductible. Thus, the deductible gradually diminishes as the size of loss increases from $51 to $499, and it disappears entirely when a loss passes the $500 threshold.

The disappearing deductible is essentially a combination of straight, percentage-of-loss, and franchise concepts. The basic objective was to preserve the premium savings function of a straight deductible without penalizing an insured for the occasional large or total loss. Although this is an appealing notion, the "50 to 500" approach did not seem to work as well as had been expected. It was difficult to explain and administratively cumbersome. Though it was once widely used in homeowners insurance, it has been largely replaced by straight or fixed-amount-per-loss deductibles, and the disappearing deductible itself seems to be disappearing from the scene.

Fixed Dollar Amount Per Year From the viewpoint of the insurance buyer, perhaps the most desirable type of deductible is one that is expressed in terms of a fixed dollar amount *per year*, irrespective of the number of losses during the year. These are referred to as "aggregate annual deductibles" or, when the aggregate aspect is implied, as "annual deductibles."

The general approach may be illustrated by an aggregate annual deductible of $5,000. Such a deductible applies to the accumulated *total* of *all* covered losses during the year. Accordingly, suppose an insured incurs separate covered losses of $1,000, $3,000, and $7,000 during the first nine months of the year. The insurer would pay nothing for the first loss, nothing for the second loss, and $6,000 for the third loss (the accumulated total loss minus the deductible = $11,000 − $5,000 = $6,000). All losses occurring during the remaining three months of the year would be paid in full, up to the policy limit(s). If the insured had been subject to a $5,000 *per-loss* deductible, the insurer would have paid nothing for the first loss, nothing for the second loss, and $2,000 for the third loss, and a $5,000 deductible would still apply to *each* additional loss thereafter. Thus, the insured might retain several times $5,000 during the course of a year.

Fixed-dollar aggregate deductibles are used extensively by health insurers in the writing of major medical expense coverage. When the policy covers a family unit, the deductible is applied per person, per year. However, in the typical policy, no more than three deductibles are applied to a family unit during any one year. For example, if a $100 annual deductible applies to each of five family members, the family unit could have no more than three deductibles (or $300) applied each year to covered medical expenses.

An aggregate annual deductible nearly always requires a higher premium than a comparable deductible amount per loss. Even so, aggregate annual deductibles have the relative advantage of enabling policyholders to forecast the maximum possible dollar impact of multiple losses during the year. The chief drawback of aggregate annual deductibles is that they are not readily available to most property-liability policyholders. In workers' compensation insurance, a type of aggregate annual deductible is available on an excess basis to employers who have formal retention programs. By negotiations, the

Exhibit 12-4
A Thirty-Day Elimination Period

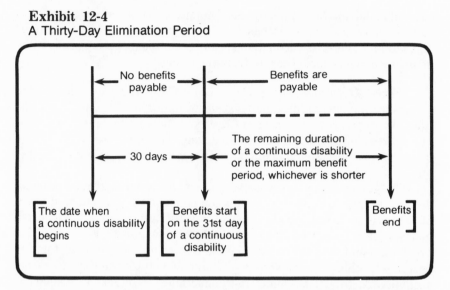

insurance buyers of large corporations, institutions, and government agencies are also able to obtain tailor-made plans that apply the annual deductible concept to some or all of their property and general liability coverages. Likewise, primary insurers are routinely able to secure annual aggregate retentions in their own contracts with reinsurers. Individuals, families, and other small insurance buyers are another matter entirely. In the standardized forms of personal and commercial coverage, annual deductibles are readily available only in major medical expense insurance. Per-loss deductibles remain as the prevailing rule in personal lines property insurance.

Elimination Period An "elimination period" is a deductible stated in days instead of dollars. Usually used with disability coverages, an elimination period is the waiting period or time interval which lies between (a) the date when a continuous disability begins and (b) the date when disability benefits first become payable. It follows that an elimination period of thirty days is the equivalent of a thirty-day deductible. The insurer would pay nothing for a disabling injury or sickness that lasted only seven days, twenty days, or twenty-nine days. Alternatively, if the insured person is disabled continuously for, say, two years and thirty days under a policy with a thirty-day elimination period, the benefits would begin on the thirty-first day of disability, and they would continue for the remaining duration of the disability, in this case two years (assuming the policy has a maximum benefit period of two years or more). A thirty-day elimination period is depicted in Exhibit 12-4.

The main purpose of an elimination period in disability insurance is to reduce the required premium by "eliminating" coverage for temporary disability of a minor nature. If a disability policy contained no elimination period pertaining to sickness, for example, the health insurer would pay income benefits for the common cold, influenza, and a host of other minor illnesses which collectively occur quite frequently. Just as a flat-dollar deductible reduces the premium for windstorm coverage, so also an elimination period reduces the premium for disability coverage. The longer the elimination period, the smaller the premium will be, as a general rule.

Elimination periods are also used in workers' compensation insurance, but here the insured employer has no choice. The elimination periods are prescribed by the applicable statute, and they apply only to the income continuation benefits payable to a disabled employee. These so-called "waiting periods" have the same duration for accidents as they do for covered diseases, within the context of any one state law, but their length varies somewhat from state to state. Most state laws prescribe elimination periods of from three to seven days. However, every state law also stipulates a "retroactive period," which makes the disability benefits payable retroactively to the first day of disability whenever the employee remains continuously disabled beyond the retroactive period. The retroactive period is longer than the elimination period in most states, ranging from two to four weeks in the larger industrial states.

Assume that a particular state law stipulates an elimination period of seven days and a retroactive period of fourteen days. Since the standard workers' compensation coverage automatically incorporates the provisions of the applicable statute, the insurer would pay no income continuation benefits to the employee who is disabled only seven days (though medical expense and other statutory benefits are payable from the first day of disability). If the employee is disabled continuously for ten days, the insurer would pay income continuation benefits for the last three days (10 ten days of disability—minus the seven days eliminated equals three days of benefits). But if the employee is disabled continuously for fifteen days, the insurer would pay income benefits for the entire fifteen—including the first seven days, retroactively.

Where the retroactive period is longer than the elimination period, as it is in most state workers' compensation laws, the elimination period operates somewhat like a modified straight deductible that is waived when the loss exceeds a specified level; the retroactive period operates somewhat like a franchise amount. The combination of two different periods makes the approach a bit different from a pure franchise deductible, in that a pure franchise deductible has just one dollar figure or percentage to serve as both the franchise amount and the deductible amount. However, in the few states where the elimination period is of the same duration as the retroactive period, the elimination period is essentially a franchise deductible which is expressed in days instead of dollars.

Although the term is seldom applied to property and liability insurance, the elimination period concept is also used in a few policies. For example, personal auto insurance policies providing theft coverage typically cover the expense of renting a temporary substitute auto to replace a stolen car. However, it is common to exclude transportation expenses incurred during the first forty-eight hours after the theft.

Boiler and machinery business interruption policies, which provide coverage for loss of earnings during a period following an accident to an insured object, typically include a "time deductible":

> If a number of hours applies, the Company shall not be liable for any loss under this Endorsement occurring during the specified number of hours immediately following the "Commencement of Liability."

Other Types of Deductible There are numerous additional types of deductible provisions, including:

- variable deductibles which decrease in amount for policyholders who enjoy claim-free years;
- aggregate deductibles which are expressed as a percentage of the accumulated total of all losses during the policy year; and,
- even per-loss deductibles which may be eliminated retroactively after the loss occurs.

There are large deductibles and small deductibles. There are deductibles that vary according to the income level of the insured. And there are deductibles that are waived under certain conditions. To be sure, the deductible concept leaves ample room for innovative variations.

General Rationale of the Deductible Concept

Though various types of deductibles appear sharply different, many meaningful generalizations may be made about the underlying rationale of the deductible concept. This is especially true when deductibles are broadly classified according to their potential impact, as either (1) large or (2) small *from the viewpoint of the insured entity.*

Whether a deductible is expressed in fixed-dollar or percentage terms, it can be converted into the estimated maximum dollar amount that the deductible might require an insured to retain in any given time period. This maximum dollar amount has virtually no meaning, however, until it is evaluated *in relation to* the financial resources of a particular insured. An uninsured loss of $2,000 might be "large" relative to the financial resources of one individual, "small" relative to the financial resources of another individual, and "petty cash" to a giant corporation or governmental unit. This suggests that the dividing line between "large" and "small" deductibles should ultimately be drawn in relation to the potential impact of each on the financial condition of a specific insured. Large deductibles tend to share common purposes, advantages, and disadvantages, whereas small deductibles tend to share distinguishably different purposes, advantages, and disadvantages.

Large Deductibles Deductibles that are quite large in relation to the financial resources of the insured entities are used mainly by corporations and governmental bodies that have formal plans of partial retention. Such plans are commonly used to treat workers' compensation loss exposures, commercial property loss exposures, and, to a lesser extent, general liability loss exposures. By definition, partial retention plans involve the purchase of excess insurance policies that contain large deductibles. The purpose of the excess insurance is to protect the insured entity against losses above the desired level of retention. The purpose of the large deductible is to enable the entity to enjoy the potential advantages of the retention technique. These potential advantages, along with the potential disadvantages, were explained in Chapter 3.

Small Deductibles Deductibles that are small in relation to the financial resources of the insured entity are used by virtually all property insurance buyers. In fact, small deductibles *should* be used as a part of every well-conceived property insurance program. From the viewpoint of rational property insurance buyers, as well as their insurers and society as a whole, the potential advantages of deductibles outweigh the potential disadvantages by a wide margin.

The primary *disadvantages* of small property insurance deductibles are said to be as follows:

(1) *Allegedly, small deductibles are not well understood by the public.* This causes disappointed claimants and ill will toward

insurers, their representatives, and the insurance mechanism generally. Most consumers have a crude but adequate understanding of how deductibles work, yet many do not seem to appreciate why deductibles are necessary or desirable, and some are not aware until after a loss that their policies contain deductibles. While this criticism is not totally lacking in merit, it could just as easily be argued that the problem is one of communication and education, not the deductible concept per se. Sophisticated corporate insurance buyers certainly understand and appreciate small deductibles, as do laypersons who make the effort. Neither deductibles nor any other policy provisions should be any more complicated than necessary. But the critics are on weak ground when they argue for the complete abolition of deductibles, if only because it would deprive everyone of a less expensive and more rational choice.

(2) *Small deductibles are believed to encourage fraud, by giving insureds a monetary incentive to inflate claims and "cover" their deductibles.* If deductibles encourage fraud and cheating, so also do income tax laws, expense accounts, fire insurance coverages, and property and liability insurance coverages generally. The survival of the entire insurance mechanism depends on the basic honesty of most persons. Abolishing deductibles is no remedy for policyholder dishonesty, in any case. The problem runs much deeper than that. The abolition of deductibles would only penalize honest persons with higher premiums. Unscrupulous persons would inevitably find other ways to "beat the system."

(3) *While straight deductibles play a useful role by eliminating coverage for small losses which are frequent in occurrence, they unduly penalize the insured who has the less frequent large or total loss.* Here, the opponents of straight deductibles have a valid point, and the industry has recognized as much by inventing the franchise type of deductible. But smaller franchise amounts are no longer readily available in personal lines of property insurance, for the reasons previously discussed. Ocean marine insurers have dealt with the aforementioned disadvantage by a policy provision that waives the straight deductible in the event of a total loss. Perhaps this kind of policy provision will someday become universal in personal lines, as well. It could also be modified to provide a contractual waiver of the deductible in the event that a loss exceeds the deductible by a stipulated large amount, in which case it would

resemble the retroactive waiting period of workers' compensation.

(4) *Another valid criticism of the typical small deductible stems from its application to each and every loss.* As explained earlier, this makes it difficult for the buyer to select an appropriate deductible amount or percentage.

The foregoing disadvantages do not make a sufficient case for those who would abolish small property insurance deductibles. They do underscore the need for some innovative improvements.

The major potential *advantages* of small deductibles are, briefly:

(1) *To the extent that property insurance policies cover windstorm, hail, fire, auto collision, theft of CB radios, auto glass breakage, and/or other perils which cause a high frequency of small losses, the application of a small deductible significantly reduces the premium that would otherwise be required.* This premium reduction is achieved in two important ways. First, by relieving the insurer of the obligation to pay all losses which are less than the deductible (and the deductible portion of larger losses, in the case of a straight deductible), a small deductible sharply reduces the aggregate payout of the insurer. Second, by relieving the insurer of the obligation to pay all losses smaller than the deductible, the deductible simultaneously eliminates the substantial administrative expenses of handling claims for such losses.

(2) *Despite the fact that the policyholder will be "out-of-pocket" for all losses smaller than the deductible amount (unless it is a franchise deductible), the rational insurance buyer allocates his or her premium dollars so as to give highest priority to insuring large losses of a catastrophic nature.* Smaller losses are easier to bear, disproportionately expensive to insure, and best handled by the retention technique. The premium dollars required for no-deductible coverage could be more wisely spent to increase the upper policy limits or buy additional coverages, or they could be invested and earmarked to pay for the uninsured portion of small losses.

(3) *Because the insured must bear the deductible portion of each loss, the insured has a financial incentive to exercise care in the prevention or reduction of losses.* It is doubtful whether a small financial stake in the loss has any appreciable influence on the prevention of some losses, such as windstorm damage to buildings, but it can provide an additional incentive to avoid

theft of personal property or minimize the amount of damage from fire or other perils.

Thus, though small property insurance deductibles do have some disadvantages, they also offer significant advantages to the policy-holder, the insurer, and society as a whole. On balance, most experts feel, the overall advantages outweigh the disadvantages, especially since two of the alleged disadvantages have no direct application to knowledgeable and honest insureds.

Uses of Deductibles in Liability Insurance

As noted earlier, large deductibles are inherent in partial retention programs, including those which are used in the treatment of workers' compensation and general liability loss exposures of large corporations. Mandatory deductibles of moderate size are also used in the writing of directors and officers, and umbrella liability coverages.

With the exception of the elimination periods which are prescribed by workers' compensation laws, small deductibles are almost never used in connection with third-party liability coverages. Why not? First, a small deductible ordinarily would permit little or no reduction in the premium charged for third-party liability coverage. Small liability claims are comparatively rare, because (1) small losses are usually paid under the medical payments, personal injury protection, or damage-to-property-of-others sections of the policy, and (2) as a practical matter, people seldom sue for small amounts. Second, to obtain a significant premium reduction, the deductible amount would have to be much larger than most policyholders are willing to retain. Third, in auto insurance, deductibles that applied to third-party liability coverages would be contrary to the basic purpose of compulsory insurance and financial responsibility laws. Such laws were enacted in the first place in an attempt to assure that third-party victims will be compensated for damages caused by negligent motorists, at least up to the minimum dollar amounts prescribed by statute, either through the negligent motorist's auto liability insurance or through equivalent forms of financial security. The underlying purpose of these statutes would not necessarily be defeated, if small deductibles of $100 or so were to be permitted in auto liability coverages. Theoretically, the aggrieved third party would still have a legal claim against the present and future assets of the negligent motorist (and/or the vehicle owner or the motorist's employer, in some cases). But pursuing such a small claim can be time-consuming or expensive to the third-party claimant. Furthermore, as a practical matter, the premium savings would be so negligible that motorists would not generally be interested in small deductibles for auto liability coverages.

In summary, large deductibles may be found in liability insurance, though to a lesser extent than in property insurance. Small deductibles are almost never found in personal types of third-party liability coverage. And the premium savings would not be significant for any type of third-party liability coverage, unless the deductible amount were to be larger than most individuals are willing to retain.

CHAPTER 13

Multiple Sources of Recovery

INTRODUCTION

Previous chapters have focused on what determines the amounts payable when a given policy of insurance serves as the sole source of recovery for a particular loss. Next to be considered are the numerous provisions providing for situations in which multiple sources of recovery may be available following a claim. Specifically, this chapter is devoted to (1) "other insurance" provisions, (2) the legal doctrine of "subrogation," and (3) a concluding summary of the various means that are used in property-liability insurance to preserve the principle of indemnity.

"OTHER INSURANCE" PROVISIONS

With the notable exception of life insurance and most individual health insurance policies, nearly all insurance policies contain provisions that limit the insurer's liability in order to:

(1) prevent duplicate benefit payments when more than one policy applies to the same loss, and
(2) provide a predetermined method of allocating the loss-payment responsibility between or among the insurers providing the coverage.

In group health insurance the antiduplication provisions are called "coordination-of-benefits provisions" (or "integration provisions," in the case of disability income insurance that is designed to supplement whatever social security benefits are payable). Their counterparts in property and liability insurance may be referred to as "other insurance" provisions or clauses. In a narrow sense, "other insurance" provisions are policy provisions that provide a predetermined method of limiting the responsibility of each insurer when more than one insurer provides coverage. This type of "other insurance" provision is usually clearly labeled as such. In this chapter, the term "other insurance provisions" will be used in its broadest possible sense, to encompass all insurance policy provisions relating to other insurance.

Several different types of "other insurance" provision may be found in property and liability policies. A policy that provides more than one type of coverage is likely to contain more than one type of other-insurance clause.

The homeowners policy, for example, contains one type of "other insurance" provision relating to property coverages and another type relating to liability coverages. The calculations required to apply "other insurance" provisions are fairly simple in many cases, when (1) *all* the policies contain identical coverages, (2) all the policies contain identical "other insurance" provisions, and (3) the latter do not conflict with one another. If any one of these three conditions is lacking, the loss settlement process can be extremely complex.

To convey the basic nature of the major types of "other insurance" provision, the following section will assume that only two non-conflicting policies are involved. A later section will summarize the general guidelines that are used to resolve conflicts among "other insurance" provisions.

Types of "Other Insurance" Provision

The various types of "other insurance" provision may be classified, according to their effect, as clauses which:

(1) *exonerate* the insurer from liability,
(2) limit the insurer's liability to a determinable *proportion* of the loss,
(3) make the policy containing the clause *excess* over other applicable insurance, or
(4) make the policy containing the clause *primary* with respect to other applicable insurance.

Of these approaches, (2) and (3) are by far the most common.

Exoneration Provisions A policy may exonerate (relieve) the insurer from liability in one of two ways. The policy's "other insurance" clause may prohibit other coverage altogether. Or, it may exclude coverage if other coverage is in force at the time of loss.

Prohibitions. Strict prohibitions of other insurance, while comparatively rare, are exemplified by a clause in the older homeowners forms. The clause reads: "Other insurance covering the described dwelling building (except insurance against perils not covered by this policy) is not permitted." Since earthquake and flood damage are not covered by homeowners policies, the policyholder could insure the dwelling for either or both of these two perils. In contrast, if the policyholder carried separate insurance on the dwelling for fire and/or some other covered peril, the insurer might be able to deny liability for a dwelling loss, the policyholder having breached an explicit condition in the homeowners form. This particular condition has been removed from most current homeowners forms.

Exclusions. Under the personal property coverage section of homeowners forms, there is an exclusion which reads: "We do not cover...articles separately described and specifically insured in this or any other insurance." The quoted exclusion is not called an "other insurance" provision, but it has the same effect. For example, if the policyholder purchased a personal articles floater to cover specific items of jewelry on a scheduled basis, this jewelry would no longer be covered under the unscheduled personal property section of the homeowners policy. The effect is to shift liability to the policy or form that is providing the scheduled jewelry coverage for an additional premium. In either case, the quoted exclusion is effectively an "other insurance" clause in the unscheduled personal property section of the homeowners policy.

Proportional Sharing Provisions To deal with the situation where two or more insurance contracts protect the same interest against the same loss, one of the most common types of "other insurance" provision has the effect of limiting each insurer's payment to a proportion of the overall loss. Variations of this general approach take the form of (1) proration by face amounts, (2) contribution by equal shares, (3) proration by amounts payable, and (4) apportionment. All of these involve loss sharing of a proportional nature; yet, each uses a different basis for determining the proportional share.

Proration by Face Amounts. The standard fire insurance policy contains a clause which is captioned "Pro Rata Liability." It is essentially an "other insurance" provision that calls for *proration by face amounts.* The relevant provision reads:

> This company (insurer) shall not be liable for a greater proportion of any loss than the amount hereby insured shall bear to the whole insurance covering the property against the peril involved, whether collectible or not.

When multiple policies cover the same insured, the same property, and the same peril, each insurer's liability is limited so that the loss is distributed equitably among the policies (whether issued by the same insurer or different insurers), and the principle of indemnity is preserved by preventing duplicate benefit payments to the policyholder.[1] If an insurer's determinable share of the loss is not collectible, perhaps because the insurer is insolvent or the insured committed fraud in obtaining the coverage, the pro-rata liability clause nonetheless limits the liability—under each policy providing collectible insurance—to that share of the loss which its face amount bears to the sum of the face amounts on all collectible *and* uncollectible policies.

To illustrate proration by face amounts, assume that a $1,000 loss is covered by insurer A under a policy with a face amount of $6,000. It is also covered by insurer B under a policy with a face amount of $4,000. The coverage of both policies is "collectible." Insurer A would pay 60 percent of the loss, or $600, while insurer B would pay 40 percent of the loss, or $400. The liability of each insurer is based upon the ratio of its face amount to the total amount of all insurance covering the same property for the same insured against the same peril (a total of $10,000, in this case). Instead of profiting from duplicate benefit payments, the insured is indemnified. However, suppose the insurance under policy A had not been collectible. Insurer B would still only pay its $400 share, even though its policy face would have been more than adequate to pay a $1,000 loss in full.

While it may seem unfair to reduce the insured's protection under policy B merely because the other insurance is uncollectible, a closer examination reveals that the approach is fair and equitable to all parties concerned. First, consider the case where policy A is uncollectible because the insured committed fraud in obtaining that policy. Since there never was an enforceable contract in existence, owing to the fraud, the courts would normally permit insurer A to "rescind" its policy all the way back to the stated inception date. This would be fair both to insurer A and to the insured who perpetrated the fraud. It could be argued then that insurer B, having received premiums for $4,000 of coverage, should be required to pay the entire $1,000 loss, just as it would have had to do if policy A had never been purchased.

The contrary view is that the pro-rata liability clause clearly expresses the agreement between the parties regarding the role of uncollectible insurance in determining insurer B's liability, and the premium charged reflects that agreement. The premium rate would have to be slightly higher, in other words, if uncollectible insurance were to be ignored in the pro-rata liability calculations. Furthermore, in most cases the insured would receive a refund of all premiums paid on policy A, when it is rescinded. To require or permit insurer B to pay the loss in full would be to defeat the purpose of the court in allowing the rescission.

Second, consider the case where policy A is uncollectible because insurer A is insolvent at the time of loss. Historically, the insured would have been out-of-pocket for the $600 portion of the loss, on the theory that he or she could have selected a financially sound insurer by the exercise of greater care. Modern public policy is reflected in the *Insurer Guaranty Funds* which have been established by statute in all fifty states. Though such statutes are not completely uniform from state to state, the policyholder in a Guaranty Fund state usually would not be out-of-pocket for the insolvent insurer's portion of the loss. It would be paid through the operation of the Guaranty Fund, and each insurer doing business in the state would be required to share the loss in proportion to its share of the statewide premium volume for the line of insurance in question.

In modern homeowners forms, the "other insurance" provision applicable to property coverages does not make any explicit reference to the matter of uncollectible insurance. The provision now reads:

> *Other Insurance.* If a loss covered by this policy is also covered by other insurance, we will pay only the proportion of the loss that the limit of liability that applies under this policy bears to the total amount of insurance covering the loss.

The provision clearly retains the traditional approach of proration by face amounts or so-called pro-rata liability. It is also clear that "the limit of liability that applies under this policy" does not affect personal property written on a scheduled basis, since it is specifically excluded elsewhere in the policy (as explained earlier). The question that cannot be answered at the time of this writing is: how will most courts interpret the phrase "the total amount of insurance covering the loss"? Is insurance that is uncollectible due to insolvency to be construed as "covering" the loss? Probably so, now that all states have established Guaranty Funds, since the desire of the legislators is to handle insolvency situations through these funds. In situations where a Guaranty Fund does not apply, the courts conceivably might take a different position. With no Guaranty Fund to protect a policyholder who is victimized by an insurer's insolvency, the courts might say that such uncollectible insurance is not really "covering" the loss, especially in view of the policy drafters' deletion of any explicit reference to uncollectible insurance. If so, the solvent insurer(s) would have to pay the otherwise uncollectible portion of their policyholder's loss.

Contribution by Equal Shares. A second form of proportional loss sharing is determined according to *contribution by equal shares.*

An example of such an "other insurance" provision may be found in the "jacket" used with general liability policies, as follows:

> If all of such other valid and collectible insurance provides for contribution by equal shares, the company shall not be liable for a greater proportion of such loss than would be payable if each insurer contributes an equal share until the share of each insurer equals the lowest applicable limit of liability under any one policy or the full amount of the loss is paid. . . .

This provision also contains additional language dealing with situations in which the other insurance does not specify contribution by equal shares.

To illustrate contribution by equal shares, assume a $60,000 claim within the scope of coverage provided by an insured's two comprehensive general liability policies: policy A with a $100,000 limit of liability for this claim, and policy B with a $25,000 limit of liability. Both policies provide for contribution by equal shares. The two policies pay equal dollar amounts until the lower of the two limits of liability, $25,000, is reached. At that point, $50,000 of the claim has been paid, leaving policy A to pay the remaining $10,000 of the claim. Had the claim been smaller—say, $30,000—each policy would have paid $15,000 toward the total. By agreement between themselves, the two insurers would have decided which was to provide investigatory and legal services, and the costs of these services would have been divided between them (in the same manner as the claims payments, unless otherwise stipulated in the policy or agreed to by the insurers).

Contribution by equal shares is justified by the practice with many kinds of insurance of charging lower rates for successively higher limits of liability, in recognition of the reduced likelihood of larger losses. In the above example, policy A had a $100,000 limit of liability and policy B had a $25,000 limit of liability. Contribution by equal shares tends to put a proportionately greater burden on the policy having the lower limit of liability, but this is equitable. While policy A provides four-fifths of the total coverage, its insurer receives considerably less than four-fifths of the total annual premium because the rate structure reflects the fact that losses between $25,000 and $100,000 are less likely than losses under $25,000 in amount. To allocate losses according to *policy limits* would be unfair to the insurer of the $100,000 policy; it would be paying 80 percent of most loss amounts, while collecting only, say, 60 percent of the total annual premium for both policies combined. Contribution by equal shares corrects this inequity by reducing the loss-sharing burden of the insurer with larger policy limits.

Proration by Amounts Payable. A third form of proportional loss sharing involves *proration by the amount which would have been payable by each policy if it had been the only policy applicable to the loss.* While this approach also results in a kind of pro-rata liability, it otherwise differs sharply from proration by face amounts. Why? Because the amounts payable by each policy are governed by the loss valuation provisions and whether it contains a coinsurance clause and/or a deductible, as well as by its policy limits. Fraud, insolvency, statutory benefit levels, or a breach of a policy condition could also be involved. Even if no other limiting factors apply, the amount payable for a partial loss is limited to the amount of the loss, which in many cases is less than the policy limit.

To take an admittedly oversimplified example, suppose a $40,000 loss is covered by insurer A under a policy with a face amount of $90,000. The loss is also (partly) covered by insurer B under a policy with a face amount of $10,000. If both policies contained an "other insurance" clause requiring proration by *face amounts*, insurer A would pay 90 percent of the loss (or $36,000) and insurer B would pay 10 percent of the loss (or $4,000). Alternatively, if both policies contained a clause requiring proration according to the *amounts payable* by each policy, standing alone, insurer A would pay 80 percent of the loss (or $32,000) and insurer B would pay 20 percent of the loss (or $8,000). Why? If the $90,000 policy would have been the only policy, its insurer would have paid no more than $40,000, the amount of the loss. If the $10,000 policy had been the only policy, its insurer would have paid no more than $10,000, its upper limit of liability. Thus, when both policies apply and contain the provision requiring proration by amounts payable, insurer A pays $40,000/$50,000 × the loss = 80 percent × the loss. Insurer B pays $10,000/$50,000 × the loss = 20 percent × the loss. Here, the $50,000 denominator is *not* the sum of the two policy faces; it is the sum of the amounts that would be payable if each policy stood by itself and the other policy did not exist.

The "other insurance" clause of the standard workers' compensation policy specifies proration by amounts payable. The reason should be obvious. The amounts payable under the relevant statute are, in effect, the policy limits.

The amounts payable approach is also used in connection with the property coverage under boiler and machinery insurance. The approach can be more equitable to the insurers than proration by face amounts. It can also be quite complex when policies have conflicting "other insurance" clauses. (In the latter situation, the boiler and machinery provision stipulates an alternative basis which is essentially a proration by face amounts.)

Apportionment. The fourth and final type of proportional loss sharing involves the so-called *apportionment clause* that is sometimes applicable when a fire policy is extended to cover additional perils. The most common is the apportionment clause in commercial and dwelling fire forms providing "extended coverage," extended coverage plus "additional named perils," or "all-risks" coverage. As explained in a previous chapter, "all-risks" coverage basically pays for all losses *except* those that are specifically excluded. The other two forms "extend" the fire policy to cover windstorm, hail, explosion, and a number of additional perils that are specifically named in the form.

The apportionment provision is divided into two distinct parts. The second part does not need to be examined at this juncture; it is essentially a complicated variation of the "amounts payable type" of "other insurance" clause. The first part of the provision is reproduced below:

> *Apportionment:* This Company shall not be liable for a greater proportion of any loss less the amount of the deductible, if any, from any peril or perils included in this policy than (A) the amount of insurance under the policy bears to the whole amount of fire insurance covering the property, or which would have covered the property except for the existence of this insurance, whether collectible or not, and whether or not such other fire insurance covers against the additional peril or perils insured against hereunder, nor (B) for a greater proportion of any loss. . . .

This part of the provision is unique in terms of its effect and its purpose. As to its effect, the provision limits the insurer's liability to no greater proportion of a loss than its total amount of coverage bears to *all fire insurance covering the property, whether or not the other policies insure the peril causing the loss.* For example, suppose insurer A provides the policyholder with a $5,000 policy covering fire and windstorm damage to a building. Insurer B provides the same policyholder (for the same building) a $5,000 policy covering fire damage only. A windstorm causes $2,000 in damage to the building. Insurer B, having provided no windstorm coverage, pays nothing for the loss. But insurer A will pay only 50 percent of the loss or $1,000 ($5,000/$10,000 × the loss = 50 percent of the loss or $1,000). The reason? Even though insurer A's policy face was larger than the loss, the apportionment clause treats the other policy *as though it provided windstorm coverage*—that is, the windstorm insurer's obligation is limited to the same proportion of loss that it would have been required to pay if *all* the fire policies on this building had likewise provided windstorm coverage.

The purpose of the first part of the apportionment clause is to encourage policyholders to insure against the additional perils as completely as they do against fire damage. If all the policies applicable to a given item of property are written to cover *exactly the same perils*, the policyholder will never be penalized by the apportionment clause. Nor will the policyholder be penalized by the purchase of separate coverage for flood, since this peril is excluded from the standard policy forms (and not subject to their apportionment clauses).

The apportionment clause no longer causes as many problems as it did in years past. First of all, the apportionment clause is no longer contained in any of the homeowners forms, nor in many of the commercial multi-peril forms, having been replaced by different types of "other insurance" clause. Second, the purchase of insurance against the extended coverage perils has become so common that what used to be an endorsement is now a part of the standard printed fire forms. Third, competent insurance producers and underwriters have become quite aware of the problems that may be created unless all fire insurance policies on a property cover identical perils. For all of the foregoing reasons, the penalty aspect of the apportionment clause seldom becomes operative, and most of the losses involving more than one policy are "apportioned" on a pro-rata liability basis.

Excess Provisions Many insurance policies contain *excess "other insurance"* provisions. This type of provision is designed to make the coverage of a policy "excess over" any other valid and collectible insurance that applies to the loss. Excess "other insurance" provisions are especially common in crime, liability, and auto coverages. For example, the relevant provision in a typical crime insurance policy reads as follows:

> If there is any other valid and collectible insurance which would apply in the absence of this policy, the insurance under this policy shall apply only as excess insurance over such other insurance. . . .

Suppose the above provision is contained in policy A, a $20,000 burglary policy. The insured also has another $10,000 burglary policy, policy B, that does not contain an "other insurance" clause. A burglar steals $8,000 worth of the insured property. Because of its excess provision, policy A would pay nothing. Policy B would pay the entire $8,000 loss. However, suppose the burglar had stolen $15,000 worth of insured property. Policy B would first pay its full limit of $10,000, while policy A would pay $5,000, the "excess over" the limit of liability of policy B. If the burglar had stolen $34,000 worth of insured property, policy B would pay $10,000, policy A would pay $20,000, and the insured would be out-of-pocket for the remaining $4,000 of uninsured loss.

Note that the insured is not deprived of the coverage of the policy containing the excess "other insurance" provision. Such a policy is excess insurance only in the sense that it does not apply until the limits of any other valid and collectible insurance have first been exhausted. If there is no other insurance, the policy acts as primary insurance. If there had been no policy B in the above illustration, for instance, policy A would have fully paid all losses from $1 to $20,000, its policy limit (ignoring any deductible or coinsurance provision). Likewise, policy A would have acted as primary insurance if (1) policy B had not been valid at the time of loss (perhaps due to fraud) or (2) the coverage of policy B had not been collectible at the time of loss (perhaps due to the insolvency of insurer B or a breach by the policyholder of a contract condition). In the latter two respects, the typical excess "other insurance" provision differs sharply from the customary pro-rata liability clause of the standard fire policy. The excess clause requires the insurer to pay up to its full policy limits, when all other insurance is either invalid or uncollectible at the time of loss. The pro-rata liability clause requires the insurer to pay only the hypothetical share it would have paid *if* all other insurance had been valid *and* collectible at the time of loss, even if one or both of the conditions are not actually met.

An excess "other insurance" *provision* is not the same thing as an excess insurance *policy*. Although the similarity in their effect makes it easy to confuse the two, they differ in several important respects.

It is helpful to think of an excess "other insurance" *provision* as an alternative to an outright prohibition of other insurance. When a policy flatly prohibits other insurance of the same type, a violation exonerates the insurer of all liability under the policy containing the prohibition. In many lines of insurance, an outright prohibition of other coverage is impractical. This penalty can also be harsh to an unwary policyholder. Compulsory insurance laws, social insurance programs, the diversity of insurance products, inter-state variations, and competition all operate to make some coverage overlaps inevitable. The intention of an excess "other insurance" clause is to provide coverage when there is no other applicable insurance. The policy only becomes excess over other insurance when other insurance applies to the loss.

In contrast, a true excess insurance *policy* never acts like primary insurance.[2] It is written subject to a large deductible amount. This same deductible amount applies, regardless of whether or not there is any other (underlying or primary) insurance. The excess policy does not pay for any loss that falls within the deductible. It merely adds a layer of protection "on top of" the deductible amount; i.e., it pays, up to its maximum limit, the amount by which a covered loss exceeds the deductible. It is intended to be an excess policy from the outset. It remains an excess policy even when there is no underlying insurance.

Excess policies are so common in liability insurance that the "other insurance" clause is often explicitly modified to accommodate their existence. The personal liability section of the homeowners policy forms will serve nicely to illustrate the point:

Other Insurance-Coverage E—Personal Liability
This insurance is excess over any other valid and collectible insurance except insurance written specifically to cover as excess over the limits of liability that apply in this policy.

Notice the explicit exception referred to in the second half of the quoted sentence. If this exception had not been made, all persons who bought both a homeowners and an excess liability policy would have had no first-dollar or underlying liability insurance to cover the exposures for which the homeowners policy was purchased in the first place. That is, in the absence of the above qualification, the homeowners liability coverage would have been excess over the upper limits of the excess liability policy. But the large deductible of the excess policy would have left the homeowner without any first-dollar liability insurance.[3] To avoid this consequence, the "other insurance" clause reaffirms that the homeowners liability coverage is intended to serve as underlying insurance in relation to exposures which are also covered by any excess liability policy.

Most excess "other insurance" provisions make the policy with the provision excess over the limits of any other valid and collectible insurance, regardless of when the other insurance became effective. A somewhat different approach is customary in ocean marine insurance. An ocean marine policy is made primary or excess *by its relative effective date*, when two or more policies are involved. For example, suppose two policies are written to cover the same cargo. According to the usual "other insurance" clause, the policy with the earlier effective date is primary. The policy with the later effective date is excess over the limits of the primary policy. If a third policy had a still later effective date, it would be excess over the second policy. However, all policies bearing the same effective date are deemed to be effective simultaneously, and the losses are shared between or among them on the basis of proration by face amounts.

Primary Provisions As should be apparent from the foregoing, the terms "excess" and "primary" may refer to (1) a different "level" of coverage or (2) the same "level" of coverage. By the operation of its large deductible, an excess policy places a "layer" of coverage on top of the upper limits of any primary or underlying policies. By the operation of its excess "other insurance" clause, a primary policy may itself become excess over the limits of other primary policies.

Alternatively, a given policy may have a clause explicitly stating that coverage is primary. That is, the given primary policy will pay its limit of liability before any other insurance policy becomes applicable to the loss in question. One example is the previously discussed ocean marine policy which becomes primary by virtue of its effective date. Another may be found in the general liability policy which contains the following "other insurance" clause:

> *Other Insurance:* The insurance afforded by this policy is primary insurance, except when stated to apply in excess of or contingent upon the absence of other insurance. When this insurance is primary and the insured has other insurance which is stated to be applicable to the loss on an excess or contingent basis, the amount of the company's (insurer's) liability under this policy shall not be reduced by the existence of such other insurance.

The clause goes on to provide for proportional loss sharing when other insurance is also written on a primary basis. The proportional sharing alternative is likewise found in policies with excess "other insurance" provisions. Just as two policies cannot simultaneously be primary, neither can two policies simultaneously be excess over one another. Therefore, an alternative sharing arrangement is frequently provided to resolve such conflicts.

With respect to "no-fault" auto or PIP (Personal Injury Protection) benefits, the "other insurance" provisions reflect the intent of the applicable law. Generally speaking, the intent is to make no-fault auto benefits excess over any comparable benefits which are payable under workers' compensation, Medicare, or compulsory temporary disability insurance statutes. On the other hand, the intent is usually to make no-fault auto benefits primary in relation to voluntary forms of health insurance. The voluntary health insurance may or may not duplicate the no-fault auto benefits, depending on the "other insurance" provision, if any, of the voluntary health insurance in question.

When two or more no-fault auto policies apply to the same accident, some laws stipulate that the vehicle owner's PIP benefits apply on a primary basis to the owner or the owner's relatives, and on an excess basis to all other eligible persons (e.g., occupants of the insured vehicle who are not relatives of the owner, or pedestrians who are struck by the insured vehicle). Other states stipulate that the owner's PIP benefits apply on a primary basis to *all* occupants of the insured vehicle. Under either kind of law, duplications of *auto* no-fault benefits are avoided. One auto policy invariably provides the no-fault benefits on a primary basis.

Except for true excess policies that are written subject to a large straight deductible, every policy will provide what is, in effect, primary coverage when it is the only policy that covers a particular loss. This can happen in several different ways:

(1) The coverage of a property insurance policy is primary when it is the only policy covering the property.

(2) Even if several policies cover the same property, a policy provides "primary" coverage when it insures against perils such as earthquake or flood, which are excluded by all the other policies of the insured.

(3) The standard workers' compensation policy provides "primary" coverage for statutory benefits when it is the only workers' compensation policy applicable, because job-connected accidents and diseases are virtually always excluded or covered on an excess basis by auto and health insurance policies. (In the few situations where two workers' compensation policies apply, the loss is prorated by amounts payable, as noted earlier).

(4) The coverage of a policy which contains an excess "other insurance" provision becomes "primary" (a) when there is no other insurance or (b) when the other insurance is not collectible or not valid at the time of loss.

(5) When the "other insurance" clause of a policy calls for proration by amounts payable, the coverage of such a policy becomes "primary" when no amounts are payable by the other policy(ies).

In each of these five situations, the coverage of a policy is or becomes "primary," apart from whether the policy explicitly contains a primary type of "other insurance" clause, because the policy is the only one that covers the loss. In practice, two or more policies often do cover the same loss, and their "other insurance" provisions are sometimes in conflict.

Conflicts Among "Other Insurance" Provisions

To illustrate the conflict that may arise, suppose each of two policies contains a clause that prohibits other insurance. Or, suppose each policy states that its coverage is to be excess over all other applicable insurance. Such conflicts would create an intolerable impasse. Were each clause to be interpreted literally, the insured would be deprived of all coverage. Or, one policy may declare that its coverage is excess, while another policy declares its coverage to be contributing. Or, one policy may provide for contribution by equal shares, while the other policy calls for proration by face amounts. Some of these conflicts have been resolved by the courts; others have not.

When all policies contain essentially identical but contradictory "other insurance" clauses, such as when all the policies are intended to provide excess coverage, or when all the policies prohibit other insurance, the courts usually have prorated liability among the insurers in some fashion believed to be equitable under the circumstances.[4] However, when two or more policies contain different types of "other insurance" provision, the court decisions have not been consistent.

Recognizing the problems created by conflicting policy provisions and inconsistent court decisions, most insurers abide by a set of principles designed to (a) allocate liability among insurers whose policies differ in scope or wording and (b) preserve protection for which insureds have paid premiums. These principles have found their latest and most complete expression in the *Guiding Principles—Casualty, Fidelity, Inland Marine—First-Party Property Losses and Claims.*[5] Developed by a number of insurance associations and promulgated on November 1, 1963, the *Guiding Principles* provide for the distribution of losses among policies that are not concurrent. This is a very complex subject which will be discussed here only with respect to its general application to "other insurance" clauses in property insurance.

As defined in the *Guiding Principles,* property insurance policies are *concurrent* if they are of the same general type (e.g., both or all fire policies, or both or all homeowners policies), insure the same interest and the identical property, and divide the exposure to a single major hazard. The policies may still be concurrent, even if they do not contain identical effective dates or limits, and apart from whether they contain deductibles or coinsurance clauses.[6] Thus, two fire insurance policies covering the same insured against loss to exactly the same property are deemed concurrent.

All situations within the general scope of the *Guiding Principles* involve "nonconcurrent" policies. Nonconcurrent policies can be of the same general type, such as fire insurance policies, but be nonconcurrent because they do not cover exactly the same property. For example, policy A may cover a building and its contents under one blanket amount of insurance, while policy B covers only contents. In addition, two or more policies of different general types (such as a fire policy and an inland marine policy, or a homeowners policy and a personal theft policy) are regarded as nonconcurrent.

Possible conflicts in "other insurance" clauses are dealt with explicitly as follows:

> These Principles provide for the equitable distribution of available insurance. As among insurance companies, the "other insurance" clause(s) which is (are) contained in a policy(ies) of the insurance, and which may include an excess provision, shall be set aside and be inoperative to the extent that it is (they are) in conflict with the purpose of these Principles. Otherwise, these Principles will not change coverage or other conditions under any policy(ies) of insurance.
>
> Further, the application of these Principles shall in no event operate

to reduce recovery to the insured below that which would have been obtained under any policy or policies covering the risk.[7]

The *Guiding Principles* establish a hierarchy of six orders of primacy among property insurance contracts. In decreasing order of primacy are insurance policies covering

(1) described articles or objects at a designated location,
(2) specifically described articles or objects without restriction as to location,
(3) described groups or classes of related articles or objects at a designated location,
(4) described groups or classes of related articles or objects without designating the location,
(5) all property at a designated location without specifying particular items or related groups or classes of property, and
(6) property without either designation of location or of particular items or related classes of property.

If two or more nonconcurrent policies are of the same order of primacy, liability for a loss is prorated in proportion to each policy's applicable limit of liability. In the *Guiding Principles*, the applicable limit of liability for each policy is considered to be the smallest of (1) the amount of insurance, (2) the amount of loss, or (3) the amount payable after applying any policy limitation.[8] Between policies with different degrees of primacy, the less primary policy becomes obligated to pay toward a loss only after the more primary policy has exhausted its limit of liability without fully paying the insured loss. If more than two policies are involved, some of them concurrent and one or more of them not, the concurrent policies are considered to be "group." Any part of the loss apportioned to a "group" of concurrent policies is shared by those policies on the basis of contribution by limits of liability for the loss.

Where contribution among nonconcurrent policies is called for, the *Guiding Principles* quite explicitly provide:

"Contribution," unless otherwise as specified in General Principle 1-G (which establishes the hierarchy of primacy described above), shall be on the basis of the applicable limit of liability under each respective policy or group of concurrent policies as though no other insurance existed, and the limit separately determined under each policy or group of concurrent policies shall be the smallest of the following:

(a) the amount of insurance
(b) the amount of loss, or
(c) the amount payable after applying any policy limitation(s)

The limits so determined of all policies or groups of concurrent policies herein declared contributing shall be added and, if the total amount exceeds the whole loss, each policy or group of concurrent policies shall pay such proportion of the loss as its limit bears to the sum of all the limits, but if the sum of the limits of liability is less than the whole loss, then each policy or group of concurrent policies shall pay its limit of liability. The determined liability of a group of concurrent policies shall be apportioned pro rata among the policies of the group.[9]

The procedure outlined here was demonstrated earlier in this chapter in connection with proration by limits of liability.

THE DOCTRINE OF SUBROGATION

If Kay negligently drives her car through a red light and strikes George's truck, his collision insurance may pay the expense of repairing the truck. However, George's insurer would probably attempt to recover the damages from Kay, or from her insurer. Once George's insurer has paid him, the insurer is "subrogated" to George's rights of recovery against Kay. The process of collecting from Kay (or her insurer) is known as "subrogation."

The doctrine of subrogation has been firmly rooted in the legal structure of the United States for well over a century. Subrogation is now recognized as a doctrine with rather broad dimensions, having been extended by the courts to embrace nearly every situation where the debt of one is paid by a nonvolunteer who is only secondarily liable for the debt.

General Meaning of Subrogation

The word "subrogation" apparently is derived from the Latin *subrogare*, which means "to put in place of another or to substitute." Substitution partially describes the process of subrogation, but it does not reveal the precise legal meaning or the substance of the current doctrine. A more accurate definition is as follows: *"subrogation is a right, equitable in origin and enforceable in common law, whereby a nonvolunteer who has made payment to another party by reason of a debt for which the nonvolunteer is only secondarily responsible, takes over that party's rights and remedies against the third party who is primarily responsible for such debt."*[10]

In the interest of precision, the above definition is necessarily rather wordy and cumbersome. Nevertheless, it does contain all of the so-called "essential elements of subrogation," namely that:

(1) the party claiming the right of subrogation shall have first paid the debt;

(2) the party claiming subrogation is not a mere volunteer, but has a legal obligation to pay the debt;

(3) the party claiming subrogation is only secondarily liable for the debt;

(4) a third party is primarily liable for the debt; and,

(5) no injustice will be done by allowing the subrogation to be exercised by the party claiming the right.

If all these elements are present, the "subrogee" is "subrogated" to whatever rights and remedies the "subrogor" may have against the third party. The *subrogee* is the nonvolunteer who is claiming the right of subrogation. The *subrogor* is the party whose rights and remedies are succeeded to—that is, the party who receives payment from the subrogee and whose rights are taken over by the subrogee.

Subrogation in Insurance

The doctrine of subrogation has a number of applications outside the field of insurance. However, it happens that insurance contracts have a natural affinity to subrogation doctrine, because the insurer agrees to pay various types of losses for which another party can often be held primarily responsible as a matter of law.

Subrogation in general liability insurance and surety bonding, due to its highly specialized nature, is reserved for study in CPCU 4. Here, the discussion will focus primarily on the application of subrogation doctrine to property insurance coverages and to the statutory benefits of workers' compensation and no-fault auto policies. In the discussion that follows, the *subrogee* is the insurer, who is secondarily liable for the debt. The *subrogor* is the insured (and the injured employee, in the case of worker's compensation to whom the debt is owed). And the third party is ordinarily the tortfeasor(s), who is primarily liable for the debt.

An Example To take a simple example, consider the insured who has auto collision insurance which is subject to a $100 deductible. A tortfeasor negligently causes $1,100 in damage to the auto covered by the collision insurance. The owner of the damaged auto could bring a negligence action directly against the guilty party. If the owner recovers the $1,100 in an action against the tortfeasor, no subrogation is involved. On the other hand, the vehicle owner could file a claim with his or her own collision insurer. Under the terms of the collision policy, the insurer would pay its insured $1,000 for the loss. Having done so, the insurer, to the extent of its payment, takes over its insured's legal rights and remedies against the negligent party. The insurer did not "volunteer" to pay the loss. Instead, it paid the loss because of its contractual obligation to its insured. This contractual payment does not relieve the negligent person from his or her liability for the damages caused. The negligent party is still primarily liable, as a matter of law. Thus, the collision insurer, having been only secondarily responsible, will attempt to recover its $1,000 payment by proceeding against the negligent party. As a matter of practice, most insurers will also assist the collision policyholder in recovering the amount of the deductible (more about this later).

Functions and Rationale In the absence of subrogation, the collision insured would receive a windfall, or the negligent party would be unjustly enriched. If the collision insured were allowed to collect from the tortfeasor, and also from the collision insurer, the insured would receive $2,100 for a $1,100 loss. If the insured collected only from the collision insurer and the insurer were to be denied subrogation rights, the tortfeasor would not be legally accountable for the wrong committed.

In contrast, the process of subrogation places the financial consequences of a wrongful act or omission on the party that the law holds primarily liable for consequences. To the extent that it achieves this central purpose, some of the most important functions of subrogation are:

(1) preventing the unjust enrichment of the third-party wrongdoer,
(2) preventing the windfall of a double recovery by the insured, thus preserving the principle of indemnity, and
(3) assuring equitable rate structures which properly allocate losses between liability and property coverages.

Moreover, subrogation recoveries are *not* a windfall gain to insurers. For each line of insurance to which subrogation applies, the amounts recovered by insurers (less the expenses of recovery) enter into the rate structure as a reduction in the incurred losses upon which the rates are based. To deny insurers the right of subrogation would cause a significant increase in the rates charged for many lines of insurance. For instance, it has been estimated that the abolition of insurer subrogation rights would require rate increases of at least 31 percent, 18 percent, and 12 percent in surety bonds, fidelity bonds, and auto collision insurance, respectively.[11]

In the case of auto collision and other property insurance coverages, the insurer's subrogation claim is most often brought as a negligence action against the tortfeasor. Since the negligent party is usually represented by a liability insurer, the subrogation proceeding is normally between two insurers. Therefore, the net subrogation recoveries of property insurers generally have the effect of yielding *lower property insurance rates* and *higher liability insurance rates* than would have been necessary in the absence of the subrogation recoveries.

Critics contend that the subrogation process (1) increases the volume of litigation and is unnecessarily expensive, (2) does not truly place the burden of loss on the negligent third parties, because they are usually protected by liability insurance, and (3) achieves a degree of rate equity which is strictly academic, because most policyholders carry both the property and the liability coverages which subrogation involves.

In point of fact, subrogation lawsuits between and among insurers are comparatively rare. Most disputes are resolved informally under the terms of the Nationwide Inter-Company Arbitration Agreement.[12] Numerous claims are handled without dispute. Industrywide figures concerning subrogation recovery expenses are not published. However, if the experience of one large insurer is any indication, aggregate subrogation recovery expenses amount to less than 2 percent of gross losses paid (and an even smaller percentage of earned premiums).

Liability insurance does relieve its insureds of the financial consequences of their torts, to the extent that both the torts and the consequences are actually covered by the policies they purchase. But this is a social disadvantage of liability insurance, not subrogation. Whether the claim against the third party is brought directly by an aggrieved person or through subrogation by the insurer, the financial resources of the defendant are theoretically immaterial to the determination of primary legal responsibility. However, one of the two types of actions is necessary to establish the defendant's liability. A denial of subrogation would either (1) relieve the defendant from legal *and* financial responsibility for his or her tort or (2) force the plaintiff to incur substantial costs in a direct action. Subrogation is a less expensive way of assuring that the primary legal responsibility for torts will come to rest where the law says it belongs. Moreover, liability insurance does not completely relieve the defendant of the financial consequences. In many cases negligent conduct will eventually require the liability insured to pay much higher premiums under merit rating or auto insurance (assigned risk) plans.

Nor is the relative equity between property and liability rates as academic as the critics contend. First and foremost, equitable rates are *required* by the rating laws of every state. Second, the buyers of property insurance are not necessarily the same people as the buyers of liability insurance. Auto liability insurance is compulsory in many states, for instance, while auto collision insurance is not legally required. In the absence of subrogation, all drivers would pay higher collision insurance rates, and all drivers would pay lower liability insurance rates. Third, subrogation is necessary to achieve a satisfactory degree of equity among insurers. The underwriting standards of different insurers vary considerably. An insurer that selects only the best drivers will have relatively good collision loss experience and lower collision rates than other insurers. This is mainly because subrogation enables the highly selective collision insurer to recover a higher percentage of the collision losses it pays. The absence of subrogation would deny both the insurer and its collision policyholders the benefits of selectivity.

Legal Foundations of Subrogation   To explain the legal foundations of subrogation, a distinction must be made between (1) the source of the right and (2) the basis of the legal action initiated under the right.

Sources of the Right.   The broad sources of the right of subrogation are (1) statutes and (2) common law. When it rests upon a statute, subrogation is accorded to insurers as a statutory right, and the nature and scope of the right are governed by the applicable statute. For instance, the typical workers' compensation statute expressly grants the right of subrogation to insurers and to qualified self-insurers. Some no-fault auto statutes also permit insurers to recover PIP benefits through subrogation. Other statutes do not. However, beyond the no-fault auto laws of some states, there are very few statutes which prohibit insurers from exercising their common law subrogation rights.

In the common law, two distinct types of subrogation are recognized. Subrogation is said to be either "equitable" or "contractual" in nature.

EQUITABLE SUBROGATION. Equitable subrogation (also called "legal" subrogation) is effected by the operation of the law, and it arises out of a condition or a relationship. Since it rests on equitable principles, equitable subrogation does not depend upon any contractual relationship between the parties. It is permitted, solely as a matter of equity, to prevent unjust enrichment. It is denied only where its exercise would work an injustice.

CONTRACTUAL SUBROGATION. Contractual subrogation (also called "conventional" subrogation) exists where the right is expressed by the parties. Since it rests on the law of contracts, its scope is measured both by the terms of the contractual agreement and by the rights the insured has against a third party. A contractual subrogation agreement must be a binding contract.

Bases of the Legal Actions.   The broad sources of the right of subrogation are statutes and common law. However, once the right of subrogation is established, the legal actions can be based upon any appropriate area of private law, according to the dictates of the particular situation. That is to say, the nature of the insurer's subrogation action will depend upon the rights and remedies which the insured has against the tortfeasor. The insured's right to recover money damages from the other party could be based upon the latter's negligence, strict liability, intentional interference, breach of contract, or failure to discharge the legal duties of an agency relationship. Likewise, the basis of the insurer's subrogation action is limited only by the extent to which the insured has a right to indemnity from the other party.

When the insured suffers property damage, the insured may or may not have the right to recover from another party. If not, there can be no subrogation by the insurer. If so, the insured's right of recovery is most often based upon the negligence of the other party. Hence, in property insurance the usual subrogation action is also based upon negligence.

Application of Subrogation to Types of Insurance Even where it is not prohibited by statute, the right of subrogation is not automatically accorded to insurers under every type of coverage they write. In the court decisions which constitute the common law, subrogation is uniformly denied to life insurers.[13] It is likewise denied under health insurance coverages, in the absence of an express policy provision. Subrogation is automatically allowed in the common law only under property-liability insurance coverages, whether valued or indemnity in nature.

With respect to health insurance coverages, the courts historically have held that insurers have no inherent or "equitable" right of subrogation. These decisions have been founded largely on the mistaken assumption that all health insurance coverages are valued in nature. But a growing number of courts will permit subrogation under health insurance coverage when (1) it is not specifically denied by statute and (2) the policy contains an explicit subrogation provision. In other words, many courts now allow "contractual" subrogation in health insurance.

Despite their views on subrogation in life and health insurance, the courts uniformly have recognized the insurer's right of subrogation under property insurance coverages, even those of a valued nature, apart from whether the policy contains an express subrogation provision. In other words, all courts allow either "equitable" or "contractual" subrogation in property insurance. Even so, most property insurance policies do contain explicit subrogation clauses or provisions.

Subrogation Provisions The various subrogation provisions can be illustrated by the language used in the standard fire policy, the workers' compensation policy, the personal auto policy, and the no-fault auto endorsement of one state. The relevant provision in the standard fire policy reads:

> *Subrogation.* This Company (insurer) may require from the insured an assignment of all right of recovery against any party for loss to the extent that payment therefor is made by this Company (insurer).

The comparable provision in the standard workers' compensation policy is as follows:

> Subrogation: In the event of any payment under this policy, the company shall be subrogated to all rights of recovery therefor of the insured and any person entitled to the benefits of this policy against any person or organization, and the insured shall execute and deliver instruments and papers and do whatever else is necessary to secure such rights. The insured shall do nothing after loss to prejudice such rights.

Under the personal auto policy, all coverages (except PIP benefits) are subject to the following subrogation provision:

> OUR RIGHT TO RECOVER PAYMENT
>
> A. If we make a payment under this policy and the person to or for whom payment was made has a right to recover damages from another we shall be subrogated to that right. That person shall do whatever is necessary to enable us to exercise our rights and shall do nothing after loss to prejudice them . . .
>
> B. If we make payment under this policy and the person to or for whom payment is made recovers damages from another, that person shall hold in trust for us the proceeds of the recovery and shall reimburse us to the extent of our payment.

Under the PIP endorsement used in one state that permits subrogation, the subrogation provision is rather extensive. It reads:

> Reimbursement and Trust Agreement. Subject to any applicable limitations set forth in the New Jersey Automobile Reparation Reform Act, in the event of any payment to any person under this endorsement:
>
> (a) the Company shall be entitled to the extent of such payment to the proceeds of any settlement or judgment that may result from the exercise of any rights of recovery of such person against any person or organization legally responsible for the bodily injury because of which such payment is made; and the Company shall have a lien to the extent of such payment notice of which may be given to the person or organization causing such bodily injury, his agent, his insurer or a court having jurisdiction in the matter;
>
> (b) such person shall hold in trust for the benefit of the Company all rights of recovery which he shall have against such other person or organization because of such bodily injury;
>
> (c) such person shall do whatever is proper to secure and shall do nothing after loss to prejudice such rights;

(d) such person shall execute and deliver to the Company such
instruments and papers as may be appropriate to secure the
rights and obligations of such person and the Company established by this provision.

This last provision reflects the statutory requirements of a particular
state. Otherwise, the wording of most no-fault insurance subrogation
provisions follows essentially the same pattern.

In a sense, the insurer's right of subrogation is independent of
policy provisions. As explained earlier, the courts have uniformly
upheld the right of the insurer to *equitable* subrogation under all
indemnity-type coverages, as well as under all property coverages of a
valued nature, even when they did not contain an express subrogation
clause. Nonetheless, nearly all property-liability policies do, in fact,
contain such provisions. Why? Express subrogation provisions are
considered necessary or otherwise desirable for the following reasons:

(1) Since workers' compensation, no-fault auto, and auto medical
payments benefits are essentially health insurance coverages,
most courts would not allow equitable subrogation. An express
subrogation provision entitles the insurer to contractual subrogation (unless it, too, is prohibited by statute or regulation);

(2) As a general rule of common law, the insurer is usually not
entitled to exercise the right of subrogation until its insured has
been *paid in full.* A strict interpretation of this rule would deny
subrogation under contracts containing deductibles, coinsurance clauses, or "other insurance" provisions when the loss is
not paid "in full." To circumvent the general rule and clarify the
intent, the typical subrogation provision stipulates that the
insurer will be subrogated *to the extent of its payment.* This is
known in the law as subrogation *pro tanto,* which means "for
as much as may be" or "as far as it goes." A *pro tanto*
subrogation right may be exercised without having first paid
the loss in full.

For example, a collision insurer may pay its policyholder the
portion of a loss in excess of the deductible and immediately
attempt to recover its payment from a negligent party. Most
insurers voluntarily follow the practice of assisting the policyholder in recovering the amount of the deductible, though the
policyholder must sometimes bear a proportional share of the
cost of recovery;

(3) Many subrogation provisions contain wording to the effect that
"the insured shall do nothing after loss to prejudice such
(subrogation) rights." Such a phrase has the minimum objective
of deterring the policyholder from signing any agreements or

otherwise doing anything which might impair the insurer's right of recovery from another party. Under certain circumstances, to be discussed in the next chapter, an insured's breach of this condition can even result in a denial of coverage; and,

(4) Some insurers fear that the failure to include an express provision in a revised policy form might be construed by the courts as a voluntary waiver of the insurer's right of subrogation, especially when such a provision was a part of earlier versions of the policy form.

These are the major reasons why property-liability policies nearly always contain subrogation provisions. Failure to include the desired provisions may impair the right of subrogation or defeat it entirely. Even where this is not the case, the provisions are believed to have other useful functions.

Insurer Waivers of Subrogation The right of subrogation has an obvious monetary value to the insurer. The policyholder cannot unilaterally waive the insurer's right of subrogation, since it is not the policyholder's right in the first place. Nor can the policyholder do anything after a loss to prejudice or impair the insurer's right of recovery against third parties. However, an insurer may expressly allow a policyholder to waive, *prior to loss*, the policyholder's right to recover from a specific third party. Or, the insurer may have the right of subrogation but refuse to exercise it *after a loss*.

Before the Loss. Limited waivers prior to loss may be permitted by inserting the following kind of clause into a property insurance policy:

> SUBROGATION: This insurance shall not be invalidated should the named Insured waive in writing prior to a loss any or all right of recovery against any party for loss occurring to the property described.

This clause is not a complete waiver of the insurer's right of subrogation. It merely permits the policyholder to participate in some noninsurance transfer agreements without invalidating the property insurance. The insurer retains its right of subrogation against any party with whom the property insured has not made such a written agreement.

For example, before a railroad will extend a sidetrack into or near a privately owned building, the railroad usually insists upon a written contract under which the building owner agrees to "hold and save harmless" the railroad for any damage to the building as a result of the sidetrack operation. Since a hold-harmless agreement of this type would adversely affect the building insurer's right of subrogation, the owner's building insurance would thereby be invalidated. Similarly, a landlord may wish to hold a tenant harmless if the tenant's negligence causes fire damage to the building. (This is quite often done when the tenant is an affiliated or a subsidiary corporation of the landlord.) Often a tenant's attorney will insist on such a hold-harmless agreement. Such an agreement would likewise invalidate the landlord's fire insurance. Both examples involve a problem which can be resolved by including the clause quoted above in the property insurance policy. In fact, though the clause once required an endorsement and sometimes an extra premium charge, it is now included automatically in many standardized property insurance forms. The clause grants the policyholder the pre-loss privilege of entering into hold-harmless agreements with specific parties. Yet, the insurer retains its subrogation rights against others, and the policyholder retains the post-loss obligation to avoid impairing the insurer's right of subrogation against them.

After the Loss.   Even when the insurer has completely preserved its legal right to subrogation, the insurer which wishes to do so may decline to exercise the right after a loss. Such declinations may take the form of (1) "knock-for-knock agreements," (2) deductible waivers, or (3) other case-by-case managerial decisions. The first is primarily of historical interest. The latter two are still quite common.

Knock-for-Knock Agreements   Knock-for-knock agreements are special, private agreements between two (or more) insurers or between an insurer and a large "self-insurer." Under the terms of the agreement, the parties voluntarily waive the exercise of subrogation rights against one another. To illustrate, suppose insurer C, an auto collision insurer, and insurer L, an auto liability insurer, are both parties to a knock-for-knock agreement. Insurer C suffers an auto collision loss which is due to the negligence of a liability policyholder of insurer L. Insurer C simply pays its collision loss and does not exercise its right to recover through subrogation. Insurer L has agreed to do likewise whenever it has a subrogation claim against a policyholder of insurer C. Under a variation of the agreement, each party agrees to pay 50 percent of the amount otherwise payable to another party to the agreement.

The basic objective of knock-for-knock agreements was to minimize subrogation lawsuits and other expenses of recovery, on the (undocumented) theory that over time the amounts an insurer collected under subrogation versus the amounts it paid out under subrogation would have been a "washout," anyway. But abuse of these special arrangements soon become commonplace. Some liability insurers would pay the claimant the amount of the collision deductible and then send the claimant to his or her own collision insurer for the balance. Conversely, some collision insurers would advise their insureds to collect from the *tortfeasor's* liability insurer rather than have a claim on their records. Not only did the knock-for-knock plans invite abuse; they distorted the loss ratios and rate structures of the participating insurers. Furthermore, the development of a Nationwide Inter-Company Arbitration Agreement proved a much better way to reduce subrogation recovery expenses and resolve disputes. It is probably fortunate, therefore, that the vast majority of knock-for-knock agreements have been set aside. Most insurers seem to have no regrets.

Deductible Waivers A deductible waiver is another matter entirely. For instance, suppose Smith carries $100 deductible auto collision coverage with a particular insurer. Jones carries auto property damage liability coverage *with the very same insurer.* Jones negligently causes $1,100 in damage to Smith's car. It would be pointless for the insurer to impose the $100 deductible on Smith, pay Smith $1,000, subrogate against Jones, recover $1,000 from itself, and then pay Smith $100 on behalf of Jones. Thus, insurers routinely waive the property insurance deductible when one of their liability insureds negligently causes property damage to one of their own property insureds (a very common situation for large insurers who have millions of auto insurance policyholders). To avoid distortion of the rate structures, the entire amount of such a loss should be included in the *liability* loss experience of the insurer. On the other hand, some insurers make it a practice to waive the collision deductible whenever two of their own policyholders are involved in an auto accident, no matter which of the two may have been negligent.

Case-by-Case Managerial Decisions When the tortfeasor is not a policyholder of the insurer, the question whether to exercise subrogation rights is decided on a case-by-case basis. There are at least four situations where insurers commonly decline to exercise their subrogation rights. Subrogation rights may not be exercised, in a given case, where the insurer fears that doing so would be likely to (1) stir up a dangerous counter demand, (2) yield no net recovery, because of the recovery costs, or because the tortfeasor is uninsured and without assets, (3) injure the insurer's reputation, or (4) embarrass a valuable insured. Particularly when amounts involved are large, decisions of this sort are often made at the upper levels of management.

SUMMARY REVIEW OF
THE PRINCIPLE OF INDEMNITY

The *principle of indemnity* is the universally accepted presupposition or assumption that the proper function of insurance is to indemnify, make whole again financially, or put the insured back into the same financial position that he or she enjoyed before the insured event occurred. Stated in the negative, the principle of indemnity means simply that a person should not profit from an insured loss.

The principle of indemnity has been referred to in this volume in several different contexts. A review of the principle is a fitting way to conclude the analysis of the amounts of recovery. It should also prove helpful in understanding the relationship between the principle of indemnity and various concepts and practices which have been discussed separately in the previous pages. Specifically, the reader's attention will be directed to (1) some apparent departures from the principle of indemnity and (2) a brief review of the devices used to implement and preserve the principle of indemnity.

Apparent Departures from the Principle of Indemnity

Allowing an insured to "profit" from a loss would violate the principle of indemnity. Thus, according to many observers, the principle is violated by valued and replacement cost coverages under which the insurance payment may exceed the actual dollar loss. Each of these contentions must be evaluated.

Valued Coverages   Under valued property insurance coverages, it is possible for the insured to profit from a *total* loss. As respects buildings, this can happen in states with valued policy laws. As respects personal property, it can happen anywhere in the world, under the valued policy forms of ocean and inland marine insurers.

In spite of the theoretical possibilities, no insurer would knowingly insure an item of property for more than 100 percent of each insured's insurable interest. Indeed, because valued policy forms potentially result in violations of the principle of indemnity, insurers are sometimes inclined to take special underwriting precautions. Appraisals of the property's insurable value are often required.

The potential for overindemnification is countered, in effect, by the widespread tendency to underinsure property in the first place. More important, inflation actually diminishes the chances of profiteering under a valued policy form. The policy limit usually remains constant during the policy period, while.the insurable value of the property is increasing. This is especially true of buildings and highly valuable personal articles, the very kinds of property which are often insured on a valued basis.

With the notable exception of arson, profiteering through valued policy forms is not as common as it might first appear. In an aggregate sense, underinsurance is probably a more serious social problem than principle-of-indemnity violations that happen to favor honest claimants.

Replacement Cost Coverages Whether or not replacement cost property insurance coverages violate the principle of indemnity is an issue that has been debated since the earliest days of fire insurance. By the late 1960s, the issue appeared to have been settled satisfactorily. Replacement cost coverage on dwellings and other buildings had become widespread, whereas personal property could usually be insured only on an actual cash value basis (with the exception of fine arts, which could be scheduled on valued policy forms).

The 1970s ushered in a period of double-digit inflation rates. Replacement cost coverage became available for residential personal property. However, highly inflated real estate values, along with a growing arson problem, caused most insurers to decline replacement cost coverage and insist on actual cash value forms for insuring older dwellings. The issue of replacement cost versus actual cash value coverage has therefore resurfaced.

At the core of the debate are the related questions of (1) whether replacement cost coverage violates the principle of indemnity and (2) if so, whether the moral hazards can be managed adequately. The answer to the first question turns on what is meant by "indemnity."

It does not overindemnify property owners to pay them on the basis of the ACV or physically depreciated value of used property. However, it would overindemnify them to pay them *more than* it would cost to replace their depreciated used property with new property. The question is, does a property owner "profit" when old property is replaced with new property of like kind and quality, without any deduction for physical depreciation? To a degree, the dwelling or commercial building owner does gain by a replacement cost settlement, *to the extent that it extends the useful lifetime* of the structure or a portion of the structure. However, a replacement cost loss settlement is not truly "profitable" to a property owner unless it increases (1) the market value of the property or (2) its value in use prior to sale. Neither may be the case, as a practical matter.

The market value of real estate includes the land, reflects the general economic conditions, depends on the relative bargaining strength of the buyer and the seller, and has no necessary relationship to the replacement cost of the building itself. Replacing all or a portion of a structure with new materials will not necessarily increase the practical market value of the real estate. Likewise, the building's use value to its owner is not altered, in the usual case, by a replacement cost loss settlement. For example, before a fire destroyed a dwelling, its owner had a home with three bedrooms, two bathrooms, and 2,500 square feet of living space. After the loss has been settled on a replacement cost basis, the owner has a home with three bedrooms, two bathrooms, and 2,500 square feet of living space (or the monetary equivalent of the former, if the owner had decided that it would be a convenient time to add another bedroom). The foregoing comments likewise apply, in a qualified way, to most items of personal property. Most insureds are honest and careful people who have no intention of making a profit from an unintended (insured) loss. It is primarily the minority, the dishonest or careless persons, who make the writing of replacement cost coverage a potentially dangerous and debatable practice from the viewpoint of insurers.

In addition to excluding specified types of personal property from the replacement cost coverage endorsement, insurers use a variety of techniques to cope with the phenomena of moral and morale hazards. Underwriting decisions and eligibility requirements limit the availability of replacement cost building coverage to dwellings and commercial buildings which are fairly new, or to those which have market values equal to or greater than a certain percentage of their replacement costs. Policy provisions allow a replacement cost settlement only if the structure is actually repaired or replaced. Some policies add the further condition that the structure must be rebuilt at the same location, if a replacement cost settlement is to apply. Older buildings which have replacement costs far greater than their market values are generally not eligible for replacement cost coverage. Actual cash value or repair cost forms must be used.

Do these underwriting safeguards and policy provisions serve to manage the moral and morale hazards adequately? In relation to windstorm and other perils of nature, they probably do. With respect to covered losses caused by persons, the degree of success is less certain.

Crimes Against Property Lamentably, so-called "crimes against property" now require more than a footnote to any discussion of replacement cost coverage and its relationship to the principle of indemnity. Incendiary fires, arson for profit, burglary, robbery, theft, and embezzlement have become a severe problem.

Incendiary and suspicious fires took 675 lives and caused an estimated $1.3 billion in property damage in 1979 alone, a dollar figure 24.5 percent higher than in the previous year.[14] Additionally, burglary, robbery, larceny, and motor vehicle theft accounted for a combined 1979 loss of $7.05 billion. Though accurate loss figures for embezzlement and other "white-collar crimes" are not available, estimates run as high as $20 billion per year. All told, crimes against property now result in losses of more than $25 billion annually, and the dollar amounts continue to grow at much higher annual rates than the overall rates of economic inflation.

To combat the arson problem, insurance industry leaders are laboring throughout the country with investigators, police and fire officials, judges, prosecutors, and other concerned citizens. An "All-Industry Committee for Arson Control" is assisting in the efforts to pass laws which (1) increase the penalties for arson and (2) facilitate the exchange of arson investigation information among insurers and law enforcement agencies, without fear of legal reprisal. Such efforts have not yet produced dramatic reductions in arson, but they do offer hope for progress.

Devices for Implementing or Preserving the Principle of Indemnity

The pages of this volume have contained separate discussions of various "devices" which share, as at least *one* of their purposes or functions, the implementation or preservation of the principle of indemnity. Although these devices include underwriting and claims practices designed to prevent insurance profiteering, our emphasis has been on policy provisions and legal doctrines which serve as limitations on the dollar amounts of recovery available under property and liability insurance contracts. In order to bring these devices together into a cohesive whole, a very brief and therefore oversimplified summary seems advisable.

When only *one property* insurance policy is involved, the following devices help to preserve the principle of indemnity by limiting the maximum amounts of recovery:

(1) the insurable interest doctrine and related policy provisions,
(2) loss valuation provisions and insurer settlement options,
(3) policy limits (including the requirements of valued policy laws),
(4) underwriting restrictions, and
(5) claims settlement practices.

When *two or more property* insurance policies are involved, or if there is more than one source of recovery, the following devices have, as one function, the preservation of the indemnity principle:

(1) to (5) (same as above),
(6) "other insurance" provisions,
(7) the doctrine of subrogation and related policy provisions, and
(8) exclusions to prevent coverage duplications.

The two groups of devices just named apply to property insurance policies and to property insurance coverages of multi-peril policies. A different set of devices applies to third-party liability insurance policies, as well as to the general liability coverages of multi-peril policies.

Violations of the principle of indemnity are perhaps best thought of as "departures" from its traditional interpretation. Such departures are not especially serious, as long as insurers are able to maintain adequate controls over moral and morale hazards. Blatant and intentional profiteering does occur, in both property and liability insurance, in spite of numerous devices which have the purpose or effect of safeguards. However, among honest persons, underinsurance is probably more serious a problem than overinsurance.

Chapter Notes

1. If each insurer has charged the same premium rate, the pro-rata liability clause also results in a situation where each insurer's share of the loss is proportionate to its share of the total premium. However, achieving relative premium equity is secondary to the loss-distribution and indemnity-preservation functions of the pro-rata liability clause.

2. The process of "layering" or stacking successive levels of coverage on top of one another is often used by large buyers of commercial liability insurance. For example, to obtain a total limit of $3 million, a corporation may buy three layers of $1 million each. The second layer of $1 million is excess over the first primary layer of $1 million, and the third layer is, in effect, excess over the second primary layer. A given layer is never primary in relation to the same or a lower level of coverage, because each layer contains its own excess "other insurance" clause.

3. The discussion of excess liability insurance assumes a "true" excess policy, to minimize the complexities. Actually, most homeowners who buy excess liability insurance have a personal umbrella policy. An umbrella policy usually provides true excess insurance over (1) the minimum underlying limits the policyholder is presumed to carry or, if larger, (2) the actual underlying limits carried by the policyholder. However, the usual umbrella policy goes one step further. It also covers some losses that are not covered by the underlying policy, but subject to a stipulated policyholder "retention limit," which is a straight deductible of a smaller amount than the deductible of the excess policy that applies to exposures covered by the underlying insurance.

4. Robert E. Keeton, *Basic Text on Insurance Law* (St. Paul: West Publishing Company, 1971), pp. 170-171, and cases cited here.

5. *Guiding Principles—Casualty, Fidelity, Inland Marine—First-Party Property Losses and Claims* (New York: Association of Casualty & Surety Companies, et al., 1963).

6. *Guiding Principles*, p. 37.

7. *Guiding Principles*, p. 111.

8. *Guiding Principles*, p. 1.

9. *Guiding Principles*, p. 3.

10. For a comprehensive treatise on the right of subrogation and its importance to insurers, see Ronald C. Horn, *Subrogation in Insurance Theory and Practice* (Homewood, IL: Richard D. Irwin, Inc., 1964).

11. See Ronald C. Horn, Chapters 11, 12, 13, and 14, which show the average subrogation recovery ratios for various types of insurance and bonds. As a percent of gross losses paid, industrywide average net subrogation recoveries were 31.3 percent (surety bonds), 18.3 percent (fidelity bonds), 12.5 percent (auto collision) and 1 percent to 3 percent for most other lines. However, these data extend only to 1960. Recent spot checks with large

auto insurers have confirmed that some insurers are now able to recover 15 percent or more of the gross losses paid under auto collision coverages. The subrogation recovery ratios for most lines of property insurance have been growing over time, mainly due to (1) the more aggressive efforts of insurers and (2) the growth of liability insurance (which helps pay the subrogation claims of property insurers).

12. Ronald C. Horn, Chapter 8 and Appendix D.
13. The reasons for denying subrogation to life insurers are beyond the scope of CPCU study, but they are analyzed in Ronald C. Horn, Chapter 3, especially pp. 36-40.
14. All statistics in this section were taken from *Insurance Facts*, 1980-81 Edition (New York: Insurance Information Institute), the sources of which were The National Fire Protection Association, the FBI, and the American Management Association. At the time of this writing, 1979 data are the most recent available.

CHAPTER 14

Contract Conditions
Affecting Insurance Coverage

INTRODUCTION

In preceding chapters, the analysis of insurance policy provisions was based on two crucial assumptions:

(1) Each policy was assumed to be a legally enforceable agreement.
(2) The insured was assumed to be in full compliance with all policy conditions.

These two assumptions were made in order to isolate the implications of each policy provision. They are also realistic and correspond to the facts in most claims situations.

While substantial compliance with policy conditions usually exists, any insured who breaches a policy condition takes the chance of reducing the amount of recovery or releasing the insurer entirely from its obligations under the contract. Such consequences can be disastrous to the insured entity and troublesome to the insurer and its representatives. The bulk of this chapter is devoted to (1) the general nature and significance of insurance policy conditions, (2) specific conditions found in property and liability policies, and (3) some of the basic principles that govern court interpretations of insurance policy conditions. To set the stage, the first section will deal briefly with the effects of an unenforceable insurance policy.

UNENFORCEABLE INSURANCE CONTRACTS

An insurance policy may be "unenforceable" for several reasons, in which case it will not be enforced by our courts of law. As explained in Chapter 8, a property insurance policy that is not supported by a valid insurable interest is "unenforceable." An insurance policy may also be unenforceable if it does not satisfy all the legal requirements of a valid and enforceable contract. For example, since a binding contract requires valuable "consideration," a policy would not be enforceable if the insured refused to pay the premium. Or, the policy may be unenforceable because the insured misrepresented a material fact, concealed a material fact, or committed an act of outright fraud in the process of obtaining the insurance. The elements of an enforceable contract are discussed in detail in CPCU 6.

If an insurance policy is unenforceable, an insurer can deny liability under the policy, leaving the insured without any coverage. If necessary, the insurer may have the policy "rescinded" by a court of law. To *rescind* a policy is to declare it null and void from the outset, because it never legally existed as an enforceable agreement in the first place. *Rescission* is not the same thing as *cancellation*. To *cancel* a policy is to acknowledge its legal validity and terminate it according to its own terms. Various state laws restrict the insurer's right to cancel specified types of property and liability policies. However, an insurer may normally contest the legal validity of a property or liability policy, at any time, for any reason which would make it unenforceable.

When an insurer refuses to pay a loss on the grounds that the insured breached a policy condition, the insurer is *not* trying to say that the policy is unenforceable. Instead, the insurer is admitting the validity of the policy and strictly enforcing its provisions.

THE GENERAL NATURE AND SIGNIFICANCE OF INSURANCE POLICY CONDITIONS

Before turning to the specific conditions that may be found in property and liability policies, the next three sections will (1) provide a general definition of a policy condition, (2) distinguish between two broad types of policy condition, and (3) summarize the general effects when a policy condition is breached by an insured.

Policy Condition Defined

An insurance policy condition is a clause or provision that qualifies an otherwise enforceable promise of the insurer. By definition, a policy condition is a provision that is contained in the policy in question. Some policy conditions are set forth in a section of the policy labeled "Conditions." Other conditions may be found almost anywhere in the forms, endorsements, or other documents that together constitute the entire contract. Thus, a policy condition is any policy provision that has the effect of qualifying the insurance contract, regardless of what it is called or where it is located in the policy.

The insurer does not make absolute or unqualified promises to perform. To the contrary, the insurer makes conditional or qualified promises of a contingent or dependent nature. The insurer makes enforceable promises to pay, furnish a legal defense, or provide other services, but *only if* (1) an insured event occurs *and* (2) the insured entity has fulfilled its contractual duties to perform specified acts and to refrain from engaging in acts that are specifically prohibited. The key word here is "if." Thus, the insurer will pay only

- *if* the insured reports losses promptly,
- *if* the insured refrains from jeopardizing the insurer's subro-gration rights,
- *if* the insured cooperates, and
- *if*....

In short, a policy condition is a provision that "attaches some strings" to the otherwise enforceable promises that are made by the insurer.

Types of Policy Condition

Policy conditions may be classified in a number of different ways. For our purposes, it will suffice to make a distinction between "conditions precedent" and "conditions subsequent."

Conditions Precedent A condition precedent is a condition that must be met *before* a right or duty becomes enforceable. Therefore, a condition precedent is a policy stipulation that must be met *before* the insurer's promise(s) will become enforceable. Note that there may be several. For example, the occurrence of an insured event is a condition precedent to the enforceability of the insurer's promise to pay property or liability losses (or provide a legal defense for the insured of a liability policy). The insured's duties to report a loss promptly, file a proof of loss, and maintain protective safeguards are also examples of conditions precedent which may be stipulated in the policy. The policy conditions that stipulate these duties will be examined later. The point here is that, if any one of these duties is stipulated in a policy condition but not fulfilled by the insured, the insurer's promise(s) will not become enforceable.

Conditions Subsequent A condition subsequent is a condition that must be met, *after* all the conditions precedent have been met, in order to avoid *releasing* the insurer from a promise that was previously enforceable. At the point in time when all the conditions precedent are fulfilled, the insurer's promise becomes enforceable. Thereafter, a breach of a condition subsequent extinguishes the contractual obligation(s) the insurer had before the breach. For example, suppose an insured event occurs under a general liability policy. The insured reports the claim promptly, gives a sworn statement, and otherwise fulfills all the conditions precedent that are stipulated in the policy. However, the policy also requires the insured to "cooperate with the insurer" in the defense of a claim. The insured who fails to cooperate breaches a condition subsequent, and the insurer may be able to withdraw its defense and deny the entire claim. Thus, an obligation that was originally enforceable against the insurer becomes unenforceable by virtue of the breach of the condition subsequent.

There are at least two reasons for distinguishing between conditions precedent and conditions subsequent. First, it is important to realize that the insured's duties do not necessarily end once an insured event has occurred and a claim has been filed. The insured must also comply with whatever conditions subsequent are stipulated in the policy. In fact, when subrogation is involved, the insured may have duties even after its loss has been paid. Second, although a breach of either type of condition may release the insurer from its obligation to perform, the courts usually make it more difficult for the insurer to deny liability for the insured's breach of a condition subsequent.

General Effects of an Insured's Breach of Condition

Most contracts of sale, along with many other contracts, involve an exchange of promises between the contracting parties. If either party violates the terms of the contract, the other party may bring a breach of contract action and collect money damages from the violator, or bring an action in equity (such as an action to require the violator to perform as originally agreed). This is not true of insurance contracts. After the premium is paid and the contract itself is otherwise enforceable, only the insured can obtain a court order to enforce the contract. If the insured breaches a condition in an enforceable policy, the insurer cannot recover money damages in a breach of contract action.[1] The insurer may at most be released from its promise(s) to perform.

When an insured breaches a policy condition, the precise effects depend on the nature and extent of the breach, the circumstances under which the breach was committed, and the court interpretations in the applicable jurisdiction. Since court decisions have not been entirely consistent, accurate generalizations are difficult to make. In the absence of a specified set of facts and a specified legal jurisdiction, it can only be said (safely) that the insurer *may* be released entirely from any obligation to perform under the contract in question. Or, if indicated in the policy condition, the amount of recovery may be reduced. The insured may or may not be required to forfeit any premiums that had been paid prior to the insurer's discovery of the breach. If the insurer has reason to believe that a court would not uphold an outright denial of liability, it may decide to pay the claim voluntarily. It may also decide to initiate a notice of cancellation, thus avoiding similar claims in the future. Furthermore, as discussed later, the insurer may be deemed by a court to have waived its right to deny liability.

SPECIFIC CONDITIONS IN PROPERTY AND LIABILITY INSURANCE POLICIES

The provisions of an insurance contract generally do not contain the words "conditions precedent" or "conditions subsequent." However, the courts treat the promised performance as conditions precedent or subsequent, wherever they may be found in the policy. Conditions, like other insurance provisions, must be clear and unambiguous. Any ambiguity or inconsistency found in a contract drafted by the insurer will be interpreted in favor of the insured. The court may also impose other doctrines to interpret policy conditions in a way that will result in granting coverage, even where the literal reading of the policy provision would lead to a denial of coverage. Some of these doctrines will be explained later in the chapter.

In the sections that follow, individual conditions involving particular policies will be examined. The content and purpose of each condition must be studied to understand its function in the contract. It also is necessary to see what actions constitute compliance. The analysis will show the application of legal principles discussed earlier.

Conditions Suspending Coverage—Continuing Promises

In this section, some examples of conditions that suspend coverage are discussed.

Property Insurance Conditions that suspend coverage are found most frequently in property insurance. Consider the following lines from the standard fire policy:

Conditions suspending or restricting insurance. Unless otherwise provided in writing added hereto this Company shall not be liable for loss occurring (a) while the hazard is increased by any means within the control or knowledge of the insured; or (b) while a described building, whether intended for occupancy by owner or tenant, is vacant or unoccupied beyond a period of sixty consecutive days; or (c) as a result of explosion or riot, unless fire ensue, and in that event for loss by fire only.

The *increase in hazard clause* and the *vacancy and unoccupancy clauses* probably are the most common examples of continuing promises that suspend the insurance entirely if they are breached. An increase in hazard must be within the control or knowledge of the insured before it will result in a suspension of coverage. Courts have liberally interpreted this condition in favor of the insured, and some have effectively changed "or" to "and" so that both knowledge *and* control are required to suspend coverage. As one court stated: "An increase of hazard as used in policy to exclude liability where insureds increase the hazard, occurs only when the insureds perform acts which are reasonably calculated to increase the risk and which the insureds know or should know will increase the risk."[2] Mere negligence or misjudgment of the insured is not enough to bring the action within the provision.

Many situations involve actions of tenants. If a tenant increases the hazard without the knowledge of the insured landlord, the condition has not been breached by the insured. The insured will not be deprived of the insurance protection, even though a loss occurs while the hazard has been increased. Statutes in a few states provide that a violation of a policy condition shall not be a defense for an insurer if the breach did not contribute to the loss. Other statutes provide that the coverage will not be suspended unless the breach was material *or* it contributed to the loss. One court stated that the insurer has the burden of proving not only the breach, but also that the breach resulted in a likelihood of appreciable prejudice to the insurer.

A condition that frequently suspends coverage is the *vacancy and unoccupancy clause.* It provides that if the premises are vacant or unoccupied for a period longer than sixty days, the insurance will be suspended. The vacancy and unoccupancy provisions are waived in writing in many property insurance policies. Nevertheless, these clauses have produced a great deal of litigation. For example, suppose that the insured is in a hospital for a period longer than sixty days. If he or she had been living alone, was the home unoccupied during the hospital stay? In general, the answer is that the premises will be considered occupied so long as there is an intent to occupy. Even here, however, the situation may invite controversy. If an insured makes use of the premises only occasionally, it may be said that they are not occupied. The courts have held that so long as the premises were suitable for the occupancy and the insured uses them for that purpose, the occupancy clause is not breached.

Vacancy is somewhat easier to handle because the premises that are vacant are stripped of furnishings. Yet, as mentioned earlier, the final answer will depend on the facts of the case. The cases range from a situation where the premises have substantially all of the furnishings to those that may have only a few chairs, a table, a cot, a refrigerator, and so on. It is a question of fact that must be decided on an individual basis. In those states that have the statutory provision discussed above, the breach would have to be material, contribute to the loss, or both.

In commercial property insurance, the vacancy and unoccupancy clause continues to be a part of the policy forms, and the courts are inclined to enforce its provisions. However, it should be noted that the following condition attempts to spell out the circumstances in which increases in hazard, and vacancy and unoccupancy do not suspend coverage.

Permits and Use: Except as otherwise provided, permission is granted:

A. to make additions, alterations and repairs. This policy insofar as it covers building(s) or structure(s) is extended to cover additions, alterations and repairs, when not otherwise covered by insurance including temporary structures constructed on site, materials, equipment and supplies therefor on or within 100 feet of the described premises; and this policy insofar as it covers contents, is extended to cover in such additions. This provision does not waive or modify any of the conditions of the Automatic Sprinkler Clause, if any, attached to this policy;

B. for such unoccupancy as is usual or incidental to the described occupancy; but vacancy is limited to the 60 day period permitted by the policy conditions ("Vacant" or "Vacancy" means containing no contents pertaining to operations or activities customary to occupancy of the building. "Unoccupied" or "Unoccupancy" means containing contents pertaining to occupancy of the building while operations or other customary activities are suspended),

C. in the event of loss hereunder, to make reasonable repairs, temporary or permanent, provided such repairs are confined solely to the protection of the property from further damage, and provided further that the named Insured shall keep an accurate record of such repair expenditures. The cost of any such repairs directly attributable to damage by any peril insured hereunder shall be included in determining the amount of loss hereunder. Nothing herein contained is intended to modify the policy requirements applicable in case loss occurs and in particular the requirement that, in case loss occurs, the named Insured shall protect the property from further damage.

Conditions relating to the standard fire policy will be discussed in greater detail in Chapter 15.

One of the more important conditions suspending coverage is found in the following condition in the general property form:

> *Protective Safeguards:* It is a condition of this insurance that the insured shall maintain so far as is within his control such protective safeguards as are set forth by endorsement hereto. Failure to maintain such protective safeguards shall suspend this insurance, only as respects the location or situation affected, for the time of such discontinuance.

Note that the particular protective safeguards that the insured must maintain will be described in an endorsement to the policy. The following clause is found in the endorsement commonly used when fire insurance is written on a building with an automatic sprinkler system. (This Automatic Sprinkler Clause is also referred to in the Permits and Use provision just quoted.)

> *Automatic Sprinkler Clause (Non-Supervisory):* In consideration of the premium at which this policy is written, based on the protection of the premises by the sprinkler system, it is a condition of this policy that the insured shall exercise due diligence in maintaining in complete working order all equipment and services pertaining to the operation of the sprinkler system which are under the control of the insured. The insured shall give immediate notice to this Company of any impairment in or suspension of the sprinkler system or services (within the knowledge of the insured). No unsprinklered additions or extensions shall be made to the building unless immediate notification is given to this Company. Permission is given in case of break, leakage, freezing conditions or the opening of sprinkler heads, to shut off the water from so much of the sprinkler system as may be imperatively necessary with immediate notification to this Company and the protection restored as promptly as possible.

The clause begins with the words, "In consideration of the premium..." because the insurance premium is reduced to reflect the loss reduction capabilities of the automatic sprinkler system. If the conditions in this clause are not met literally, the fire insurance will be suspended.

Another condition is seen in a mercantile open stock burglary policy:

> *Declarations:* By acceptance of this policy the Insured agrees that the statements in the declarations are the agreements and representations of the Insured, that this policy is issued in reliance upon the truth of such representations and that this policy embodies all agreements existing between the Insured and the Company or any of

its agents relating to this insurance.

If for reasons beyond the Insured's control

(a) The Insured fails to maintain the alarm system stated in the declarations but, until such alarm system has been fully restored to proper working condition, the Insured provides at least one watchman within the premises at all times when the premises are not open for business and such watchman is in addition to any number of watchmen specified in the declarations, or

(b) the Insured fails to maintain any other service or equipment stated in the declarations,

the insurance under this policy shall apply only in the reduced amount which the premium for this insurance would have purchased, in accordance with the Company manual as of the commencement of such failure, in the absence of any agreement of the Insured to maintain such service or equipment.

In this condition, instead of suspending the coverage entirely, the amount of recovery is merely reduced. Maintenance of an alarm system nevertheless becomes a condition precedent to full recovery. A different approach is taken in the storekeepers burglary and robbery policy. There, if the safe is not locked, the condition precedent is not met, and there is no coverage whatsoever for the loss.

A very clear condition suspending coverage is found in a boiler and machinery policy:

Inspection: The Company shall be permitted but not obligated to inspect, at any reasonable times, any Object designated and described in a Schedule or Endorsement forming a part of the policy. Neither the Company's right to make inspections nor the making thereof nor any report thereon shall constitute an understanding on behalf of or for the benefit of the Insured or others, to determine or warrant that such Object is safe or healthful.

Suspension: Upon the discovery of a dangerous condition with respect to any Object, any representative of the Company may immediately suspend the insurance with respect to an Accident to said Object by written notice mailed or delivered to the Insured at the Address of the Insured, as specified in the Declarations, or at the location of the Object as specified for it in the Schedule or Endorsement. Insurance so suspended may be reinstated by the Company, but only by an Endorsement issued to form a part of this policy and signed by an officer of the Company. The Insured shall be allowed the unearned portion of the premium paid for such suspended insurance, pro rata, for the period of suspension.

Loss control under boiler and machinery insurance invariably involves close inspections of the "objects" (items eligible for coverage) of the insured. The quoted condition permits an inspector to suspend coverage immediately upon the discovery of a dangerous condition. It is expected that the insured would be very cooperative in promptly correcting a serious hazard, in view of the potential severity of a boiler explosion.

As the condition points out, there is no obligation or requirement imposed on the insurer to make inspections. However, an inspection by competent personnel is one of the most valuable features of this insurance.

Liability Insurance Liability insurance policies generally have fewer conditions suspending coverage than property lines. A few examples of conditions suspending coverage can be found in the personal auto policy, which states:

> We do not provide liability coverage for any person ... for that person's liability arising out of the ownership or operation of a vehicle while it is being used to carry persons or property for a fee ... (or) while employed or otherwise engaged in the business or occupation of a. selling; b. repairing; c. servicing; d. storing; or e. parking; vehicles designed for use mainly on public highways ....

Notice and Proof of Loss

There is a slight variation between (1) the requirements for prompt notice and the filing of a proof of loss in property policies and (2) the requirement for reporting accidents, occurrences, and claims in liability policies. This section will give a short analysis of these property and liability requirements. The situations that excuse literal compliance will be distinguished from those that do not.

> *Your Duties After Loss:* In case of a loss to which this insurance may apply, you shall see that the following duties are performed:
>
> a. give immediate notice to us or our agent, and in case of theft also to the police. In case of loss under the Credit Card coverage also notify the credit card company;
>
> b. protect the property from further damage, make reasonable and necessary repairs required to protect the property, and keep an accurate record of repair expenditures;
>
> c. prepare an inventory of damaged personal property showing in detail, the quantity, description, actual cash value and amount of loss. Attach to the inventory all bills, receipts and related documents that substantiate the figures in the inventory;
>
> d. exhibit the damaged property as often as we reasonably require and submit to examination under oath;
>
> e. submit to us, within 60 days after we request, your signed, sworn statement of loss which sets forth, to the best of your knowledge and belief:
>
> (1) the time and cause of loss;
> (2) interest of the insured and all others in the property involved and all encumbrances on the property;
> (3) other insurance which may cover the loss;
> (4) changes in title or occupancy of the property during the term of the policy;

(5) specifications of any damaged building and detailed estimates for repair of the damage;

(6) an inventory of damaged personal property described in 2c;

(7) receipts for additional living expenses incurred and records supporting the fair rental value loss;

(8) evidence or affidavit supporting a claim under the Credit Card, Forgery and Counterfeit Money coverage, stating the amount and cause of loss.

Property Insurance The purpose of the insured's notice of loss to the insurer is to allow the insurer to form an adequate estimate of its liabilities and to enable it promptly to begin investigating the claim. The conditions requiring notice and proof of loss vary according to the type of coverage afforded by the insurance policy. In property insurance, a typical notice is found in the standard fire policy:

Requirements in case loss occurs: The insured shall give immediate written notice to this Company of any loss, protect the property from further damage, forthwith separate the damaged and undamaged personal property, put it in the best possible order, furnish a complete inventory of the destroyed, damaged and undamaged property, showing in detail quantities, costs, actual cash value and amount of loss claimed; and within sixty days after the loss, unless such time is extended in writing by this Company, the insured shall render to this Company a proof of loss, signed and sworn to by the insured, stating the knowledge and belief of the insured as to the following: the time and origin of the loss, the interest of the insured and of all others in the property, the actual cash value of each item thereof and the amount of loss thereto, all encumbrances thereon, all other contracts of insurance, whether valid or not, covering any of said property, any changes in the title, use, occupation, location, possession or exposures of said property since the issuing of this policy, by whom and for what purpose any building herein described and the several parts thereof were occupied at the time of loss and whether or not it then stood on leased ground, and shall furnish a copy of all the descriptions and schedules in all policies and, if required, verified plans and specifications of any building, fixtures or machinery destroyed or damaged. The insured, as often as may be reasonably required, shall exhibit to any person designated by this Company all that remains of any property herein described, and submit to examinations under oath by any person named by this Company, and subscribe the same; and, as often as may be reasonably required, shall produce for examination all books of account, bills, invoices and other vouchers, or certified copies thereof if originals be lost, at such reasonable time and place as may be designated by this Company or its representative, and shall permit extracts and copies thereof to be made.

Liability Insurance General liability and auto liability insurance have produced quite a bit of litigation concerning the notice condition of the policy. Reflecting the public interest in claim administration, a court recently noted that the efficient and economical administration of liability insurance requires early knowledge of claims in order that proper investigation can be made.[3] The requirement is that the insured must give notice "as soon as practicable." The notice must contain particulars sufficient to identify the insured and furnish reasonably obtainable information respecting time, place, and circumstances of the accident. Names and addresses of injured parties, as well as available witnesses, also should be furnished.

Courts are more likely to enforce the notice requirement under liability contracts than under property contracts, because lack of prompt investigation prejudices the insurer's ability to defend the insured. With the passage of time, evidence and witnesses become more difficult to obtain. What were originally minor injuries may become magnified and complicate settlement. Prompt notice also helps prevent and minimize future losses, thereby furthering the interests of the insured, the insurer, and the public in general. Furthermore, timely notice facilitates control of claims, promotes favorable settlements, and reduces litigation expenses and awards for damages. As a result, any delay that frustrates the purpose of the notice provision of the insurance contract is deemed to be prejudicial. The following notice requirement from a special multi-peril policy illustrates a typical notice condition:

Insured's Duties in the Event of Occurrence, Claim or Suit:

1. In the event of an occurrence, written notice containing particulars sufficient to identify the insured and also reasonably obtainable information with respect to the time, place and circumstances thereof, and the names and addresses of the injured and of available witnesses, shall be given by or for the insured to the Company or any of its authorized agents as soon as practicable.
2. If claim is made or suit is brought against the insured, the insured shall immediately forward to the Company every demand, notice, summons or other process received by him or his representative.

A question sometimes arises as to whether the injured person can report the accident information to the insurer and thereby legally satisfy the notice condition. This question arises most frequently in connection with auto insurance. Under financial responsibility laws, the injured claimant has been treated, in effect, as a third-party beneficiary of auto liability coverage. Some states have statutes that liberalize the notice requirement of the policy insofar as the injured claimant is concerned. Some states have even enacted "direct action statutes" that permit an action directly against the insurer.

It is obvious that the injured party is vitally interested in preserving the insurer's obligation to its insured. However, the third-party beneficiary's claim could be defeated if the insured failed to give the required notice.

The purpose of the notice is to give the insurer an opportunity to make an investigation. It does not matter how the notice gets to the insurer. Hence, the injured person can properly give such notice and prevent the consequences of a breach of the condition by the insured. The third party may not have as many details as are available to the insured, and in such cases the courts are inclined to soften the timeliness standards. In general, the notice under the policy of liability insurance can be given by anyone, so long as reasonable and timely notice is given to the insurer. The notice section requires that the insured forward notices or legal papers *immediately.* The courts require strict compliance with this provision, because a failure to enforce the provision would probably result in prejudice to the insurer. For example, if suit is filed and notice to the insurer is delayed, a default judgment may be entered. Any defenses that would have been available are thereby lost. Many plaintiffs' attorneys, aware that such a breach of notice may release the insurer from liability, will forward suit papers routinely to the insurer at the time the summons is served. If they are about to take a default judgment and have not notified the insurer in advance, they will postpone action to give the insurer time to answer and make an appearance. If a default judgment has been taken and then it is discovered that the insurer had not been notified in accordance with this policy condition, they may offer to reopen the judgment to give the insurer an opportunity to answer and to defend the suit. Otherwise, all that the plaintiff may have is a judgment against an uninsured debtor. If the suit papers reach the insurer in time to prevent a default judgment, the courts are generally agreed that there has been compliance with the word "immediately."

Excused Delay. Early cases held that a delay of thirty days in giving notice of a claim or suit was conclusively presumed to be prejudicial. However, current cases allow the insured to show mitigating circumstances which excuse delay. Thus, a court will consider whether the insured's actions were reasonable under the circumstances of the case. There is an attempt to apply an objective standard of "whether a reasonable person would have inferred from the facts that an insured event had occurred." It may be argued that the need to "discover" whether or not a covered tort has occurred implies a more subjective standard by which the insured would be excused for a delay in making a report, unless the insured knows of the event.[4] This is quite different from the objective standard of the reasonable person.

In most of the cases involving relatively short delay, the insurer is required to show prejudice. Thus, in cases where there were delays ranging from a few days to as much as four months, and the insured was able to show extenuating circumstances, courts have held that there was no breach of the notice condition.

There are many cases where the insured is not aware of the potential liability loss. It does the insured little good to know about the requirements of the notice provision of the contract if he or she does not know *what* to report. In a case where an insured's attorney advised that he did not think the insured would be held liable in damages, the court agreed that this was a reasonable excuse for a delayed notice.[5] In another case, notice was given under a homeowners policy three months after an accidental shooting by the insured's son while hunting. After the son's arrest, an attorney advised the insured that the homeowners policy provided coverage. The trial court found no "substantial breach of the notice requirement."[6]

Among business people, excuses for nonfulfillment of the notice condition may be more difficult to sustain. Business people are expected to be more knowledgeable than the typical unsophisticated consumer. The burden of explaining the delay in reporting to the insurer rests on the insured, and business people have to exercise that standard of reason common to business people. For example, if the insured is a lawyer and a former claims adjuster, the insured will be held to a strict standard of what constitutes "reasonable notice."

Unexcused Delay. Delay that is "prejudicial" to the insurer is usually not excused by the courts. The insured's failure to give prompt notice makes the claim defense substantially more dangerous, onerous, or troublesome for the insurer. For example, a claim of prejudice was sustained when a late report of an auto accident was due to a misunderstanding between a husband and wife. The insurer was unable to take photographs and talk with witnesses while the facts were still fresh. One witness died of unrelated causes before the insurer was able to interview her.

Ordinarily, an insurer raises the defense of "prejudice" by pointing to a long delay in reporting. In one case the report was delayed twenty-two months. The long delay in the circumstances was enough to raise the presumption of prejudice, and then it was up to the insured to produce evidence of justification or other mitigating circumstances.

The manner in which prejudice is handled varies considerably among the states.

- In one state, absent some excuse or mitigating circumstances, the judge, rather than the jury, is to decide the question of whether the notice given by the insured fulfilled the notice requirements.[7]
- In one state the insurer has to prove breach of the notice provision and a "likelihood of appreciable prejudice" therefrom

in order to fulfill the reasonable expectations of the purchaser "so far as its language will permit."[8]

● In contrast, another state places the burden of proving an absence of prejudice on the person claiming liability.

● Yet another position says that a presumption of prejudice exists if the delay is in itself unreasonable.[9]

● Finally, some courts require two types of findings. The first is a finding of whether or not the notice itself was unreasonably delayed. If so, there then has to be a second finding on whether the delay was prejudicial to the insurer.[10]

Obviously, if the delay is excused it does not matter whether the insurer is prejudiced. If the delay is *not* excused *and* the insurer has *not* been prejudiced, the insurer is not allowed to avoid its obligation under the contract.

In general, prejudice is one of the factors that determines what is a reasonable time to give a liability insurer notice of a claim. Prejudice constitutes a basic element of an insurer's denial of payment based on the nonfulfillment of the notice condition.

Medical Payments Benefits Auto insurance, homeowners insurance, and other policies provide for medical payments for injuries. In general, claims relating to health insurance of this type have great potential for fraud and abuse. The insurer must determine whether the insured is ill or disabled, whether the treatment claimed is necessary, and whether the medical bills are reasonable. The subjectivity of injury complaints places heavy reliance on the integrity of the injured party, as well as on the persons and institutions that administer health care. Insurers find timely information to be of great value in controlling claims costs. A typical medical payments notice condition is taken from a special multi-peril policy:

Medical Reports; Proof and Payment of Claim: As soon as practicable the injured person or someone on his behalf shall give to the Company written proof of claim for medical expense, under oath if required, and shall, after each request from the Company, execute authorization to enable the Company to obtain medical reports and copies of records. The injured person shall submit to physical examination by physicians selected by the Company when and as often as the Company may reasonably require. The Company may pay the injured person or any person or organization rendering the services and the payment shall reduce the amount payable hereunder for such injury. Payment hereunder shall not constitute an admission of liability of any person or, except hereunder, of the Company.

The usual "as soon as practicable" provision is used with medical payments coverage. A difficulty sometimes arises when the injured party is also a bodily injury claimant under the same policy and the claimant is represented by a lawyer. Some lawyers are reluctant to release medical information to the insurer under such circumstances. However, the insurer is not in a position to demand the medical reports because of the adversary position. At the same time, neither is it obligated to make medical payments until it gets the reports and supporting bills.

Mitigation of Loss

Some policy conditions require the insured to take steps to "mitigate" or lessen the damage or loss after an insured event occurs. Clauses requiring protection against further loss usually apply only to property insurance. Occasionally there is also such a provision in the liability section of a policy.

Property Insurance Under the typical notice provision of property insurance contracts, besides giving notice to the insurer, the insured is obligated "to protect the property from further damage." Most of the general property forms, under the "Permits and Use" section, provide for "reasonable and necessary" repairs to protect property from further damage. The policy is merely making explicit what previously had been implicit in the law. Every claimant is required by common law to mitigate damages, although some courts have ignored this tenet where insurance is involved. The standard fire policy, in line 21, also includes under "perils not covered," "neglect of the insured to use all reasonable means to save and preserve the property at and after the loss or when the property is endangered by fire in neighboring premises."

The policy injunction to take "reasonable steps" to protect the property from further damage is not something that requires specialized knowledge. Nor does it require heroic action on the part of the insured. However, loss exposure recognition requires expertise. Not everyone is able to identify potential hazards. In property situations, the need for an inspection of any remaining property is usually evident. The nature of that inspection will depend on the circumstances. A structural engineer can be expected to recognize a condition in a building that needs protective measures. Someone not competent to make such an analysis would be excused from identifying the problem, but not from the notice requirement, if there was obvious damage.

The language of the contract describes what loss prevention activities are expected. For instance, one dwelling form has the following "mitigation of loss" provision:

> *Your Duties After Loss:* In case of a loss to which this insurance
> may apply, you shall see that the following duties are

performed:...protect the property from further damage, make reasonable and necessary repairs required to protect the property, and keep an accurate record of repair expenditures . . . .

This same policy also excludes from coverage loss caused directly or indirectly by the neglect of the insured to protect the property after a loss or when endangered by a peril insured against. Protective measures that an insured might use include:

- removal of contents when an insured peril threatens to cause damage;
- drying and oiling wet tools to prevent rusting;
- prompt disposition of perishables, either by sale or by locating them in cold storage;
- separation of the damaged from the undamaged and the dry from the wet property;
- covering exposed property with emergency tarps or plastic;
- draining plumbing in cold weather; or
- disconnecting electric power if the building is seriously damaged.

The policy places these duties upon the insured. However, recovery of protection or mitigation expenses may be allowed only if the policy so provides. The courts have sometimes been reluctant to charge the insurer with such costs even if they are incurred for the insurer's benefit, without a provision assuming such liability. A duty to take a particular course of action may be imposed on the insured by court interpretation, even if the policy is silent in regard to such duty.

Under a typical auto physical damage coverage, the insured is also obligated to mitigate the loss:

... to recover for loss to a covered auto or its equipment you must do the following:
a. Permit us to inspect and appraise the damaged property before its repair or disposition.
b. Do what is reasonably necessary after loss at our expense to protect the covered auto from further loss.
c. Submit a proof of loss when required by us.
d. Promptly notify the police if the covered auto or any of its equipment is stolen.

The duty to prevent further damage is narrowly construed. In a sense, the clause runs contrary to the usual property insurance policy, which covers accidental loss even if caused by the insured's negligence. Despite the narrow construction, the clause serves a useful purpose. It prevents what (in effect) would be an abandonment of the damaged property to the insurer. In case of an accident, the insured cannot abandon the auto at the side of the road where it is exposed to the possibility of being "stripped" or set on fire.

On occasion, an insured may insist on special repairs, such as new parts or a new paint job, because the wrecked auto was left exposed to the weather. The insurer may not be liable for damage to the interior of the auto under such circumstances. There is always the possibility that the insured will claim that the insurer's refusal to allow the requested repairs prevented the insured from moving the auto into a garage for repairs. The insurer's conduct also has to be reasonable. However, if the insured acts in a reasonable manner, subsequent damage will be covered. In a case where the insured collided with a telephone pole, the insured thought that only the fender and bumper were damaged. In fact, the brake fluid line was severed and a tire deflated. The insured drove the auto in its damaged condition, and it caught on fire and burned. The insurer was held responsible to pay damages.[11]

Similarly, it is common on gravel roads (and roads under construction) for stones to strike the underside of an auto and the oil pan. While the insured might get out and inspect the underside of the auto after striking a rock, he or she might not crawl beneath the vehicle and check it closely, and the inspection might reveal no damage. However, a rock may in fact have ruptured the oil pan. The insured, unaware of the damage, may continue to drive the auto and burn up the engine. Such losses generally are covered.

Multiple ownership of property may create an especially severe application of loss mitigation provisions. In one case, one of the dwelling's co-owners, a former husband, set fire to the house. It was held that the wife could not recover her half interest, on the grounds that there was a joint contractual obligation to preserve the insured property "at and after loss." In a more recent case, a former husband set fire to the house and incinerated himself in the fire. The court permitted recovery of one-half interest by the wife. This court held that the husband's tort—fraud—is several and separate and not joint. The court refused to follow the concept of contractual obligation to preserve the insured property.[12] If the courts continue to hold to the contractual obligation theory, the results can be harsh.

There are cases also that suggest that the conduct of a partner in a partnership may affect the interests of the other partners. This entire area of law suggests that a clearer expression of intention of the parties to the contract may be necessary. For example, a co-owner of property could insist that his or her interest be covered, regardless of the conduct of the other co-owners. That is essentially the situation when a mortgagee's interest is insured under the standard mortgage clauses.

Liability Insurance The 1966 general liability policies had a provision that the insured shall "promptly at his own expense take all reasonable steps" to prevent further loss. The purpose of this provision was to direct the insured to eliminate a hazard related to premises or products that might go on injuring people. However, the clause was very difficult to interpret in the context of occurrence-basis policies and was dropped from later policy revisions. The requirement that "bodily injury" or "property damage" be neither expected nor intended by the insured is considered a persuasive reminder of the insured's obligation to try to prevent further injury or damage after an accident. Furthermore, it is likely that an insured who allows serious controllable hazards to persist will soon have its coverage discontinued by the insurer.

Cooperation with the Insurer

The cooperation condition requires the insured to cooperate with the insurer. Failure to give notice promptly may be a breach of the cooperation condition. However, cooperation goes farther than mere notice.

Property Insurance Under property insurance contracts, the insured has the duty to assist the insurer in adjusting the loss. The insured must supply information about the property and circumstances of its loss. There may be a need to inventory and display the damaged property. The insurer may need to have drawings, specifications, photographs, fire and police department records, deeds, receipts, bills of sale, and any other information pertinent to the loss. Some contracts require the insured to maintain records of the property to assist in adjusting any loss. Although the standard fire policy specifically requires the insured to prepare inventory records of both damaged and undamaged property after a loss, strict compliance with this provision is rare. In cases involving coinsurance clauses, it may be necessary.

Cooperation with the insurer under a property insurance contract normally does not depend on third parties. In the normal situation, the named *insured* must perform the conditions precedent in order to activate the *insurer's* liability. As shown under "notice and proof of loss," if the insured is remiss in some detail, normally a correction or addition of supplemental material will be allowed. The concepts of fair dealing and good faith between the parties are implicit.

Liability Insurance The situation is quite different in liability insurance, because third parties outside of the contract are involved, and time may be crucial. A failure to cooperate may cause irreparable damage to any of the parties in the liability situation.

The typical assistance and cooperation condition of a liability contract reads:

> The insured shall cooperate with the company and, upon the company's request, assist in making settlements, in the conduct of suits and in enforcing any right of contribution or indemnity against any person or organization who may be liable to the insured because of bodily injury or damage with respect to which insurance is afforded under this policy; and the insured shall not, except at his own cost, voluntarily make any payment, assume any obligation or incur any expense other than for first aid to others at the time of accident.

The above provision is a continuation of the "Insured's Duties in the Event of Occurrence, Claim or Suit." The requirement to give notice promptly is only one of the duties required of the insured. The insured also has a duty in regard to the quality of information included in the notice. These provisions are intended to guarantee to insurers the opportunity and right to prepare their defenses adequately. *Cooperation* means a fair and frank disclosure of information reasonably demanded. If an insured does not comply or did not frankly disclose the information to which the insurer was entitled, there is a breach of this condition.

There are two aspects to the problem of noncooperation. One deals with the insured's failure to comply with the contract provision. The other deals with what the insurer has done to secure cooperation from an apathetic, inattentive, or vanished policyholder. Further, liability insurance is intended in part to protect members of the public who may be injured through negligence. Indeed, auto liability insurance is made mandatory in many states. It would greatly weaken the practical usefulness of policies designed to afford public protection if the insurer could disclaim liability merely by showing the disappearance of its insured, without full proof of proper efforts by the insurer to locate and secure the cooperation of its insured.

Prejudice to Insurer. The success of an insurer's defense based on a breach of the assistance and cooperation clause generally rests on a finding that:

(1) the condition has been breached, and
(2) the breach has prejudiced the insurer.

How these issues are handled by the courts was discussed in detail under the section "Notice and Proof of Loss." In this section, references to the breach of the cooperation clause and prejudice must be understood in the light of the previous discussion. The insurer must show that it has suffered "substantial prejudice." This means that the insured's conduct adversely affects the insurer's interest in some substantial and material way. The insured's noncooperation requires proof that the insured in bad faith refused or neglected to cooperate with the insurer, and that the noncooperation caused substantial prejudice to the insurer's preparation of a defense to a claim against the insured. If an insured intentionally or through indifference furnishes false information of a material nature, either before or at trial, a breach of this condition exists.

This can best be illustrated by the typical procedural rules imposed during a trial. Frequently, false information is involved in auto liability cases. The insured is trying to protect one who might have been intoxicated or who did not have permission to drive. Assume that the case has gone to trial on the belief that the parties were telling the truth when, in fact, they were not. During the trial, the true facts emerge. Generally, the insured is both a party to the legal action and a key trial witness. However, trial rules normally do not permit an attorney, representing the insured, to impeach the credibility of the insured who is the witness and also a party to the litigation. A court may be aware that an attorney provided by an insurance company may face a conflict of interest because the attorney's legal obligation to a client who has not been telling the truth conflicts with the attorney's economic responsibilities to the insurer. However, a court will seldom allow an insured's attorney to withdraw from the case because of this conflict of interest. Hence, when an attorney provided by an insurer discovers that the insured's untruthfulness may be contrary to the insurer's financial interests, there is a need for a prompt decision on what the attorney should do.

If, in the course of investigation, the insurer is convinced that the insured has not been telling the entire truth or is concealing facts, the insurer cannot simply deny coverage for breach of the cooperation condition of the policy. Instead, it must confront the insured with what the investigation has revealed. It may be that the insured is correct and the investigation faulty. But, assuming that the investigation correctly suggests there was false information, the insured must be given an opportunity to correct the earlier misrepresentation. If he or she persists in the original story and the insurer is actually prejudiced, it *may* have a defense. Note that the word used in the previous sentence was *may*. If the insured maintains that he or she was sober at the time of the accident and the investigation conclusively reveals that the insured was drunk, is the insurer actually prejudiced? It now knows the condition of the insured at the time of the accident. Would it help the defense of the liability claim for the insured to recant and admit to being drunk? It is doubtful that any court would find prejudice in this situation. If an insured corrects a misrepresentation in adequate time and the insurer has adequate time to evaluate its liability and prepare for trial, there is no breach of the cooperation condition. One court provided a guide for the insured to follow in cooperating with the insurer by stating:

> Good faith ... in telling and adhering to the truth at all times is the keystone of the cooperating arch. The insured must not prejudicially embarrass or cripple his insurer in its defense by switching from one version of the facts to another or blow hot and cold to suit his convenience or that of the third party.[13]

An example may be helpful. An insured told the insurer that the brakes on the car failed, but at trial he testified that he had been operating the car at a speed too fast to make a turn even if the brakes were working. During the trial he did not remember whether he had applied brakes at all. The cooperation clause was clearly breached by such conduct.

Collusion. The insured's collusion with the claimant (or with the claimant's attorney) is such a serious violation of the assistance and cooperation clause that in some jurisdictions the insurer may not be required to show prejudice. If collusion is shown, courts have been careful to protect the rights of the insurer. If the insured acted in bad faith, it is not required that the insurer show that the trial result was affected.

For example, a person insured under a farmers comprehensive liability policy denied to the insurer that he had started a fire that burned a railroad bridge. Suit was started by the railroad. Railroad adjusters persuaded the insured to admit to starting the fire in exchange for the railroad's agreement not to levy execution on the farmer in excess of the policy limits. The misrepresentation to the insurer was held to be a breach of the assistance and cooperation clause of the contract.[14]

Excused Conduct. Not all contacts with the plaintiff attorney or the claimant are collusive. Courts have upheld the insureds in cases where they had a duty to their children and arranged for attorneys to represent the children in an action against the insured. If the insured discloses to the claimant (or his or her attorneys) acts that show negligence, it is not collusion or a breach of the cooperation clause of the contract.

Demands by insurers for cooperation are not always successful. In liability insurance, the insured can be involved in situations that are criminal, as well as civil. An insurer cannot demand from an insured disclosures that might be incriminating. For example, an insured facing murder or manslaughter charges cannot be expected to reveal details that would help to convict him or her. However, the insured cannot remain silent, and must indicate to the insurer why he or she cannot make certain disclosures. If the insured is represented by an attorney, this is rarely a problem, because the attorney will insist on being present at any questioning of the insured. The reasons for refusing to discuss certain details quickly become obvious and should tell the insurer what it needs to know about potential testimony at a trial.

Another problem frequently encountered is whether an insured fails to cooperate if he or she pleads guilty to a traffic or other criminal charge. In some cases, claims personnel may specifically counsel against such a plea. While such a guilty plea is an admission against the insurer's interest and affects the defense of the case, it is not a refusal to cooperate. At this point there is a conflict of interest, and the insured must be allowed to take whatever steps best suit his or her own interests and not those of the insurer. Further, if there is clear evidence of aggravated negligence, it is rather pointless for the insurer to be concerned about the insured's conduct in the criminal proceedings, since it has adequate facts on which to make its own evaluation.

Questions have been raised in regard to possible breaches of the cooperation condition when an insured makes statements such as "It is all my fault" or "I was not looking" or some other statement that has an adverse effect on a possible defense. While they may be admissions against interest, they are not assumptions of liability or agreements to pay the claim. An assumption of liability needs an agreement with all of the principles of contract being present. If the insured's actions lead the claimant to change his or her position, there theoretically may be a breach, but no cases have been found to suggest such a result. There have been attempts to claim a breach of the cooperation condition in cases where the insured gave facts of the accident to the claimant, his or her attorney, and other interested parties. However, the courts point out in such situations that the insurer cannot expect the insured to lie or otherwise distort the truth when speaking with other persons.

Attendance at Trial. If there is a good defense to the plaintiff's claim for liability, it will generally depend on the insured's testimony during trial. Therefore, the insured has an affirmative duty to be available during trial. If the insured attempts to obstruct the insurer's handling of the claim, it is a clear violation of the cooperation clause of the contract, and it will defeat coverage if prejudicial. The presence at the trial of an insured who was unquestionably intoxicated when involved in an accident can hardly be called essential to the case. But if the insured flatly refuses to attend trial without a reasonable excuse, it will be a violation. Most cases reflect the situations where the insured could not be located before trial.

Although an insured has an obligation not to prejudice the insurer's ability to defend the claim or control the settlement negotiations, the insured should cooperate readily. The insurer must use reasonable diligence to locate an insured and secure attendance at the trial. This is to prevent collusion between the insured and plaintiff. Exactly what that "diligence" means will be a question of fact to be determined from all of the circumstances concerning the efforts to locate the insured. If the insured disappears and the insured's testimony is vital to a successful defense of the case, the insurer may have no choice but to allow the case to go by default. If the plaintiff and/or the plaintiff's attorney knows of the whereabouts of the insured, and knows that the insurer is having difficulty locating the insured, they must notify the insurer of the whereabouts of the insured. Otherwise, they cannot later complain if the insurer disclaims liability.

Most policies provide that the insurer will pay the expenses for attendance at trial plus up to some stated limit such as $25 or $50 per day for lost wages. The amount limited for the lost pay may add to an insured's reluctance to attend trial, particularly if the trial is expected to last a week or more. Some authorities feel that there is nothing wrong with the idea of reimbursement up to the actual wages, without regard to the stated limit. Some insurance companies do so. It would be different if the insurer started offering some sort of a bonus for attendance at trials. That might even suggest "buying" witnesses favorable to the insurer. But asking an insured to attend trial at considerable sacrifice may not be fair to the insured. Under the cooperation clause of the contract, the insured is generally required to assist in "making settlements, in the conduct of suits, attend hearings, assist in securing and giving evidence and obtaining the attendance of witnesses." All expenses incurred at the request of the insurer are payable under the "supplemental payments" section of the policy.

Preservation of Insurer Defenses (Nonwaiver Agreements—Reservation of Rights). Whenever the insurer becomes aware of a possible breach of cooperation clause it must be careful. Actions taken by the insurer may constitute a "waiver" (a voluntary relinquishment of a known right). For example, failure of the insurer to agree on a trial date offered by a plaintiff may waive its right to require the insured's cooperation. Moreover, unless the insured's failure to cooperate causes real prejudice to the insurer, the court may not permit avoidance of the contract. If at any time the insurer becomes aware of a breach of the cooperation clause but continues to defend the insured after the breach without some precaution, it will be held to have waived its rights under the clause.

A genuinely difficult problem arises when the insurer discovers the lack of cooperation during the trial. Trial counsel are not always familiar with the complexities of this condition. In a situation where the insured changes his or her story concerning the facts previously given to the insurer and relied on by it for the defense, the problem requires proper and prompt action at that exact time. Many courts will not permit counsel to withdraw from the case. As explained earlier, the insurer is not a party to the suit in most states. The attorneys are representing only the insured (the defendant) in the suit. The insured and not the insurer is their only recognized client. The law of the state must be examined carefully to determine what courses of action are permissible, and the insurer's counsel must be familiar with the law. About the only safe course that is available is to serve a so-called "reservation of rights" immediately, and to so inform the court. Attorneys who are not prepared to deal with this contingency often have continued the defense of the case while they await instructions from their insurer. Such action may waive the potential defense of breach of the cooperation clause in the insurance contract.

To preserve their defenses, insurers have several options. They can withdraw from the case entirely and leave the insured to handle the matter. This is often dangerous because the insurer gives up all further control of the case. If the injuries are serious, there is a potential of a very high verdict that cannot be contested later. Another route, and the one most commonly used, is to reserve the insurer's rights to deny coverage because of noncooperation but to continue handling the case in the usual manner. This allows time to decide on final strategy.

Reservation of rights is done under two types of action. One is the use of the *nonwaiver agreement*. Under a nonwaiver agreement, the insured agrees that investigation and determination of the value of the claim by the insurance company do not constitute an admission that the insurance company has assumed liability. Claims personnel may find a nonwaiver agreement difficult to obtain from the insured. The agreement is highly technical and must specify the basis for the defense raised. By its language it suggests that the insurer will likely disclaim coverage. The insured is likely to ask questions about its meaning and what the insurance company intends to do. If the insured refuses to sign the agreement, the insurer must agree to accept coverage, deny coverage outright or take some legal action. If it fails to do so and further handles the claim, it will have waived its defense. If, however, the claim adjuster or producer "explains" the document in such a way as to lead the insured to believe that it is a mere routine and not very important, and the insured is persuaded to sign it, the document has been so weakened that its effectiveness is in question.

A better method of preserving an insurer's defenses is to send the insured a *reservation-of-rights letter*. This is a unilateral instrument and does not involve insurer personnel in any explanation. In most cases, the insured will consult his or her own attorney about the consequences of the unilateral action taken by the insurer. Confrontation with the insured is avoided. The attorney, generally, will not want to push for a prompt decision from the insurer. If he or she does, the insurer may elect to withdraw from the claim entirely. If the insurer does withdraw, the insured's attorney will have deprived the client of the benefit of the insurer's handling of the claim.

As pointed out earlier, a reservation of rights does not guarantee the insurer an airtight defense, even in a case of genuine breach of the cooperation clause. If a case becomes long and drawn out, the insurer may have to reevaluate the situation from time to time and consider the potential of waiver. If the case has not been settled for a long period of time and there have been continuing contacts with the insured, it is likely that the activity of the insured that led to the breach may be cured or corrected.

Subrogation

The doctrine of subrogation was thoroughly discussed in the previous chapter. It is mentioned here in order to remind the reader that the usual subrogation provision forbids the insured from doing anything *after a loss* that would adversely affect the insurer's right of subrogation against third parties. Thus, the subrogation clause serves as an important condition subsequent. If this condition is breached by the insured, the insurer may be released entirely from any liability under the policy.

Appraisal and Arbitration

Appraisal deals with the establishment of value. *Arbitration* means the submission of disputes to a third party, other than a court of law. Appraisal and arbitration, when required, are conditions precedent to any claim against the insurer.

Appraisal Once coverage has been established in property insurance claims, the main area of potential disputes between an insured and insurer is the determination of the amount of the loss. Insureds may have an exaggerated sense of value, whereas claims personnel may have an unrealistically narrow view of the worth of a claim. The appraisal condition of the policy is a mechanism to take disputes away from the insurer and the insured and put them into the hands of impartial third parties to establish the amount of loss. For the insured, it means getting away from the impersonal and sometimes "faceless financial giant" who, in the eyes of the insured, is removed from "reality." It enables the insured to meet, face to face, with people who have the final authority to determine value or amount of the loss. By the same token, the appraisal condition allows the insurer to bring in third parties to resolve exaggerated values on the part of the insured. Overall, the condition has performed its function well when required. Lest it be overemphasized, however, it should be noted that the vast majority of property losses are settled without appraisal.

The real difficulties with the appraisal provision have been constitutional. In general, no insurance contract can contain any condition, provision or agreement which prohibits to the insured the right of trial by jury on any substantive question of fact. This limits the appraiser to determining the amount of the loss.

Appraisal conditions are essentially the same in all policies. The following is the condition in the physical damage section of one auto insurance form:

> *Appraisal:* If we and you do not agree on the amount of loss, either may demand an appraisal of the loss. In this event, each party will select a competent appraiser. The two appraisers will select an umpire. The appraisers will state separately the actual cash value and the amount of loss. If they fail to agree, they will submit their differences to the umpire. A decision agreed to by any two will be binding. Each party will:
>
> 1. Pay its chosen appraiser; and
> 2. Bear the expenses of the appraisal and umpire equally.
>
> We do not waive any of our rights under this policy by agreeing to an appraisal.

Under the quoted provision, either party can make a demand for an appraisal. The appraisers, in turn, select an umpire. After selection of appraisers and the umpire, each appraiser then makes an evaluation of each item in dispute. If the two appraisers do not agree on any item, they submit that item to the umpire for final determination. A determination by any two of the appraisal panel is binding.

The appraisal award is subject to attack for the same reasons as a contract. Thus, a palpable mistake of law, fraud, collusion, dishonesty, unfairness, or the reference of any matter to chance or lot may void the award. Mere inadequacy of the award is not a ground for voidance unless it is so grossly inadequate as to reflect a mistake, misfeasance, or a deliberate attempt to defraud.

The insured is obligated to make the demand for an appraisal within a reasonable time. But, as discussed under "Notice and Proof of Loss," many situations involving delay are excused. Using several theories, courts occasionally have required the insurer to pay a loss even though the insured has not strictly fulfilled the obligation under this condition. If an insurer denies liability, it has been held to have waived its rights to require appraisal after suit has been brought. In other cases, the insurer has been held liable because of conduct inconsistent with the policy requirements. In one case, the insurer had engaged in protracted negotiations. Meanwhile, the property was deteriorating and the insured sold it. It was then that the insurer made a demand for appraisal. The court decided that the insurer had waived its rights to demand appraisal.

Arbitration The steps to set up an arbitration proceeding are outlined in the policy condition. For example, the uninsured motorists coverage section of an auto insurance policy contains the following arbitration provision:

Arbitration: If we and a covered person do not agree:
1. Whether that person is legally entitled to recover damages under this Part; or
2. As to the amount of damages;

either party may make a written demand for arbitration. In this event, each party will select an arbitrator. The two arbitrators will select a third. If they cannot agree within 30 days, either may request that selection be made by a judge of a court having jurisdiction. Each party will:
1. Pay the expenses it incurs; and
2. Bear the expenses of the third arbitrator equally.

Unless both parties agree otherwise, arbitration will take place in the county in which the covered person lives. Local rules of law as to procedure and evidence will apply. A decision agreed to by two of the arbitrators will be binding as to:
1. Whether the covered person is legally entitled to recover damages; and
2. The amount of damages. This applies only if the amount does not exceed the minimum limit for bodily injury liability specified by the financial responsibility law of the state in which your covered auto is principally garaged. If the amount exceeds that limit, either party may demand the right to a trial. This demand must be made within 60 days of the arbitrators' decision. If this demand is not made, the amount of damages agreed to by the arbitrators will be binding.

The arbitration provision of the uninsured motorist coverage was put in to expedite the disposition of claims outside of the court system. It offered a speedy and economical method for the resolution of disputes. When it was first introduced, it encountered considerable hostility from the courts, as well as from the organized bar, and it has been the subject of much litigation. Some of this has been due to dissatisfaction with an award itself, but there also have been a number of suits attacking the impartiality of the arbitrators. There have been cases where arbitrators were clearly hostile to the concept of arbitration or even incompetent to handle the subject matter in controversy.

The constitutional objections to appraisal are applicable also to arbitration. In an effort to encourage arbitration, some states have removed the prohibitions against it and allow all issues to be arbitrated if such requirement is set forth in a policy condition. However, the majority of the states confine mandatory arbitration to specified issues.

Experience has indicated that arbitration has served the purposes for which it was established. Proponents were disappointed over the hostility that was encountered and the limitations that have been placed upon it. Most observers indicate that the majority of arbitrators perform their duties faithfully and competently. There do not appear to be any significant differences in the amounts awarded. They are comparable to court or jury verdicts. This is as it should be. The results are obtained more quickly, and the cost is substantially less than litigation, as a general rule. However, until the legislatures and the courts eliminate the general prohibitions and hostility towards arbitration, its use will remain limited.

Suits Against the Insurer

The final, albeit drastic, action available to an *insured* to compel payment of the insurance company's obligation is a suit in a court of law. Contract provisions dealing with suits seek to prevent unreasonable delays and reinforce other contract provisions that serve as preconditions to suits.

Property Insurance   A typical provision in a special multi-peril policy reads:

> *Suit:* No suit shall be brought on this policy unless the insured has complied with all the policy provisions and has commenced the suit within one year after the loss occurs.

Provisions in the standard fire policy also place a one-year limitation on the filing of suit against the insurer. In either case, it should be noted that the condition specifically requires compliance with all the terms of the policy.

The one-year limitation in the SMP condition starts from the time the loss occurs. There are many instances where a later suit is permitted. Yet, there are courts that have adhered strictly to the wording of the condition. For example, in one case, the loss was discovered but the insured did not realize the loss was from a covered peril. After some delay, the loss was reported and finally suit brought within one year of the realization that there was coverage. The court sustained the insurer's defense that the suit was barred by the condition "within twelve months next after inception of the loss."

Liability Insurance Liability policies commonly require, as a prerequisite to the filing of a suit, "full compliance with all the terms of this policy" and that "the amount of the insured's obligation to pay shall have been finally determined." Some states have statutes that are known as "direct action" statutes. They permit a filing of liability suits by the plaintiff against the insurer, as well as against the insured. The reason for this is to eliminate a second suit by the successful plaintiff after he or she recovers a judgment against the insured. There has been concern that this type of statute exposes the insurer to the open hostility of the jury.

Liability policies do not have a specified time within which suit must be brought against the insurer, whether by the insured or the plaintiff. Under some circumstances, the statute of limitations will apply. If so, the plaintiff will have to file suit within the specified period. There are cases that may involve protracted litigation between insured and claimant. Others may involve minors who have right to bring suit against the insured after they attain their majority. However, if the insurer denies coverage, the insured may have to file a special kind of action, called a declaratory judgment action, to determine the question of coverage within the period provided by the statute of limitations. A denial of coverage and successful prosecution of the declaratory judgment action does not foreclose the eventual suit by the third party claimant, unless it was a party to the action. But the denial of coverage generally means that the insurer will not provide the insured with a defense if suit is filed. By filing the special action, the insured hopes to convince a court that there is coverage and force the insurer to assume the handling of the defense to suits that may be filed.

As an alternative to filing a declaratory judgment action, the insured may undertake the defense of the liability claim by employing his or her own counsel. If there is a verdict against an insured who is otherwise solvent, he or she may pay off the judgment and then sue the insurer on the contract for the amount of the judgment and the cost of the defense. Sometimes the insured is unable to furnish the defense, and the plaintiff may secure a default judgment against the insured. Sometimes the final verdict, particularly if it goes by default, will exceed the policy limits. The insured, faced by a personal judgment, (amount of the verdict) may assign the judgment to the plaintiff. When the plaintiff gets the assignment from the insured, the entire amount will be claimed from the insurer. The insurer *may* have to pay more than its policy limit. The ramification of excess verdicts is beyond the scope of this chapter. However, the problems posed by a denial of coverage and a potential excess verdict point out the dangers to an outright denial of coverage without having a court resolve the question of coverage and duty to defend prior to the trial of the liability claim.

As pointed out earlier, handling the insured's defenses under a nonwaiver agreement or a reservation of rights gives at least some protection to the insurer from potentially unpleasant results.

Concealment and Fraud in Connection with Claim

Moral and morale hazards are particularly important in property insurance and, therefore, the condition dealing with fraud and concealment is important. One homeowners form has the following such clause:

> *Concealment or Fraud:* We do not provide coverage for any insured who has intentionally concealed or misrepresented any material fact or circumstance relating to this insurance.

The same provision is contained in lines 1 through 6 of the standard fire policy. In a few states, there are statutes that apply to a proof of loss, and, in order for a misrepresentation to defeat a claim, the statutes require that it be fraudulent and material to the liability of the insurer. The insurer may not have to prove intent. It is enough if the facts which were material to the policy were within the knowledge of the insured. Facts used with reckless abandon can give rise to a presumption of fraud. Generally, it becomes a jury question. If the insured presents a proof of loss with an exaggerated claim and can only prove a small percentage of the amount claimed, it raises a presumption that the proof of loss is false and prepared in a fraudulent manner. That presumption then can be made conclusive if the insurer can present evidence that the amount of the loss and the amount claimed are highly disparate, and the explanation offered is not believable. The conclusion that can be drawn is that fraud has been perpetrated; it will enable the insurer to deny the claim.

To deny coverage, the insurer does not have to show that it has relied on the fraudulent representation. It is enough to show that the insured attempted to defraud the insurer. The provision against fraud has withstood attacks that it is against public policy. All that the insurer has to demonstrate is that there was a willful concealment or misrepresentation of a material fact, before or after a loss. What amounts to a fraud, concealment, or false swearing becomes a question for the court. Mere exaggeration or some minor but good faith error in a proof of loss is generally not held to be false swearing. Many insureds receive help in preparing proofs of loss. In such cases it would be manifestly unfair to allow an insurer to defeat the claim because of an error. In most cases, the insurance company has a duty to bring the insured's attention to such error and give it an opportunity to submit a corrected proof of loss. As one court observed about an exaggerated claim, it must be so "extravagant" as to lead to the conclusion that it was not due to a mistake in judgment but to an intention to defraud.

Many of the cases that involve this condition of the policy develop when the insurer becomes suspicious and begins to ask questions. There have been cases of a proof of loss submitted on a six-room house that shows enough destroyed furniture to equip a much larger house. When questions concerning the proof are raised, the requirement to submit to examinations under oath, line 116 of the fire policy, are enforced. Numerous cases show that if the insured simply refuses to submit to the examination, the courts will uphold the insurer's right to make such examination. In other cases, an insured will appear for the examination with an attorney and then refuse to answer questions which would show the fraud in the proof of loss. This too is a violation that will defeat the coverage.

SOME DOCTRINES GOVERNING COURT INTERPRETATIONS OF INSURANCE POLICY PROVISIONS

The courts are reluctant to penalize an insured for conduct which deviates slightly from the literal wording of a policy condition. Like any other policy provision, a condition is interpreted within the context of the entire policy. Furthermore, various legal doctrines are used by the courts in applying policy language to specific factual situations. The following paragraphs summarize some of the major legal doctrines that influence the courts in reaching their ultimate decisions.

Doctrine of Adhesion

The typical insurance policy is legally classified as a "contract of adhesion." A *contract of adhesion* is a written contract that is drafted by only one of the contracting parties. It is merely "adhered to" by the other party, in the sense that the other party played no role in drafting its specific provisions. If there are any ambiguities in a contract of adhesion, they are interpreted against the draftor of the instrument and in favor of the other party. Accordingly, in the usual insurance policy, all ambiguities are resolved in favor of the insured. They are construed against the insurer in recognition of its superior bargaining power. As one court put it:

> If semantically permissible, the contract will be given such construc-
> tion as will fairly achieve its objective of securing indemnification to
> the insured for the losses to which the insurance relates. If the
> insurer uses language which is uncertain, any reasonable doubt will
> be resolved against it; if the doubt relates to extent or fact of

coverage, whether as to peril insured against, the amount of liability or the person or persons protected, the language will be understood in its most inclusive sense, for the benefit of the insured.[15]

In short, if a policy provision can reasonably be interpreted in more than one way, it will be interpreted in the way that favors the insured. A policy provision that can reasonably be interpreted in more than one way is deemed to be ambiguous regardless of the original intent of the drafters. Whether a policy provision is ambiguous is ultimately a question of fact for the courts to decide. If the courts believe it is ambiguous, it is ambiguous.

Particularly in the 1960s, judges began to insist on making insurance policies easy to read and to understand. There were attacks on the "fine print" in policies and demands that exclusions and conditions had to be in the same size type as the insuring agreements. Similar demands have come from consumer and business groups. An executive of a major U.S. corporation stated in a speech, critical of the complexities of insurance contracts, that insurance companies should issue one "simple" policy that would insure *everything*. Yet, his own company would not and could not manufacture complex equipment or sell *everything* with one simple contract.

The fact is that few insureds ever read an entire insurance contract; and, no matter how simply written, fewer still can fully understand its terms. Courts are expecting insurers to make substantially complex insurance problems exceedingly simple. A few courts have been sympathetic to insurers who have tried to simplify contracts. Others have seemed hostile in interpreting new contracts, though drafters had made genuine efforts at simplification and ease in understanding.

Doctrine of Reasonable Expectations

The "doctrine of reasonable expectations" is another effort to balance the rights of insureds with those of insurers. Judge Learned Hand wrote in 1947, concerning the language on an interim receipt, "An underwriter might so understand the phrase when read in its context, but the application was not submitted to underwriters; it was to go to persons utterly unacquainted with the niceties of life insurance and who would read it colloquially. It is the understanding of such persons that counts."[16] Thus, courts are looking at insurance practices and policies and are asking a fundamentally simple question: What would a reasonable person expect in this situation? Hence, the doctrine of honoring *reasonable expectations* developed. In 1966, a New Jersey court pointed out that in an earlier case it had "stressed that insureds are entitled to the measure of protection necessary to fulfill their 'reasonable expectations' and they should not be subjected to technical encumbrances or to hidden pitfalls."[17] The courts feel an obligation to assist insureds in obtaining such benefits as reasonable persons would have expected under the same circumstances. It should be noted that other courts have rejected this doctrine.

Doctrine of Substantial Performance

Closely related to the doctrine of reasonable expectations is the equitable doctrine of "substantial performance," which applies to those insureds who have undertaken to perform their contracts in all material and substantial particulars in an honest and faithful manner. It becomes a factual question to be evaluated from all of the circumstances surrounding a case. The insured must be able to demonstrate that there was no willful omission or departure from the contract. This doctrine recognizes that a condition must be performed as outlined in the contract of insurance, but that there are circumstances where literal performance may be excused.

Although strict compliance with all of the conditions was required in early insurance contracts, this requirement has been relaxed by legislative intervention, competitive business practices, and judicial interpretation. Today, the doctrine of substantial performance is used, instead of literal compliance, as the minimum standard which must be met by the insured. As long as the insured is acting honestly and in good faith, substantial compliance with the policy provisions is usually adequate, and the insurer will not be allowed to deny liability on the grounds of the insured's failure to abide by a narrower interpretation of the policy requirements.

Doctrine of Unconscionable Advantage

The law abhors giving one party an "unconscionable advantage" over another. For example, the insurer cannot take unconscionable advantage of an insured by delaying negotiations with a claimant until the statute of limitations for the filing of a suit has run out. There is an implied covenant of good faith in every insurance contract. This convenant demands that the insurer deal fairly with all its insureds.

In one case an insured sent written notice of a fire loss, including detailed inventories of items lost in the fire. The information was more complete than that required by the proof of loss. The insurer never requested a form proof of loss, despite inquiries about the status of the claim from the insured. In the meantime the insurer proceeded to pay the mortgagee its interest under the policy, without any proof of loss, and then denied the insured's claim for failure to file the proof of loss.

Fortunately a court prevented the insurer from taking unconscionable advantage of this insured.

Where the insured is trying to preserve the contract but finds some clause objectionable, difficult, or almost impossible to perform, the courts have come to the aid of the insured. Sometimes the court opinions candidly recognize the principle of unconscionability. Often, it is the only rationale for the decision.

Doctrines of Waiver and Estoppel

Generally speaking, "waiver" is the voluntary relinquishment of a known right. "Estoppel" refers to conduct that is inconsistent with a claimed position. An insurer may *voluntarily waive* its right to deny liability under a policy. Or, if an insured entity, to its own detriment, was justified in relying on the representations or conduct of the insurer, the insurer may be *estopped* from denying liability. The latter is sometimes called "waiver by estoppel" (or involuntary waiver, which is technically a contradiction of terms). Waiver and estoppel play a large role in policy cancellations involving nonpayment of premiums and acceptance of premiums after a loss has occurred. For example, in a case where one agent knew of a policy cancellation before a loss but another agent accepted a late payment of the premium, the insurer was held to have waived its defense. Similarly, an insurer paid a small loss by mistake while the policy had been canceled for nonpayment of premium. The court held that it was estopped from denying coverage for a second loss that occurred shortly thereafter. In these cases, note, the insurer's conduct is inconsistent with its position that the insured has no coverage. The insurer is estopped from denying liability.

The insured may be able to show that the insurer had customarily accepted later premium payments without a lapse of coverage, or that a producer explained that a late payment would reinstate a policy without any lapse of coverage. An insured also may produce evidence that, in the course of dealing with the insurer for a number of years, the insurer had always sent the insured a second notice, but that a second notice was not sent in the case at hand. By relying on the second notice, the insured failed to pay the premium due at the time the loss occurred. The insured may also be able to show that the insurer had accepted late premiums as a regular business practice. It is obvious that a court cannot permit an insurer to reinstate coverage only for those insureds who had no losses during the lapsed period. Proof of its business practices would be held to be an election to reinstate all policies without lapse of coverage. It is everywhere agreed that the insurer may accept a late premium payment after knowledge of an existing breach of conditions. In doing so, it demonstrates its intention to regard the contract as continuing in full force. Insurers customarily issue renewal policies and bill the insured later. That creates a debt relationship with the customer. Clearly, there is no breach of the condition to pay the premium for that policy in such a situation.

Before an insured can be said to breach a condition, he or she has to be placed in a position to know about its provisions. Where an insurance policy was delivered to the mortgagee and only an abbreviated copy given to the insured, the insured was not bound by the policy's notice requirement. The insurer would be estopped from requiring such compliance.

If the insurer takes action which makes the notice requirement meaningless, the defense of failure to fulfill the notice condition of the policy may be waived by the insurer. For example, if the insurer notifies the insured that there is no coverage for the accident, presumably it knows what it is talking about and does not need any further details. That was the case when an insured reported the accident to an insurer's agent and the insurer promptly denied coverage. The insurer refused to take over defense of suits. Later it tried to claim prejudice by the delay in the fulfillment of the notice provisions. The insurer was held to have waived the defense. As a practical matter, modern claim handling procedures make the formal reporting of claims almost obsolete. Most reports reach the insurer by telephone and, if the claim is very serious, claim personnel are immediately assigned to conduct an investigation. In all cases there very likely will be a request for a written report, for control purposes, if for no other reason. However, the insurer cannot later claim a breach of the "notice" condition, when it started its investigation without the written report.

The insurer must act in a timely manner in preparing the defense of its insured. In a case where the insurer delayed making preparation for defense, the insured became concerned, took steps to settle the claim, and then sued the insurer for the amount of the settlement. The court held that the insurer had waived its right to rely on the clause prohibiting the insured from settling. Thus, if the insurer breaches its duty to use reasonable care to obtain cooperation of the insured, it cannot later complain. If a default judgment has been obtained, the insurer has a duty to notify the insured and seek revision of the default. If it fails to do so, a waiver of the defense of noncooperation may result. A waiver may also result where the insurer breaches its duty to defend. It cannot later complain about the action that the insured may have taken to protect his or her own interest. Finally, when an insurer discovers facts which indicate that the insured has breached the cooperation clause of the insurance contract, it must act promptly to notify the insured of the position it intends to take. If it fails to do so, it may be waiving its defense under this clause.

A Concluding Note

It should not be inferred that insurance policy provisions have become meaningless. To the extent that a policy has a clear meaning and places reasonable demands on the insured, most courts will enforce its terms in accordance with the underwriting intent. In fact, most claims are resolved without litigation. When an insurance policy's rights and duties are at issue in a formal lawsuit, the courts will be influenced by the above doctrines in interpreting the policy and applying it to a specific set of facts.

Chapter Notes

1. In cases where an auto liability policy has been provided to meet the requirements of a financial responsibility or compulsory insurance statute, the insurer *may* be held liable to third-party claimants, in spite of the insured's failure to meet specified policy conditions. If so, the insurer may have the right to obtain reimbursement from its insured. But this is not quite the same as collecting damages for a breach of contract. If the insured had breached the very same condition but the third party was liable, the insurer could not collect damages from its insured.

2. Plaza Equities Corp. v. Aetna Casualty and Surety Co., D.C. NY (1974), 372 F. Supp. 1325.

3. Greenway v. Selected Risks Ins. Co., D.C. App. (1973), 307 A. 2d 753, quoting Waters v. Amer. Auto Ins. Co., 124 U.S. App. D.C. 197, 363, F. 2d 684.

4. For delay, generally, see 44 Am. Jur. 2d & 1474 and *Appleman's Insurance Law and Practice*, 1731-1747; 4731-4747.

5. St. Paul Fire and Marine Ins. Co. v. Petzold (1969), 418 F. 2d 303.

6. Abington Mut. Fire Ins. Co. v. Drew (1969), 109 NH 464, 254 A. 2d 829.

7. Clute v. Harder Silo Co. Inc. A.D. (1973), 345 NY S. 2d 251, 42 A.D. 2d 818.

8. Cooper v. Govt. Empl. Ins. Co., 51 NJ 86, 237 A. 2d 870 (1968). Also see Billington v. Interinsurance Exch., 71 CA 2d 728, 456 P. 2d 982, 79 Cal. Rptr. 326 (1969).

9. Lumbermen's Mut. Cas. Co. v. Oliver (1975), NH, 335 A. 2d 666. Also see *Appleman's Insurance Law and Practice*, 4731

10. State Farm v. Johnson, 315 A. 2d 585 and 320 A.2d 345.

11. Centennial Cas. Co. v. Snyder, 142 CO 198, 350 P. 2d 337 (1960).

12. Howell v. Ohio Casualty Ins. Co., 124 NJ Super. 414, 307 A. 2d 142, Modified 130 NJ 350, 327 A. 2d 240.

13. Annis v. Annis, 250 MN 256, 84 N.W. 2d 527 (1957).

14. Western Mut. Ins. Co. v. Baldwin, 258 IA 460, 137 N.W. 2d 918 (1965).

15. Continental Casualty Co. v. Phoenix Construction Co., 46 CA 2d 423, 296 P. 2n 801.

16. Gaunt v. John Hancock Mutual Life Ins. Co., 160 F. 2d 599, Cert. denied 331 U.S. 849 (1947).

17. Gerhardt v. Continental Ins. Cos., 48 NJ 291, 225 A. 2d 328 (1966).

CHAPTER 15

The Standard Fire Policy

INTRODUCTION

This final chapter is devoted to (1) the current significance and historical development of fire insurance, (2) the general structure of fire insurance contracts, and (3) an analysis of the standard fire insurance policy. The primary objective of the chapter is to illustrate the practical application of the principles and concepts explained in Chapters 8 through 14. Overlaps with previous material will be minimized by omitting or de-emphasizing such topics as deductibles, insurance-to-value provisions, "other insurance" illustrations, and the legal aspects of the insurable interest and subrogation doctrines.

In keeping with the primary objective, the chapter will stress a systematic procedure for coverage analysis. The brief introductory sections are to confirm the inherent importance of fire insurance and underscore its basic role in property insurance generally.

THE SIGNIFICANCE AND DEVELOPMENT OF FIRE INSURANCE

The potential loss of property from fire is perhaps the most easily recognized property loss exposure. The magnitude of fire losses is also easy to appreciate in terms of both frequency and severity. Homes, commercial buildings, industrial structures, contents of residences, and the inventories of mercantile, manufacturing, warehousing, and service operations are readily identified loss exposures. The fire peril, whether arising out of natural causes, negligence, or arson, is too frequently the generator of loss. The significance of the fire peril is dramatized by the overall dimensions of fire losses and the premiums of the fire insurance industry.

Fire Losses

On the average, over 8,500 fires occur per day in the United States.[1] Annual fire losses to real and personal property exceed $4.85 billion. The National Safety Council estimated that 5,800 persons were killed by fires in this country in 1979. While most fires are due to either natural causes or negligence, arson or incendiarism is estimated currently to account for nearly 30 percent of all building fires. The trend of fire losses in dollar terms has been generally upward over recent years.

Historical Perspective

Private fire insurance began to be available in the seventeenth century. Following the catastrophic London fire of 1666, which destroyed 85 percent of the city, Nicholas Barbon, an entrepreneur engaged in housing development, began a speculative business operation involving residential construction and sales. Each sale included an agreement to repair or rebuild any house damaged or demolished by fire. The scheme met with such widespread acceptance that Barbon, in 1667, opened a private commercial fire insurance business which he named "The Phoenix Fire Office." This ancestral firm was the origin not only of the private fire business, but also of the fire mark and private fire brigade concepts as well.

The Phoenix Fire Office maintained (as did other insurance operations that soon developed) a group of men trained and equipped to fight fires in (and protect from the spread of fires) only those houses or properties insured by the company. The Fire Office placed on each insured dwelling a distinctive metal insignia or "mark." This was the birth of the fire mark.

Fire marks played an important part in the history of fire insurance. They were normally not placed upon a building until it was actually insured, and they were promptly removed if a policy was canceled or not renewed. Made of lead, brass, cast iron, copper, tin, or zinc, the marks were often painted in vivid colors and intricate designs. One of the more popular designs, used by both English and American companies for over 200 years, showed a pair of clasped hands. This design was used by both the "Hand-In-Hand Fire and Life Insurance Society" and the "Friendly Insurance Society." Other well-known fire marks include the Green Tree on the shield of the Green Tree Mutual

Insurance Company and the eagle emblem of the Insurance Company of North America.

Early developments of the fire insurance concept in the United States came about in the first part of the eighteenth century in the form of fire fighting organizations. Most such organizations were simply groups of neighbors who banded together to fight local fires. Others were volunteer fire fighting companies that fought fires in hopes of being rewarded by the homeowner whose building was saved by their efforts. The Union Fire Company, of which Benjamin Franklin was a founding member, was the first of the community-supported type to be established. It was formed in 1730.

While these early fire fighters were successful in controlling many fires, they were unable to do anything for the people who suffered losses from the fires that were not controlled. As cities grew in size, the problem of monetary losses from fire became more important.

To address this problem, Benjamin Franklin founded, in 1752, America's first incorporated fire insurance company, the Philadelphia Contributionship for the Insurance of Houses from Loss by Fire. The company was run like a neighborhood fire fighting squad. Each member contributed a sum of money to reimburse any member who suffered a fire loss to "insured property." The company is still in operation today.

From such a humble beginning as Barbon's initial scheme in 1666, the fire insurance business and the standard fire policy have evolved. Over 200 years of private fire insurance experience is reflected in today's fire insurance products, procedures, and systems.

Development of the Standard Fire Policy

During the first 100 years of its development in the United States, the fire insurance business was characterized by simple contracts written by insurers who knew their insureds well. Most insurers confined their operations to a relatively small geographical area and to insureds with whom the underwriters of the firm were familiar. Insurance was sold primarily through home office employees, without the assistance of agents or brokers. The fire insurance contract was extremely brief, including little more than the description of the property, the amount of the coverage, the period of coverage, and a premium citation. Insurance operations were characterized by individual underwriting and mutual understanding between insured and insurer. The importance of fire insurance lay not so much in the language of the agreement, the written policy, but in the mutual understanding between the parties as to what they sought to achieve.

As commerce increased and fire insurance grew into a larger, more sophisticated business, simplicity in product form and marketing methods began to bow to complexity. The prosperity experienced by commercial fire insurance brought on increased competition and more creative marketing systems. The result was a decentralization of underwriting activities, a lessening of firsthand knowledge in the selection process, and marketing through producers who often were significantly detached from the home office of the insurer.

By the second half of the nineteenth century fire insurers had encountered numerous problems—drastic rate cutting, unfavorable legislation, arson, and the use of highly combustible construction materials. In response, insurers pushed ever harder for more efficient fire fighting equipment, professional fire fighting companies, and building codes based on fire prevention concepts. They also made their first attempts at writing a standard fire policy for all companies to use.

Fire insurance companies that survived the New York fire of 1835 recognized the inherent danger of restricting operations to a limited geographical area. Consequently, they expanded their geographical underwriting boundaries. Selling and servicing policies throughout the nation proved difficult for home offices located in major cities; the property being insured or the damage caused by each fire was not readily available for examination. This led companies to pay agents in various states and towns to handle the policy sales and claims handling for them. For this reason, fire insurers have been given credit for instituting the American Agency System.

While such agents did alleviate some of the difficulties that distance had created, they also created some new problems. A company could not supervise the honesty of the agents or determine whether the out-of-state insurance applications contained accurate information. Moreover, the physical separation of the insured from the insurer depersonalized the insurer's relationship with its insureds and left insurers more subject to moral hazards. To alleviate these concerns, fire insurers issued policies filled with provisions designed to protect insurance companies from unwittingly accepting undesirable business and paying unjust claims.

Unfortunately, such policies became filled with restrictions, exclusions, exceptions, small type, confusing sentences, and undefined terms. Insureds often found they could not collect on their policies because of unseen exclusions buried deep in the fine print. Insurers found it hard to negotiate claim settlements because their policy conditions had become nullified, or otherwise modified, by widely differing court decisions. As stated in a court decision of 1873:

> Forms of applications and policies...of a most complicated and elaborate structure, were prepared, and filled with covenants, exceptions, stipulations, provisos, rules, regulations and conditions, rendering the policy void in a great number of contingencies.... Some of the

most material stipulations were concealed in a mass of rubbish on the
back side of the policy and the following page, where few would
expect to find anything more than a dull appendix, ... As if it were
feared that ... some extremely eccentric person might attempt to
examine and understand the meaning of the involved and intricate net
in which he was to be entangled—it was printed in such small type
and in lines so long and so crowded that the perusal of it was made
physically difficult, painful and injurious. Seldom has the art of
typography been so successfully diverted from the diffusion of
knowledge to the suppression of it. There was ground for the
premium payer to argue that the print alone was evidence ... of a
fraudulent plot.[2]

Lack of Uniformity

As early fire insurance developed in the mid- to late-1800s and early
1900s, a great deal of product differentiation came about. Individual
insurers went their own way in developing customized fire insurance
contracts. There was a general lack of cooperation among insurers in
terms of developing a common form or even guidelines toward a
generally acceptable agreement. Such product competition and customi-
zation led to a "hodgepodge" of fire insurance contracts which resulted
in consumer confusion. Fire insurance became an enigma to many
insureds, and the insurance industry was increasingly viewed with
suspicion.

The absence of standardization as to form and wording among fire
insurance contracts gave rise to numerous problems both for insureds
and insurers. As is partially true today, consumers knew what they
thought the agreement was supposed to do; however, most consumers
had not studied the policy in detail and were not at all certain of the
implications of all of the provisions therein. At the same time, with
insurers developing their own contracts without reference to any
common wording, fire insurance contracts were too often ambiguous.
As a result, problems came about in terms of interpretation of
coverage, litigation, and settlement of loss where dual coverage
existed. It became apparent that uniformity was a desirable goal. The
need for a shorter, simpler standard fire policy became increasingly
apparent.

Contract Standardization

The first serious attempt to develop a standard policy is believed to
have been undertaken by the National Board of Fire Underwriters in
1868. Massachusetts was the first state actually to adopt a standard
form for the writing of fire insurance. Very soon after its development,
the Massachusetts standard policy gained wide use and was made

mandatory for all companies writing business in the state after 1880. The New York legislature adopted a standard policy in 1887. This policy was the result of collaboration within the insurance industry. While formerly designated the "General Standard Fire Policy," it was popularly known as the "1886 form" (even though adopted in 1887).

Not for another thirty-one years did another major development take place in the evolution of the standard fire policy. Then, in 1916, the National Convention of Insurance Commissioners (now the National Association of Insurance Commissioners), following several years of deliberation, recommended a new standard form. This new form significantly decreased the number of clauses found in the "1886 form" that dealt with moral hazard and substituted "while clauses" which had the effect of suspending coverage if certain events occurred. The old form contained "if clauses" which voided coverage once a violation occurred. Other changes also were recommended and, in 1918, New York adopted the resulting "200 line form" which became known as the "Commissioners' form."

It was almost two decades before another significant step occurred in the development of the standard fire policy. In 1936, a committee of the National Association of Insurance Commissioners recommended revision of the 1918 form. Recommended changes in the policy included (1) the addition of lightning and fire caused by riot as perils covered, (2) the modification of the policy to an "interest" contract which did not require that the insured be the sole and unconditional owner of the property in order to have coverage, (3) the allowing of assignment of the policy with the insurer's consent, (4) the providing for the liberalization of vacancy and unoccupancy clauses to allow such conditions if for less than sixty days, and (5) the addition of a stipulation that in the event of loss (and multiple coverage) the loss would be prorated among insurers according to the face amounts of the coverage, whether collectible or not. On July 1, 1943, New York adopted this "165 line form." It became and is still popularly known today as the New York standard fire policy, or simply the standard fire policy.

The 1943 New York Standard Fire Policy

The 1943 New York standard fire policy is now used in nearly all states. In most of these states it is made "standard" or "approved" by reference in the insurance code of the state or by insurance department regulation. In a few states, the contract is statutory, i.e., the exact wording of the policy is incorporated into a state statute. Variations or modifications of the standard form are found in several states, most notably in California, Massachusetts, Minnesota, and Texas. Minor variations are required in Florida, Georgia, Hawaii, Indiana, Kansas, Maine, Missouri, New York, North Dakota, South Carolina, and Vermont. In these latter states, most of the policy variations relate to the declarations page, or to provisions such as perils covered or cancellation. In only a few states are there major variations in the body of the contract (the "165 lines").

Current Importance of the Standard Fire Policy

The standard fire policy is not a complete contract. In order to be complete, it must be combined with at least one additional "form" which defines and explains important aspects of coverage. Nevertheless, an understanding of the terms and conditions of the standard fire policy is critical to an understanding of property insurance in general.

The standard fire policy is the basis of many dwelling and commercial fire forms. For this reason alone, a comprehensive study of the standard fire policy is warranted. In addition, it should be recognized that, within the area of property insurance, a majority of the basic insurance concepts—insurable interest, indemnity, actual cash value, subrogation, pro-rata sharing of loss among multiple insurers, and appraisal—were conceived, nurtured, and first legally defined in relation to the standard fire policy. The Homeowners 76 policies, Dwelling 77 policies, the various businessowners policies, and the 1977 revised special multi-peril forms no longer contain the standard numbered lines of the New York standard fire policy in many states. The equivalent of most standard fire policy terms and conditions, however, are invariably included.

General Structure of the Standard Fire Policy

The standard fire insurance policy contains an insuring agreement, the name of the person or firm to be insured, the period of coverage, information concerning the identification and location of specific property being insured, the amount of the premium, and the "165 lines" of provisions, stipulations, and conditions. The standard fire policy becomes a complete contract only after the attachment of an additional "form," which describes the physical nature of the insured property, applicable extensions of coverage, circumstances or situations to which the insurance applies, and special conditions unique to the type of exposure covered. The form most commonly utilized to make the standard fire policy a complete contract is the general property form. For the illustrative purposes of this chapter, it will be presumed that the general property form or some other appropriate form has been attached to the basic policy.

As is generally true of property and liability insurance contracts, the standard fire policy is composed of five basic parts: declarations, insuring agreement, exclusions, conditions, and miscellaneous provisions. In the standard fire policy there is no clear distinction made to set off these five basic parts—that is, no boldface type or heading identifies them.

Physically, the standard fire policy may be set up in one of two ways. The first is to insert a declarations page into a "jacket" which contains the insuring agreement on one page and the 165 lines on another. The second way is to print the insuring agreement on the declarations page as illustrated in Exhibit 15-1 and place the 165 lines on a succeeding page as shown in Exhibit 15-2. In either case, additional forms are attached. Also in either case, about two-thirds of a page is devoted to information identifying (1) the insured, insurer, and the policy number; (2) the inception and duration of the insurance; and (3) the subject(s) of the insurance coverage, the perils insured against, the rates charged for each unit of coverage, the total premium charged for the coverage, and the specific items of property insured. This page is commonly referred to as the "declarations" because most of the information comes from statements made by the insured or selections of coverage and peril options made by the insured.

The insuring agreement of the standard fire policy may also be found on the declarations page. The insuring agreement is, in general, a statement in broad terms of what the insurer agrees to do under the contract.

The second page of the standard fire policy consists of the 165 lines. These provisions, stipulations, and conditions are standardized by statute, insurance code, or insurance commissioner regulation, and they set forth definitions, limitations, exclusions, and procedures for loss adjustment.

AN ANALYSIS OF
THE STANDARD FIRE POLICY

The remainder of this chapter analyzes the standard fire policy in order to illustrate the application of the systematic framework for policy analysis that has been developed in the previous six chapters. The discussion here will also inevitably provide an introduction to fire insurance principles that form the basis of personal and commercial property insurance coverages.

Modified slightly for the purpose of expositional convenience, the systematic policy analysis procedure will be used here to consider, in this order:

Exhibit 15-1
Standard Fire Policy Declarations and Insuring Agreement

STANDARD FIRE INSURANCE POLICY for Alabama, Alaska, Arizona, Arkansas, Colorado, Connecticut, Delaware, District of Columbia, Florida, Georgia, Hawaii, Idaho, Illinois, Indiana, Iowa, Kansas, Kentucky, Louisiana, Maine, Maryland, Michigan, Mississippi, Missouri, Montana, Nebraska, Nevada, New Hampshire, New Jersey, New Mexico, New York, North Carolina, North Dakota, Ohio, Oklahoma, Oregon, Pennsylvania, Rhode Island, South Carolina, South Dakota, Tennessee, Utah, Vermont, Virginia, Washington, West Virginia, Wisconsin and Wyoming.

No.   NONASSESSABLE

STANDARD FIRE POLICY

Insured's ⌈
Name
and
Mailing ·
Address
         ⌊   ⌋

Policy
Term: INCEPTION (Mo. Day Year)   EXPIRATION (Mo. Day Year)   YEARS

$_____
Div. on Exp. Pol.   Renewal of

It is important that the written portions of all policies covering the same property read exactly alike. If they do not, they should be made uniform at once.

INSURANCE IS PROVIDED AGAINST ONLY THOSE PERILS AND FOR ONLY THOSE COVERAGES INDICATED BELOW BY A PREMIUM CHARGE AND AGAINST OTHER PERILS AND FOR OTHER COVERAGES ONLY WHEN ENDORSED HEREON OR ADDED HERETO

Item No.	DESCRIPTION AND LOCATION OF PROPERTY COVERED Show address (No., Street, City, County, State, Zip Code), construction, type of roof and occupancy of building(s) covered or containing property covered. If occupied as a dwelling state if building is a seasonal or farm dwelling. If commercial state exact nature of product (and whether manufacturer, wholesaler or retailer) or the service or activity involved.	Protection Class	Dwelling Business Only			
			No. of Families	Feet From Hydrant	Miles From Fire Dept.	Zone
1.						

Item No.	PERIL(S) INSURED AGAINST AND COVERAGE(S) PROVIDED (INSERT NAME OF EACH)	Per Cent of Co-Insurance Applicable	Deductible Amount	Amount of Insurance	Rate	Prepaid or Installment Premium Due At Inception	Installment Premium Due At Each Anniversary
1.	FIRE AND LIGHTNING			$		$	$
	EXTENDED COVERAGE			x x x x x x x			

Special provision applicable only in State of Mississippi—**Total Insurance**—See form attached—
Item 1, $_____ ; Item 2, $_____ ; Item 3, $_____   TOTAL(S) |$ |$

Special provision applicable only in State of So. Carolina—**Valuation Clause**—See form attached—
Item , $_____ ; Item , $_____ ; Item , $_____   TOTAL PREMIUM FOR POLICY TERM PAID IN INSTALLMENTS |$

Subject to Form No(s).   **attached hereto.**
                        INSERT FORM NUMBER(S) AND EDITION DATE(S)

Mortgage Clause: Subject to the provisions of the mortgage clause attached hereto, loss, if any, on building items, shall be payable to:

                        INSERT NAME(S) OR MORTGAGEE(S) AND MAILING ADDRESS(ES)

		AGENT
COUNTERSIGNATURE DATE	AGENCY AT	

IN CONSIDERATION OF THE PROVISIONS AND STIPULATIONS HEREIN OR ADDED HERETO AND OF the premium above specified, this Company, for the term of *years specified above* from *inception date shown above* At Noon (Standard Time) to *expiration date shown above* At Noon (Standard Time) at location of property involved, to an amount not exceeding the amount(s) above specified, does insure *the insured named above* and legal representatives, to the extent of the actual cash value of the property at the time of loss, but not exceeding the amount which it would cost to repair or replace the property with material of like kind and quality within a reasonable time after such loss, without allowance for any increased cost of repair or reconstruction by reason of any ordinance or law regulating construction or repair, and without compensation for loss resulting from interruption of business or manufacture, nor in any event for more than the interest of the insured, against all **DIRECT LOSS BY FIRE, LIGHTNING AND BY REMOVAL FROM PREMISES ENDANGERED BY THE PERILS INSURED AGAINST IN THIS POLICY, EXCEPT AS HEREINAFTER PROVIDED,** to the property described herein while located or contained as described in this policy, or pro rata for five days at each proper place to which any of the property shall necessarily be removed for preservation from the perils insured against in this policy, but not elsewhere.
   Assignment of this policy shall not be valid except with the written consent of this Company.
   This policy is made and accepted subject to the foregoing provisions and stipulations and those hereinafter stated, which are hereby made a part of this policy, together with such other provisions, stipulations and agreements as may be added hereto, as provided in this policy.

TA8-3

Exhibit 15-2
Standard Fire Policy "165 Lines"

1 **Concealment,** This entire policy shall be void if, whether
2 **fraud.** before or after a loss, the insured has wil-
3 fully concealed or misrepresented any ma-
4 terial fact or circumstance concerning this insurance or the
5 subject thereof, or the interest of the insured therein, or in case
6 of any fraud or false swearing by the insured relating thereto.
7 **Uninsurable** This policy shall not cover accounts, bills,
8 **and** currency, deeds, evidences of debt, money or
9 **excepted property.** securities; nor, unless specifically named
10 hereon in writing, bullion or manuscripts.
11 **Perils not** This Company shall not be liable for loss by
12 **included.** fire or other perils insured against in this
13 policy caused, directly or indirectly, by: (a)
14 enemy attack by armed forces, including action taken by mili-
15 tary, naval or air forces in resisting an actual or an immediately
16 impending enemy attack; (b) invasion; (c) insurrection; (d)
17 rebellion; (e) revolution; (f) civil war; (g) usurped power; (h)
18 order of any civil authority except acts of destruction at the time
19 of and for the purpose of preventing the spread of fire, provided
20 that such fire did not originate from any of the perils excluded
21 by this policy; (i) neglect of the insured to use all reasonable
22 means to save and preserve the property at and after a loss, or
23 when the property is endangered by fire in neighboring prem-
24 ises; (j) nor shall this Company be liable for loss by theft.
25 **Other Insurance.** Other insurance may be prohibited or the
26 amount of insurance may be limited by en-
27 dorsement attached hereto.
28 **Conditions suspending or restricting insurance. Unless other-**
29 **wise provided in writing added hereto this Company shall not**
30 **be liable for loss occurring**
31 (a) while the hazard is increased by any means within the con-
32 trol or knowledge of the insured; or
33 (b) while a described building, whether intended for occupancy
34 by owner or tenant, is vacant or unoccupied beyond a period of
35 sixty consecutive days; or
36 (c) as a result of explosion or riot, unless fire ensue, and in
37 that event for loss by fire only.
38 **Other perils** Any other peril to be insured against or sub-
39 **or subjects.** ject of insurance to be covered in this policy
40 shall be by endorsement in writing hereon or
41 added hereto.
42 **Added provisions.** The extent of the application of insurance
43 under this policy and of the contribution to
44 be made by this Company in case of loss, and any other pro-
45 vision or agreement not inconsistent with the provisions of this
46 policy, may be provided for in writing added hereto, but no pro-
47 vision may be waived except such as by the terms of this policy
48 is subject to change.
49 **Waiver** No permission affecting this insurance shall
50 **provisions.** exist, or waiver of any provision be valid,
51 unless granted herein or expressed in writing
52 added hereto. No provision, stipulation or forfeiture shall be
53 held to be waived by any requirement or proceeding on the part
54 of this Company relating to appraisal or to any examination
55 provided for herein.
56 **Cancellation** This policy shall be cancelled at any time
57 **of policy.** at the request of the insured, in which case
58 this Company shall, upon demand and sur-
59 render of this policy, refund the excess of paid premium above
60 the customary short rates for the expired time. This pol-
61 icy may be cancelled at any time by this Company by giving
62 to the insured a five days' written notice of cancellation with
63 or without tender of the excess of paid premium above the pro
64 rata premium for the expired time, which excess, if not ten-
65 dered, shall be refunded on demand. Notice of cancellation shall
66 state that said excess premium (if not tendered) will be re-
67 funded on demand.
68 **Mortgagee** If loss hereunder is made payable, in whole
69 **interests and** or in part, to a designated mortgagee not
70 **obligations.** named herein as the insured, such interest in
71 this policy may be cancelled by giving to such
72 mortgagee a ten days' written notice of can-
73 cellation.
74 If the insured fails to render proof of loss such mortgagee, upon
75 notice, shall render proof of loss in the form herein specified
76 within sixty (60) days thereafter and shall be subject to the pro-
77 visions hereof relating to appraisal and time of payment and of
78 bringing suit. If this Company shall claim that no liability ex-
79 isted as to the mortgagor or owner, it shall, to the extent of pay-
80 ment of loss to the mortgagee, be subrogated to all the mort-
81 gagee's rights of recovery, but without impairing mortgagee's
82 right to sue; or it may pay off the mortgage debt and require
83 an assignment thereof and of the mortgage. Other provisions

84 relating to the interests and obligations of such mortgagee may
85 be added hereto by agreement in writing.
86 **Pro rata liability.** This Company shall not be liable for a greater
87 proportion of any loss than the amount
88 hereby insured shall bear to the whole insurance covering the
89 property against the peril involved, whether collectible or not.
90 **Requirements in** The insured shall give immediate written
91 **case loss occurs.** notice to this Company of any loss, protect
92 the property from further damage, forthwith
93 separate the damaged and undamaged personal property, put
94 it in the best possible order, furnish a complete inventory of
95 the destroyed, damaged and undamaged property, showing in
96 detail quantities, costs, actual cash value and amount of loss
97 claimed; **and within sixty days after the loss, unless such time**
98 **is extended in writing by this Company, the insured shall render**
99 **to this Company a proof of loss,** signed and sworn to by the
100 insured, stating the knowledge and belief of the insured as to
101 the following: the time and origin of the loss, the interest of the
102 insured and of all others in the property, the actual cash value of
103 each item thereof and the amount of loss thereto, all encum-
104 brances thereon, all other contracts of insurance, whether valid
105 or not, covering any of said property, any changes in the title,
106 use, occupation, location, possession or exposures of said prop-
107 erty since the issuing of this policy, by whom and for what
108 purpose any building herein described and the several parts
109 thereof were occupied at the time of loss and whether or not it
110 then stood on leased ground, and shall furnish a copy of all the
111 descriptions and schedules in all policies and, if required, verified
112 plans and specifications of any building, fixtures or machinery
113 destroyed or damaged. The insured, as often as may be reason-
114 ably required, shall exhibit to any person designated by this
115 Company all that remains of any property herein described, and
116 submit to examinations under oath by any person named by this
117 Company, and subscribe the same; and, as often as may be
118 reasonably required, shall produce for examination all books of
119 account, bills, invoices and other vouchers, or certified copies
120 thereof if originals are lost, at such reasonable time and place as
121 may be designated by this Company or its representative, and
122 shall permit extracts and copies thereof to be made.
123 **Appraisal.** In case the insured and this Company shall
124 fail to agree as to the actual cash value or
125 the amount of loss, then, on the written demand of either, each
126 shall select a competent and disinterested appraiser and notify
127 the other of the appraiser selected within twenty days of such
128 demand. The appraisers shall first select a competent and dis-
129 interested umpire; and failing for fifteen days to agree upon
130 such umpire, then, on request of the insured or this Company,
131 such umpire shall be selected by a judge of a court of record in
132 the state in which the property covered is located. The ap-
133 praisers shall then appraise the loss, stating separately actual
134 cash value and loss to each item; and, failing to agree, shall
135 submit their differences, only, to the umpire. An award in writ-
136 ing, so itemized, of any two when filed with this Company shall
137 determine the amount of actual cash value and loss. Each
138 appraiser shall be paid by the party selecting him and the ex-
139 penses of appraisal and umpire shall be paid by the parties
140 equally.
141 **Company's** It shall be optional with this Company to
142 **options.** take all, or any part, of the property at the
143 agreed or appraised value, and also to re-
144 pair, rebuild or replace the property destroyed or damaged with
145 other of like kind and quality within a reasonable time, on giv-
146 ing notice of its intention so to do within thirty days after the
147 receipt of the proof of loss herein required.
148 **Abandonment.** There can be no abandonment to this Com-
149 pany of any property.
150 **When loss** The amount of loss for which this Company
151 **payable.** may be liable shall be payable sixty days
152 after proof of loss, as herein provided, is
153 received by this Company and ascertainment of the loss is made
154 either by agreement between the insured and this Company ex-
155 pressed in writing or by the filing with this Company of an
156 award as herein provided.
157 **Suit.** No suit or action on this policy for the recov-
158 ery of any claim shall be sustainable in any
159 court of law or equity unless all the requirements of this policy
160 shall have been complied with, and unless commenced within
161 twelve months next after inception of the loss.
162 **Subrogation.** This Company may require from the insured
163 an assignment of all right of recovery against
164 any party for loss to the extent that payment therefor is made
165 by this Company.

IN WITNESS WHEREOF, this Company has executed and attested these presents; but this policy shall not be valid unless countersigned by the duly authorized Agent of this Company at the agency hereinbefore mentioned.

(1) Insured Entities
(2) Insured Events
    (a) Covered Properties
    (b) Covered Locations
    (c) Covered Time Periods
    (d) Covered Causes
    (e) Covered Consequences
(3) Limitations on the Amounts of Recovery
(4) Policy Conditions

In order to focus on these topics, the discussion will once again presuppose that all of the contract enforceability requisites and insurable interest requirements have been met. Examples and explanations of concepts discussed earlier have been reduced to a bare minimum.

Insured Entities

The insuring agreement of the standard fire policy states that it insures the named insured. However, the standard fire policy will actually insure only named persons or entities that also have an insurable interest in the properties covered. The fire policy is a personal contract which covers the *interests* of the entities insured, not the property per se.

Named Insured The named insured under the standard fire policy is any party identified on the declarations page as a named insured. Such party or parties may be an individual, more than one individual, an informal business association, a partnership, a governmental agency, a charitable organization, an educational institution, or a corporate entity. Regardless, it is extremely important that the parties whose interests are to be insured actually be named in the contract in some fashion.

A policy may be written without a named insured when it is stated that it is "for whom it may concern." Such a situation is useful when the insurance may be needed for an unknown individual such as a consignee, or for the benefit of numerous and changing persons, such as customers of a bailee.

A party not specified as an insured normally has no legal right to recover directly under the fire insurance policy, even if he or she has an insurable interest in the property at the time of loss. This is true even though the insurer may benefit from not having to pay to the total face of the contract (due to the fact that the insured actually named does not have an insurable interest equal to the full amount of insurance). Therefore, for certainty of protection, all parties having an interest in the insured property should be named in the declarations, with the exception of legal representatives of the insured.

Legal Representatives   The insuring clause of the fire contract automatically provides coverage for the "legal representatives" of the insured. The term "legal representatives" appears in the insuring agreement of the fire contract in order to circumvent the termination of the policy by the death, bankruptcy, or mental incapacity of the insured. The term "legal representatives" is intended to cover the administrators or executors of an insured who dies during the policy term, or the person legally appointed to supervise the affairs of an insane or otherwise legally incompetent person. Heirs do not automatically fall within this legal representatives designation. However, an assignee or a receiver in insolvency and a trustee in bankruptcy of a corporation are legal representatives within the meaning of the term of the fire contract.

Assignability   As is true of most property and liability insurance contracts, the fire contract may be assigned, but only with the written consent of the insurer. The policy insuring agreement specifically states this limitation: "Assignment of this policy shall not be valid except with the written consent of (the insurer)."

The effect of the assignment clause is to reemphasize the personal nature of the insurance contract and to make it clear that the insurer reserves the right to choose with whom it does business.

Mortgagee Protection   The relationships with any mortgagee are governed by lines 68 through 85 of the standard fire policy:

> *Mortgagee interests and obligations.*   If loss hereunder is made payable, in whole or in part, to a designated mortgagee not named herein as the insured, such interest in this policy may be cancelled by giving to such mortgagee a ten days' written notice of cancellation.
>
> If the insured fails to render proof of loss such mortgagee, upon notice, shall render proof of loss in the form herein specified within sixty (60) days thereafter and shall be subject to the provisions hereof relating to appraisal and time of payment and of bringing suit. If this Company shall claim that no liability existed as to the mortgagor or owner, it shall, to the extent of payment of loss to the mortgagee, be subrogated to all the mortgagee's rights of recovery, but without impairing mortgagee's right to sue; or it may pay off the mortgage debt and require an assignment thereof and of the mortgage. Other provisions relating to the interests and obligations of such mortgagee may be added hereto by agreement in writing.

If a mortgagee has an interest in the property and is to be protected under the policy, it should be named in the space provided in the declarations. This *could* also be done simply by including the name as an insured, such as "First National Bank, first mortgagee." However, it is better to name the mortgagee as subject to the mortgage clause. The standard fire policy provides that if loss is made payable in whole or in part to a designated mortgagee not named as the insured, ten days' written notice of cancellation must be given to such mortgagee. In those states where regulation or statute requires ten days' prior notice to the named insured, this provision is of no particular advantage to the mortgagee over the insured. In other states it is. It not only gives the mortgagee the right of independent notice but also allows time in which the mortgagee might arrange for alternative insurance on his or her interest.

The "mortgagee interests and obligations" clause further provides that, if the insured does not file proof of loss, the mortgagee may do so within sixty days after being notified. The mortgagee's interest is therefore given additional protection. The mortgagee does not necessarily suffer because of oversights on the part of the named insured in relation to the payment of premium or in providing proof of loss.

The mortgagee interests and obligations clause in the standard contract is not sufficient to protect fully a mortgagee's interest. Greater protection may be acquired by attaching the so-called "standard mortgage clause" to the policy. This clause is automatically included in many of the forms which may be attached to the standard fire policy. The standard mortgage clause defines the interest and obligations of the mortgagee, beyond those cited in the policy itself. It promises to indemnify the mortgagee as its interest appears; it further provides that the mortgagee shall be protected against any act on the part of the mortgagor that may invalidate the insurance.

Standard Mortgage Clause. The mortgage clause specifically recognizes the mortgagee's interest and agrees to protect that interest (as it may appear) regardless of acts or omissions on the part of the mortgagor, who is the named insured. Whether the mortgage clause is attached to the fire policy as an endorsement or is part of an attached form, its wording is very similar. The following example of a mortgage clause has been taken from the general property form:

> Loss or damage, if any, under this policy, shall be payable to the mortgagee (or trustee), named on the first page of this policy, as interest may appear, under all present or future mortgages upon the property herein described in which the aforesaid may have an interest as mortgagee (or trustee) in order of precedence of said mortgages, and this insurance, as to the interest of the mortgagee (or trustee) only therein, shall not be invalidated by any act or neglect of the mortgagor or owner of the within described property, nor by any foreclosure or other proceedings or notice of sale relating to the property, nor by any change in the title or ownership of the property, nor by the occupation of the premises for purposes more hazardous

than are permitted by this policy; provided, that in case the mortgagor or owner shall neglect to pay any premium due under this policy, the mortgagee (or trustee) shall, on demand pay the same.

Provided, also, that the mortgagee (or trustee) shall notify this Company of any change of ownership or occupancy or increase of hazard which shall come to the knowledge of said mortgagee (or trustee) and, unless permitted by this policy, it shall be noted thereon and the mortgagee (or trustee) shall, on demand, pay the premium for such increased hazard for the term of the use thereof; otherwise this policy shall be null and void.

This Company reserves the right to cancel this policy at any time as provided by its terms, but in such case this policy shall continue in force for the benefit only of the mortgagee (or trustee) for 10 days after notice to the mortgagee (or trustee) of such cancellation and shall then cease, and this Company shall have the right, on like notice, to cancel this agreement.

Whenever this Company shall pay the mortgagee (or trustee) any sum for loss under this policy and shall claim that, as to the mortgagor or owner, no liability therefor existed, this Company shall, to the extent of such payment, be thereupon legally subrogated to all the rights of the party to whom such payment shall be made, under all securities held as collateral to the mortgage debt, or may, at its option, pay to the mortgagee (or trustee) the whole principal due or to grow due on the mortgage with interest, and shall thereupon receive a full assignment and transfer of the mortgage and of all such other securities; but no subrogation shall impair the right of the mortgagee (or trustee) to recover the full amount of said mortgagee's (or trustee's) claim.

The above example of the standard mortgage clause is the generally accepted form. Though largely self-explanatory, several of its provisions warrant specific note.

Generally, if the mortgage clause is attached, the mortgagee will also be named on the declarations page of the fire policy. While the mortgage clause in lines 68 through 85 of the standard fire policy is somewhat redundant when the standard mortgage clause is also attached, the latter clause specifically provides that:

... the interest of the mortgagee (or trustee) only therein, shall not be invalidated by any act or neglect of the mortgagor or owner of the within described property, nor by any foreclosure or other proceedings or notice of sale relating to the property, nor by any change in the title or ownership of the property, nor by the occupation of the premises for purposes more hazardous than are permitted by this policy....

This clause does provide, however, that the mortgagee shall notify the insurer of any known change of nature in occupancy or increase in hazard, in which case the insurer may insist on an additional premium. The clause also provides that, in the event of a cancellation, coverage shall continue for the benefit of the mortgagee for a ten- or twenty-day period, depending on the particular form of the clause used.

The application of the standard mortgage clause to a loss under the fire policy is relatively simple. For example, if (1) the insured were to have dwelling coverage in the amount of $30,000 on his or her home which was encumbered by a $22,000 mortgage, and (2) there occurred a $12,000 insured loss to the dwelling structure, then the insurer would customarily pay the amount of the loss in a joint draft payable to both parties as mortgagee and mortgagor. Strictly speaking, the mortgagee (secured creditor) is entitled to all of the proceeds of the insurance under the provisions of the standard mortgage clause. Customarily, however, proceeds of such insurance are given to the mortgagor to make his or her collateral whole and to continue as mortgagor for the full amount of the mortgage balance. In the event that the mortgagee keeps the proceeds of the insurance, the mortgage will be credited or reduced by the amount of the $12,000 payment.

One might feel that the ability of the mortgagee to keep all proceeds of insurance up to the extent of the mortgage debt is inequitable to the insured-mortgagor, who may need such proceeds in order to repair or rebuild his or her property. The mortgagor might suffer hardship under the provisions of the clause. Nevertheless, the legality of the situation is such that the mortgagee (secured creditor) does have the right to receive benefit of the insurance and apply it toward the reduction of the balance of the mortgage. It might be noted that this is also compatible with the typical insurance clause in most mortgage instruments currently used. In such "insurance clauses," it is provided that, to the extent of the mortgage debt, insurance proceeds may either be applied to the reduction of that debt or paid to the mortgagor directly, *at the option of the mortgagee.*

Insured Events

Covered Properties In order to understand fully what property is covered under the standard fire policy, one must look not only to the declarations page of the policy, but also to the 165 lines of text. The declarations page notes the items or types of property covered, both real and personal. The 165 lines then excludes and excepts from coverage certain property that might otherwise be covered.

While land itself is generally not a subject of insurance, permanent improvements thereto (buildings and related structures) definitely are important subjects of insurance. Also, personal property such as contents of residences, business stock, inventories, goods in process, machinery, and equipment are important subjects of insurance.

Items Noted in Declarations. The basic items insured under the standard fire policy are generally identified by descriptive terms like "building" or "contents" in a space provided on the declarations page of the contract. Specific dollar amounts for the particular property insured are itemized. For example, a typical policy might have a specified building limit of $32,000. If various buildings at a common location are to be insured under a single policy, they may be listed as separate items or as a group. Generally, personal property at any one location is given a single aggregate value on the declarations page of the contract. In insuring the physical property which is the subject of coverage under the fire policy, and in selecting amounts of coverage by item, the basic division is between each "building" and the "contents" of the buildings on the described premises.

Since the standard fire policy affords coverage to described property at a specified location, it follows that property must be described in a definite manner. Many court cases involving ambiguity in the terms of fire policies concern the description of the subject of insurance. Such ambiguity, as would be expected, is resolved by considering the intention of the parties.

The words used in the declarations to describe the property are intended to identify the subject of insurance; they are ordinarily not intended to be specific. The words must be broad enough to include all property the parties intend to cover, yet not so broad as to be vague and misleading. Thus, on a policy designed for a mercantile exposure, the contents may be described as "furniture and fixtures, stock consisting chiefly of hardware and personal property of the insured." By custom or normal usage, all property customarily kept in the insured premises or required by the nature of its occupancy is insured without any specific description. Thus, flammable solvents incidental to the dry cleaning business would be considered normal contents for that type of business, since the form's definition of contents usually provides for inclusion of such incidental supplies and equipment.

Mistakes in identifying the insured building do happen. In practice, the courts interpret the policy to cover any building the parties intended to insure, despite an inaccurate description of that property. A converted dwelling, for example, described as a schoolhouse and used as a school was held to be sufficiently well described to identify the building. Nevertheless, good practice would dictate that the description be accurate enough to avoid ambiguity. The word "building" includes all equipment and fixtures attached to it, if so defined by the form.

Excluded and Excepted Properties. The standard fire policy does not cover certain types of property. Specifically, in lines 7 through 10 of the contract, deeds, evidences of debt, money, currency, accounts, bills, and securities (the acronym "DEMCABS" is frequently used to aid in remembering these excepted properties) are excluded from coverage:

Deeds
Evidences of debt
Money
Currency
Accounts
Bills
Securities

Unless specifically added by a form attached to the fire contract, or named in the declarations, the contract also does not cover bullion or manuscripts:

> *Uninsurable and excepted property.* This policy shall not cover accounts, bills, currency, deeds, evidences of debt, money or securities; nor, unless specifically named hereon in writing, bullion or manuscripts.

The two principal reasons for excluding such property from coverage are (1) the relative ease with which they can be concealed, and (2) the difficulty of determining their value. It would be hard to prove the amount of money destroyed in a fire, or to trace money or bonds taken away before a fire.

All of the excepted properties under the fire policy are items of personal property. In addition, their major value is largely intangible in nature, deriving from their importance as media of exchange, legal claims, evidence of ownership, or from their subjective value. The fact that such properties are excluded or excepted from coverage under the standard fire policy does not mean that they are uninsurable. Forms attached to the fire contract usually do extend coverage to records of account, to the extent of the cost of the blank paper and actual expenses of transcribing; indirect losses resulting from the destruction of account records may be insured under a separate contract, such as an accounts receivable policy; the potential loss of money and securities may be insured under a money and securities insurance form; and, manuscripts may be covered by a valuable papers and records policy.

Covered Locations The insuring agreement of the standard fire policy specifies that property described in its declarations will be insured:

> ... while located or contained as described in this policy or pro-rata for five days at each proper place to which any of the property shall necessarily be removed for preservation from the perils insured against in this policy, but not elsewhere.

This clause effectively limits locations to which coverage may apply (except during removal).

Described Premises. The declarations page of the fire policy provides space for indicating the specific location(s) of the property to be insured. This information is essential for rating, underwriting, and claims settlement purposes.

While it is not necessary in a fire insurance policy (or in any other insurance contract, for that matter) to give a complete legal description of the location of the real property (metes and bounds, government survey, or recorded subdivision lot and block legal description), as would be required in a deed to convey title to realty, the more detailed and complete the description, the better. The location should be specified in such detail that there is no ambiguity. In practice, a correct street address will normally suffice.

The 1943 standard fire policy covers the property only when located in the place described. The statement of location is a material fact and an integral part of the definition of the insured property. Any significant variance from this definition might enable the insurer to deny coverage. As an illustration, when a policy covers a stock of flour in a warehouse, the insurer is not liable for loss while the flour is situated at a location other than the one described in the policy. However, it is common for the various *forms* attached to the standard fire policy to liberalize the location restriction in the basic policy, usually by providing some limited extensions of coverage for property while off the described premises.

Property Removed to Protect. The last part of the insuring clause of the standard fire policy provides coverage "pro rata for five days at each proper place to which any of the property shall necessarily be removed for preservation...." The effect of this clause is to extend coverage to *any* location. For example, if an insured's home (or his or her neighbor's home) were to catch on fire, endangering personal property, such property, if removed to locations other than the described premises, would still be insured while removed.

If the insured were to remove some of his or her personal property threatened by fire and store it in a friend's garage. coverage would apply at the location of the garage for a five-day period. The fire policy clearly states that coverage will apply at each proper place to which the property shall necessarily be removed for preservation. The effect of this clause is to extend coverage temporarily to any proper or reasonable place in the event that the property is endangered by an *insured* peril. This could conceivably mean worldwide coverage. Moreover, during removal, this property is insured against loss from virtually any cause.

Covered Time Periods

Term of Policy. Most fire policies are written for a term of one year, although terms of less than one year or terms of three years are not uncommon. For a particular policy, the term is specified in the declarations and referred to in the insuring agreement: "... for the term of years specified above...."

Time of Inception. Unless designated otherwise, coverage under the standard fire policy begins at noon, standard time, and ends at noon, standard time at the location of the property. While it might be argued that noon is not the most convenient time to end coverage from the viewpoint of commerce, there is a general belief that there is more likely to be a witness to the inception of a fire at noon than at midnight. Thus, in an effort to minimize disputes as to when a fire started, it was general custom that all property insurance contracts with the fire contract as a base are made to begin and end at noon. In many states now, however, most property insurance policies change the time of inception and expiration to "12:01 A.M." standard time at the location of the property. Most future property insurance contracts will probably adopt the 12:01 A.M. inception time, which is commonly used with liability insurance.

In the absence of any express provision to the contrary, the day the policy begins is the day of the acceptance of the agreement by the insurer or its representative. The contract may, however, be made effective at the time the negotiations began or at some other time. The general common-law view is that the specific day of delivery of the policy to the applicant is relatively immaterial to the existence of an enforceable contract. Coverage is effective once the application is accepted by the insurer. The fact that the policy is not physically completed or mailed to the prospective insured is not of great importance.

Binders. An insurance producer very often has the power to "bind" an insurer. Agency agreements frequently provide that the producer has the right to obligate the company to coverage at *any* hour. A binder is frequently restricted to thirty or sixty days, and it is usually issued for even shorter periods. Some state laws limit the time for which a binder is valid. If the insurance is required for only a short time, the policy supposedly represented by the binder would probably never be issued.

A statement is usually included in a written binder which indicates that it automatically terminates upon (1) the issuance of the regular policy applied for or (2) the day following notification of refusal to underwrite coverage. In addition, there is often a statement expressly acknowledging that the policy applied for is an inherent part of the binder.

Renewal of Coverage. The standard fire policy runs for its stated, pre-agreed term. It is not perpetual. However, the fire contract, as is true of most insurance contracts written on a term basis, may be renewed. Though semi-automatic renewal of fire insurance—especially on dwellings—is commonplace, the standard fire policy itself does not address the issue of renewal. Absent a statute to the contrary, neither party is under an obligation to renew the agreement. It is clear that a renewed contract is a new contract. If the nature of the exposure (description of property, location of property, use and occupancy, and so forth) is not changed, there is usually no problem with renewal. When significant changes are to be made, there may be problems; and renewal may be a more cumbersome and less-than-automatic process. Renewal of coverage does not enlarge, restrict, or change the terms of the original policy, unless change is specifically provided for. Any new endorsements should be examined closely by the insured to verify that the new contract provides the agreed-upon coverage.

Cancellation of Policy. As discussed in previous chapters, cancellation is an important right of an insurer. It is, in effect, a post-selection underwriting device. In lines 56 through 67 of the standard fire policy, the cancellation provisions of the policy are defined. They specifically allow the insured or the insurer to cancel coverage, though the requirements placed on the two parties differ:

> *Cancellation of policy.* This policy shall be cancelled at any time at the request of the insured, in which case this Company shall, upon demand and surrender of this policy, refund the excess of paid premium above the customary short rates for the expired time. This policy may be cancelled at any time by this Company by giving to the insured a five days' written notice of cancellation with or without tender of the excess of paid premium above the pro rata premium for the expired time, which excess, if not tendered, shall be refunded on demand. Notice of cancellation shall state that said excess premium (if not tendered) will be refunded on demand.

The insured may cancel at any time. All he or she need do is request cancellation by oral or written notice. Such cancellation may become effective as soon as the notice reaches the insurer, if so desired by the insured. If an insured does cancel, the premium on the unexpired portion of the policy term will be returned on a "short rate" basis, producing a lower than pro-rata refund. Such a penalty is fair and proper, since the extra expense and reduced investment earnings attributable to canceling a short-term policy equitably should be borne by the insured when it is he or she who actually cancels. It is a general principle of contract law that the party to a contract who is willing to continue the contract shall not be disadvantaged through the inability or unwillingness of the other party to continue the contract. A more pragmatic reason for the short rate penalty is to discourage cancellations and the changing of insurers or contracts.

The insurer may also cancel at any time, but it must give the insured written notice five days before the effective date of cancellation. Because of this requirement, insurers frequently cancel by registered or certified mail, so as to have proof of receipt of notice of cancellation by the insured. The common-law view is that the five-day period of notice required prior to cancellation begins at midnight of the day that notice of cancellation is received and runs for five full days thereafter, ending at midnight of the fifth day following receipt of notification. In the event of cancellation by the company, the return premium is calculated on a pro rata basis for the unexpired term. It is important to note that the five-day notice requirement in the standard fire policy is commonly modified by legislative action or by forms attached to the policy. In many states, ten days' notice is now required. Many forms also dictate a modification to ten days, apart from any statute, so as to coincide with the notice given to mortgagees.

The cancellation provision is of great importance to the standard fire policy. Were it not for this kind of provision, the policy could not legally be discontinued in mid-term unless both insured and insurer were to agree. There are several reasons why the insurer or the insured might wish to exercise a right to cancel. For the insured, common reasons would include the sale of the covered property, a desire to acquire coverage elsewhere for a lower premium, or dissatisfaction with the services received from the present insurance producer or company. The insurer might find, subsequent to the issuance of the policy, that undesirable moral, morale, or physical hazards exist in relation to the subjects insured; or, the insurer might simply decide to withdraw from a line of business or particular geographical area. Whatever the reason for the cancellation of an insurance contract, it has been a generally accepted principle in relation to fire insurance that neither the insured nor the insurer need give justification or reasons for its cancellation.

The importance of the regulatory influence on the cancellation clause of the standard fire policy should not be overlooked. By statute or regulation, state legislatures or state insurance commissioners may vary the five-day notice requirement. For example, in many states a ten-day notice requirement is mandatory for the fire policy. Also, in a growing number of states, cancellation by the insurer must now be based on some justifiable reason, such as nonpayment of premium, fraud, recklessly increasing the hazards surrounding the properties insured, or illegality of contract.

Covered Causes The standard fire policy is a named-perils contract. That is, perils or causes of loss insured against are specified in the insuring agreement of the contract. The insurance company insures: "Against all DIRECT LOSS BY FIRE, LIGHTNING AND BY REMOVAL FROM PREMISES ENDANGERED BY THE PERILS INSURED AGAINST. . . ."

The Fire Peril. The word "fire" is not defined in the contract. However, the meaning of the term "fire" has been well established by court decisions. The usual definition of fire is "oxidation sufficiently rapid to cause a flame or glow."

Combustion that does not cause a flame does not constitute a fire. Heating, charring, scorching, and smoke can exist without the occurrence of a fire. Similarly, the decomposition of animal or vegetable matter can cause loss without any ignition. The consensus of court decisions on the definition of fire is well summarized as follows:

> Fire means combustion accompanied by visible light or heat. Combustion without visible heat or light is not fire. However, the glow need not be observed. If the heat which took place could only be the proximate result of a fire, then the fire, even though actually unobserved, will be held to have occurred.[3]

Friendly Versus Hostile Fires. Under the law, there are two different kinds of fires: "friendly" and "hostile." A *friendly fire* is a deliberately ignited flame or glow that stays within its intended confines, such as fires within heating, cooking, and lighting units. *Hostile fires* are those that escape their intended confines. Although the policy does not specifically say so, the standard fire policy covers only hostile fires. Any damage caused by a fire within its confines, such as smoking or scorching, is not usually considered to be covered under the standard fire policy because the cause of the loss was a friendly fire. Likewise, when fire is used as an agent in a manufacturing process, damage to the material being processed is not covered unless the fire escapes its confines. When a boiler is allowed to go dry, the damage to the boiler caused by the overheating of the regular furnace fire is not covered because the fire is friendly.

Lightning. The standard fire policy covers direct loss by lightning. Under most fire contracts before the 1943 standard policy, lightning coverage was obtained by endorsing the policy and paying an additional premium. A few courts interpreted lightning coverage into early fire policies by viewing lightning as "fire from the heavens." However, the general view was that, if no specific lightning peril endorsement had been added, damage due to lightning was excluded under fire contracts, unless fire ensued, and then only the damage done by the fire was covered.

Coverage of the lightning peril is important. Frequently, when lightning strikes, it may damage property so severely before fire ensues that relatively little of the damage can be attributed to the fire loss. Furthermore, lightning often strikes and damages building structures without any fire ensuing.

Lightning is a discharge of atmospheric electricity. It is so viewed under the fire policy and is not interpreted to include artificially generated (i.e., man-made) electricity. Damage caused by lightning is covered under the contract, as is damage due to fire resulting from lightning. Damage by electrical current artificially generated is not covered by the standard fire policy, though *fire* growing out of an electrical malfunction is covered.

Removal from Premises. As previously noted, the standard fire policy covers "removal from premises endangered by perils insured against in the policy...pro rata for five days at each proper place to which any of the property shall be necessarily removed for preservation from the perils insured against in this policy...." The effect of this clause is to give virtually "all-risks" coverage to insured property removed to another location if it was moved in order to preserve it from damage by an insured peril. The time limitation on this coverage is short (five days), but it can prove to be very valuable protection. Because the act of "removal" increases the chance of loss, some people consider "removal" to be a hazard, rather than a peril.

As will be noted later, it is an obligation of the insured to make reasonable efforts to protect his or her property from damage or destruction. The policy, in effect, says that when an insured takes steps to remove property from imminent damage by perils insured against, any loss occurring as a result of removal under such circumstances will be a valid claim. The coverage is quite broad. Almost any conceivable loss would be covered during the process of removal, including loss by breakage, rain, flood, or even theft. For example, if an insured's home kitchen were to catch fire and the insured were to remove various pieces of furniture to the yard where they suffer rain damage, the rain damage to the furniture would be covered. Or, if a fire in a house next door to the insured dwelling were threatening the insured's property and a neighbor, helpfully removing a fine painting from the insured's premises, stumbled, ripping the canvas of the artwork, such a loss also would be covered.

During removal, theft, which is an otherwise specifically excluded peril in the fire contract, is covered. Numerous court decisions support the view that the theft of property removed from a burning building is the proximate result of fire and, therefore, is covered under the fire policy.

Excluded Perils. There are some situations in which the standard fire policy does not provide insurance against fire, lightning, and removal. Lines 11 through 24 describe the events to which the coverage does not apply:

> *Perils not included.* This Company shall not be liable for loss by fire or other perils insured against in this policy caused, directly or indirectly, by: (a) enemy attack by armed forces, including action taken by military, naval or air forces in resisting an actual or an immediately impending enemy attack; (b) invasion; (c) insurrection; (d) rebellion; (e) revolution; (f) civil war; (g) usurped power; (h) order of any civil authority except acts of destruction at the time of and for the purpose of preventing the spread of fire, provided that such fire did not originate from any of the perils excluded by this policy; (i) neglect of the insured to use all reasonable means to save and preserve the property at and after a loss, or when the property is endangered by fire in neighboring premises; (j) nor shall this Company be liable for loss by theft.

Reasons for excluding these losses are briefly examined below.

"WARTIME" PERILS. The so-called "wartime" perils of enemy attack, invasion, insurrection, rebellion, revolution, civil war, and usurped power are excluded. Such exposures are considered uninsurable by most private insurers in fire insurance.

ORDER OF CIVIL AUTHORITY. The "order of civil authority" exclusion appears reasonable, especially when the limited scope of this exclusion is considered. Destruction of insured property by civil authorities to prevent the spread of fire remains covered, provided that such fire did not originate from any of the causes excluded from coverage under the policy. In order for an insurer to escape liability under the fire contract by reason of the civil authority clause, the burden of proof rests on the insurer to show that (1) the fire damage was *not* "caused, directly or indirectly, by: .... order of any civil authority..." to prevent the spread of *a fire already in progress* or (2) the fire originated from one of the wartime perils. The insurer would seldom be able to deny liability in peacetime, because civil authorities seldom burn or order the burning of a building (or its contents) unless the purpose is to prevent the spread of fire. About the only time they do so for another purpose is when a law enforcement officer burns a building to "smoke out" a dangerous criminal. Such a fire is not covered; its purpose is not to prevent the spread of fire. Avoiding liability for such fires would be the only reason for the civil authority exclusion, if fire is the only covered peril, since the wartime perils are excluded anyway. However, when perils such as explosion and collapse are added to the policy, the civil authority exclusion is also necessary to avoid coverage for destruction of a condemned building by means other than fire.

NEGLECT OF THE INSURED AT OR AFTER LOSS. Under the standard fire policy, the insurer is not liable for damage caused by the insured's neglect in preserving property. The effect of this clause is to prevent the insured from collecting for property damaged or destroyed if there were a reasonable chance to prevent such damage or destruction.

While such neglect on the part of the insured does not void the policy, it relieves the insurer from liability for that part of the loss attributable to the neglect. For example, if an insured's office building suffered a small roof fire which caused structural damage to the roof and, two weeks later, rain came through the resulting opening in such amounts as to damage the interior of the building and its contents, the insurer would likely have to pay only for the fire damage to the roof, not for the subsequent damage to the interior and contents. Even though fire might be considered the proximate cause of such a loss, the loss was also aggravated or affected in magnitude by the intervening neglect of the insured, i.e., the insured's failure to use reasonable means to save and preserve the property from further loss. If the insured had made a real effort in attempting temporary repairs in the roof and the rain damage still occurred, the entire loss would likely have been covered.

The general rule in regard to such losses is stated quite succinctly in Couch's *Cyclopedia of Insurance Law*: "An insured is obligated to protect his property at the time of the fire and after the fire and if he fails to do so, the insurer is not liable under the protection clause of the policy."[4] Whether or not the insured exercised reasonable care or due diligence to protect property exposed to loss is ultimately a question of fact for a jury.

THEFT. Among the excepted perils, theft is specifically noted. This exclusion was more appropriate before enabling laws were passed to permit multiple line policies. Before then, in many states a fire insurance policy by law could not insure against theft. Modern property insurance forms often include theft with other perils insured against in the contract. Theft which occurs during removal from a premises endangered by an insured peril is covered under the fire policy, apart from whether theft per se is a named peril in the contract.

EXPLOSION AND RIOT. The explosion peril is excluded from coverage in lines 36 and 37 of the fire policy:

> as a result of explosion or riot, unless fire ensue, and in that event for loss by fire only.

Notice that explosion and riot per se are not covered under the fire contract; however, if an explosion or riot occurs and a fire results, the damage or destruction that can be specifically attributable to the resulting fire loss would be covered. The explosion exclusion had led to great confusion, partly because it is difficult to determine which peril caused which part of a loss when both fire and explosion are involved. Determination of whether fire caused the explosion or whether explosion caused the fire may thus be a major issue of determining coverage under the standard fire policy. Fortunately, "extended coverage," which includes coverage of the explosion and riot perils (among other perils), is usually in a form attached to the basic fire policy.

NUCLEAR EXPOSURE. While nuclear reaction was virtually an unknown peril at the time of development of the 1943 New York standard fire policy, loss due to nuclear explosion would be excluded under the explosion clause. In addition, in 1957, a nuclear reaction, radiation, and contamination exclusionary endorsement was adopted for nationwide use. It is now attached to virtually all fire contracts, either as a specific endorsement or as part of some other attached form.

Nuclear Clause and Nuclear Exclusion No. 1

Nuclear Clause (Applicable to all Fire Policies): The word "fire" in this policy or endorsements attached hereto is not intended to and does not embrace nuclear reaction or nuclear radiation or radioactive contamination, all whether controlled or uncontrolled, and loss by nuclear reaction or nuclear radiation or radioactive contamination is not intended to be and is not insured against by this policy or said endorsements, whether such loss be direct or indirect, proximate or remote, or be in whole or in part caused by, contributed to, or aggravated by "fire" or any other perils insured against by this policy or said endorsements; however, subject to the foregoing and all provisions of this policy, direct loss by "fire" resulting from nuclear reaction or nuclear radiation or radioactive contamination is insured against by this policy.

Nuclear Exclusion No. 1 (Applicable to all Policies to which the Extended Coverage Endorsement is attached): Loss by nuclear reaction or nuclear radiation or radioactive contamination, all whether controlled or uncontrolled, or due to any act or condition incident to any of the foregoing, is not insured against by this Extended Coverage Endorsement, whether such loss be direct or indirect, proximate or remote, or be in whole or in part caused by, contributed to, or aggravated by windstorm, hail, explosion, riot, riot attending a strike, civil commotion, aircraft, vehicles or smoke; and nuclear reaction or nuclear radiation or radioactive contamination, all whether controlled or uncontrolled, is not "explosion" or "smoke."

Other Perils. Provision is made in the standard fire policy for the inclusion of perils other than fire, lightning, and removal from the premises. Lines 38 through 41 state:

Other perils or subjects. Any other peril to be insured against or subject of insurance to be covered in this policy shall be by endorsement in writing hereon or added hereto.

The most common use of this provision is the addition of "extended coverage."

EXTENDED COVERAGE. Extended coverage "extends" the scope of the fire policy to cover the additional perils of windstorm, hail, explosion, riot, riot attending a strike, civil commotion, loss by aircraft, loss by vehicles, and smoke. Insuring these perils once required a separate endorsement, but they are now included automatically in most of the forms which are attached to complete the fire insurance contract. Some of these perils are defined in a limited or narrow way. Others have fairly literal meanings. In any case, the extended coverage perils are like any other covered perils. Their meanings can be understood only by studying the entire policy, along with the applicable court interpretations.

"BROAD" FORMS. Beyond the extended coverage perils, the insured may further extend the policy to cover an additional group of specified perils. For example, one so-called "broad form" covers loss by the extended coverage perils *and* vandalism and malicious mischief; falling objects; the weight of ice, snow, or sleet; collapse of buildings; damage by burglars; freezing of plumbing, heating, and air conditioning systems; and several additional perils.

SPECIAL OR "ALL-RISKS" FORMS. The insured may instead purchase a so-called "special form," which covers buildings for "all risks of physical loss ... except as otherwise excluded or limited." This form effectively converts the fire policy from a named-perils basis to an all-risk basis of coverage. Some property insurance forms provide "all-risks" coverage on buildings and named-perils coverage on personal property. "All-risks" coverage is the broadest and most expensive coverage available. The cost of named-perils coverage increases as the number of covered perils increases.

Covered Consequences The basic consequence covered by the standard fire policy is *direct* loss by the perils of fire or lightning. The "direct loss" limitation is important. Direct loss constitutes actual physical damage to, or destruction of, the insured property. Direct loss also includes damage to property where a covered peril is the *proximate cause* of the loss, such as damage by smoke from a hostile fire. In addition, water damage resulting from an attempt to extinguish a fire in the subject property would constitute a direct loss. The doctrine of proximate cause was explained fully in an earlier chapter.

Direct loss means actual physical damage to or destruction of tangible property. It excludes indirect loss, such as loss of earnings from operations, loss of rental income, or extra expenses which often result from direct losses. It is important to note, however, that such indirect losses may be insurable under indirect loss coverages, such as business interruption insurance, rental value insurance, rents insurance, and extra expense insurance, via forms attached to the basic fire contract.

Limitations on the Amounts of Recovery

Throughout the fire contract, there are a number of phrases and stipulations which have the effect of limiting the insurer's contractual liability. Several of these limitations are referred to in the insuring clause of the contract; however, they also appear elsewhere.

Policy Limits The limit of liability stated on the declarations page is the maximum amount for which the insurer can be held liable. Its actual liability in many loss situations is often much less, even if the concerned property is totally destroyed by fire.

Under the insuring agreement of the standard fire policy, the insured is covered for the face amount of the policy:

> ... to the extent of the actual cash value of the property at the time of loss, but not exceeding the amount which it would cost to repair or replace the property with material of like kind and quality within a reasonable time after such loss, without allowance for any increased cost of repair or reconstruction by reason of any ordinance or law regulating construction or repair, and without compensation for loss resulting from interruption of business or manufacture, nor in any event for more than the interest of the insured....

The form used to complete the contract will also contain sublimits on specified types of property and specified types of losses. The face amount of the policy and the various sublimits are collectively the "policy limits." Thus, when only one policy is involved, the maximum amount of recovery is the *smallest of:*

(1) the applicable policy limit(s)
(2) the actual cash value of the property at the time of loss (except where valued policy laws require the payment of the agreed-upon value for a total loss)
(3) the cost to repair or replace the property with material of like kind and quality, *or*
(4) the insured's legally insurable interest in the property at the time of loss

The amount of recovery may be reduced by the operation of a deductible and/or coinsurance provision, if either or both are applicable by virtue of an attached form or endorsement.

"Other Insurance" Provisions   Another policy clause which affects insurance under the standard fire policy is the *"other insurance" clause*, lines 25 through 27:

> *Other Insurance.*   Other insurance may be prohibited or the amount of insurance may be limited by endorsement attached hereto.

This provision allows an insurer to prohibit (in an endorsement) other policies of insurance applying to the same property. Violation of such a prohibiting endorsement could void the policy, although the law is not uniform on this point. The underlying reason for this clause is to prevent overinsurance of certain types of property.

The intent of this clause is not to prevent several different persons from being insured under separate policies, but rather to prevent the same insured from securing several different policies without the knowledge of the insurer(s). The clause may be used to prevent duplicate policies insuring the same insurable interest, insuring against the same perils and covering the same property.

In Chapter 13, the subrogation rights which an insurer may have following a loss were discussed in detail. The doctrine of subrogation is a major supporting element of the concept of indemnity. The principle of indemnity could be violated if an insured could collect from both the insurer and some third party responsible for the loss. Thus, the right of subrogation provides for the substitution of the insurer in place of the insured for the purpose of claiming indemnity from a third party (or the third party's liability insurer).

Notice that the standard fire policy provides actual cash value coverage and contains the usual insurer settlement options of ACV coverage. Again, by endorsement or attachment of the appropriate form, the ACV coverage may be converted to a replacement cost basis of loss valuation. The insurer loss settlement options would be altered accordingly.

The foregoing comments assume that just one policy applies. Also to be considered are the situations involving multiple insurers.

Residential property is usually insured under a single insurance contract, and the allocation of losses among multiple insurers is not encountered. On the other hand, when large property values are involved, as is often true with commercial, industrial, institutional, and governmental property, the same property may be insured with more than one insurance company. The amount for which each company is liable in event of a loss is determined by the following lines of the standard fire policy:

> *Pro rata liability.*   This Company shall not be liable for a greater proportion of any loss than the amount hereby insured shall bear to the whole insurance covering the property against the peril involved, whether collectible or not.

increase the chances of loss caused by children playing around or within the premises, adult trespassers, vandals, burglars, or other parties with no interest in the property insured. In addition, it is obvious that unoccupied premises are far less likely to receive any benefit from the insured's actions following a loss. Therefore, what could have been a small, containable fire loss might turn into a much greater one. A building is *vacant* when there is an absence of both people and furnishings or other contents from the building. *Unoccupancy* refers merely to the absence of people from the premises. Thus, a dwelling could be unoccupied even though it actually contained all furniture and fixtures necessary for normal living accommodations. Some insurance students remember which is which by noting that the "No Vacancy" sign outside a motel should really read, "No Unoccupancy."

The words "vacancy" and "unoccupancy" have been the subject of so much litigation that some elaboration of the brief definitions is in order. For instance, "... 'unoccupied' ... [implies] a situation in which the insured building or premises are without an occupant of the kind, and during the time, contemplated by the intention of the parties as indicated by the terms and descriptions of the policy.[5] However, a temporary absence (in at least one case, extending several "winter vacation" months) does not render the dwelling "unoccupied." The intention to return is controlling. On the other hand, in most instances the insurer need not prove that the condition resulted in an increase in hazard.

The wording of the policy is clear in relation to the vacancy or unoccupancy provision. Either vacancy *or* unoccupancy beyond a period of sixty consecutive days will suspend coverage. The policy, in effect, considers the increase of hazard associated with both vacancy and unoccupancy to be similar. It also recognizes that temporary vacancy or unoccupancy not exceeding sixty consecutive days is compatible with the implicit underwriting standards of the fire contract. For planned vacancies or unoccupancies in excess of the sixty-day threshold, a "vacancy or unoccupancy endorsement" may be added to the fire contract, for an additional premium, thereby extending coverage indefinitely and negating the application of the vacancy or unoccupancy clause in the policy. It should also be noted that most dwelling and commercial property forms which might be attached to the basic fire policy modify the vacancy or unoccupancy limitation.

Fraud and Concealment Apparently, when the standard fire policy was originally drafted, its provision relating to concealment or fraud on the part of the insured was considered so important as to be entered as the first item (lines 1 through 6) among the 165 lines.

Concealment, fraud. This entire policy shall be void if, whether before or after a loss, the insured has wilfully concealed or misrepresented any material fact or circumstance concerning this insurance or the subject thereof, or the interest of the insured therein, or in case of any fraud or false swearing by the insured relating thereto.

The effect of the concealment and fraud provision in the fire policy is to give the claims adjuster contractual support for disclaiming liability if an insured *"wilfully"* withholds facts which are material to the insuring of the exposure. Such concealment and fraud may occur before the inception of coverage, or it may be occasioned by an insured who has sworn falsely in proofs of loss, or has otherwise sought to defraud the insurer. The word "wilfully" is very important to the provision. Prior to the 1943 New York standard fire policy, this adverb did not usually appear in fire contracts. Its presence makes it necessary for the insurer to prove that the insured intended to conceal or defraud the insurer. Innocent concealment or misrepresentation due to oversight or ignorance is not sufficient to deny liability through this policy provision. Intention of the insured becomes important and, of course, is difficult to prove.

Concealment has been defined as failure to disclose known facts or as "silence when obligated to speak." The prevailing view, in relation to fire insurance, is that the insured must reveal only material facts, and that a contract can be voided only if the concealment was material and intentional. Often, accessibility to inspection is a key in determining whether a contract may be voidable on the basis of a material concealment. If the insurer or its representative could have inspected and found out the facts for itself in the normal course of business, the insured is usually not held responsible for declaring the facts. For example, if an insured was unaware that the wiring in his or her home was not up to building code standards, the insurer would likely be held to the coverage in the event of loss caused by such faulty wiring. In addition, there are certain facts relevant to fire insurance underwriting which the insured need not affirmatively dislcose. For example, facts of general knowledge need not be pointed out to the insurer. Thus, if an insured orders fire insurance coverage on his or her dwelling property located halfway between two neighboring towns, furnishing the proper rural address, the insured is not obligated to volunteer the information that no fire department will respond to calls in that area. The insured also need not disclose facts which should be reasonably known to the insurer, such as the age of the building, condition of the wiring, or the nature of the foundation.

While a concealment does not appear in writing, a representation often does. A misrepresentation is an incorrect or false statement relating to the insurance or the subjects of insurance. Clearly, a representation is a collateral inducement to the making of the insurance contract. It has the legal effect of allowing the insurer to declare the contract voidable only if (1) false, (2) relied upon, and (3) material. The common law distinguishes between a *misrepresentation of fact* and a *misrepresentation of opinion*, saying that a misrepresentation of fact may allow avoidance of a contract if material, while a misrepresentation of opinion may render a contract ineffective only if material and fraudulent. For example, if an insured, in applying for a fire insurance contract, misstates the age of the building structure on his or her property by several years, it is not likely that such a mistake would be material to the exposure. In addition, if it were only an estimate of age, it would be mere opinion. As another example, consider the exterior construction of a dwelling, which is clearly an important underwriting criterion in fire insurance. If a prospective insured were asked over the telephone to indicate whether a house was of brick or frame construction, and the insured answered brick—not knowing that the house was indeed brick veneer and therefore ratable as frame—there would be no intentional misrepresentation.

Two legal references do a good job of summarizing the common-law view of the concealment and fraud provision of the standard fire policy. In the words of the court in one case:

> If there is a willful misrepresentation of a material fact, or concealment thereof, on the part of the insured in the proof of loss, examination pursuant to the policy, or otherwise, the policy is void in accordance with its terms.[6]

In the words of Couch:

> Where a representation is intentionally false, and calculated to mislead the insurer into issuing a policy and is material, the policy is avoided whether the insurer or its agent knew or did not know of its falsity, such result being in conformity with the general principle that fraud vitiates all contracts.[7]

Requirements if Loss Occurs   Much of the second column of the 165 lines portion of the standard fire policy relates to requirements that apply to the insured following loss. Lines 90 through 97 state:

> *Requirements in case loss occurs.*   The insured shall give immediate written notice to this Company of any loss, protect the property from further damage, forthwith separate the damaged and undamaged personal property, put it in the best possible order, furnish a complete inventory of it in the best possible order, furnish a complete inventory of the destroyed, damaged and undamaged property, showing in detail quantities, costs, actual cash value and amount of loss claimed. . . .

These lines indicate that the insured is obligated to do certain things immediately (within a reasonable time) after a loss, including (1) protecting the property from further damage, (2) giving written notice of the loss to the company, (3) separating the damaged and undamaged personal property and putting it in its best possible order, and (4) furnishing certain detailed information.

Protection of Property. The requirement that the insured protect property from further damage following a loss may prove to be of great importance to the insurer. The effect of this clause is to make postloss loss reduction activities a definite obligation of the insured following a fire. For example, if an insured's residence were partially destroyed by fire and he or she were to vacate the premises without taking any precautions to protect the remaining contents from pilferage, the insurer would not be obligated to pay for such additional loss. The protection-of-property clause merely reaffirms the fact that the fire policy insures against direct loss by fire or other specified perils. It is not an indirect loss coverage applying to loss resulting from the insured's failure to protect the property from further damage. In practice, the insured should not be reluctant to take steps to prevent further damage, as such costs commonly are paid as part of the loss payable under the fire policy.

Proof of Loss. Lines 97 through 113 relate primarily to requirements as to proof of loss:

> ... and within sixty days after the loss, unless such time is extended in writing by this Company, the insured shall render to this Company a proof of loss, signed and sworn to by the insured, stating the knowledge and belief of the insured as to the following time and origin of the loss, the interest of the insured and of all others in the property, the actual cash value of each item thereof and the amount of loss thereto, all encumbrances thereon, all other contracts of insurance, whether valid or not, covering any of said property, any changes in the title, use, occupation, location, possession or exposures of said property since the issuing of this policy, by whom and for what purpose any building herein described and the several parts thereof were occupied at the time of loss and whether or not it then stood on leased ground, and shall furnish a copy of all the descriptions and schedules in all policies and, if required, verified plans and specifications of any building, fixtures or machinery destroyed or damaged.

Specifically, unless the time has been extended in writing, proof of loss must be sent to the insurance company within sixty days after the occurrence of loss. Such proof of loss must be signed and sworn to by the insured. The proof of loss should state the knowledge and belief of the insured as to several things bearing on the loss: (1) how the loss occurred, (2) all interest in the property at the time of the loss,

(3) relative values lost and saved, (4) encumbrances, (5) insurance, and (6) any other pertinent facts. As noted earlier, fraud on the part of the insured in submitting a claim is grounds for avoiding the contract. This section of the policy makes it possible for the insurer to demand that the insured furnish supporting evidence, such as descriptions or schedules of all insurance policies and, if required, detail of all properties destroyed.

Examination Under Oath. In addition to the proof of loss requirement, in lines 113 through 122 the insurer reserves the right to examine the insured under oath and to examine his or her books and records as well as the remains of any property insured under the policy.

> The insured, as often as may be reasonably required, shall exhibit to any person designated by this Company all that remains of any property herein described, and submit to examinations under oath by any person named by this Company, and subscribe the same; and, as often as may be reasonably required, shall produce for examination all books of account, bills, invoices and other vouchers, or certified copies thereof if originals be lost, at such reasonable time and place as may be designated by this Company or its representative, and shall permit extracts and copies thereof to be made.

This gives the insurer access to full information concerning the loss, the extent of the insured's interest in the property damaged or destroyed, the total amount of damage or destruction, and other information necessary to prove or verify the magnitude of loss. The contract provides the insurer with the right to request that the insured submit to examination under oath by any person named by the company. It also provides that the insured shall furnish any books of account, bills, invoices, or other vouchers at such reasonable time as the insurer may designate.

Unfortunately, in fire insurance as in many other insurance fields, the cause or dimensions of losses are sometimes called into question by the existence of moral hazard on the part of the insured. The examination under oath provision of the standard fire policy is an important process by which the insurer might attempt to bring the true facts surrounding a loss or its magnitude to the surface. Sometimes fire losses or claims are unusually suspicious. There may be suspicion of arson. The amount of damage claimed by the insured following a loss may be highly questionable. It may become necessary to reconstruct the exposures to loss prior to the occurrence of a covered peril, in order to properly arrive at a valid award for indemnity. Reviewing the books of account of a business may allow the insurer to uncover evidence that suggests an underlying motive for fraud.

The right to require examination under oath may be a potent tool of the insurer in protecting itself from the payment of unjust claims.

For example, following a loss, if an insurer were to notify the insured of its intentions to examine him or her under oath in the form of a deposition, specifying an exact time and location for the taking of such testimony and indicating who would hear such testimony, the insured is required to comply with the request. If not, the insurer has a defense against the claim. Technically, an examination under oath differs from a pretrial examination or deposition which is taken under the purview of court rule. The primary difference is that, even though an insured who is required to submit to an examination under oath may bring along his or her own attorney or counsel, the insured's attorney, while having the right to object to certain questions raised, has no right actually to offer evidence or to cross-examine the insured.

Appraisal Agreement. The standard fire policy allows both the insured and the insurer to demand an appraisal procedure when they disagree as to the amount of the loss or as to the required payment to indemnify the insured. Lines 123 through 140 state:

> *Appraisal.* In case the insured and this Company shall fail to agree as to the actual cash value or the amount of loss, then, on the written demand of either, each shall select a competent and disinterested appraiser and notify the other of the appraiser selected within twenty days of such demand. The appraisers shall first select a competent and disinterested umpire; and failing for fifteen days to agree upon such umpire, then, on request of the insured or this Company, such umpire shall be selected by a judge of a court of record in the state in which the property covered is located. The appraisers shall then appraise the loss, stating separately actual cash value and loss to each item, and, failing to agree, shall submit their differences, only, to the umpire. An award in writing, so itemized, of any two when filed with this Company shall determine the amount of actual cash value and loss. Each appraiser shall be paid by the party selecting him and the expenses of appraisal and umpire shall be paid by the parties equally.

The process is really quite simple. Each party selects a competent and disinterested appraiser. Such an appraiser need not have any particular qualifications other than meeting the general criteria of "competent and disinterested." These appraisers may then proceed to negotiate or arbitrate the disagreement as to actual cash value or the amount of the loss in such a manner as they think proper. There are no requirements that any strict procedures of judicial investigation be followed. If for some reason the appraisers are not able to agree on dollar amounts, a third-party umpire may be called in. If the two appraisers or either appraiser and the umpire at any time agree, the decision as to amount is determined. Such decisions as to fair awards by appraisers or appraiser and umpire are usually binding on both insurer and insured, unless it can be shown that the determination was influenced by fraud or mistake. While the entire appraisal procedure can occasionally be costly, usually it is not. In any case, each party to the dispute is responsible for any payment required to its own appraiser, and the parties share equally in any fee which goes to the umpire.

Loss Settlement. Under the "company's options" stated in lines 141 through 147, the insurer is given the option to take all or any part of the property at the agreed or appraised value, or to repair, rebuild, or replace the property damaged or destroyed.

> *Company's options.* It shall be optional with this Company to take all, or any part, of the property at the agreed or appraised value, and also to repair, rebuild or replace the property destroyed or damaged with other of like kind and quality within a reasonable time, on giving notice of its intention so to do within thirty days after the receipt of the proof of loss herein required.

This is just another way of saying that the insured is required to give up the damaged property should the insurer exercise this option by giving notice of its intention to do so within thirty days after the receipt of proof of loss (and so doing within a reasonable time after the notice is given).

Lines 148 and 149, relating to abandonment of property by the insured, are very straightforward. This provision simply states that the insured may not abandon property to the insurer:

> *Abandonment.* There can be no abandonment to this Company of any property.

The abandonment provision amplifies the previous seven lines by emphasizing the fact that it is the insurance company that elects the basis of settlement. The insurance company has the option to take salvage at the agreed value, but the abandonment clause makes it clear that the insurer cannot be forced to take salvage, and the insured cannot abandon any property to the insurer.

Under the provisions of lines 150 through 156, the insurer is required to pay a claim within sixty days after proof of loss is received and ascertainment of the loss is made, either by agreement or by appraisal procedure:

> *When loss payable.* The amount of loss for which this Company may be liable shall be payable sixty days after proof of loss, as herein provided, is received by this Company and ascertainment of the loss is made either by agreement between the insured and this Company expressed in writing or by the filing with this Company of an award as herein provided.

It should be noted that the sixty-day limit is a maximum; most losses are paid well within this period.

Suit Against the Company If there is a dispute involving whether liability exists, a court action may be initiated, regardless of the action of appraisers. Lines 157 through 161 state:

> *Suit.* No suit or action on this policy for the recovery of any claim shall be sustainable in any court of law or equity unless all the requirements of this policy shall have been complied with, and unless commenced within twelve months next after inception of the loss.

The effect of this policy provision is to shorten the statute of limitations on the time within which a party to the contract may bring suit.

For example, in several states, the statute of limitations applying to contracts is five years. The standard fire policy provision shortens this period to a mere twelve months. Except in jurisdictions which specifically require otherwise by state statute, the shorter limitation period stated in the policy prevails. In order for an insured to sue under a fire policy, there are thus two general requirements which must be met: (1) all conditions to the policy must be complied with, and (2) legal action must commence within twelve months following the occurrence of loss.

CONCLUSION

This concludes the discussion of the parts, terms, and conditions of the standard fire policy. It should be emphasized again that the standard fire policy is not a complete insurance contract, that it cannot stand alone, but must be complemented by the addition of other forms, some of which add perils, some of which modify the policy provisions, and all of which define the subject of insurance and add further terms and conditions.

The standard fire policy and the extended coverage endorsement are extremely important coverages to the entire property insurance field. While many modern property insurance forms do not include the 165 lines of the standard fire policy specifically within their confines, most of the provisions and stipulations of that contract (and the common-law interpretations thereof) are implicitly a part of such coverages. If one is to understand the property insurance field, from a product or policy standpoint, one must first understand the conditions and stipulations of the standard fire policy. All dwelling fire forms, commercial fire forms, homeowners policies, and business multi-peril contracts are outgrowths of the 1943 standard fire policy, as far as their property coverages are concerned.

Chapter Notes

1. Data presented in this section are taken from *Insurance Facts*, 1980-81 Edition (New York: Insurance Information Institute.)
2. Delancy V. Rockingham Farmers Mutual Insurance Company (1873) 52 N.H. 581, 587.
3. H. Schumacher Oil Works v. The Hartford Fire Insurance Co., 239 F.2d. 836.
4. George J. Couch, *Cyclopedia of Insurance Law*, 2nd ed. (Rochester: Lawyers Co-Operative Publishing Company, 1960), section 42:505.
5. 43 Am. Jur. 2d. 897.
6. Werber Leather Coat Co. v. Niagara Fire Insurance Co., 254 App. Div. 298, 5 N.Y.S. 2d.1.
7. Couch, section 35:109.

Bibliography

AICPA Professional Standards, Vol. 3. New York: American Institute for Certified Public Accountants, September 1975.

Athearn, James. *Risk and Insurance.* 2nd ed. New York: Appleton-Century-Crofts, 1969.

Baglini, Norman A. *Risk Management in International Corporations.* New York: Risk Studies Foundation, 1976.

Bickelhaupt, David L. *General Insurance.* 10th ed. Homewood, IL: Richard D. Irwin, 1979.

Bird, Frank E., Jr. and Germain, George L. *Damage Control.* New York: American Management Association, 1966.

Breslin, Cormick L. and Troxel, Terrie E. *Property-Liability Insurance Accounting and Finance.* Malvern, PA: American Institute for Property and Liability Underwriters, Inc., 1978.

Brightman, W. T., Jr. "What the Underwriting Company Can Offer." *Insurance Costs and Controls: A Reappraisal,* AMA Management Report No. 19, pp. 36-37.

Close, D. B. and O'Connell, J. J. "A Guide to Formulation of Risk Management Policy Statements." *CPCU Annals,* September 1976, pp. 195-200.

Couch, George J. *Cyclopedia of Insurance Law.* 2nd ed. Rochester, NY: The Lawyers Cooperative Publishing Co., 1962.

Craven, Douglas I. *Guidelines for Developing an Insurance Manual.* New York: Risk and Insurance Management Society, 1975.

Criddle, A. Hawthorne. "A Theory of Risk Discovery." *National Insurance Buyer,* Vol. 6, January 1959, pp. 8, 14-18, 31, 35, 39.

_____. "The Use of Financial Statements in Corporate Risk Analysis." *Identifying and Controlling the Risks of Accidental Loss.* AMA Report No. 73. New York: American Management Association, 1962.

Denenberg, Herbert S.; Eilers, Robert D.; Melone, Joseph J.; and Zelten, Robert A. *Risk and Insurance.* 2nd ed. Englewood Cliffs, NJ: Prentice-Hall Publishing Co., 1974.

Denenberg, Herbert S. "The Legal Definition of Insurance." *The Journal of Insurance,* Vol. 30, September 1963, pp. 323-328.

Fayol, Henri. *General and Industrial Management.* New York: Pitman Publishing Corp., 1949.

Geisel, Jerry and McIntyre, Kathryn J. "Carnation Co. Loses Tax Fight Over Captive." *Business Insurance,* 16 March 1981, pp. 1 and 75.

Gordis, Philip. *Property and Casualty Insurance.* 23rd ed. Cincinnati: The Rough Notes Co., 1976.

315

Greene, Mark R. *Risk and Insurance*. 4th ed. Cincinnati: South-Western Publishing Co., 1977.

Greider, Janice E. and Beadles, William T. *Law and the Life Insurance Contract*. 4th ed. Homewood, IL: Richard D. Irwin, 1979.

Grimaldi, John V. and Simonds, Rollin H. *Safety Management*. 3rd ed. Homewood, IL: Richard D. Irwin, 1975.

Guiding Principles—Casualty, Fidelity, Fire, Inland Marine—First-Party Property Losses and Claims. New York: Association of Casualty & Surety Companies, et al., 1963.

Haddon, William, Jr. "The Basic Strategies for Reducing Damage from Hazards of All Kinds." *Hazard Prevention*, September/October 1980, pp. 8-12.

———————. "On the Escape of Tigers: An Ecologic Note." *Technology Review*, May 1970.

Hammond, J. D.; Shapiro, Arnold F.; and Shilling, N. *The Regulation of Insurer Solidity Through Capital and Surplus Requirements*. Summary Report NSF Grant APR75-16550. University Park, PA: The Pennsylvania State University, April 1978.

Heinrich, H. W. *Industrial Accident Prevention*. 4th ed. New York: McGraw-Hill Book Co., 1959.

Horn, Ronald C. *Subrogation in Insurance Theory and Practice*. Homewood, IL: Richard D. Irwin, 1964.

Ingley, A. J. "Problems of Risk Analysis." *The Growing Job of Risk Management*. AMA Management Report No. 70. New York: American Management Association, 1962, pp. 137-398.

Insurance Executives Association. *Report on Floods and Flood Damage*, May 1952.

Insurance Facts, 1980-81 edition. New York: Insurance Information Institute.

Keeton, Robert E. *Basic Text on Insurance Law*. St. Paul: West Publishing Co., 1971.

Kimball, Spencer L. and Denenberg, Herbert S, eds. *Insurance, Government and Social Policy*. Homewood, IL: Richard D. Irwin, 1969.

Kimball, Spencer L. and Pfenningstorf, Werner. "Administrative Control of the Terms of Insurance Contracts: A Comparative Study." *Indiana Law Journal*, Vol. 40, No. 2, Winter 1965, pp. 143-231.

———————. "Legislative and Judicial Control of the Terms of Insurance Contracts: A Comparative Study of American and European Practice." *Indiana Law Journal*, Vol. 39, No. 4, Summer 1964, pp. 675-731.

Krogh, Harold D. "The Securities Investor Protection Corporation: Financial Stringency in Securities Firms." *CPCU Annals*, Vol. 30, No. 1, March 1977, pp. 78-85.

Lalley, Edward P. *Self Assumption, Self Insurance and the Captive Insurance Company Concept*. New York: Risk and Insurance Management Society, 1975.

Lewis, J. R. "A Critical Review of the Federal Riot Reinsurance System." *Journal of Risk and Insurance*, Vol. 38, No. 1, March 1971, pp. 29-42.

MacDonald, Donald L. *Corporate Risk Control*. New York: The Ronald Press Co., 1966.

Mehr, Robert I. and Cammack, Emerson, *Principles of Insurance*. 7th ed. Homewood, IL: Richard D. Irwin, 1980.

Mehr, Robert I. and Hedges, Bob A. *Risk Management: Concepts and Applications*. Homewood, IL: Richard D. Irwin, 1974.

_____. *Risk Management in the Business Enterprise.* Homewood, IL: Richard D. Irwin, 1963.

Patterson, Edwin W. *Essentials of Insurance Law.* 2nd ed. New York: McGraw-Hill Book Co., 1957.

Petersen, Dan. *Techniques of Safety Management,* 2nd ed. New York: McGraw-Hill Book Co., 1978.

Pfeffer, Irving. *Insurance and Economic Theory.* Homewood, IL: Richard D. Irwin, 1956.

"Poll: Owners Want Competition Curbs." *The National Underwriter, Property & Casualty Insurance Edition,* 23 July 1976, pp. 1, 28.

Potter, F. W. "Presidential Address." *Proceedings of the National Convention of Insurance Commissioners,* Vol. 1, 1914, p. 14.

Reis, Frederick M. "Corporations and the Captive Insurer." *Proceedings of the 12th Annual Insurance Conference.* The Ohio State University, 1961.

"Report of Rates and Rating Organizations Subcommittee" (F1). *Proceedings of the National Association of Insurance Commissioners,* Vol. 1, 1969.

Riegel, Robert; Miller, Jerome S.; and Williams, C. Arthur, Jr. *Insurance Principles and Practices: Property and Liability.* Englewood Cliffs, NJ: Prentice-Hall Publishing Co., 1976.

The Risk and Insurance Manager Position: A Study of Responsibilities and Compensation. Conducted for the Risk and Insurance Management Society, Inc. Princeton: Sibson and Company, Inc., 1978.

Simonds, Rollin H. and Grimaldi, John V. *Safety Management.* Rev. ed. Homewood, IL: Richard D. Irwin, 1963.

Simpson, Laurence P. *Handbook on the Law of Contracts.* 2nd ed. St. Paul: West Publishing Co., 1965.

Smith, Michael L. "Selection of Deductibles in Property and Liability Insurance." Ph.D. dissertation, Univ. of Minnesota, 1974.

"Strategies to Reduce Damage from Environmental Hazards." *Status Report,* Vol. 15, No. 17, 21 November 1980.

"Tax Court Affirms IRS Veto of Captives in Carnation Co. Test Case." *Business Insurance,* 8 January 1979, pp. 1 and 86.

United States Statutes at Large, 1970-71, Part 2 (Washington DC), pp. 1788-1790.

"View on Crime, Riot Cover Sought." *The National Underwriter, Property & Casualty Insurance Edition,* 6 March 1981, p. 1.

Wenck, Thomas L. "The Historical Development of Standard Policies." *Journal of Risk and Insurance,* Vol. 35, No. 4, December 1968, pp. 537-550.

Williams, C. Arthur, Jr. and Heins, Richard M. *Risk Management and Insurance.* 4th ed. New York: McGraw-Hill Book Co., 1981.

Williams, Walter. "The Valued Policy and Value Determination." *Insurance Law Journal,* No. 457, February 1971, pp. 71-78.

Winter, William D. *Marine Insurance.* 3rd ed. New York: McGraw-Hill Book Co., 1952.

Zuger, Martin. "What Is the Public *Really* Telling Us?" *The Journal of Insurance,* May/June 1980, p. 35.

Index

F